Lecture Notes in Computer Science   9820

Commenced Publication in 1973
Founding and Former Series Editors:
Gerhard Goos, Juris Hartmanis, and Jan van Leeuwen

More information about this series at http://www.springer.com/series/7409

Hans Jochen Scholl · Olivier Glassey
Marijn Janssen · Bram Klievink
Ida Lindgren · Peter Parycek
Efthimios Tambouris · Maria A. Wimmer
Tomasz Janowski · Delfina Sá Soares (Eds.)

Electronic Government

15th IFIP WG 8.5 International Conference, EGOV 2016
Guimarães, Portugal, September 5–8, 2016
Proceedings

 Springer

Editors

Hans Jochen Scholl
University of Washington
Seattle, WA
USA

Olivier Glassey
Université de Lausanne
Lausanne
Switzerland

Marijn Janssen
Delft University of Technology
Delft, Zuid-Holland
The Netherlands

Bram Klievink
Delft University of Technology
Delft, Zuid-Holland
The Netherlands

Ida Lindgren
Linköping University
Linköping
Sweden

Peter Parycek
Donau-Universität Krems
Krems
Austria

Efthimios Tambouris
University of Macedonia
Thessaloniki
Greece

Maria A. Wimmer
Universität Koblenz-Landau
Koblenz, Rheinland-Pfalz
Germany

Tomasz Janowski
United Nations University
Guimarães
Portugal

Delfina Sá Soares
University of Minho
Guimarães
Portugal

ISSN 0302-9743   ISSN 1611-3349 (electronic)
Lecture Notes in Computer Science
ISBN 978-3-319-44420-8   ISBN 978-3-319-44421-5 (eBook)
DOI 10.1007/978-3-319-44421-5

Library of Congress Control Number: 2016947387

LNCS Sublibrary: SL3 – Information Systems and Applications, incl. Internet/Web, and HCI

Printed on acid-free paper

This Springer imprint is published by Springer Nature
The registered company is Springer International Publishing AG Switzerland

Preface

Under the auspices of the International Federation for Information Processing (IFIP) Working Group 8.5 (Information Systems in Public Administration), or IFIP WG 8.5 for short, the dual IFIP EGOV-ePart Conference 2016 presented itself as a high-caliber five-track conference and a doctoral colloquium dedicated to research and practice on electronic government and electronic participation.

Scholars from around the world have used this premier academic forum for over 15 years, which has given it a worldwide reputation as one of the top two conferences in the research domains of electronic, open, and smart government, and electronic participation.

This conference of five partially intersecting tracks presents advances in the socio-technological domain of the public sphere demonstrating cutting-edge concepts, methods, and styles of investigation by multiple disciplines.

The Call for Papers attracted over 135 submissions of completed research papers, work-in-progress papers on ongoing research (including doctoral papers), project and case descriptions, as well as four workshop and panel proposals. Among the full research paper submissions, 24 papers (empirical and conceptual) from the General EGOV Track, the Open Government and Open/Big Data Track, and the Smart Governance/Government/Cities Track were accepted for Springer's LNCS EGOV proceedings, whereas another 14 completed research papers from the General ePart Track and the Policy Modeling and Policy Informatics Track are published in LNCS ePart proceedings (vol. 9821).

The papers in the General EGOV/Open-Big Data/Smart Gov Tracks were clustered under the following headings:

- Foundations
- Benchmarking and Evaluation
- Information Integration and Governance
- Services
- Evaluation and Public Values
- EGOV Success and Failure
- Governance
- Social Media
- Engagement
- Processes
- Policy-Making
- Trust, Transparency, and Accountability
- Open Government and Big/Open Data
- Smart Government/Governance/Cities

As in previous years, IOS Press published accepted work-in-progress papers and workshop and panel abstracts in a complementary open-access proceedings volume. In 2016, this volume covers over 60 paper contributions, workshop abstracts, and panel summaries from *all* tracks, workshops, posters, and the PhD colloquium.

As in the past and per the recommendation of the Paper Awards Committee under the lead of the honorable Prof. Olivier Glassey of the University of Lausanne, Switzerland, the dual IFIP EGOV-ePart 2016 Conference Organizing Committee again granted outstanding paper awards in three distinct categories:

- The most interdisciplinary and innovative research contribution
- The most compelling critical research reflection
- The most promising practical concept

The winners in each category were announced in the award ceremony at the conference dinner, which has always been a highlight of each dual IFIP EGOV-ePart conference.

The dual IFIP EGOV-ePart 2016 conference was jointly hosted in Guimarães, Portugal, by the University of Minho (UMinho) and the United Nations University Operating Unit on Policy-Driven Electronic Governance (UNU-EGOV). Established in 1973, UMinho operates on three campuses, one in Braga, and two in Guimarães, educating approximately 19,500 students by an academic staff of 1,300 located in eight schools, three institutes, and several cultural and specialized units. It is one of the largest public universities in Portugal and a significant actor in the development of the Minho region in the north of Portugal. UNU-EGOV is a newly established UN organization focused on research, policy, and leadership education in the area of digital government, located in Guimarães and hosted by UMinho. The organization of the dual conference was partly supported by the project "SmartEGOV: Harnessing EGOV for Smart Governance," NORTE-01-0145-FEDER-000037, funded by FEDER in the context of Programa Operacional Regional do Norte.

Although ample traces of Celtic and Roman presence and settlements were found in the area, Guimarães became notable as the center of early nation building for Portugal in the late eleventh century, when it became the seat of the Count of Portugal. In 1128, the Battle of São Mamede was fought near the town, which resulted in the independence of the Northern Portuguese territories around Coimbra and Guimarães, which later extended further south to form the independent nation of Portugal. Today, Guimarães has a population of about 160,000. While it has developed into an important center of textile and shoe industries along with metal mechanics, the city has maintained its charming historical center and romantic medieval aura. It was a great pleasure to hold the dual IFIP EGOV-ePart 2016 conference at this special place.

Many people make large events like this conference happen. We thank the over 100 members of the dual IFIP EGOV-ePart 2016 Program Committee and dozens of additional reviewers for their great efforts in reviewing the submitted papers. Delfina Sá Soares of the Department of Information Systems at the UMinho and Tomasz Janowski of the UNU-EGOV and their respective teams in Guimarães, Portugal, were major contributors who helped organize the dual conference and manage zillions of details locally. We would also like to thank the University of Washington organizing team members Kelle M. Rose and Daniel R. Wilson for their great support and administrative management of the review process and the compilation of the proceedings.

September 2016

Hans Jochen Scholl
Olivier Glassey
Marijn Janssen
Bram Klievink
Ida Lindgren
Peter Parycek
Efthimios Tambouris
Maria A. Wimmer
Tomasz Janowski
Delfina Sá Soares
Yannis Charalabidis
Mila Gascó
Ramon Gil-Garcia
Panos Panagiotopoulos
Theresa Pardo
Øystein Sæbø
Anneke Zuiderwijk

Organization

Conference Lead Organizer

Hans Jochen Scholl   University of Washington, USA

General E-Government Track Chairs

Marijn Janssen   Delft University of Technology, The Netherlands (Lead)
Hans Jochen Scholl   University of Washington, USA
Maria A. Wimmer   University of Koblenz-Landau, Germany

General eParticipation Track Chairs

Efthimios Tambouris   University of Macedonia, Greece (Lead)
Panos Panagiotopoulos   Queen Mary University of London, UK
Øystein Sæbø   Agder University, Norway

Open Government and Open and Big Data Track Chairs

Bram Klievink   Delft University of Technology, The Netherlands (Lead)
Marijn Janssen   Delft University of Technology, The Netherlands
Ida Lindgren   Linköping University, Sweden

Policy Modeling and Policy Informatics Track Chairs

Maria A. Wimmer   University of Koblenz-Landau, Germany (Lead)
Yannis Charalabidis   National Technical University, Greece
Theresa Pardo   Center for Technology in Government,
         University at Albany, SUNY, USA

Smart Governance, Government and Cities Track Chairs

Peter Parycek   Danube University Krems, Austria (Lead)
Mila Gascó   Escuela Superior de Administración y Dirección
         de Empresas (ESADE), Spain
Olivier Glassey   Université de Lausanne, Switzerland

Chair of Outstanding Papers Award

Olivier Glassey   Université de Lausanne, Switzerland

PhD Colloquium Chairs

Ida Lindgren   Linköping University, Sweden (Lead)
Ramon Gil-Garcia   Centro de Investigación y Docencia Económicas, Mexico
Anneke Zuiderwijk   Delft University of Technology, The Netherlands

Program Committee

Suha Al Awadhi   Kuwait University, Kuwait
Renata Araujo   UNIRIO, Brazil
Jansen Arild   University of Oslo, Norway
Karin Axelsson   Linköping University, Sweden
Frank Bannister   Trinity College Dublin, Ireland
Jesper Berger   Roskilde University, Denmark
Lasse Berntzen   Buskerud and Vestfold University College, Norway
Paul Brous   Delft University of Technology, The Netherlands
Wojciech Cellary   Poznan University of Economics, Poland
Bojan Cestnik   Temida d.o.o., Jožef Stefan Institute, Slovenia
Yannis Charalabidis   National Technical University, Greece
Soon Ae Chun   City University of New York, USA
Wichian Chutimaskul   King Mongkut's University of Technology Thonburi,
                         Thailand
Peter Cruickshank   Edinburgh Napier University, UK
Todd Davies   Stanford University, USA
Sharon Dawes   Center for Technology in Government, University
                         at Albany/SUNY, USA
Fiorella de Cindio   Università di Milano, Italy
Robin Effing   University of Twente, The Netherlands
Elsa Estevez   United Nations University, Macao
Sabrina Franceschini   Regione Emilia-Romagna, Italy
Iván Futó   National Tax and Customs Administration, Hungary
Mila Gascó   ESADE, Spain
Katarina Gidlund   Midsweden University, Sweden
J. Ramon Gil-Garcia   Centro de Investigación y Docencia Económicas, Mexico
Olivier Glassey   Université de Lausanne, Switzerland
Göran Goldkuhl   Linköping University, Sweden
Dimitris Gouscos   Laboratory of New Technologies in Communication,
                         Education and the Mass Media, University of Athens,
                         Greece
Joris Hulstijn   Delft University of Technology, The Netherlands
Johann Höchtl   Danube University Krems, Austria
M. Sirajul Islam   Örebro University, Sweden
Tomasz Janowski   UNU Operating Unit on Policy-Driven Electronic
                         Governance, Portugal
Marijn Janssen   Delft University of Technology, The Netherlands
Carlos Jiménez   IEEE e-Government, Spain

Marius Rohde Johannessen	University College of Southeast Norway, Norway
Luiz Antonio Joia	FGV/EBAPE - Escola Brasileira de Administração Pública e de Empresas, Brazil
Nikos Karacapilidis	University of Patras, Greece
Bram Klievink	Delft University of Technology, The Netherlands
Roman Klinger	University of Stuttgart, Germany
Ralf Klischewski	German University in Cairo, Egypt
Helmut Krcmar	Technische Universität München, Germany
Robert Krimmer	Tallinn University of Technology, Estonia
Juha Lemmetti	Tampere University of Technology, Finland
Azi Lev-On	Ariel University Center, Israel
Ida Lindgren	Linköping University, Sweden
Euripidis Loukis	University of the Aegean, Greece
Luis Luna-Reyes	University at Albany, SUNY, USA
Ulf Melin	Linköping University, Sweden
Gregoris Mentzas	National Technical University of Athens, Greece
Michela Milano	Università di Bologna, Italy
Yuri Misnikov	Institute of Communications Studies, University of Leeds, UK
Gianluca Misuraca	European Commission, JRC-IPTS, Italy
Catherine Mkude	University of Koblenz, Germany
Carl Moe	Agder University, Norway
José María Moreno-Jiménez	Universidad de Zaragoza, Spain
Morten Nielsen	Tallinn University of Technology, Estonia
Nadine Ogonek	Westfälische Wilhelms-Universität, Institut für Wirtschaftsinformatik, Germany
Adegboyega Ojo	Insight Centre for Data Analytics, National University of Ireland, Ireland
Panos Panagiotopoulos	Queen Mary University of London, UK
Eleni Panopoulou	University of Macedonia, Greece
Theresa Pardo	Center for Technology in Government, University at Albany, SUNY, USA
Peter Parycek	Danube University Krems, Austria
Marco Prandini	Università di Bologna, Italy
Barbara Re	University of Camerino, Italy
Nicolau Reinhard	University of São Paulo, Brazil
Andrea Resca	Cersi-Luiss "Guido Carli" University, Italy
Michael Räckers	European Research Center for Information Systems (ERCIS), Germany
Gustavo Salati	Faculdade de Ciências Aplicadas da Unicamp, Brazil
Rodrigo Sandoval Almazan	Universidad Autonoma del Estado de Mexico, Mexico
Rui Pedro Santos Lourenço	Universidade de Coimbra, Portugal

Sabrina Scherer	University of Koblenz-Landau, Germany
Hans J. Scholl	University of Washington, USA
Gerhard Schwabe	Universität Zürich, Switzerland
Luizpaulo Silva	UNIRIO, Brazil
Maria Sokhn	University of Applied Sciences of Switzerland, Switzerland
Henk Sol	University of Groingen, The Netherlands
Mauricio Solar	Universidad Tecnica Federico Santa Maria, Chile
Maddalena Sorrentino	University of Milan, Italy
Witold Staniszkis	Rodan Systems, Poland
Leif Sundberg	Mid Sweden University, Sweden
Delfina Sá Soares	University of Minho, Portugal
Øystein Sæbø	University of Agder, Norway
Efthimios Tambouris	University of Macedonia, Greece
Dmitrii Trutnev	e-Government Technologies Center of ITMO University, Russian Federation
Jolien Ubacht	Delft University of Technology, The Netherlands
Jörn von Lucke	Zeppelin Universität Friedrichshafen, Germany
Elin Wihlborg	Linköping University, Sweden
Andrew Wilson	University of Brighton, UK
Maria Wimmer	University of Koblenz, Germany
Chien-Chih Yu	National ChengChi University, Taiwan
Anneke Zuiderwijk	Delft University of Technology, The Netherlands

Additional Reviewers

Ayman Alarabiat	Ansgar Mondorf
Jonathan Bright	Alessia Caterina Neuroni
Claudia Cappelli	Ann O'Brien
Gabriel Cavalheiro	Giulio Pasi
Sunil Choenni	Joachim Pfister
Bettina Distel	Dhata Praditya
Felipe Díaz-Sánchez	Fadi Salem
Silja Eckartz	Birgit Schenk
Marcelo Fornazin	Ralf-Martin Soe
Tupokigwe Isagah	Leonardo Sonnante
Naci Karkin	Matthias Steinbauer
Martin Karlsson	Gabriela Viale Pereira
Barbara Kieslinger	Gianluigi Viscusi
Mehmet Kilic	Christian Voigt
Thomas Josef Lampoltshammer	Erik Wende
Hannu Larsson	Sergei Zhilin

Contents

E-Government Foundations

Making Sense of Indices and Impact Numbers: Establishing Leading EGOV Scholars' "Signatures"

Hans J. Scholl$^{(\boxtimes)}$

University of Washington, Seattle, USA
jscholl@uw.edu

Abstract. From its earliest stages on, scholars immersed in Electronic Government Research (EGR) have cared for the study domain's reputation and academic standing. With the publication of "Forums for Electronic Government Scholars" a few years ago, it was established, which academic outlets in EGR (both journals and conferences) the most prolific and influential scholars in the domain preferred, and how these outlets were rated by the very same scholars. Based on sources such as the Electronic Government Reference Library (EGRL) and Google Scholar, various counts and indices have now become publicly available, which make possible to trace each EGR scholar's productivity and impact at any point in time. However, quantitative citation counts and index numbers, while important, can be misleading for various reasons. This study presents a complementary approach to identify each leading EGR scholar's "signature" and argues that citation numbers, indices, and signatures when taken together present a far more informative picture of scholarly impact and influence than citation and index numbers alone.

Keywords: Google Scholar · Citation index · Citation count · h-index · i10-index · Electronic Government Reference Library · EGRL · Version 11.5 · Electronic Government Research · EGR · Publication outlets · Academic impact · EGOV scholars · Tenure and promotion · Trends in EGOV research · Scholarly signature · EGOV-List

1 Introduction

Periodic evaluation of academic job performance has been characterized as substantial and central elements in academic life [14] and an important criterion in hiring, tenure, and promotion decisions [16]. Both the criteria and procedures for academic tenure and promotion may differ between types of academic institutions (for example, research universities, doctorate-granting universities, comprehensive universities, and Liberal Arts colleges) [16]. Differences in evaluation criteria may also exist between disciplines as well as between academic systems (for example, the US versus the French, or German systems). However, three main areas appear to be evaluated although with varying weight and emphasis: research, teaching, and service. At research universities the highest weight is regularly put on research [14, 16], and lower weights are attributed to a scholar's performance in teaching and service [12].

© IFIP International Federation for Information Processing 2016
Published by Springer International Publishing Switzerland 2016. All Rights Reserved
H.J. Scholl et al. (Eds.): EGOV 2016, LNCS 9820, pp. 3–18, 2016.
DOI: 10.1007/978-3-319-44421-5_1

When academic tenure and promotion committees evaluate a scholar's relative performance in research, mainly three factors are considered: productivity, impact, and individual signature.

The first factor, *productivity* typically refers to a scholar's quantitative annual publication output at ranked and institutionally accepted outlets, which provide high-quality, double-blind peer reviews of submitted work. When inspecting a scholar's publication output across time periods, evaluators expect to find a so-called publication rhythm, that is, a pattern of uninterrupted publications, which are seen as documenting steady and ongoing research involvement [11].

The second factor, scholarly *impact* has traditionally been measured in terms of number of citations [2, 11, 12]. However, significant differences exist between disciplines with regard to the mean of citations for the most senior researchers [11]. While senior social scientists may have lifetime citation numbers in the three to four thousands, senior researchers in the natural sciences may have citation numbers of over five times as many. The use of citation numbers as a proxy for measuring scholarly impact has repeatedly been criticized for its tendency towards inflation as a result of self-citations as well as the effect of multiple co-authorships, which function as citation accelerators [2]. Furthermore, the "lucky punch," that is, a single massively cited publication might represent the lion's share of a scholar's overall citation number effectively hiding a weak publication rhythm. Last, the traditional citation indices, for example, Thomson Reuters' Web of Science accounted only for journal citations omitting and neglecting other important publication outlets such as conferences, which penalizes disciplines, in which journals play an inferior role, for example, in Computer Science. The increasingly accepted Google Scholar citation index, therefore, includes journal and conference citations among others as well as the h-index [13] and the i10-index, which indicates the number of publications cited at least ten times [21].

The third factor, scholarly *signature*, has become a more important measure and analytical lens in recent years, whereby published work is analyzed also along the lines of identifiable individual contribution to the academic body of knowledge. Much scholarly work is multi-co-authored as opposed to single authorships [1]. Hiring, tenure, and promotion committees take a look at the mix of single-authored papers versus co-authored papers and lead co-authored papers versus non-lead co-authored papers. Also, the average number of co-authors is taken into account. The absence of single-authored or lead co-authored publications suggests an unidentifiable scholarly signature, whereas a significant number of single-authored and of lead co-authored publications reveals an identifiable scholarly signature.

In this study, productivity, impact, and individual scholarly signature of leading scholars in Electronic Government Research (EGR) are analyzed. EGR is a multi-disciplinary study domain, which is neither owned nor dominated by a single discipline. As a consequence the accepted standards of inquiry vary. The object of the study is to inform tenure and promotion-seeking EGR scholars about the landscape of scholarship in the study domain and provide orientation with regard to productivity, impact, and individual signature. It is also intended to help hiring, tenure, and promotion committees in their evaluation of candidates.

The paper is organized as follows: First, the current literature on the subject is briefly reviewed; then, the research questions are presented followed by the methodology section. Next, the findings are presented, which are then discussed in the succeeding section. Finally, the paper concludes that the EGR study domain has reached a new plateau of productivity, impact, and identifiable individual signatures of leading EGR scholars which suggests that the study domain can maintain its solid academic standing as a multidisciplinary endeavor.

2 Literature Review

This review is concise, since the number of publications on EGR scholarship and publication trends is relatively low.

A number of bibliometric analyses based on the Electronic Government Reference Library (EGRL) has focused on the topical trends in EGR and on the profile of the scholarly community [18–22, 24]. Topical trends and researcher profiles in EGR were also studied by different means and data sources such as select journals and other outlets [7–9, 17]. According to these studies EGR has so far mainly centered on topics such as organizational transformation, citizen participation, improvement of government services, technical design of e-government systems, institutional architectures and interoperability, policy and governance, and more recently also on topics such as cloud services, social media, transparency, and big and open data.

When attempting to size the active EGR community two indicators were used. The EGOV-List listserv subscriber count tallied 1,200 members, while the co-author count of the EGRL showed over 3,800 entries [20]. The EGOV-List also contains a couple hundred non-academic subscribers, whereas a large number of co-authors have only one or two entries in the EGRL. In contrast, the innermost circle of EGR scholars, that is, scholars with at least 18 publications or more was reported significantly smaller, that is, 51 scholars [21]. This led to size the active EGR community in the bracket of five to eight hundreds. Scholl's 2014 study also reported on the academic impact of EGR scholars in the so-called core or "inner circle" of the study domain by detailing and comparing respective Google Scholar citation numbers, and h and i10 indices for the first time.

The Google Scholar citation counts along with the h and i10 indices are seen as more representative of a scholar's overall impact than the sum of journal-based citation counts multiplied by the respective journal's impact factor, since as mentioned above this approach unduly ignores the impact of conference publications altogether, which appears as highly problematic for a number of disciplines that appreciate conference publications significantly over journal publications.

Finally, the report also provided a breakdown of top-51 EGR contributors by geography revealing that the vast majority of leading researchers in this domain of study were still located in either Europe or North America. Interestingly, the European share among the top-51 EGR scholars had increased to almost 61 % while the North American share had fallen to under 30 % in the period between 2009 and 2013 from the previous five-year interval [21].

In summary, over the past decade the study domain has significantly grown in numbers of publications, numbers of scholars, and slightly grown also in number of disciplines involved. Thereby, the domain has gained excellent reputational standing across academia. Meanwhile publications like "Forums for Electronic Government Scholars" [24] have reportedly influenced hiring, tenure, and promotion decisions of EGR scholars in positive ways. Such cases, however, also identified a gap in understanding and a need for clarifying the meaning and comparability of various factors and indices of individual scholarly signature and individual impact.

3 Research Questions and Methodology

3.1 Research Questions

Based on bibliographic data derived from the EGRL (version 11.5, December 2015), it was possible to update the 2014 list of major contributors and most prolific EGR scholars along with these scholars' academic impact (based on Google Scholar indices). Furthermore, the individual scholar's "signature," that is her/his unique and individual contribution and impact, could be determined, which leads to the following three research questions:

> *Research Question #1* (RQ #1): What cumulative publication output have the leading EGR scholars produced, and how has it changed?
> *Research Question #2* (RQ #2): What are leading EGR scholars' Google Scholar indices such as citation numbers, h-index, and i10 index, and how have they changed?
> *Research Question #3* (RQ #3): In light of the cumulative publication output and the Google Scholar indices, what are leading EGR scholars' individual contributions ("signatures"), and how can they be determined?

3.2 Data Selection and Analysis

Data Selection. The data source for this study was the Electronic Government Reference Library (EGRL, version 11.5, December of 2015) [22]. This reference library is a well established and acclaimed source of peer-reviewed academic EGR articles in the English language, which on average is updated every six months (see http://faculty. washington.edu/jscholl/egrl/history.php). The publishers of the EGRL aspire (see http://faculty.washington.edu/jscholl/egrl/criteria.php) to consistently capture at least 95 % of the eligible peer-reviewed and published EGR literature. EGRL version 11.5 contained a total of 7,899 references, an increase of 1,616 references (or, 25.7 %) over EGRL version 9.5 (6,283 references), which was the basis of the previous analysis two years before.

Data Extraction and Preparation. The EGRL version 11.5 was prepared with the EndNote reference manager, version X7.5.1.1 (Build 11194 – see http://endnote.com); it was used to export the references into the standard tagging Refman (RIS) file format, which is widely used to format and exchange references between digital libraries. As in the previous study, by means of the tags, for example, "TY - JOUR" for publication type journal, or, "AU - Bertot" for an author's name, references were extracted and prepared for further processing and analysis. Data needed cleaning and harmonizing. For example, author names were found in different forms with regard to first names (abbreviated or full, with or without middle names, or initials). Furthermore, diacriticals needed to be exchanged against plain UTF-8 characters. Author names containing multiple terms (first name, middle name, last name) were concatenated by double equal symbols (==) between the terms so to avoid separation in subsequent analyses of term frequencies. Pre-analysis data preparation and harmonization was performed in part with TextEdit version 1.11 (Build 325) as well as with Mac Excel 2008 version 12.2.3 (Build 091001). All terms were converted to lowercase and diacriticals were removed except for dashes and double equal symbols.

Data Analysis. The analysis was mainly carried out using the R statistical package (version 3.0.3, GUI 1.63 Snow Leopard build (6660)). For text mining under R the tm package version 0.5–10 by Feinerer and Hornik [10, 15] was downloaded from the Comprehensive R Archive Network (CRAN) (see http://cran.us.r-project.org – accessed 3/12/2014) and used. Frequencies of author names were counted. For authors with frequency counts greater than or equal to 20 (18 before, or, +11.1 % over the previous study), which represented the most prolific 60 scholars in EGR (up from 51).

For each author in the top 60, the number of co-authors was counted for each publication in the EGRL providing a scholar's average number of co-authors per publication. Furthermore, for each author in the top 60, the number of single authorships and lead co-authorships was counted providing a single/lead author index, that is, the ratio of single/lead (co-)authored publications over all publications of the respective author.

An additional (manual) data collection was performed with regard to individual author's Google Scholar entry. For each scholar in the list the citation count, the h- and the i10-indices were recorded if publicly available (http://scholar.google.com/ - accessed March 7, 2016). For EGR scholars without a published publication profile, the Google Scholar citation counts and respective indices could have been counted and calculated; however, until now it is preferred that scholars publish their profile themselves, which is strongly recommended because the data is publicly available anyway.

It is also noteworthy, that in several cases the Google Scholar counts were erroneous, for example, for one EGOV scholar's citation count was overrepresented by a staggering 811 citations (or, 35.5 %). However, other citation counts were also found identifiably inflated, yet not to this order of magnitude as in the aforementioned case. It is suggested that EGR scholars carefully review their Google Scholar data, once published, and manually eliminate counting errors and citation inflation.

Finally, for each EGR scholar in the top 60, the number of single authorships or lead co-authorships was counted for the top-10 most cited publications in Google Scholar as another indicator of individual "signature."

4 Findings

Findings are presented in the order of the research questions.

4.1   Cumulative Scholarly Publication Output in EGR (RQ #1)

As recently presented elsewhere [23], within only two years the core or "inner circle" of EGR expanded from 51 to 60 scholars (18 %) defined by tallying a cumulative minimum of 20 peer-reviewed publications, which represents an increase of 11.1 publications for making it into the EGR core group.

It is also noteworthy that since the last publication of an bibliometric evaluation in EGR, the body of EGR-related knowledge increased from 6,283 publications in 2013 to 7,899 in late 2015, that is, an increase of 25.7 % within just two years [23].

As Table 1 indicates, the ranking of the top-6 cumulatively most prolific EGR scholars remained the same compared with 2014, while a group of four scholars (Reddick, Charalabidis, Dwivedi, and Grönlund) moved up into the top-10. In 2016 it required at least 45 peer-reviewed EGRL-recorded publications to rank among the top-10 most prolific EGR scholars, whereas two years earlier 36 publications would have provided that same ranking.

Table 1. Cumulative publication output by top-20 most prolific EGR scholars (early 2016)

Rank	Name		# of Entries in EGRL v11.5 (March 2016)	# of Entries in EGRL v 9.5 (March 2014)	Rank (March 2014)
1	Marijn Janssen, TU Delft, The Netherlands	(—)	122	85	1
2	Ramon Gil-Garcia, CTG, SUNY Albany, USA	(—)	97	81	2
3	Theresa A. Pardo, CTG, SUNY Albany, USA	(—)	86	78	3
4	Hans Jochen Scholl, University of Washington, Seattle, USA	(—)	75	62	4
5	Maria A. Wimmer, University of Koblenz, Germany	(—)	67	51	5
6	Vishanth Weerakkody, Brunel University, Uxbridge, UK	(—)	61	50	6
7	Christopher G. Reddick, University of Texas, San Antonio, USA	↑	56	36	10
8	Yannis Charalabidis, University of the Aegean, Samos, Greece	↑	52	40	8
9	Yogesh K. Dwivedi, Swansea University, UK	↑	51	29	14
10	Ake Grönlund, Örebro University, Sweden	↑	45	29	14
11	Sharon S. Dawes, CTG, SUNY Albany, USA	↓	42	42	7
12	Ann Macintosh, University of Leeds, UK	↓	41	37	9
	Luis F. Luna-Reyes, UDLA, Puebla, Mexico	↓	41	34	11
14	Efthimios Tambouris, University of Macedonia, Thessaloniki, Greece	↑	39	28	17
15	Paul T. Jaeger, University of Maryland, College Park, USA	↓	36	32	12
	Björn Niehaves, Hertie School of Governance, Berlin, Germany	↓	36	32	12
	Konstantinos Tarabanis, University of Macedonia, Thessaloniki, Greece	↑	36	26	20
18	John C. Bertot, University of Maryland, College Park, USA	↓	34	28	17
19	Kim N Andersen, Copenhagen Business School, Denmark	↓	31	29	14
20	Jörg Becker, University of Münster, Germany	↓	30	28	17

Interestingly, the minimum publication number for reaching a top-10 ranking increased by 25 % matching the overall increase in EGR publications for the period studied. Focus on other areas of research or a slowdown of publication output due to retirement or leave of absence appear as the most likely explanations among other reasons. EGR scholars Dwivedi (9), Tarabanis (15) and Becker (20) have traditionally published in other areas than EGR. In the case of Dwivedi, it appears that a major shift in favor of EGR has occurred. The cumulatively top-20 most prolific EGR scholars had fairly wide ranges of productivity over the two-year period studied ranging from no increase to a 75.9 % increase.

As discussed before the percentage-related increases describe the emphasis (or, de-emphasis, respectively) of EGR scholars with regard to their EGR-related publi cation output. While the mean percentage increase of publications for top-20 most prolific EGR scholars was 26.7 % (that is, slightly higher than the average increase in EGR publications), the median percentage increase was 21.2 %, and the mode 12.5 %.

In summary, the majority of top-20 most prolific scholars is still actively, and as the percentage numbers unveil, even massively engaged in EGR, and this group strongly contributes to the increase of the body of academic knowledge in the study domain. It is also worth mentioning that among the top-20 most prolific EGR scholars one finds a number of current or former editors-in-chief of leading EGR journals (Janssen and Bertot/GIQ, Weerakoddy/IJEGR, and Reddick/IJPADA) as well as organizers of leading conferences (Scholl/HICSS EGOV and IFIP EGOV, Janssen and Wimmer/IFIP EGOV). While no change was observed among the top-6 EGR contributors, some changes were noticed in the remainder of the top-20 rankings.

4.2   Leading EGR Scholars' March 2016 Google Scholar Indices (RQ #2)

In this section the various Google Scholar indices are presented for the top-20 most prolific scholars in the domain. However, when it comes to interpreting citation numbers and indices, two particular circumstances have to be considered.

(1) As Scholl pointed out in an earlier study [21], several most prolific EGR scholars have large numbers of publications (and, therefore, citations and credentials) outside EGR. It would be greatly misleading if these numbers were used in direct comparison with those of mostly or solely EGR-focused scholars. Although the EGR-related citations for these scholars could be manually counted and the respective indices calculated, for the purpose of this study it was decided to ignore these cases, which are Dwivedi, Tarabanis, Irani, and Becker. Instead the next most prolific authors were included as long as their citation numbers and indices were available from Google Scholar. This appears justifiable since despite rela- tively large EGR publication numbers, the relative fraction of citations and indices relating to EGR publications was still found minor relative to the remainder of the respective scholar's work. However, admittedly in domain analyses the use of indices clearly shows its weaknesses for those scholars who work across multiple domains and disciplines. In future studies, cases such as Dwivedi's might there- fore become more problematic in comparative analyses like this one, since a strong shift of focus towards EGR like in Dwivedi's case might make it necessary to individually calculate the EGR-related impacts (and signatures).

(2) Another adjustment had to be made, since Grönlund, Macintosh, and Jaeger had not made public their Google Scholar citations and indices. In the absence of official numbers in these cases the next most prolific scholars were included in this analysis instead, as long as their Google Scholar citations and indices were published (see also [23]).

As further mentioned above, while citation indices have been criticized also from various other perspectives [1, 2, 11], they have nevertheless become a part of scholarly life, and in particular, evaluation of impact. In Tables 2, 3, and 4, the Google Scholar citation numbers, the h-indices, and the i10-indices are presented.

Table 2. Google Scholar citation numbers for leading EGR scholars (as of march 7, 2016); note: Grönlund, Macintosh, and Jaeger unpublished/not included

Rank	Name, Affiliation, Country	Change in %	Google Scholar Citations (March, 2016)	Google Scholar Citations (April, 2014)
1	John C. Bertot, University of Maryland, College Park, USA	43.7%	5096	3547
2	Marijn Janssen, TU Delft, The Netherlands	84.2%	4733	2570
3	Theresa A. Pardo, CTG, SUNY Albany, USA	70.7%	4350	2548
4	Ramon Gil-Garcia, CTG, SUNY Albany, USA	83.9%	3868	2103
5	Lemuria Carter, North Carolina A & T State University, Greensboro, USA	63.1%	3328	2041
6	Sharon S. Dawes, CTG, SUNY Albany, USA	40.5%	3235	2302
7	Hans Jochen Scholl, University of Washington, Seattle, USA	65.1%	2627	1591
8	Eric W. Welch, Arizona State University, Phoenix, USA	56.1%	2619	1678
9	Vishanth Weerakkody, Brunel University, Uxbridge, UK	61.3%	2591	1606
10	Maria A. Wimmer, University of Koblenz, Germany	41.4%	2338	1654
11	Björn Niehaves, Hertie School of Governance, Berlin, Germany	68.5%	2328	1382
12	Victor J. J. M. Bekkers, Erasmus University Rotterdam, The Netherlands	n/a	2285	n/a
13	Kim N Andersen, Copenhagen Business School, Denmark	44.1%	2024	1405
14	Anthony Cresswell, CTG, SUNY Albany, USA	42.1%	1984	1396
15	Christopher G. Reddick, University of Texas, San Antonio, USA	63.7%	1835	1121
16	Luis F. Luna-Reyes, University at Albany	82.0%	1749	961
17	Albert Meijer, Utrecht University, The Netherlands	92.4%	1712	890
18	Soon Ae Chun, City University of New York, USA	61.3%	1679	1041
19	Flavio Corradini, University of Camerino, Italy	n/a	1605	n/a
20	Ralf Klischewski, German University Cairo, Egypt	19.9%	1565	1305

Table 2 shows the citation counts for leading EGR scholars as found on Google Scholar on March 7, 2016. Across the board EGR scholars' citation counts grew rapidly within the relatively short reposting period of two years. Citation counts increased between 19.9 % and 92.4 %. The rank order of the most highly cited six scholars did not change; however, Janssen and Gil-Garcia had the highest percentage increases in the top echelon.

Table 3 shows the h-index for leading EGR scholars from the same data collection. Also in this case, the top-6 EGR scholars' rankings have remained unchanged. Percentage increases range between 12.5 % and 57.1 %.

In comparison, Table 4 presents the i10-index, again from the same data collection. Rankings are by and large similar to the other two indices. Also, in the case of the i10-indices, the average percentage increase equals almost 42 %.

In summary, as the Google Scholar indices reveal the study domain's leading scholars have significantly increased their overall impact across all three measures, the citation counts, the h-index, and the i10-index. Quite a number of EGR scholars are listed in *all* tables so far presented.

Table 3. Google Scholar h-index for leading EGR scholars (as of march 7, 2016); note: Grönlund, Macintosh, and Jaeger – unpublished/not included

Rank	Name, Affiliation, Country	Change in %	h-index (March 2016)	h-index (April 2014)
1	John C. Bertot, University of Maryland, College Park, USA.	15.6%	37	32
2	Marijn Janssen, TU Delft, The Netherlands	29.6%	35	27
3	Ramon Gil-Garcia, CTG, SUNY Albany, USA	40.9%	31	22
4	Theresa A. Pardo, CTG, SUNY Albany, USA	24.0%	31	25
5	Vishanth Weerakkody, Brunel University, Uxbridge, UK	26.1%	29	23
6	Sharon S. Dawes, CTG, SUNY Albany, USA	12.5%	27	24
7	Hans Jochen Scholl, University of Washington, Seattle, USA	25.0%	25	20
8	Maria A. Wimmer, University of Koblenz, Germany	20.0%	24	20
9	Björn Niehaves, Hertie School of Governance, Berlin, Germany	26.3%	24	19
10	Kim N Andersen, Copenhagen Business School, Denmark	29.4%	22	17
11	Albert Meijer, Utrecht University, The Netherlands	37.5%	22	16
12	Soon Ae Chun, City University of New York, USA	16.7%	21	18
13	Yannis Charalabidis, University of the Aegean, Samos, Greece	53.8%	20	13
14	Christopher G. Reddick, University of Texas, San Antonio, USA	33.3%	20	15
15	Luis F. Luna-Reyes, University at Albany	25.0%	20	16
16	Efthimios Tambouris, University of Macedonia, Thessaloniki, Greece	25.0%	20	16
17	Euripidis Loukis, University of the Aegean, Samos, Greece	46.2%	19	13
18	Dimitrios Askounis, National Technical University of Athens, Greece	n/a	18	n/a
19	Adegboyega Ojo, National University of Ireland Galway, Republic of Ireland	n/a	12	n/a
20	Rodrigo Sandoval-Almazan, State Autonomous University of Mexico, Toluca, Mexico	57.1%	11	7

4.3   Identifying Leading EGR Scholars' Individual "Signatures" (RQ #3)

A scholar's so-called academic publication rhythm, impact, and reputation (and with those her/his unique "signature") are not only evidenced (a) by the sheer number of publications [5] along with citation numbers and indices, but also (b) by participating in and co-organizing academic conferences, workshops, and colloquia domestically and around the world at various levels, (c) by serving on editorial boards, (d) by receiving external and internal funding for research, (e) by invited talks at renowned venues, (f) by requests for reviewing journal/conference articles, book manuscripts, and grant proposals, (g) by holding offices with professional academic organizations, (h) by participating in public events and publishing websites, and also (i) by receiving national or international awards such as fellowships, residencies, prizes, and other honors (see [3]).

While a scholar's unique "signature" needs to be considered along these various indicators, the authorship of publications itself, however, already provides a good sense of "signature": Consider, for example, a scholar who mostly publishes as a single author as opposed to a scholar who never publishes in the capacity of a single author. Or, consider an author who while publishing collaborative work with others mostly has the lead authorship, as opposed to a co-author who never appears in a lead author role, just to consider some extremes. Conventions for listing co-author names in the sequence of names vary across academic disciplines.

Table 4. Google Scholar i10-index for leading EGR scholars (as of march 7, 2016)); note: Grönlund, Macintosh, and Jaeger – unpublished/not included

Rank	Name, Affiliation, & Country	Change in %	i10-index (March 2016)	i10-index (April 2014)
1	Marijn Janssen, TU Delft, The Netherlands	59.7%	115	72
2	John C. Bertot, University of Maryland, College Park, USA	n/a	98	n/a
3	Ramon Gil-Garcia, CTG, SUNY Albany, USA	40.0%	70	50
4	Theresa A. Pardo, CTG, SUNY Albany, USA	23.2%	69	56
5	Vishanth Weerakkody, Brunel University, Uxbridge, UK	35.4%	65	48
6	Björn Niehaves, Hertie School of Governance, Berlin, Germany	65.8%	63	38
7	Victor J. J. M. Bekkers, Erasmus University Rotterdam, The Netherlands	n/a	61	n/a
8	Maria A. Wimmer, University of Koblenz, Germany	31.7%	54	41
9	Hans Jochen Scholl, University of Washington, Seattle, USA	35.9%	53	39
10	Flavio Corradini, University of Camerino, Italy	n/a	49	n/a
11	Sharon S. Dawes, CTG, SUNY Albany, USA	23.7%	47	38
12	Yannis Charalabidis, University of the Aegean, Samos, Greece	58.6%	46	29
13	Soon Ae Chun, City University of New York, USA	33.3%	44	33
14	Euripidis Loukis, University of the Aegean, Samos, Greece	87.0%	43	23
15	Albert Meijer, Utrecht University, The Netherlands	40.0%	42	30
16	Ralf Klischewski, German University Cairo, Egypt	13.9%	41	36
17	Christopher G. Reddick, University of Texas, San Antonio, USA	53.8%	40	26
18	Efthimios Tambouris, University of Macedonia, Thessaloniki, Greece	30.0%	39	30
19	Luis F. Luna-Reyes, University at Albany, USA	60.9%	37	23
20	Anthony Cresswell, CTG, SUNY Albany, USA	19.4%	37	31

The "sequence-determines-credit" approach (SDC) appears as the most prevalent norm in many disciplines, according to which the name's mention in the sequence of co-author names indicates the relative weight of individual contribution to the collaborative effort from highest to lowest [4, 6, 25]. This norm also appears to be the most prevalent in the study domain of EGR despite the variety of contributing disciplines. A special case under this norm is the publication of two co-authors, which would suggest equal contribution unless the alphabetical order of names is reversed, or the lead co-authorship of an alphabetically first-listed author is indicated otherwise. Other norms include the "equal contribution" norm (EC), which attributes citation numbers and impacts proportionally to the number of contributors, and the "first-last-author-emphasis" norm (FLAE), which is used in some areas of biological and medical research, as well as the "percent-contribution-indicated" approach (PCI), where authors acknowledge their contributions to the publication in percentage figures [25]. The latter two apparently play no role in EGR. Consequently, for this analysis a combined SDC/EC approach has been used.

Number of Co-authors. Among the top-20 most prolific and predominantly EGR-dedicated researchers the preferences with regard to co-authoring vary widely. Based on the EGRL version 11.5 in this top group the average number of co-authors per peer-reviewed contribution amounts to 2.90 (mode: an adjusted 2.65/median: 2.85).

Number of co-authorships range from 1.50 to 4.80. For example, whereas at the one end of the spectrum Reddick (1.50) and Wimmer (2.04) occasionally publish with co-authors, although, not many, at the other end of the spectrum Askounis (3.80) and Charalabidis (4.80) appear to regularly publish with quite a number of co-authors (average co-author counts in parentheses). While in the former two cases a significant individual contribution can be inferred, in the latter cases the individual co-author's contribution remains unclear.

Number of Single and Lead Authorships. As mentioned above single and lead authorships are indicators of high individual contributions to publication output and impact. Also in this category, the top-20 most prolific and predominantly EGR-dedicated researchers demonstrate widely different preferences. The spectrum ranges from an 0.88 index (that is, in 88 % of the publications the author is either a single or the lead author) to zero (that is, not a single sole or lead authorship could be identified). On average the top-20 most prolific authors have a lead of single authorship in about every other publication (mean = 0.51, median = 0.49, and median = 0.35).

Number of Single or Lead-authored Publications in Top-Ten Cited. While the former two categories already provide a good grasp of an individual scholar's signature, when looking at a scholar's top-ten most-highly cited publications in Google Scholar, the number of single and lead co-authored publications among the top ten reveal the individual impact even more clearly. Maximum and range were found at 8, that is, in case of the maximum value, 8 of 10 most highly cited publications were single of lead authored. The median and mode were 6, and the mean was 5.45. However, these descriptive statistics suggest leading EGR scholar truly lead also in terms of documented impact in this category, a few scholars predominantly gain their top-ten citation counts from publications, in which they had no lead whatsoever. The average of single and lead-authored publications is 4.8 and the median 5.

As a result, when taking into consideration the three impact (or signature) categories of (1) number of co-authors, (2) number of single and lead authorships, and (3) number of single or lead-authored publications in top-ten cited, citation and impact indices can be adjusted accordingly, which is shown for citation counts in Table 5.

When multiplying the gross citation number with the single/lead authorship index, an adjusted index results, which more adequately represents the scholar's impact in terms of citations. As Table 5 reveals adjustments made on this basis can significantly reduce or increase a scholar's impact figures. Similar adjustments could easily be made in the same fashion for h-indices and i10-indices (see gross numbers in Tables 3 and 4), which for space constraints cannot be shown here. Further adjustments can also be made for average number of co-authors regarding citation counts, h-indices, and i10-indices by dividing the respective count/index by the average number of co-authors as discussed above. Again, for space constraints these adjustments are not shown here.

Finally, for the most highly cited EGR scholars in Google Scholar the number of single/lead authorships within their respective top-ten most highly cited publications are also shown in Table 5 (rightmost column), which is a profound indicator of scholarly impact along with the other adjusted indices.

In summary, the three impact and signature categories discussed above allow for adjustments and informed interpretations of gross citation counts and indices. Adjusted

Table 5. Most-cited EGR scholars' adjusted citation indices, lead authorship indices, co-authorship indices, and top-ten cited index; note: Grönlund, Macintosh, and Jaeger unpublished/not included

Rank	Name, Affiliation, Country	Avg # of single or lead co-author-ships	Adjusted Google Scholar Citations (March, 2016)	Google Scholar Citations (March, 2016)	Un-adjust-ed Rank	Avg # of Co-Auth ors	# of single or lead-author ed in top-ten cited
1	John C. Bertot, University of Maryland, College Park, USA	0.88	4459	5096	1	3.00	8
2	Marijn Janssen, TU Delft, The Netherlands	0.61	2887	4733	2	2.68	5
3	Sharon S. Dawes, CTG, SUNY Albany, USA	0.65	2103	3235	6	2.40	8
4	Victor J. J. M. Bekkers, Erasmus University Rotterdam, The Netherlands	0.85	1942	2285	12	2.00	6
5	Hans Jochen Scholl, University of Washington, Seattle, USA	0.72	1891	2627	7	2.36	6
6	Ramon Gil-Garcia, CTG, SUNY Albany, USA	0.46	1779	3868	4	2.73	3
7	Christopher G. Reddick, University of Texas, San Antonio, USA	0.85	1560	1835	15	1.50	8
8	Theresa A. Pardo, CTG, SUNY Albany, USA	0.35	1523	4350	3	3.65	2
9	Kim N Andersen, Copenhagen Business School, Denmark	0.75	1518	2024	13	2.70	8
10	Lemuria Carter, North Carolina A & T State University, Greensboro, USA	0.45	1498	3328	5	2.25	6
11	Eric W. Welch, Arizona State University, Phoenix, USA	0.50	1310	2619	8	2.20	6
12	Ralf Klischewski, German University Cairo, Egypt	0.75	1174	1565	20	1.90	7
13	Maria A. Wimmer, University of Koblenz, Germany	0.48	1122	2338	10	2.04	6
14	Albert Meijer, Utrecht University, The Netherlands	0.65	1113	1712	17	2.15	7
15	Luis F. Luna-Reyes, University at Albany, USA	0.55	962	1749	16	3.35	7
16	Soon Ae Chun, City University of New York, USA	0.50	840	1679	18	2.80	4
17	Björn Niehaves, Hertie School of Governance, Berlin, Germany	0.35	815	2328	11	2.90	5
18	Flavio Corradini, University of Camerino, Italy	0.50	803	1605	19	3.25	4
19	Vishanth Weerakkody, Brunel University, Uxbridge, UK	0.29	751	2591	9	2.95	3
20	Anthony Cresswell, CTG, SUNY Albany, USA	0.15	298	1984	14	3.75	0

counts and indices reveal more accurately the true impact of scholars, not just EGR scholars.

5 Discussion, Future Research, and Concluding Remarks

It has been the object of this investigation to update and further analyze the individual scholarly productivity of leading EGR scholars, determine their scholarly impact in terms of citations and citation indices, and introduce the concept of scholarly signature into EGR.

5.1   Remarks on Productivity and Unadjusted Impact

Overall Productivity. From the end of 2005 the volume of publications (see http://faculty.washington.edu/jscholl/egrl/history.php) in the English language in peer-reviewed outlets has grown more than eight-fold, which represents a compound annual growth rate of 21.6 %. In the reporting period since the last investigation in 2014, the number of entries into the EGRL had grown by more than a quarter indicating that the academic output in EGR has maintained its relatively strong growth pattern suggesting that the study domain is well established and topically sound. Major contributors to the continued overall growth are the leading scholars in EGR, whose average growth in publication output equals the overall average. This steady growth helps explain the continued sustainability of five journals and four major international conferences in EGR without a detectable effect of compromising the quality of publications; on the contrary, for example, the acceptance rates at leading conferences such as the HICSS EGOV track have decreased over the years.

Individual Productivity. Instruments such as the EGRL and Google Scholar make possible to closely track scholars' publication output individually and also identify individual scholars' publication behavior (in terms of preferred co-authors, number of co-authors, topics, outlets, and overall publication rhythm, among other measures). This provides an unprecedented and timely transparency to EGR scholars as well as to hiring, tenure, and promotion committees. While such transparency and measurability might be unwelcome to some, the vast majority of individual contributors shows remarkable levels of consistent performance. However, high productivity alone can only be an initial indicator, which in and by itself is not considered a sufficient measure of academic performance and contribution.

Unadjusted Impact. Ever since Google Scholar made individual scholarly profiles publishable in 2012, the impact of scholarly work became more readily identifiable to a wide audience. As reported, erroneous citation counts can still be identified and eliminated. The margin of error in terms of h-index and i-10 index appears to be far smaller for obvious reasons. Despite these known deficiencies, by and large, the Google Scholar service appears to have gained in reputation over the years and now informs hiring, promotion, and tenure committees around the world. However, for reasons discussed above, in particular, the citation counts can be fairly misleading if taken at face value.

5.2   Remarks on Adjusted Impact and Signature

Adjusted Impact. The adjustments presented above account for the number of co-authors and the number of single and lead authorships in publications. Obviously, the former presents a straightforward way to adjust indices by dividing the various counts and indices by the average number of co-authors on a publication and distributing the results evenly. This approach effectively curtails the phenomenon of citation count inflation by inflating the number of co-authors. However, it might also unduly misrepresent the contributions of lead co-authors. Therefore, a more accurate measure appears to be the recognition of single and lead authorships in multi-authored work. When multiplying the various citation counts and indices with the individual single/lead-authorship averages a far more accurate picture appears. Both adjustments taken together provide some significance. For example, in a case with an average of five co-authors per publication and very low or even no single/lead authorships it is hard to determine any individual contribution that stands out. In contrast, in case of a low average number of co-authors and a high number of single/lead authorships the high individual contribution would be undeniable. This would still hold in cases with high average numbers of co-authorships and high numbers of lead authorships. A case in point is Bertot with an average of three co-authors but a record of 88 % of lead authorships. In summary, the number of single and lead authorships along with the number of average co-authors per publication provide meaningful adjustments to otherwise potentially inflated citation counts and indices.

Signature. While these two adjustments already provide the contours of a scholar's "signature," another measure helps sharpen its silhouette: As discussed above, when counting the number of single and lead-authored contributions, for example, in the top-ten highest-cited Google Scholar publication per scholar, more evidence of individual impact and contribution emerges. It is remarkable that mean, median, and mode were all at or around 6 for the number of single/lead-authored publication in the top-ten most highly cited publications in the group of most prolific EGR scholars, which indicates a strong signature and individual impact of scholars in this group. On the other hand, low numbers (equal or lower than three) also point at a relatively weak signature in terms of genuine individual contributions to the earned citation count.

5.3   Making Sense of the Citation Counts and Indices

Multiple Perspectives. In the introduction performance evaluations and comparisons were portrayed as an inevitable and integral part of academic life. Performance evaluations do not only inform hiring, tenure, and promotion decisions, but rather also are an important control element for assuring the quality of academic outcomes and products. No single yardstick produces reliable and all-encompassing indicators, which would span across multiple disciplines and domains. Even inside a discipline or domain, a single measure would be highly problematic. However, in EGR, even if multiple criteria such as productivity, Google Scholar citation counts, h-indices, and i10-indices were taken just at face value, the results would still be inaccurate to unacceptable degrees. Adjustments like those discussed above appear as far more accurate measures. Rather than suggesting to simply replace the unadjusted figures by adjusted ones, it is held that all measures considered together provide a better overall grasp of the evaluation at hand than any of them in isolation. Finally, when reviewing the collective work and impact of leading EGR scholars, de-facto standards of inquiry and "good" research also begin to emerge. This will be the subject of a future study.

Other Future Research. Previous studies on the subject were reportedly used in hiring, tenure, and promotion decisions. It is expected that this will also be the case for this report. Future research is intended to establish how the various studies on academic job performance and evaluations have influenced and been used in hiring, tenure, and promotion cases throughout EGR and its contributing disciplines.

References

1. Acedo, F.J., Barroso, C., Casanueva, C., Galán, J.L.: Co-authorship in management and organizational studies; an empirical and network analysis. J. Manag. Stud. **43**, 957–983 (2006)
2. Altbach, P.G.: The tyranny of citations. Int. High. Educ. **43**, 3–5 (2006)
3. Anonymous: Research Expectations Within the Humanities. Webpage, University of South Florida (2015)
4. Anonymous: Guidance on Authorship in Scholarly or Scientific Publications. Yale University (2016)
5. Bedeian, A.G.: Lesson learned along the way: twelve suggestions for optimizing carrer success. In: Frost, P.J., Taylor, M.S. (eds.) Rhythms of Academic Life: Personal Accounts of Careers in Academia, pp. 1–10. Sage Publications, Thousand Oaks (1996)
6. Brückner, C., Birbaum, S.A., Salathé, M.: Authorship in scientific publications: analysis and recommendations. PDF, Scientific Integrity Committee of the Swiss Academies of Arts and Sciences (2013)
7. Dwivedi, Y., Weerakkody, V.: A profile of scholarly community contributing to the International Journal of Electronic Government Research. Int. J. Electr. Gov. Res. **6**, 1–11 (2010)
8. Dwivedi, Y.K.: An analysis of e-Government research published in Transforming Government: People, Process and Policy (TGPPP?). Transforming Gov.: People Process Policy **3**, 7–15 (2009)
9. Dwivedi, Y.K., Singh, M., Williams, M.D.: Developing a demographic profile of scholarly community contributing to the Electronic Government, an International Journal. Electr. Gov. Int. J. **8**, 259–270 (2011)
10. Feinerer, I.: tm: Text Mining Package. R package version 0.5–7.1 (2012)
11. Goodall, A.: The place of citations in today's academy. Int. High. Educ. (2015)
12. Green, R.G.: Tenure and promotion decisions: the relative importance of teaching, scholarship, and service. J. Soc. Work Educ. **44**, 117–128 (2008)
13. Hirsch, J.E.: An index to quantify an individual's scientific research output. Proc. Natl. Acad. Sci. U.S.A. **102**, 16569–16572 (2005)
14. Holden, G., Rosenberg, G., Barker, K.: Bibliometrics: a potential decision making aid in hiring, reappointment, tenure and promotion decisions. Soc. Work Health Care **41**, 67–92 (2005)
15. Meyer, D., Hornik, K., Feinerer, I.: Text mining infrastructure in R. J. Stat. Softw. **25**, 1–54 (2008)
16. Park, B., Riggs, R.: Tenure and promotion: a study of practices by institutional type. J. Acad. Librariansh. **19**, 72–77 (1993)
17. Rana, N.P., Williams, M.D., Dwivedi, Y.K., Williams, J.: Reflecting on e-Government research. Int. J. Electr. Gov. Res. **7**, 64–88 (2011)
18. Scholl, H.J.: Profiling the EG research community and its core. In: Wimmer, M.A., Scholl, H.J., Janssen, M., Traunmüller, R. (eds.) EGOV 2009. LNCS, vol. 5693, pp. 1–12. Springer, Heidelberg (2009)
19. Scholl, H.J.: Electronic government: a study domain past its infancy. In: Scholl, H.J. (ed.) E-government: Information, Technology, and Transformation, vol. 17, pp. 11–32. M.E. Sharpe, Armonk (2010)
20. Scholl, H.J.: Electronic government research: topical directions and preferences. In: Wimmer, M.A., Janssen, M., Scholl, H.J. (eds.) EGOV 2013. LNCS, vol. 8074, pp. 1–13. Springer, Heidelberg (2013)

21. Scholl, H.J.: The EGOV research community: an update on where we stand. In: Janssen, M., Scholl, H.J., Wimmer, M.A., Bannister, F. (eds.) EGOV 2014. LNCS, vol. 8653, pp. 1–16. Springer, Heidelberg (2014)
22. University of Washington, The Information School. http://faculty.washington.edu/jscholl/egrl/
23. Scholl, H.J.: EGOV Scholarship and EGOV Forums: An Update, pp. 1–11 (under review) (2016)
24. Scholl, H.J., Dwivedi, Y.K.: Forums for electronic government scholars: insights from a 2012/2013 study. Gov. Inf. Q. **31**, 229–242 (2014)
25. Tscharntke, T., Hochberg, M.E., Rand, T.A., Resh, V.H., Krauss, J.: Author sequence and credit for contributions in multiauthored publications. PLoS Biol. **5**, e18 (2007)

Cross-Context Linking Concepts Discovery in E-Government Literature

Bojan Cestnik[1,2(✉)] and Alenka Kern[3]

[1] Temida d.o.o., Ljubljana, Slovenia
bojan.cestnik@temida.si
[2] Jozef Stefan Institute, Ljubljana, Slovenia
[3] Housing Fund of the Republic of Slovenia, Public Fund, Ljubljana, Slovenia
alenka.kern@ssrs.si

Abstract. To conduct their business, organizations are nowadays challenged to handle huge amount of information from heterogeneous sources. Novel technologies can help them dealing with this delicate assignment. In this paper we describe an approach to document clustering and outlier detection that is regularly used to organize and summarize knowledge stored in huge amounts of documents in a government organization. The motivation for our preliminary study has been three-fold: first, to obtain an overview of the topics addressed in the recently published e-government papers, with the emphasis on identifying the shift of focus through the years; second, to form a collection of papers related to a preselected terms of interest in order to explore the characteristic keywords that discriminate this collection with respect to the rest of the documents; and third, to compare the papers that address a similar topic from two document sources and to show characteristic similarities and differences between the two origins, with a particular aim to identify outlier papers in each document source that are potentially worth for further exploration. As a document source for our study we used E-Government Reference Library of articles and PubMed. The presented case study results suggest that the document exploration supported by a document clustering tool can be more focused, efficient and effective.

Keywords: Document clustering · Linking concepts discovery · E-government · Public housing · Social media

1 Introduction

Every modern organization in both government and private sector needs to process, organize and store information that is required to conduct its business. In this task, ontologies typically play a key role in providing a common understanding by describing concepts, classes and instances of a given domain. They are frequently built manually by extracting common-sense knowledge from various sources in some sort of representation. Many computer programs that support manual ontology construction have been developed and successfully used in the past, such as Protégé [1].

Since manual ontology construction can be a complex and demanding process, there is a strong need to provide at least partially automated support for the task. With the emergence of new text and literature mining technologies, large corpora of

© IFIP International Federation for Information Processing 2016
Published by Springer International Publishing Switzerland 2016. All Rights Reserved
H.J. Scholl et al. (Eds.): EGOV 2016, LNCS 9820, pp. 19–30, 2016.
DOI: 10.1007/978-3-319-44421-5_2

documents can be processed to semi-automatically construct structured document clusters [2]. Resulting document clusters can be viewed as concepts (classes, topic descriptions) that can be used to describe domain properties in the form of topic ontologies. In recent years, various tools that help constructing document clusters from texts in a given problem domain were developed and successfully implemented in practice [2]. One example of such tool that enables interactive construction of clusters of text documents in a selected domain is OntoGen [3]. It can be used to extract concepts from input documents and organize them into high-level topics. By using modern data and text processing techniques OntoGen supports individual phases of ontology construction by suggesting concepts and their names and defining relations between them [4].

Literature mining is a process of applying data mining techniques to sets of documents from published literature. Essentially, literature mining is a technique used to tame the complexity of high dimensional data and extract new knowledge from the available literature. It can be used in many ways and for various purposes, also, for example, when dealing with problems spawning from economic crisis that the society is facing in our time. For instance, in [5] the authors analyze and compare innovation in public and private sectors. They identify three factors for improved interest for innovation in public sector. First, the requirements and expectations of the public sector services have grown considerably. Second, the number of complex problems that the public sector has to face in the areas like public safety, poverty reduction, and climate mitigation has also grown. And third, innovative capabilities of governments and localities play an important role in the competitive globalization game [5].

Documents that are of interest for an organization might come from various sources. They can be stored in the organization's Intranet storage, or can reside in a more or less organized form and format on the Internet. Among many publicly accessible potential sources we can identify semi-structured Semantic Web entities and Linked Data sources, as well as more organized public libraries such as Medline and PubMed [6], E-Government Reference Library [7], and Google Scholar [8]. A general text processing management and ontology learning process from text consists of several steps [e.g. 2]. First, the documents (natural language texts) and other resources (e.g. semi-structured domain dictionaries) are obtained from designated sources. Then, they are preprocessed and stored on text processing server. In the next step, domain ontology is built with ontology learning and ontology pruning algorithms. In the last step, the constructed ontology is visualized, evaluated and stored on a repository for further use and exploration.

The main motivation for our case study was to demonstrate how the text processing can be used for public documents and government data. We wanted to present the utility and evaluation of the approach from the interested parties' (i.e. public bodies) viewpoint. In particular, our aim was to offer some interesting insights, such as how the document clustering technology can be used to identify mutual subsets of papers from one context (document source) that were more close to the subset of papers from the other context. Such a cross-context approach to linking term discovery has been introduced in medical field [e.g. 9–11] and has been used to identify hidden relations between domains of interest with a great success.

In the case study described in this paper we used E-Government Reference Library of articles [7] and PubMed [6] as a document source. In the first experiment we obtained an overview of the topics addressed in the recently published e-government papers. In particular, we were interested in the shift of focus of the papers through the years; the keywords describing document clusters gave us clues about which topics are trending in certain time periods. In the second experiment we formed a cluster of papers related to a preselected term (in our case we used two arbitrarily selected terms: "social media" and "housing") in order to explore the characteristic keywords that discriminate this cluster with respect to the rest of the documents. The underlying assumption was that while it is often easy to automatically collect data, it requires considerable effort to link and transform them into practical information that can be used in concrete situations. In the third experiment we combined the papers addressing the similar topic from two document sources, e-Government Reference Library and PubMed. Then, we identified characteristic similarities and differences between the two origins, with a particular aim to identify outlier papers that are worthy of further exploration for finding potential cross-context concept links. Here, the underlying assumption was that while the majority of papers in a given domain describe matters related to a common understanding of the domain, the exploration of outliers may lead to the detection of interesting associating concepts among the sets of papers from two disjoint document sources. In addition, focusing on a potentially interesting subset of outlier papers might considerably reduce the size of article corpora under investigation. The presented case study results suggest that the document exploration aided by OntoGen can, in comparison to the traditional manual one, be more focused, efficient and effective.

This paper is organized as follows. In the Sect. 2 we describe the construction of the input sets of documents. In the Sect. 3 we describe the methods used in the study and present three cases in which OntoGen was used to generate and visualize clusters of documents with similar properties. In Sect. 4, we assess and discuss the main lessons learned from the case study. The paper is concluded in Sect. 4.

2   Document Sources

Documents and papers that are of interest for an organization can be obtained from many publicly accessible sources on the Internet. There are several semi-structured Semantic Web entities and Linked Data sources, as well as more organized public libraries such as Medline and PubMed [6], E-Government Reference Library [7], and Google Scholar [8]. Majority of the contemporary published papers can be, depending on the copyright issues, obtained in an electronic form from the Internet. It is particularly useful when a set of documents from a selected domain is available in some sort of standard format.

One such example is E-Government Reference Library – EGRL – [7] that in the current version 11.5 contains 9.690 references of peer-reviewed articles predominantly in English language. It is available in XML format for public download and use. Another example of a resource of papers on the Internet is PubMed [6], which contains papers largely from the medical field.

The first step in the process of text mining and document clustering is retrieval and preprocessing of text documents. For our study we took 7.810 documents from the EGRL library in XML format as an input for further processing. Text mining and document clustering methods were shown to produce useful results on scientific papers when used on titles and abstracts [12]. Therefore, in the preprocessing phase we excluded the papers that contain only title in the XML file and included only those library papers that have also their abstracts available. There are 5.223 such papers in the library. Each relevant paper was described with the year of publication, the title and the abstract. Short statistics of the included papers according to the year of publication is shown in Table 1. The first input document collection was used in the experiments described in Subsects. 3.1 and 3.2.

To process the papers that address a similar topic from two document sources we prepared the second input document collection from the PubMed papers responding to the search string "social media" and "government". The criteria for the search were arbitrarily selected with the aim to focus on the papers related to "government" topic and narrow the number of retrieved papers. Note that any other specific topic of interest can be used instead of "social media". The concrete search query was "government AND social AND (media OR network)". As a result, we obtained 9.690 papers, from which 5.327 papers had abstracts and were published after the year 2004. The second input document collection was used together with the first document collection in the experiment, described in Subsect. 3.3.

Table 1. Number of papers from E-Government Reference Library [7] by the year of publication. In the last two columns the papers with included abstract are given.

Publication year	All papers		With abstracts	
	Number	%	Number	%
2002 and before	502	6.4	283	5.4
2003	288	3.7	211	4.0
2004	404	5.2	270	5.2
2005	465	6.0	243	4.7
2006	353	4.5	93	1.8
2007	592	7.6	210	4.0
2008	353	4.5	297	5.7
2009	687	8.8	449	8.6
2010	650	8.3	428	8.2
2011	702	9.0	431	8.3
2012	793	10.2	469	9.0
2013	763	9.8	682	13.1
2014	698	8.9	606	11.6
2015	560	7.2	551	10.5
Total	7.810	100.0	5.223	100.0

3 Document Clustering with OntoGen

The process of forming clusters of documents from a set of documents and naming them by key words can be considered as creating topic ontology in a domain under study. Ontologies include descriptions of objects, concepts, attributes and relations between objects. They conceptualize and integrate the domain terminologies that can be identified in text. Therefore, ontologies reflect the content and the structure of the knowledge as it can be recognized through the use of terms in the inspected collection of texts. Note that the documents that are used in the construction of topic ontologies must be carefully selected before they are processed and considered for analyses.

Ontologies for a given domain can be constructed manually using some sort of language or representation. In manual extraction, an expert seeks common sense concepts and organizes them in hierarchical form. Since manual ontology construction is a complex and demanding process, several computerized programs have been created that support semi-automatic construction of ontologies from a set of documents [e.g. 2]. Based on text mining techniques that have already been proved successful for the task, OntoGen [4] is a tool that enables the interactive construction of ontologies from text in a selected domain. Note that OntoGen is one representative of the tools that help constructing ontologies from texts. With the use of machine learning techniques, OntoGen supports individual phases of ontology construction by suggesting concepts and their names, by defining relations between them and by the automatic assignment of text to the concepts. The most descriptive words of each concept are obtained by the SVM [13] from the documents grouped in each cluster.

The input for OntoGen is a collection of text documents. Documents are represented as vectors; such representation is often referred to as Bag of Words (BoW) representation [14]. In the BoW vector space model, each word from the document vocabulary stands for one dimension of the multidimensional space of text documents. This way, the BoW approach can be employed for extracting words with similar meaning. Therefore, it is commonly used in information retrieval and text mining for representing collections of words from text documents disregarding grammar and word order, which enables to determine the semantic closeness documents. BoW vector representation can also be used to calculate average similarity between the documents of a cluster. The similarity is also called cosine similarity, since the similarity between two documents is computed as cosine of the angle between the two representative vectors.

3.1 Topic Focus Shift Through Time

In the first experiment we set a goal to acquire an overview of the topics (keywords) prevailingly addressed in the recently published e-government papers. In particular, we were interested in the shift of topic focus of the papers through the years. The characteristic keywords describing document clusters, which were generated automatically with OntoGen, gave us clues about which topics are trending in certain time periods. By using OntoGen users can construct a complex ontology more efficiently and in shorter time period than manually. They can create concepts, organize them into topics and also assign documents to concepts. Simultaneously, they have full control over whole process (therefore semi-automatic) by choosing or revising the suggestions provided by the system [3].

We constructed a topic ontology with OntoGen from the abstracts of 5.223 papers from EGRL [7], shown in Table 1 and Fig. 1. The topics represent temporal divisions (clusters) of documents according to the year of publication and are labeled with the most descriptive words. The topic ontology from Fig. 1 can be regarded as a structure of folders for the input set of papers. In such way it can enrich our prior knowledge about the domain, motivating creative thinking and additional explanations of the constructed concepts. Moreover, the descriptions of clusters (keywords) in Fig. 1 can be used to analyze trends in the published topics. For example, keyword "media" (or "social media") appeared in the descriptions only after year 2011 and gained more importance after 2013. Keyword "citizens" is spotted from 2005 on, while "cities" gained importance in 2015 with the smart cities initiative. Many other interesting relations can be observed directly from Fig. 1. Note that average similarity measure for each cluster is also shown in Fig. 1.

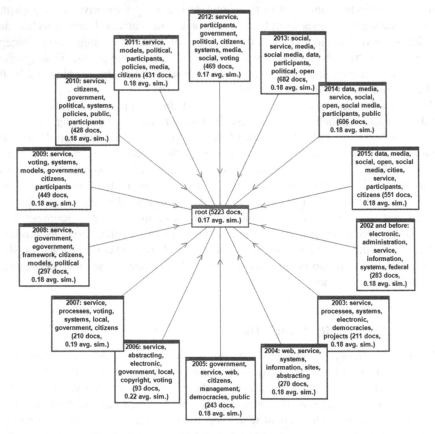

Fig. 1. 5.223 papers from EGRL library clustered according to the year of publication. Each cluster is described with SVM [13] keywords that characterize the contained papers.

3.2   Grouping Papers by Selected Characteristic Keywords

In the second experiment we generated a special cluster of papers related to a prese-lected term (in our case we used two arbitrarily selected terms: "social media" and "housing") in order to explore the characteristic keywords that discriminate this cluster with respect to the rest of the documents. The underlying assumption was that while it is often easy to automatically collect data, it requires considerable effort to link and transform them into practical information that can be used to help decision makers in concrete situations. As input we took the abstracts of 5.223 papers from EGRL and manually (overriding OntoGen's document similarity feature) constructed four clusters. In the first cluster we included documents containing term "social media" (503 papers); the remaining 4.720 documents were included in the second cluster. In the third cluster we included documents containing term "housing" (21 papers); the remaining 5.202 papers were included in the fourth cluster. Then, we generated SVM keyword descriptions for each cluster that distinguish it from its counterpart cluster (the first from the second, and the third from the fourth cluster). The goal was to explore the characteristic keywords that discriminate the documents in one cluster with respect to the rest of the documents. In our case, we wanted to identify common concepts (keywords) between the two clusters, since "social media" and "housing"are both topic of high interest for our organization, and pinpoint the most relevant papers describing the two topics.

The four clusters and descriptions are shown in Fig. 2. The cluster for "social media" is described with the following keywords: "social, media, social media, net-works, political, social networks, community, twitter, participants, citizens", while the remaining cluster is described by "service, systems, government, models, data, citizens, public, information, participants, processes". The cluster for "housing" is described with the following keywords: "housing, community, service, digital, divide, digital divide, social, citizens, website, government website", while its counterpart cluster is described by "service, government, systems, citizens, models, public, data, participants, political, social". The descriptions of two distinguished clusters share two common keywords: "social"and "citizens". The central document for "social media" ncluster is the document with id 1998 [15], while the central document for "housing" cluster is the document with id 6588 [16]. The two documents were used for more detailed pre-liminary study of the two topics and for finding new, potentially uncovered ideas for social media applications in housing.

3.3   Combining Papers from Two Document Sources

In the third experiment we combined the papers addressing the similar topic from two document sources, e-Government Reference Library and PubMed. Our aim was to identify characteristic similarities and differences between the papers from the two origins. In particular, we were interested in outlier papers that are worthy of further exploration for finding potential cross-context concept links [e.g. 11]. Here, our assumption was that while the majority of papers in a given domain describe the matters related to a common understanding of the domain, the exploration of outliers

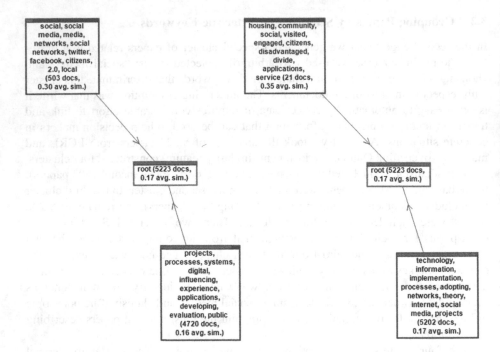

Fig. 2. Two document clusters for preselected terms "social media" (left) and "housing" (right). The characteristic keywords that discriminate the two clusters with respect to the rest of the documents are shown in the rectangles.

may lead to the detection of interesting associating concepts among the sets of papers from two disjoint document sources. In addition, focusing on a potentially interesting subset of outlier papers might considerably reduce the size of article corpora under investigation, which might also help decision-makers narrowing down the mere quantity of papers to read for further study.

For practical purposes, we have joined the first and the second input document collections to obtain 10.550 papers with abstracts. Then, we have constructed with OntoGen two clusters of documents based on their similarity. I the papers from the two sources were completely different, the two clusters would most probably contain the documents from one document source, respectively. However, the situation depicted in Fig. 3 shows that this assumption is only partially correct. The two top level clusters are labeled "health, careful, patients" and "service, citizens, government". The first cluster (lets denote in with P) contains 8.416 documents, while the second one (denoted with E) contains 5.734 documents. Second level clusters reveal that in cluster P there is a majority of papers (4.749) from PubMed and only a minority (67 papers in cluster denoted P-E) of papers from eGov field. The situation is reversed in cluster E: here, the majority is from eGov (5.156 papers) and slightly bigger minority from PubMed (578 papers in cluster denoted E-P).

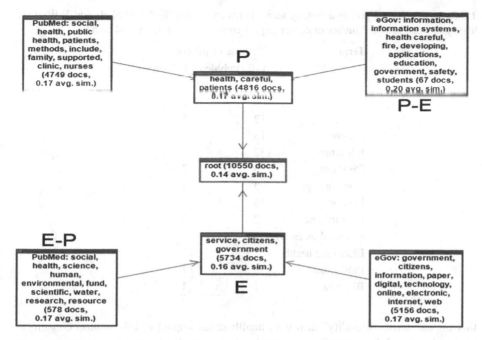

Fig. 3. Combining papers from two sources: e-Government Reference Library and PubMed. Clusters containing outlier documents are shown in bottom-left and top-right rectangle.

In cluster P-E there are 67 documents from EGRL library that are described with keywords "information, information systems, health careful, fire, developing, applications, education, government, safety, students". They are "outliers" from eGov (EGRL) library because they are more similar to PubMed documents. Clearly, they prevailingly deal with the health-related issues. On the other hand, in cluster E-P there are 578 documents from PubMed that are more similar to EGRL library documents. The can be described with the following keywords: "social, health, science, human, environmental, fund, scientific, water, research, resource".

In our preliminary study we took into account the outlier papers from both P-E and E-P clusters and formed combined blended input document collection for further analysis. Our aim was to investigate the potential of outlier clusters for uncovering linking concepts between the two fields in our further work. In order to reduce the search space, the white list of interesting potential linking concepts for further consideration (shown in Table 2) that was prepared with OntoGen and further refined and validated by the domain expert.

All the listed terms appear to be interesting to the domain expert that was included in the process. The identified outlier papers for each term seem worth for further exploration. For example, the single outlier paper from EGRL that contains the term "family" states how job clarity, effective communications with management, a participatory management approach, organizational support of career development, opportunities for advancement, and **family-friendly policies** are all significant variables affecting the job satisfaction of IT employees [17]. The two papers from EGRL

Table 2. The list of potential linking terms between outliers E-P (PubMed) and P-E (eGov library of documents). Number of outlier papers containing each term is shown.

Term	Number of papers	
	E-P (PubMed)	P-E (eGov)
Safety	14	5
Media	96	2
Privacy	12	1
Family	13	1
Education	32	7
Disability	6	2
Disadvantage	3	1
Economy	13	1
Low income	2	2
Financial incentive	3	1
Electronic health	1	3
Public fund	9	1
Big data	1	1

that include term "disability" deal with health status impact to information consumers [18] and regional disparities in occurrences of diseases due to unsafe water resources in China [19]. We have observed that the last paper is indexed also in the PubMed library. When considering "disadvantage" as a linking term, the outlier document indexed in EGRL that deals with poverty and health in the good society [20] was identified. It is actually a book published by Palgrave Macmillan and is definitely worth reading and referencing in further studies. Last but not least, we found two outlier documents containing term "big data". The first document indexed in PubMed deals with big data analysis framework for healthcare and social sectors in Korea [21], while the second document is indexed in EGRL and deals with incentivizing health information exchange [22].

4   Conclusion

In this paper we describe three experiments in using text processing and clustering methods to model and visualize existing but often overlooked knowledge that is hidden in documents and papers. The issue addressed is the information integration in e-Government domain ontologies and their visualization through the similarity maps. The ontologies were constructed semi-automatically with the computational support of OntoGen [3] using scientific papers from EGRL [7] and PubMed as input. The use of OntoGen has enabled a quick insight into a given domain by semi-automatically generating the main ontology concepts from the domain's documents.

Our observations show that ontologies help gaining understanding in a given subject area. Therefore, using tools for semi-automatic ontology construction from textual data can significantly speed up the process of becoming acquainted with the domain of interest. We can first generate top-level domain ontology concepts and thus obtain a general overview and understanding of the domain, and only then concentrate on reading an extra load of information. In such a way, semi-automatically constructed ontologies actually helped us to review and understand the variety of topics of interest prior to further investigation.

Encouraged by the growing demands for public innovation, one of the aims of this article was also to explore technological possibilities for supporting creative processes in public sector. In order to exploit existing but often overlooked knowledge that is hidden in public information we investigated the potential of text processing and document clustering. In the third experiment we focused on identifying outlier documents from two document sources (PubMed and EGRL libraries), since the exploration of outliers may lead to the detection of interesting associating concepts among the two sets of documents. We have demonstrated that focusing on a potentially interesting subset of outlier papers considerably reduces the size of document corpora under investigation. Our observations show that using tools for semi-automatic ontology construction from text can significantly speed up the process of becoming acquainted with the domain of interest, thus making the process more focused and effective.

Acknowledgement. The presented work was partially carried out for the Housing Fund of the Republic of Slovenia, Public Fund. The authors wish to thank the Fund's management for their continuous cooperation and support.

References

1. Gennari, J., Musen, M.A., Fergerson, R.W., Grosso, W.E., Crubezy, M., Eriksson, H., Noy, N.F., Tu, S.W.: The evolution of protégé: an environment for knowledge-based systems development. Int. J. Hum.-Comput. Stud. **58**(1), 89–123 (2003)
2. Kietz, J.U., Mädche, A., Mädche, E., Volz, R.: A method for semi-automatic ontology acquisition from a corporate intranet. In: EKAW-2000 Workshop "Ontologies and Text", Juan-Les-Pins (2000)
3. Fortuna, B., Grobelnik, M., Mladenić, D.: System for semi-automatic ontology construction. In: Demo at ESWC 2006, Budva, Montenegro (2006)
4. Fortuna, B.: OntoGen: Description. http://ontogen.ijs.si/index.html. Accessed 15 Dec 2015
5. Sørensen, E., Torfing, J.: Enhancing collaborative innovation in the public sector. Adm. Soc. **43**(8), 842–868 (2011)
6. PubMed, 15 December 2015. http://www.ncbi.nlm.nih.gov/pubmed
7. Scholl, H.J.: E-Government Reference Library (EGRL) version 11.5 (2015). https://catalyst. uw.edu/webq/survey/jscholl/22768. Accessed 3 Jan 2015
8. Google Scholar (2016). https://scholar.google.com/. Accessed 15 Dec 2015
9. Swanson, D.R., Smalheiser, N.R., Torvik, V.I.: Ranking indirect connections in literature-based discovery: the role of medical subject headings (MeSH). J. Am. Soc. Inf. Sci. Technol. **57**(11), 1427–1439 (2006)
10. Weeber, M., Vos, R., Klein, H., de Jong-van den Berg, L.T.W.: Using concepts in literature-based discovery simulating Swanson's Raynaud–fish oil and migraine–magnesium discoveries. J. Am. Soc. Inf. Sci. Technol. **52**(7), 548–557 (2001)

11. Petrič, I., Cestnik, B., Lavrač, N., Urbančič, T.: Outlier detection in cross-context link discovery for creative literature mining. Comput. J. **55**(1), 47–61 (2012)
12. Cestnik, B., Urbančič, T., Petrič, I.: Ontological representations for supporting learning in business communities. In: Smrikarov, A. (ed.) e-Learning 2011: proceedigs of the International Conference on e-Learning and the Knowledge Society, pp. 260–265. ASE Publishing House, Bucharest (2011)
13. Ayed, Y.B., Fohr, D., Haton, J.-P., Chollet, G.: Keyword spotting using support vector machines. In: Sojka, P., Kopeček, I., Pala, K. (eds.) TSD 2002. LNCS (LNAI), vol. 2448, pp. 285–295. Springer, Heidelberg (2002)
14. Sebastiani, F.: Machine learning in automated text categorization. ACM Comput. Surv. **34**(1), 1–47 (2002)
15. Effing, R., van Hillegersberg, J., Huibers, T.W.: Social media participation and local politics: a case study of the Enschede council in the Netherlands. In: Wimmer, M.A., Tambouris, E., Macintosh, A. (eds.) ePart 2013. LNCS, vol. 8075, pp. 57–68. Springer, Heidelberg (2013)
16. Sipiror, J., Ward, B.: Bridging the digital divide for e-government inclusion: a United States case study. Electron. J. e-Gov. **3**(3), 137–146 (2005)
17. Kim, S.: IT employee job satisfaction in the public sector. Int. J. Public Adm. **32**(12) (2009). Special Issue: Reforms of Welfare Administration and Policy
18. Goldner, M.: How health status impacts the types of information consumers seek online. Inf. Commun. Soc. **9**(6), 693–713 (2006)
19. Carlton, E.J., Liang, S., McDowell, J.Z., Li, H., Luo, W., Remais, J.V.: Regional disparities in the burden of disease attributable to unsafe water and poor sanitation in China. Bull. World Health Organ. **90**(8), 578–587 (2012)
20. Cattell, V.: Poverty, Community, and Health: Co-operation and the Good Society. Palgrave Macmillan, New York (2011)
21. Song, T.M., Ryu, S.: Big data analysis framework for healthcare and social sectors in Korea. Healthcare Inf. Res. **21**(1), 3–9 (2015)
22. Jarman, H.: Incentivizing health information exchange: collaborative governance, market failure, and the public interest. In: Proceedings of the 15th Annual International Conference on Digital Government Research, pp. 227–235. ACM, New York (2014)

Open Statistics: The Rise of a New Era for Open Data?

Evangelos Kalampokis[1,2](✉), Efthimios Tambouris[1,2], Areti Karamanou[1,2], and Konstantinos Tarabanis[1,2]

[1] University of Macedonia, Thessaloniki, Greece
{ekal,tambouris,akarm,kat}@uom.gr
[2] Centre for Research and Technology – Hellas, Information Technologies Institute, Thermi, Greece

Abstract. A large part of open data concerns statistics, such as demographic, economic and social data (henceforth referred to as Open Statistical Data, OSD). In this paper we start by introducing *open data fragmentation* as a major obstacle for OSD reuse. We proceed by outlining data cube as a logical model for structuring OSD. We then introduce *Open Statistics* as a new area aiming to systematically study OSD. Open Statistics reuse and extends methods from diverse fields like Open Data, Statistics, Data Warehouses and the Semantic Web. In this paper, we focus on benefits and challenges of Open Statistics. The results suggest that Open Statistics provide benefits not present in any of these fields alone. We conclude that in certain cases OSD can realise the potential of open data.

Keywords: Open data · Statistical data · Open statistics · Linked data · Data analytics

1 Introduction

Today an increasing number of public authorities, international organisations and even enterprises publish Open Data [1,2]. Open Data refers to data that *can be freely used, re-used and redistributed by anyone*[1]. In the public sector, opening up government data aims to increase transparency and boost economic growth. Indeed, estimates suggest that the potential of Open Data is tremendous [3]. For example, a study conducted by the McKinsey Global Institute estimated the global annual economic potential value of Open Data to \$3 trillion [4]. Against this general euphoria however, studies reveal that publishing open data does not automatically provide benefits [5,6]. Thus, we are still far from suggesting that the potential of open data has been realised. On the contrary, further research is needed in promising areas.

---

[1] http://opendefinition.org.

© IFIP International Federation for Information Processing 2016
Published by Springer International Publishing Switzerland 2016. All Rights Reserved
H.J. Scholl et al. (Eds.): EGOV 2016, LNCS 9820, pp. 31–43, 2016.
DOI: 10.1007/978-3-319-44421-5_3

In this respect, an obvious route for further research is to understand the nature of open data. Policy documents and research in the area suggest that a large part of open data is numerical and, more specifically, concerns statistics [7]. Examples include demographics (e.g. census data), social data (e.g. on unemployment and poverty), economic data (e.g. number of new businesses) etc. In this paper we refer to these as Open Statistical Data (OSD). The fact that OSD is a large part of open data was the main motivation for our research. OSD are numerical hence can be easily processed and visualised while significant knowledge already exists in areas such as statistics and data warehouses.

In this paper, we present Open Statistics as a new field to systematically investigate OSD and the creation of value from them. Open Statistics reuse methods from diverse fields like Open Data, Semantic Web, Statistics, Machine Learning and Data Warehouses. More specifically, Open Statistics use existing knowledge on Open Data (such as processes and formats used to publish open data) as background environment. In this environment, Open Statistics reuse but, more importantly, in many cases redefines and extends existing methods from other areas, e.g. for data integration, analysis and visualisation. As a result, Open Statistics provide benefits that go much beyond what was possible in each separate field. This suggests that Open Statistics can actually constitute a significant field of research that, under certain conditions, could enable realising the full potential of Open Data.

The research work that we present in this paper is exploratory [8] as we aim to scope out the magnitude of Open Statistics and to provide and initial understanding about it. In general, exploratory research is research conducted for a problem that has not been clearly defined. It often occurs before we know enough to make conceptual distinctions or posit an explanatory relationship [9]. As a result, we include the following activities in our approach:

- Study datasets from two open data portals at different administrative levels. In particular we focus on the UK's national open data portal[2] and the European Union's open data portal[3] and we study statistical datasets related to *unemployment*.
- Review literature related to research areas overlapping with Open Statistics. In particular, we reuse existing knowledge from (a) Open Data because open statistical data is a major part of them, (b) Data Warehouse and Online Analytical Processing (OLAP) because data cube model seems appropriate to conceptualise OSD, (c) Statistics as a valuable way to create value out of OSD, and (d) Linked Data as a vital technological enabler to achieve the full potential of Open Statistics.

The rest of this paper is organised as follows. In Sect. 2 we present the existing situation in OSD. In Sect. 3 we present a major challenge for OSD reuse, namely data fragmentation. In Sect. 4 we outline the data cube model. In Sect. 5 we introduce Open Statistics and show how it is related to other fields of study.

---

[2] http://data.gov.uk.
[3] http://www.europeandataportal.eu/.

In Sect. 6 we illustrate the benefits of Open Statistics while in Sect. 7 we present the relevant challenges. Section 8 presents the main conclusions of the work and directions of future research.

2   Existing Situation

Today, opening government data is a political priority in many countries worldwide including the USA and the EU. As a result, an exponentially increasing amount of government data is rapidly opening. International organizations (such as the World Bank) also open up their data. A five-star model has been proposed by Tim Berners-Lee to evaluate the maturity of open data[4].

More specifically, OSD is currently provided by governments and organisations through data portals at the international, European, national or regional level. At the international level, organisations provide OSD related to countries in data portals such as the World Bank data portal[5], the Organisation for Economic Cooperation and Development (OECD) data portal[6] and the United Nations Educational, Scientific and Cultural Organisation (UNESCO) data portal[7]. At the European level, OSD are provided through the official European Data Portal[8] and the data portal of Eurostat[9]. At the national level, OSD are provided by the national open data portals (e.g. the data.gov.uk in the UK) but also by the National Statistical Offices (e.g. the Office for National Statistics[10] in the UK). Finally, at the regional level, OSD are published by local agencies, cities or even boroughs of cities in local data portals such as the data portal of the city of Brussels[11] and the data portal of the Camden borough of London[12]. Finally, data portals also serve as single points of access and, apart from providing data regarding their administrative level, they also provide links to datasets that are published at data portals of lower levels.

3   Open Statistical Data Fragmentation

As already stated, a large part of open data are numerical thus potentially easy to process and visualise. In reality however studies suggest that open data reuse is limited. In this section, we investigate practical obstacles for OSD reuse. We do not consider obstacles related to legal and organisational issues at the side of the publishers. Instead, we concentrate on the side of the end user, who is interested to reuse open data.

---

[4] https://www.w3.org/DesignIssues/LinkedData.html.
[5] http://data.worldbank.org/.
[6] http://stats.oecd.org/.
[7] http://opendata.unesco.org/.
[8] http://europeandataportal.eu/.
[9] http://ec.europa.eu/eurostat/data/database.
[10] http://ons.gov.uk.
[11] http://opendata.brussel.be/.
[12] http://opendata.camden.gov.uk/.

For the purposes of this research, we searched two major open government data portals, namely the UK data portal and the European data portal. In both case, according to our scenario, we were interested to reuse open data about *unemployment*.

We first searched the UK data portal for datasets using the keyword *unemployment*. This resulted in 122 results, which provided access to 56 files and 610 links to other portals (e.g. to the UK's Office for National Statistic) and thus to other files. We opened and examined these files one by one and find out that only 13 out of 56 are relevant to unemployment and that 7 out of 13 provide structured numeric values in a machine readable format.

Most importantly, however, those datasets measure unemployment based on different characteristics (also called dimensions). For example, we found datasets for unemployment in different geospatial levels (e.g. in the city of London, in the Camden borough, or in the different wards of Camden), age groups, gender or time duration (e.g. annual, quarterly or monthly unemployment). Relative datasets also measure unemployment using different units of measure (e.g. unemployment rate or thousands of unemployed people). Finally, different datasets may employ different methods for measuring unemployment e.g. based on the UK's Office for National Statistics (OSN) estimations, based on the number of people that claim Job Seekers Allowance (JSA) or based on the International Labour Organization's (ILO) model.

We then searched European data portal using *unemployment* keyword. This search returned 120 datasets mainly from Eurostat. Again, those datasets describe unemployment using different dimensions and units of measures. Different datasets also measure unemployment in different context (e.g. in the context of education and training or in regional statistics). This also means that these datasets are located in different parts of the portals.

In summary, our research revealed that searching the two open data portals for useful data on unemployment results in large numbers of datasets and links.

We call *open data fragmentation* the situation where collections of relevant open data are broken down into many pieces that are not close together. This definition is actually an adaptation of the definition of data fragmentation in computing.

Unemployment is not the only case where relevant data are fragmented. In the case of OSD, fragmentation is actually the rule rather than the exception. Therefore, we suggest that in order for OSD (and therefore Open Data in general) to be useful the problem of open data fragmentation has to be sufficiently addressed. We acknowledge that other obstacles already mentioned in the literature are also important. However, in this paper we concentrate on overcoming the obstacle of open data fragmentation.

4   The Data Cube Model

The study of datasets in both the UK and the European open data portals reveals that (a) OSD can be conceptualised using the traditional data cube (or just cube) model that was initially introduced in Data Warehouses and that (b) different datasets provide fragmented views of a cube.

Although research in data warehouses is active for more than two decades, concepts and systems lack a uniform theoretical basis with regards to models that define data cubes and operations that are performed on data cubes [10–14]. In general, however, a data cube is specified by a set of dimensions and a set of measures. The dimensions create a structure that comprises a number of cells, while each cell includes a numeric value for each measure of the cube. Let us consider as an example a cube from Eurostat with three dimensions, namely time in years, geography in countries, and age group, that measures the employment rate. An example of a cell in this cube would define that the percentage of unemployed people between 25 and 49 years old in France in 1999 is 10.2 % (Fig. 1). This conceptual cube could have been created using numeric values from multiple datasets.

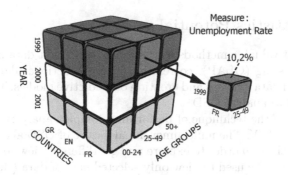

Fig. 1. Open statistical data modelled as a cube

5 Open Statistics

Open Statistics is a field aiming to systematically study Open Statistical Data (OSD). The main idea behind Open Statistics is that we concentrate only on Open Data that are actually statistics. This is a large part of all Open Data but clearly not all Open Data are OSD.

Open Statistics mainly capitalise on existing knowledge on Open Data and mainly Open Government Data. The majority of the existing body of knowledge in those areas is applicable in Open Statistics although in some cases some precaution is necessary. In this environment, methods from three other areas are reused and in some cases redefined. These are Data Warehouses and OLAP, Statistics and the Semantic Web (mostly Linked Open Data).

Open Statistics reuse the concept of data cubes for OSD logical organisation. It shows how data are logically connected and not necessarily how they are physically connected.

Open Statistics also reuse Online Analytical Processing (OLAP) methods, such as slicing and dicing. In some cases however those methods are redefined since OLAP was initially introduced in a close environment. In Open Statistics we have the possibility of performing operations not needed before. For example, searching for similar data cubes in the same or different open data portal is an essential operation to overcome open data fragmentation.

Open Statistics involve analysing OSD with statistical methods, such as Pearson's correlation, linear regression, and logistic regression, and techniques such as panel data analysis and even statistical learning analysis in order to explain or predict phenomena. In the context of Open Statistics the exploitation of these methods and techniques will be redefined.

Finally, Open Statistics capitalise on the Linked Open Data technology (LOD) and more specifically on the LOD implementation of the data cube model, termed RDF Data Cube (QB) vocabulary. This provides the necessary technological infrastructure for Open Statistics.

6   Open Statistics Potential

Some of the most valuable methods that are used to exploit data include Online Analytical Processing (OLAP), correlation of cross-sectional data, time-series correlation, panel data analysis and creation of predictive models. These methods can also be used to analyse OSD.

OLAP refers to the technique of performing complex analysis over the information stored in a DW. The multidimensional nature of OSD allows performing OLAP on top of them in order to explore and get different views of the data. For example, OLAP can be used to view only selected part of data (slice or dice), to view a reoriented view of the data (pivot) or to navigate among different levels of the data along a specific dimension (drill-down or roll-up).

Cross-sectional data [15] provide observations of phenomena at a single point of time. Correlation of cross-sectional data can be, hence, used in statistics to measure and interpret the extent to which two measured variables are related to each other within a single point of time. Linear regression is the mostly used method to explore the correlation between two measured variables. Cross-sectional data correlation can be used to assess possible associations between different phenomena described by OSD e.g. unemployment rate and poverty rate in the UK in 2015.

Correlation can be also used to measure and interpret the relationship between measured variables over time. In this case, correlation is applied in data that are modeled as time-series. OSD can be easily formulated as time series data as they usually measure the same phenomenon at successive time intervals. Time-series correlation can then be applied in order to explore the relationship between different phenomena over time e.g. unemployment rate and poverty rate in the UK over the last ten years.

Panel data [16] (or longitudinal data) can be used to model multi-dimensional data over time. Panel data are able to contain observations of multiple phenomena over multiple time periods. Panel data can be used on top of OSD to explore how a measured variable changes over time. For example, panel data can be used to explore the relationship between unemployment rate in all countries of Europe and the poverty rate in all countries of Europe the last ten years.

Predictive models arc created and assessed in the context of predictive analytics in order to make empirical predictions using data and statistical or data mining methods [17]. In general, the goal of predictive models is to predict the output of a variable value (Y) for new observations given their input values (X) based on historical data. OSD can be used as historical data for the creation as well as the assessment of predictive models.

According to our view Open Statistics introduce two types of OSD exploitation: the *problem-driven* approach and the *data-driven* approach.

The problem-driven approach follows the traditional data exploitation paradigm that aims to solve a well-defined problem. In this case, one of the main challenges is to discover the appropriate data and Open Statistics can support this task. For example, a problem-driven type of scenario could be the following: *"I would like to explore a phenomenon"*. In this scenario, if we consider as an example the phenomenon of unemployment in European countries, the first requirement towards exploring unemployment would be to discover all relevant OSD. These can be datasets that measure unemployment from different European countries and in various time periods, provided by a single or various data portals. Relevant OSD can be then combined to provide a single view of unemployment and then analysed using different methods of analysis to produce interesting results. OLAP analysis, for example, could be used to view unemployment in Italy, Greece and Spain in years 2014 and 2015.

Another problem-driven type of scenarios could be the following: *"I would like to explore the relationship between two or more phenomena"*. For example, we would like to explore the relationship between unemployment and poverty in the countries of Europe. Towards this end, we need again to discover relevant OSD. Once we have the datasets, we can combine them and then apply on them methods such as cross-sectional correlation, time-series correlation or panel data analysis.

As a result, the most important task in problem-driven scenarios is the discovery of relevant data. In the new reality of Open Statistics the vision is to facilitate the discovery of this relevant data. Hence, the main benefit of Open Statistics in this approach is that it will allow the easy and effective discovery of relative OSD that can be then analysed using the methods of analysis described above in order to solve specific problems.

The data-driven approach is a bottom-up approach compelled by OSD. Specifically, this approach aims at identifying unexplored results starting from a dataset at hand. A data-driven type of scenarios could be the following: *"I would like to explore phenomena out of OSD"*. In order to solve this problem, we could start from a single dataset and then search for relevant datasets, combine and analyse them in order to discover possible relationships or other interesting conclusions.

In data-driven scenarios the benefits of Open Statistics can be even greater since the different methods of analysis that can be applied on OSD need to be redefined. Specifically, starting from a specific dataset, OLAP can be used to enhance this dataset by finding relevant datasets (e.g. that measure the same variable in a different year). This will facilitate the inspiration of innovative solutions or unexpected results that were not known before. Moreover, correlation (cross-sectional or time series) could be used to identify unexpected relationships with other datasets. Starting again from a specific dataset, data-driven correlation and panel data in Open Statistics will allow to go bottom-up and identify and create new and, maybe, unexpected relationships with other datasets. Finally, OSD can be used as the basis for the creation and assessment of predictive models. These predictive models could then be reused by different applications, in the same way that open data is reused.

7 Open Statistics Challenges

This section presents a preliminary analysis of the main challenges towards the vision of Open Statistics.

7.1 Data Integration

A big challenge in Open Statistics is related to overcoming the data fragmentation problem. OSD integration is required in order to be able to achieve the vision of Open Statistics. Data integration is the problem of combining data residing at different sources, and providing the user with a unified view of these data [18]. Because, however, OSD can be conceptualised as cubes, the data integration problem in Open Statistics can be though as the problem of combining cubes.

Although cubes integration has being studied in data warehouses literature for more than a decade [13,19,20], OSD have introduced new requirements in the area. Traditionally, an organisation had a collection of measures that were important to its operation. These measures were organised in a data warehouse. In Open Statistics, however, data providers make available for reuse in an ad-hoc manner multiple datasets that can actually comprise parts of a bigger cube with multiple measures, dimensions, and hierarchies. On the other hand, however, users may need data that require the integration of these datasets or even the data cubes that can be created by integrating the datasets. Moreover, in most of the traditional theoretical frameworks cubes integration was only presented as part of a generic framework aiming at conceptualise cubes and thus they do not describe in detail cubes integration. As a result, cube integration has to be studied under this new perspective.

An interesting case of OSD integration involve the expansion of an initial cube by using data from other cubes. For example, in terms of our first scenario, we can expand a dataset about unemployment in European countries in different years by reusing cubes with unemployment data in lower geographical level. This will result in a new cube with data of unemployment in two levels of geography (Fig. 2).

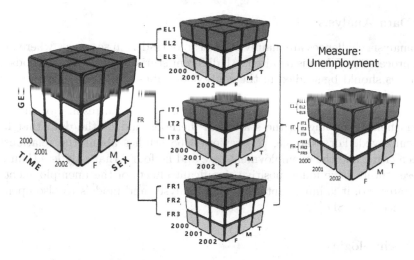

Fig. 2. Cube integration that enables the expansion of an initial cube

A second interesting case of OSD integration involves the creation of a cube from the intersection of two other cubes. For example, in terms of the same scenario, we integrate two cubes with the same dimensions but with different values of dimensions. The resulted cube contains only the intersection of these values as presented in Fig. 3.

These types of cube integration pose some interesting requirements that need to be further analysed and formally defined.

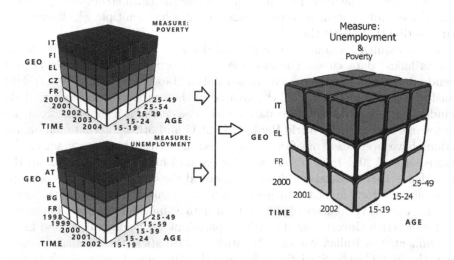

Fig. 3. Cube integration that enables the intersection of two cubes

7.2   Data Analysis

Data analysis challenges are mainly related to data-driven scenarios where automatic processing of data is required. All different statistical analysis methods and techniques should be studied in the context of cubes and specific requirements that would enable automated and massive analyses should be defined.

Moreover, different analyses could present controversial results for the same phenomenon depending on the statistical methods and/or the data that have been employed. For example, [21] reviewed 68 studies about the relationship between crime and the unemployment rate and he found that only less than half of these studies have found positive significant effects of the unemployment on crime rates. So, it is important statistical analyses and models to also open up and connect to OSD [22].

7.3   Technologies

Linked data technologies has been early proposed as the most effective way for opening up data on the Web [23]. In the case of OSD this is particular true as it will not only facilitate data integration but also enable the realisation of data-driven scenarios that require automatic data processing [24].

The RDF Data Cube (QB) vocabulary [25] is a *W3C* standard for publishing data cubes on the Web using the RDF (Resource Description Framework) and the linked data principles. The core class of the vocabulary is the *qb:DataSet* that represents a cube. A cube is connected to a *qb:DataStructureDefinition* which in turn contains a set of components that can be a *qb:DimensionProperty*, a *qb:MeasureProperty* or a *qb:AttributeProperty*. The first one defines the dimensions of the cube, the second the measures, while the third structural metadata such as the unit of measurement. Finally a cube has multiple *qb:Observation* that describe the cells of the cube.

At the moment, a number of statistical datasets are freely available on the Web as linked data cubes. For example, the European Commission's Digital Agenda provides its Scoreboard as linked data cubes. An unofficial linked data transformation of Eurostat's data[13], created in the course of a research project, includes more than 5,000 linked data cubes. Few statistical datasets from the European Central Bank, World Bank, UNESCO and other international organisations have been also transformed to linked data in a third party activity[14]. Census data of 2011 from Ireland and Greece and historical censuses from the Netherlands have been also published as linked data cubes [26,27]. Moreover, many official efforts launched by governmental organisations (owning the data) are using the QB vocabulary to publish their data as linked data cubes. For example, the Scottish Government, the UK Department for Communities and Local Government, the Italian National Institute of Statistics, the Flemish Government, the Irish Central Statistics Office and the European Commission's Digital Agenda have published their data using the QB vocabulary.

---

[13] http://eurostat.linked-statistics.org.
[14] http://270a.info.

Although all the above efforts use the same vocabulary, they often adopt different practices, thus hampering the data integration. The result is the creation of cubes that cannot be integrated despite the use of linked data technologies [28]. Interoperability conflicts that hamper data integration have been extensively studied in the context of relational databases and data warehouses. Examples of such conflicts include naming, structural, data scaling, data precision, and data representation conflicts [11, 29–31]. It is essential, however, to identify all the types of conflicts that may hamper data cube integration in the context of Open Statistics and linked data. Moreover, it is important to come up with and agree on best practices to be followed by statistical data publisher in order to overcome these types of conflicts.

Finally, software tools that support important functionalities related to linked data cubes creation and exploitation have been recently developed [32,33]. However, we need to overcome challenges related to performance especially in the case of exploiting cubes from multiple data stores [34].

8   Conclusion

An increasing number of public authorities and international organisations publish Open Data. Despite the great expectations of open data movement, studies reveal that publishing open data does not automatically provide benefits. At the same time, policy documents and research in the area suggest that a large part of open data is numerical and, more specifically, concerns statistics.

In this paper, we introduced Open Statistics as a new field to systematically investigate Open Statistical Data. Open Statistics reuse methods from diverse fields like Open Data, Semantic Web, Statistics, Data Warehouses, and OLAP.

Towards this end, we initially studied datasets in both the UK and the European open data portals. We concluded that (a) OSD can be conceptualised using the traditional data cube (or just cube) model that was initially introduced in Data Warehouses and that (b) different datasets provide fragmented views of a cube.

Thereafter we presented the potential of Open Statistics and we described how OSD redefines traditional statistical analysis methods such as OLAP, panel data, and statistical learning. We also presented challenges related to the achievement of Open Statistics. The challenges were categorised in three categories, namely data integration, data analysis, and technology.

In summary, the results suggest that Open Statistics provide benefits not present in any of these fields alone. We conclude that in certain cases OSD can realise the potential of open data.

Acknowledgments. This work is funded by the European Commission within the H2020 Programme in the context of the project OpenGovIntelligence (http:// OpenGovIntelligence.eu) under grand agreement No. 693849.

References

1. Kalampokis, E., Tambouris, E., Tarabanis, K.: A classification scheme for open government data: towards linking decentralized data. Int. J. Web Eng. Technol. **6**(3), 266–285 (2011)
2. Attard, J., Orlandi, F., Scerri, S., Auer, S.: A systematic review of open government data initiatives. Gov. Inf. Q. **32**(4), 399–418 (2015)
3. Susha, I., Zuiderwijk, A., Janssen, M., Gronlund, A.: Benchmarks for evaluating the progress of open data adoption: usage, limitations, and lessons learned. Soc. Sci. Comput. Rev. **33**(5), 613–630 (2014)
4. Manyika, J., Chui, M., Bughin, J., Dobbs, R., Bisson, P., Marrs, A.: McKinsey Global Institute D (2013)
5. Janssen, M., Charalabidis, Y., Zuiderwijk, A.: Benefits, adoption barriers and myths of open data and open government. Inf. Syst. Manag. **29**(4), 258–268 (2012)
6. Kalampokis, E., Tambouris, E., Tarabanis, K.: Linked open government data analytics. In: Wimmer, M.A., Janssen, M., Scholl, H.J. (eds.) EGOV 2013. LNCS, vol. 8074, pp. 99–110. Springer, Heidelberg (2013)
7. European Commission: Guidelines on recommended standard licences, datasets and charging for the reuse of documents, C240/1, 24 July 2014
8. Bhattacherjee, A.: Social Science Research: Principles, Methods, and Practices, Open Access Textbooks (2012)
9. Shields, P., Rangarajan, N.: A Playbook for Research Methods: Integrating Conceptual Frameworks and Project Management. New Forum Press Inc., Stillwater (2013)
10. Romero, O., Abell, A.: A survey of multidimensional modeling methodologies. Int. J. Data Warehous. Min. **5**(2), 1 (2009)
11. Tseng, F.S., Chen, C.W.: Integrating heterogeneous data warehouses using XML technologies. J. Inf. Sci. **31**(3), 209–229 (2005)
12. Niemi, T., Hirvonen, L., Jrvelin, K.: Multidimensional data model and query language for informetrics. J. Am. Soc. Inf. Sci. Technol. **54**(10), 939–951 (2003)
13. Datta, A., Thomas, H.: The cube data model: a conceptual model and algebra for on-line analytical processing in data warehouses. Decis. Support Syst. **27**(3), 289–301 (1999)
14. Chaudhuri, S., Dayal, U.: An overview of data warehousing and OLAP technology. ACM SIGMOD Rec. **26**(1), 65–74 (1997)
15. Dielman, T.E.: Pooled cross-sectional and time series data: a survey of current statistical methodology. Am. Stat. **37**(2), 111–122 (1983)
16. Hildreth, C.: Combining cross section data and time series. Cowles Commission Discussion paper, No. 347, 15 May 1950
17. Shmueli, G.: To explain or to predict? Stat. Sci. **25**(3), 289–310 (2010)
18. Lenzerini, M.: Data integration: a theoretical perspective. In: Proceedings of the 21st ACM SIGMOD-SIGACT-SIGART Symposium on Principles of Database Systems, pp. 233–246. ACM (2002)
19. Agrawal, R., Gupta, A., Sarawagi, S.: Modeling multidimensional databases. In: Proceedings of the 13th International Conference on Data Engineering, pp. 232–243 (1997)
20. Perez, J., Berlanga, R., Aramburu, M., Pedersen, T.: Integrating data warehouses with web data: a survey. IEEE Trans. Knowl. Data Eng. **20**(7), 940–955 (2008)
21. Chiricos, T.: Rates of crime and unemployment: an analysis of aggregate research evidence. Soc. Prob. **34**(2), 187–212 (1987)

22. Kalampokis, E., Karamanou, A., Tambouris, E., Tarabanis, K.: Towards a vocabulary for incorporating predictive models into the linked data web. In: Proceedings of the 1st International Workshop on Semantic Statistics (SemStats 2013) Within 12th International Semantic Web Conference (ISWC 2013), Sydney, Australia, vol. 1549. CEUR-WS (2013)

23. Bizer, C., Heath, T., Berners-Lee, T.: Linked data the story so far, In: Semantic Services, Interoperability and Web Applications: Emerging Concepts, pp. 205–227 (2009)

24. Tambouris, E., Kalampokis, E., Tarabanis, K.: Processing linked open data cubes. In: Tambouris, E., Janssen, M., Scholl, H.J., Wimmer, M.A., Tarabanis, K., Gascó, M., Klievink, B., Lindgren, I., Parycek, P. (eds.) EGOV 2015. LNCS, vol. 9248, pp. 130–143. Springer, Heidelberg (2015)

25. Cyganiak, R., Reynolds, D., Tennison, J.: The RDF Data Cube Vocabulary. W3C Recommendation. World Wide Web Consortium (W3C), 16 January 2014

26. Petrou, I., Papastefanatos, G., Dalamagas, T.: Publishing census as linked open data: a case study. In: Proceedings of the 2nd International Workshop on Open Data, Ser. WOD 2013, pp. 4:1–4:3. ACM, New York (2013)

27. Mero-Peuela, A., Ashkpour, A., Rietveld, L., Hoekstra, R., Schlobach, S.: Linked humanities data: the next frontier? In: Proceedings of the 2nd International Workshop on Linked Science 2012, A Case-Study in Historical Census Data, vol. 951 (2012)

28. Kalampokis, E., Roberts, B., Karamanou, A., Tambouris, E., Tarabanis, K.: Challenges on developing tools for exploiting linked open data cubes. In: Proceedings of the 3rd International Workshop on Semantic Statistics (SemStats 2015) within the 14th International Semantic Web Conference (ISWC 2015), Bethlehem, Pennsylvania, USA, 11–15 October 2015, vol. 1551. CEUR-WS (2015)

29. Kim, W., Seo, J.: Classifying schematic and data heterogeneity in multidatabase systems. Computer 24(12), 12–18 (1991)

30. Batini, C., Lenzerini, M., Navathe, S.B.: A comparative analysis of methodologies for database schema integration. ACM Comput. Surv. (CSUR) 18(4), 323–364 (1986)

31. Berger, S., Schrefl, M.: FedDW global schema architect: UML-based design tool for the integration of data mart schemas. In: Song, I.-Y., Golfarelli, M. (eds.) DOLAP, pp. 33–40. ACM, Maui (2012)

32. Kalampokis, E., Nikolov, A., Haase, P., Cyganiak, R., Stasiewicz, A., Karamanou, A., Zotou, M., Zeginis, D., Tambouris, E., Tarabanis, K.: Exploiting linked data cubes with opencube toolkit. In: Proceedings of the ISWC 2014 Posters and Demos Track a Track Within 13th International Semantic Web Conference (ISWC 2014), Riva del Garda, Italy, 19–23 October 2014, vol. 1272. CEUR-WS (2014)

33. Salas, P.E.R., Da Mota, F.M., Breitman, K.K., Casanova, M.A., Martin, M., Auer, S.: Publishing statistical data on the web. Int. J. Semant. Comput. 6(4), 373–388 (2012)

34. Kalampokis, E., Tambouris, E., Tarabanis, K.: ICT tools for creating, expanding, and exploiting statistical linked open data, Stat. J. IAOS (2016, in press)

Open Government

Open Data Innovation Capabilities: Towards a Framework of How to Innovate with Open Data

Silja Eckartz, Tijs van den Broek, and Merel Ooms[✉]

TNO, The Hague, The Netherlands
{silja.eckartz,merel.ooms}@tno.nl

Abstract. Innovation based on open data lags behind the high expectations of policy makers. Hence, open data researchers have investigated the barriers of open data publication and adoption. This paper contributes to this literature by taking a capabilities perspective on how successful open data re-users create value out of the available data sources. First, a framework of IT, organization and skills capabilities required to innovate with data is derived from literature. Second, a case study including a survey and interview with managers from 12 frontrunners in the Netherlands was conducted. The analysis reveals that skills are valued the highest closely followed by organizational capabilities. Setting up a multi-disciplinary team with motivated employees and giving this team the mandate to experiment with data, is essential when innovating with open data. Theoretically, this study contributes to open data research by offering a new capabilities perspective on the organizational level. Our results highlight the importance of entrepreneurship theories to explain value creation with open data. Practically, our study suggests that digital skills and start-ups are important to the open government data policies.

Keywords: Open data · Re-use · Public sector innovation · Value of data and apps · Capabilities

1 Introduction

An increasing number of government agencies release open data to spur economic growth through the development of new digital services or increasing organizational productivity. McKinsey [1] estimates that open data may provide 900 billion US dollar additional annual economic growth in Europe compared to an economy without open data. To unlock this potential, more and more data sources, ranging from transport to educational data, are available in open data portals throughout Europe. However, the question remains how to further exploit the economic potential of open data. Currently, innovation based on open data sets seems to lag behind the high expectations of policy makers. Hence, previous research took stock of barriers to the publication and use of open data. This paper contributes by taking a capabilities perspective to study how successful open data re-users create both economic as well as social value out of the available data sources. What can we learn from these frontrunners? Hence, the central research question is: *"What capabilities are most important to create value out of open data?"*

© IFIP International Federation for Information Processing 2016
Published by Springer International Publishing Switzerland 2016. All Rights Reserved
H.J. Scholl et al. (Eds.): EGOV 2016, LNCS 9820, pp. 47–60, 2016.
DOI: 10.1007/978-3-319-44421-5_4

The gap between open data provision and usage is reflected in IS research. To date, most attention has been paid to barriers at the side of open data providers, which are predominantly government agencies [2–5]. Recently, scholars have started to examine the impediments that open data re-users experience [5]. However, most of these studies focus on the technical barriers related to opening, finding and using data that hinder usage [5, 6]. Several scholars urge for more research on the non-technical barriers, such as those related to business cases, management support and organizational culture, that open data re-users experience [7, 8]. Only a few studies examine the capabilities that open data re-users need to create economic value from data [9, 10]. Jetzek et al. [9] describe capabilities as *"the collective ability of individuals and organizations to use and re-use open data"* and focus on access to open data and data literacy. Complementing Jetzek et al. [9], we aim to study open data innovation capabilities related to data re-use focused on the organizational level.

Our paper contributes to open data research in two ways. First, we synthesize information systems (IS) and innovation management (IM) literature on capabilities for data-driven innovation to develop a conceptual framework. To complement current open data research, this framework includes IT, organizational and people-related capabilities. Second, we present the results of the study of 12 Dutch frontrunners in innovation based on open data to test the conceptual framework. The study includes a questionnaire and semi-structured interviews with the CIOs and/or technical managers of the 12 organizations.

The practical implications of this study are twofold. First, we formulate the capabilities required for organizations that want to start to innovate with open data, e.g. by developing new services or improving their current practices. Firms may use the insights to develop an open data innovation plan that includes technical and non-technical measures. Second, policy makers may use the insights of this paper to develop policy instruments that stimulate data-driven innovation. For example, our research may fuel policy debate about the digital skills that organizations need.

2   An Open Data Innovation Capabilities Framework

A literature review identified IS and IM journal articles and conference papers that study capabilities needed for data-driven innovation. Keywords for our search included combinations of the words e-Skills, capabilities, innovation, "data-driven", "digital skills", "data re-users" and barriers. We found 19 relevant studies that examined capabilities for data-driven innovation. The studies are mentioned in the tables below.

We clustered the results of our literature review around three main types of capabilities: IT related capabilities, organizational capabilities and skills. Each capability type was identified in literature as influencing the data innovation capacity of an organization. Within each concept we distinguish a number of categories and sub categories, presented in the sections below.

In contrast to previous research [10], the selected IS and IM studies point at the importance of non-technical capabilities to innovate with data. This reflects the general notion in innovation management that three quarter of innovations' success is related to non-technical factors [11]. Furthermore, many capabilities are related to small or medium-sized enterprises and not to large enterprises, for example entrepreneurship and agility.

2.1 IT Capabilities

With respect to IT capabilities we found three categories that influence the data innovation potential of an organization: (1) Infrastructure and enabling technologies that include all hardware and software that is needed to collect, store, analyze and visualize open data, (2) An IT strategy that includes planning, data management and governance, and measures to secure data, and (3) Interoperability that includes capabilities on working with standards and ability to integrate IS. Table 1 provides an overview of the IT capabilities, how they are defined in literature and a list of studies that mention them.

Table 1. Overview of IT capabilities identified

Category	Capabilities	Definition	Studies
Infrastructure & enabling technology	Hardware & software	General IT infrastructure (incl. tools and applications) needed to create value from data	[5, 9, 10, 12, 13]
	Data analytics	Technologies (software and tools) for data search, discoverability and mining	[5, 12, 14–16]
	Data output/visualization	Technologies for showing insights from data analytics, including visualization and reporting technologies	[10, 14, 15]
IT strategy	Planning	Vision and IS portfolio management, knowledge management, architecture	[9, 13, 17–19]
	Data management	Data lifecycle management, technical data manipulation	[12, 14, 18]
	Data governance	Processes and policies including data quality and usability	[7, 12, 15]
	Security	System and data security processes and mechanisms	[20]
Interoperability	Standards	Interoperability/standards	[5, 15]
	System integration	Systems integration, IT integration	[14, 15]

2.2 Organizational Capabilities

With respect to organizational capabilities we found four categories that influence the data innovation potential of an organization: (1) Strategic capabilities that includes top management support for data-driven innovation and the ability to change decisions and policies based on open data, (2) Tactical capabilities that include the mixing of disciplines over organizational silos, allocation of resources, and ability to adapt organizational processes based on data, (3) Operational capabilities that include entrepreneurship and R&D, and (4) cultural capabilities that include a culture focused on innovation and agility. Table 2 provides an overview of the organizational capabilities, how they are defined in literature and a list of relevant IS and IM studies.

2.3   Skills

With respect to skills we found two categories that influence the data innovation potential of an organization: (1) Hard skills, and (2) Soft skills. Where hard skills can be defined as more technical skills such as programming or data analytics skills and soft skills as more non-technical such as interdisciplinary cooperation and entrepreneurship. Table 3 provides an overview of the capabilities, how they are defined in literature, and a list of relevant IS studies.

Table 2. Overview of organizational capabilities identified

Category	Capabilities	Definition	Studies
Strategic	Leadership	Top management support	[14, 20]
	Governance	Data-driven policies and decision-making	[13, 14, 16, 17]
Tactical	Multi-disciplinarity	Integration capability, multi-disciplinary teams	[12, 18, 21, 22]
	Coordination capability	Enhanced knowledge across boundaries, resource allocation, asset orchestration	[9, 16]
	Processes	Data-driven processes across entire organization, performance management based on data	[13, 15–17, 20]
Operational	Entrepreneurial orientation	Ability to recognize value of information, imitate competitors and commercialize value of information	[10, 20–23]
	Develop new ideas	Research and development, creativity and ideas	[10, 19, 23]
Culture	Innovation culture	e-Awareness, socialization (shared ideology and collective identity), communication	[7, 9, 14, 17, 22, 24]
	Agility	Degree of adaptability of the firm, change management, improvisational organizational capability	[14, 17, 18, 23]

3 Methods

To answer our research question, we studied 12 leading open data re-users in the Netherlands. We decided to sample cases from the Netherlands as the research team had access to Dutch cases and the Netherlands has a lively open data community with governments opening up more and more datasets. However, despite the Dutch central government wishes the Netherlands to be an open data frontrunner in Europe, policy evaluations indicate that this still requires significant effort.[1] The open data frontrunners in this study were selected based on their presence as showcase in national and European open data research (e.g. the former ePractice portal and the European Commission's join up community) or because they have won national and European app awards. Furthermore, we selected cases that vary in size and sector to avoid selection bias. The selection process resulted in a longlist of 17 Dutch frontrunners of which 12 respondents finally participated in our research. Frontrunner only participated in the survey. The response rate of 71 % can be qualified as very high, which indicates that respondents were highly involved with the topic and therefore more inclined to

Table 3. Overview of skills identified

Category	Capabilities	Definition	Authors
Hard skills	e-literacy	Computer science skills, utilization, architecture skills, e-user skills	[14, 20, 22, 24, 25]
	Data literacy	Interoperability, semantic webs, linked data skills	[5, 12, 22, 24]
	Programming skills	Different programming languages, hacking machine learning, NLP, Mapreduce/	[5, 12, 22, 25]
	Data analytics	Knowledge of data models, cleaning, integration and analysis	[5, 12, 22, 24]
	Research skills	Research and analysis skills/statistics	[5, 9, 12, 16, 25, 26]
	Data output skills	Communication skills: story telling with data, data journalism and visualization	[12, 25]
Soft skills	Management skills	e-Leadership skills, decision quality	[16, 24]
	Customer and service focus	Service provisioning and receiving, customer focus.	[26]
	Interdisciplinary cooperation	People integration, knowledge management, Inter-disciplinary domain knowledge	[5, 14, 15]
	Entrepreneurship	Proactivity, e-Business, competitive actions	[14, 16, 17, 20, 24]

---

[1] See the report by the Dutch Court of Audit (2016) on trends in open data, p. 42, available at http://www.rekenkamer.nl/dsresource?objectid=23808&type=org.

participate. Our research targeted the frontrunners' technical managers, innovation managers, CIOs or CTOs. Usually, only one respondent per case was contacted.

We used a two-step approach to measure the capabilities in our conceptual framework. First, we operationalized the capabilities in the framework in a question-naire that included seven questions on the organization, their application of open data and which capabilities they find most important. We tested and improved the questions on comprehensiveness. The questions in the survey asked respondents to rate the importance of each capability to the success of creating value out of open data on a five-point Likert scale (ranging from very unimportant to very important). In addition to the closed questions, we allowed respondents to add their own capabilities and explain why they are important. After we received the answers on the questionnaire, we contacted each respondent within one week after filling in the questionnaire for a semi-structured interview. In this interview, we asked respondents to explain their answers: why are certain capabilities important or not important at all in their view? Interviews were conducted by phone and varied in length from 15 to 45 min. The questionnaire (in Dutch) and interview protocol are available on request.

Table 4 below provides an overview of the frontrunners that participated in our research.

An analysis of the cases shows that two third of our respondents have more than 3 years' experience with open data. About half of our cases are organizations with less than 10 employees. Only 2 cases are large organizations.

Most organizations (91.7 %) use open data to develop new products or services or improve existing products (58.3 %). Half of the organizations aim to develop societal value with open data. Examples of societal value created by the organizations are insight in quality of schools or the plans of the local government in your neighborhood. Our respondents focus less on the optimization of internal processes and decision support with open data. This might be related to the relatively small average size of the organizations (mainly SMEs).

4   Results

In this section we describe how respondents rated and explained the importance of IT, organizational and people-related capabilities for the use of open data. The focus in this paper is more on the underlying reasons that organizations have for finding certain aspects important in relation to data innovation than to have representative scores. This is reflected in the modest amount of respondents. Therefore, the figure does not present representative numbers but a reflection of the average of our respondent group (Fig. 1).

4.1   Information Technology Capabilities

The factors that were found to be most important are data governance (4.40, on a scale from 1 to 5), followed by data management (4.25) and interoperability (4.22). The factors that received the lowest scores were Hardware and Information Systems (3.42) and having an IS strategy and planning in place (3.42).

Table 4. Description of cases

Case	Description and goal of open data usage	Respondent function	Size (nr of employees)	Type of organization	Years of experience with open data usage
A	Development and improvement of new products and services based on open data.	Chief concept creation	11–50	App developer	More than 5 years
B	Development and improvement of new products and services based on open data.	Big data consultant & engineer	11–50	Data/IT consulting	About a year
C	Find and compare all schools in the NL. Development of new products (App) in order to create societal value.	Owner	1–10	App developer	3–5 years
D	Publishing data as well as using data to improve internal processes and develop new services.	Enterprise architect	1001–5000	Energy grid provider	1–3 years
E	Development and improvement of new products and services based on open data. Create societal value.	Co-founder and creative director	11–50	App provider	More than 5 years
F	Consulting and development of new products and services based on (open) data.	Chief marketing	11–50	Solution provider big data	More than 5 years
G	New services (app) based on open data.	Director	1–10	App provider	3–5 years
H	Mainly data provider, using some other (e.g. geo) data to improve their services.	Specialist data management	5001–10000	Governmental organization	More than 5 years
I	Use data to provide new services (air quality measures) and create societal value.	Data architect	1001–5000	Governmental organization	More than 5 years

(Continued)

Table 4. (*Continued*)

J	Provide new services (expected need for roadside assistance) based on open weather data.	Chief technology officer	1–10	Deep-learning start-up (spin-off)	1–3 years
K	Consulting and development of new products and services based on (open) data. App gives shippers real-time information on berth availability.	Co-founder	1–10	App provider	1–3 years
L	Provides software, consultancy and data services based on open geographical data sets.	Manager consultancy & content	1001–5000	Solution provider big data	More than 5 years

Looking at a higher level, we can conclude that IT capabilities related to the handling of open data are perceived as most important. First, data governance, which describes the processes and policies that ensures that important data assets are formally managed, is essential for data re-users as it ensures that data can be trusted and that data owners are accountable for risks, for example a low data quality. Specifically, the ability to judge data quality was mentioned by most respondents as being essential to evaluate if data can actually be used. Knowing who the data owner is, how the maintenance of the data is deployed and who is responsible for the quality of the data are success factors when innovating with open data. Another factor related to data governance is to define rules on how to deal with new technological developments related to the data, e.g. cloud storage. Second, respondents rated data management, which comprises all the disciplines related to managing data as a valuable resource, as a very important IT capability when innovating with open data. It is important to specify how data are stored, manipulated and processed, in particular when open data are combined with proprietary data for new services. Third, innovation often means that data re-users need to be able to access different datasets and link them in new ways. Hence, interoperability, semantic standards and system integration are important capabilities, or as one of the respondents indicated: *"without standards there is no integration"*. The ability to handle different open data standards (both open source and proprietary) is important to ensure that data can actually be reused, e.g. data is readable, actual and relevant. The availability of standards makes the reuse of open data faster and more efficient. Data re-users need to be familiar with and their information systems need to be compatible with the latest data standards of the data providers. These standards are domain specific and require domain knowledge.

Data analytics technologies, such as software and tools were found to be important but as they are widely (commercially) available, this factor is not considered a challenge anymore. The same holds for hardware and software which are seen as a

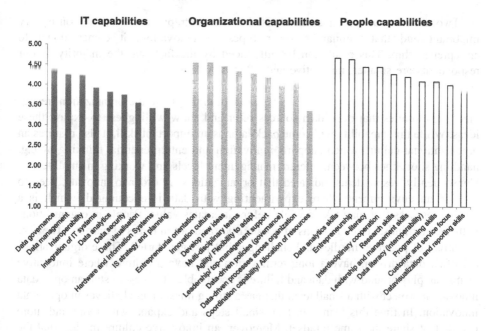

Fig. 1. Overview of how capabilities were rated on a scale from 1 to 5

prerequisite for data innovation but are also considered as given and thus not a challenge anymore to invest in. Of all IT capabilities, having the right hardware and software is deemed the least important. However, just having the right hardware and software does not guarantee that they are used to their full potential. Hardware and software becomes an important capability when privacy, security and ethical questions of the use open data start to arise. With respect to data security it is important that the infrastructure used ensures that the data is stored securely and that data access is in line with access policies. Last, an IT strategy and planning seems to be less relevant to our respondents, which might be biased due to the relatively high amount of small and innovative firms in our sample.

4.2   Organizational Capabilities

The organizational capabilities that were found to be most important by our respondents are entrepreneurial orientation (4.55, on a scale from 1 to 5) and an innovative organizational culture (4.55), followed by the organizational capability to develop new ideas (4.45). The organizational capability that was perceived by far as least important for data-driven innovation is the organization's capability to efficiently allocate resources (3.36).

We divided the organizational capabilities into strategic, tactical, operational and cultural capabilities. Based on the questionnaire and interviews we conclude that the operational and cultural organizational capabilities are considered to be most important when innovating with open data.

Two third of our respondents indicated that an entrepreneurial orientation is very important and that, similar to other types of innovation, it comes down to entrepreneurship. This result can be influenced by the fact that the majority of our respondents are smaller, innovative and often more entrepreneurial organizations. To create value out of open data, organizations need teams that are capable of making links between different subjects, develop a network in and outside the organization, recognize opportunities that open data sources offer and show willingness to exploit these ideas. While this capability will come back later as an important skill, it also requires an organizational culture which supports innovation and entrepreneurial thinking by e.g. handling short lines between different management levels and working in small teams. Consequently, respondents indicated that organizations, in order to innovate, need to provide an environment where experimenting with data is encouraged, which is a creative process that may take a while before it creates value. People in organizations with such a mindset think in terms of possibilities and not in terms of barriers. They are not afraid of potential hurdles and challenges but just get started. These organizations are often data driven, have a long term vision and have a culture where innovative teams can play around with data and failure is acceptable. It is best to start an open data innovation project with a small team that has a strong mission and believes in open data innovation. In time this team can take small steps and expand with more and more people that share the same mindset. Moreover, an innovative culture implies that the costs of the innovation e.g. data applications are positioned as costs for the business, not as costs for the IT department. Thus, making the business responsible for data innovation is essential for its success. As the context and challenges around the data might constantly change it is essential to have a learning, agile organization that can quickly adapt to changes in the provision of data.

Multidisciplinary teams are crucial in the open data innovation process, as organizations need people with both technical knowledge and people that understand the domain context of the data and the needs of potential customers. Teams need to understand the bigger picture of the data and be able to talk across boundaries of systems and organizations. Multidisciplinarity helps teams to understand and translate technical complex concepts in something that is visually appealing.

Our respondents indicated that central leadership in itself is less important to innovate, but having mandate and budget from top management is very relevant for the success of an open data innovation. Although innovation initiatives and ideas are most likely to develop on business level it is very important to have a data driven vision at board level to move from an experimental phase to a next phase where innovations are further deployed and implemented. Our interviewees further mentioned that organizations should use successful examples as inspiration to stimulate the re-use of open data in their own organization. Central coordination of resources and activities as well as asset orchestration was found to be the least important in supporting the innovation. Most of the small innovative and entrepreneurial organizations in our sample did not recognize this capability as being important. However, coordinated actions might be valuable for organizations to match the supply and demand of data and stimulate the dialog between data owners and re-users. The management of an organization might want to play a catalyst role in this.

We find that the larger organizations in our sample find it important that the overall organization is ready and willing to support processes and decision-making based on open data. If an organization really wants to innovate with data it should let go of its classical decision making process and use the results of its data innovation to form its own decisions and policies.

Relationship management is a capability that was not initially considered based on our literature analysis and questionnaire, but based on the interviews the ability to engage with external stakeholders (e.g. end-users) is found to be important to be able to innovate. Often, the availability of open data sets is a first step, and close collaboration between the data provider and user is necessary to take the next steps and create value. As one of the respondents said: *"Do not think in organizational silos but look across organizational boundaries when innovating with data."*

4.3 Skills

The factors that got the highest scores and are found to be the most important skills are data analytics skills (4.67 on a scale from 1 to 5) and entrepreneurship (4.64) followed by general e-literacy (4.45) and the capability of people to cooperate between disciplines (4.45). The factor that received the lowest score and was found to be less but still important when innovating with open data are data visualization and reporting skills (3.83). This shows that a successful organization or team consists of people with data analytics skills in combination with entrepreneurship skills and who are able to combine knowledge from several disciplines.

Regarding technical or hard skills, our respondents foremost stressed that it is important to *"employ people who can detect patterns in data, who are creative and have a high quantitative skills"*. Even though respondents valued a team with a diverse set of skills, most team members should have a basic understanding of data (e.g. experience with working with large databases) and good analytical skills to actually make technical sense out of the data. One respondent noted that *"it is more important to have mathematicians than having only programmers. The latter you can simply hire"*.

General IT skills, such as programming, are still important when you innovate with open data: *"if you do not have your IT Skills in order, then you are not part of the game anymore"*. However, IT skills just qualify, but a deep understanding and creativity with data gives a competitive advantage. Consequently, open data re-users need employees that have R&D skills to experiment (or 'play' as respondents qualified this skills) and test how different data sources can provide value or insights about the problems they want to address. More specifically, employees need to think in large distributed systems and make complex data combinations (from both open and closed data source).

Regarding non-technical or soft skills, having employees who are team players is key. Respondents valued employers that are open to the ideas of others and who are willing to learn. These quick learners need to be good networkers with a mindset to create new ecosystem, that are a able set up new collaborations with new parties and defend and their business decisions taken based on data. Additionally, it is important to have people with the capacity to think in terms of customer needs. Business models based on open data are often still a challenge. For example, one of the respondents see applications based on open data as a showcase to get to know new customers and sell additional data services. Hence, it is important to start early in the process with the identification of customer needs and business potential.

5 Discussion

Comparing the three types of capabilities we see that all were found to be important but accents differ. On average skills are valued the highest (4.27) closely followed by organizational capabilities (4.19). IT capabilities are with a score of 3.86 rated the lowest by our respondents. This may indicate that investing in technology and other IT related capabilities that allow you to process and analyze data may not be enough when you want to create value from the re-use of open data. It is seems even more important to focus on skills and organizational capabilities. For example, a lack of employees with the right skills is the biggest barrier to open data innovation.

Although we address the three capabilities in isolation there are many interdependencies between the capabilities. Future quantitative studies with a higher number of respondents may conduct factor analysis to cluster capabilities into a more coherent set of open data innovation capabilities. In addition, some capabilities are present on multiple levels. For example, entrepreneurial orientation (organizational) and an entrepreneurial mindset (people) are very similar and probably overlap. Respondents stress the importance of an emergent innovation strategy: you need to keep your goal in mind, but how and what IT resources are needed may change rapidly. Organizations need to know where they are going, however this does not need to be planned completely in an IT strategy. This finding may contradict with IS Strategy literature that emphasizes the importance of a well-planned IT strategy that are more important to large organizations. SMEs employ more emergent and flexible strategies. Furthermore, we find that frontrunners focus strongly on open innovation: networks are important in the innovation process to make optimal use of partners' competences and be able to complement each other in the open data innovation process.

While open data is in some aspects different from internal, proprietary organizational data some experts expect that the barriers related open data are largely the same. However, open data may be less sensitive to privacy risks than proprietary data. The value of open data may be the highest when an open data sets are combined with proprietary datasets. Such a combination can bring new insights which would not have been possible without open data.

The small number of organizations studied and the focus on the Netherlands is a limitation of our research which does not allow us to generalize the results to a larger amount of organizations in different national contexts. The surveys and interviews, however, provide interesting insights for future research on the re-use of open data. Future research may expand the number of cases in different countries over a longer period of time. A longitudinal study is required to study how dynamic capabilities may change over time, for example along the maturity of the data innovator.

6 Conclusion

This paper aims to study which capabilities are required to innovate successfully with open data. We present an open data innovation capabilities framework based on a literature review on capabilities for data driven innovation. Our analysis of 12 Dutch open data front runners reveals that for innovation with data to happen it is not enough to just make more and more open data available by government agencies and focus on IT capabilities at the side of data re-users.

Theoretically, we contribute by offering a capabilities perspective on open data innovation that complements earlier studies on the barriers of data availability and re-use [2–5]. As data-driven innovation seems to require entrepreneurship, open data research may benefit from theories in entrepreneurship literature, such as dynamics capabilities or causation/effectuation, to better explain the value creation process [27].

Practically, digital skills and digital entrepreneurship policies are as important as persuading governments to open-up data. Policy makers may need to set up stimulating programs that are aimed at educating more employees and entrepreneurs with the right set of skills. Organizations aiming to create more value out of open data may follow the following lessons from frontrunners: (1) Set up a multi-disciplinary team with motivated and creative employees, give this team the mandate to experiment with data, and let them formulate an emergent data strategy and get top management support to create a stable innovation environment. (2) Take an entrepreneurial approach: Recognize and exploit opportunities and strive for an open and experimental culture. When successful, the start-up team may motivate and engage more teams within the organization. (3) Think outside organizational boundaries and silos. Set up new inter-organizational networks with complementing skills and experience. The social interaction between employees from a variety of organizations and domains may inspire innovation. Furthermore it is essential that data users and suppliers keep discussing their data needs and ensure that open data is more reliable and usable for external stakeholders, decreasing the risks for data innovators regarding data quality and availability.

References

1. Manyika, J.: Open Data: Unlocking Innovation and Performance with Liquid Information. McKinsey, New York (2013)
2. Huijboom, N., Van den Broek, T.: Open data: an international comparison of strategies. Eur. J. ePract. **12**(1), 4–16 (2011)
3. van Veenstra, A.F., van den Broek, T.A.: Opening moves – drivers, enablers and barriers of open data in a semi-public organization. In: Wimmer, M.A., Janssen, M., Scholl, H.J. (eds.) EGOV 2013. LNCS, vol. 8074, pp. 50–61. Springer, Heidelberg (2013)
4. Zhang, J., Dawes, S.S., Sarkis, J.: Exploring stakeholders' expectations of the benefits and barriers of e-government knowledge sharing. J. Enterp. Inf. Manag. **18**(5), 548–567 (2005)
5. Zuiderwijk, A., et al.: Socio-technical impediments of open data. Electron. J. e-Gov. **10**(2), 156–172 (2012)
6. IODC: Enabling the Data Revolution: An International Open Data Roadmap (2015)

7. Attard, J., et al.: A systematic review of open government data initiatives. Gov. Inf. Q. **32**(4), 399–418 (2015)
8. LaValle, S., et al.: Big data, analytics and the path from insights to value. MIT Sloan Manag. Rev. **52**, 21 (2013)
9. Jetzek, T., Avital, M., Bjorn-Andersen, N.: Data-driven innovation through open government data. J. Theoret. Appl. Electron. Commer. Res. **9**(2), 100–120 (2014)
10. Venkatraman, N.V., et al.: Theorizing digital business innovation: platforms and capabilities in ecosystems (2014). SSRN 2510111
11. Volberda, H.: Concurrentie en Innovatie Monitor, Erasmus University Rotterdam (2005)
12. Hemerly, J.: Public policy considerations for data-driven innovation. Computer **46**(6), 25–31 (2013)
13. Norris, D.M., Baer, L.L.: Building organizational capacity for analytics (2013). EDUCAUSE http://www.educause.edu/library/resources/building-organizationalcapacity-analytics
14. Cosic, R., Shanks, G., Maynard, S.B.: A business analytics capability framework. Australas. J. Inf. Syst. **19**, S5–S19 (2015)
15. Jia, L., Hall, D., Song, J.: The conceptualization of data-driven decision making capability (2015)
16. Sharma, R., Mithas, S., Kankanhalli, A.: Transforming decision-making processes: a research agenda for understanding the impact of business analytics on organisations. Eur. J. Inf. Syst. **23**(4), 433–441 (2014)
17. Knabke, T., Olbrich, S.: Exploring the future shape of business intelligence: mapping dynamic capabilities of information systems to business intelligence agility (2015)
18. Kung, L., et al.: Managing big data for firm performance: a configurational approach (2015)
19. Kusiak, A.: Innovation: a data-driven approach. Int. J. Prod. Econ. **122**(1), 440–448 (2009)
20. Kamioka, T., Tapanainen, T.: Organizational use of big data and competitive advantage–exploration of antecedents (2014)
21. Chang, Y.-C., et al.: How do established firms improve radical innovation performance? The organizational capabilities view. Technovation **32**(7), 441–451 (2012)
22. Kabir, N., Carayannis, E.: Big data, tacit knowledge and organizational competitiveness. In: Proceedings of the 10th International Conference on Intellectual Capital, Knowledge Management and Organisational Learning: ICICKM 2013. Academic Conferences Limited (2013)
23. Knight, G.A., Cavusgil, S.T.: Innovation, organizational capabilities, and the born-global firm. J. Int. Bus. Stud. **35**(2), 124–141 (2004)
24. Mitrovic, Z.: Building Open Data Capacity through e-Skills Acquisition
25. Davenport, T.H., Patil, D.: Data scientist. Harvard Bus. Rev. **90**, 70–76 (2012)
26. Maruyama, H., et al.: Developing data analytics skills in Japan: status and challenge. 日本経営工学会論文誌 **65**(4E), 334–339 (2015)
27. Bharadwaj, A., et al.: Digital business strategy: toward a next generation of insights. MIS Q. **37**(2), 471–482 (2013)

Open Data Research in the Nordic Region: Towards a Scandinavian Approach?

Iryna Susha[1(✉)], Paul Johannesson[2], and Gustaf Juell-Skielse[2]

[1] Department of Informatics,
Örebro University School of Business, 702 81 Örebro, Sweden
iryna.susha@oru.se
[2] Department of Computer and Systems Sciences, Stockholm University,
Postbox 7003, 164 07 Kista, Sweden
{pajo,gjs}@dsv.su.se

Abstract. Since 2009 open data has been growing into a specialized research area, including in the Nordic countries. Historically Information Systems research from this region has managed to develop a distinct identity on the international research arena. Hence, the expectation is that also in the context of open data there exists room for unique contributions of Nordic researchers. However, no systematic overview exists yet of the open data research conducted in these countries or of the emerging research community. This paper, therefore, aims to fill this gap by conducting a comprehensive literature review. Our study focuses on the following aspects: (1) which perspectives and topics are examined and (2) which empirical settings and methods are applied in Nordic open data research. Finding answers to these questions will enable us to propose a future research agenda and thereby stimulate debate in the Nordic open data research community.

Keywords: Open data · Open government data · Open government · Literature review · Scandinavian · Nordic

1 Introduction

Since 2009 governments around the world have been implementing programs to provide public sector information online in the open data format. Open data refers to data which is legally and technically open, i.e. it can be accessed, reused, and redistributed freely by anyone and it is available in machine-readable and bulk form (Open Data Handbook n.d.). Open data programs are driven by expectations that open government data will be reused by actors outside the government and thereby deliver a wide range of benefits, such as economic growth and increased transparency.

Responding to these rapid developments, in the past five years the field of open data has been growing into a specialized research area. Presently all major e-government conferences (IFIP Electronic Government, International Conference on Theory and Practice of Electronic Governance, International Conference on Digital Government Research, and European Conference on e-Government) host dedicated open data tracks, and a number of special issues focusing on open data problems and themes have

© IFIP International Federation for Information Processing 2016
Published by Springer International Publishing Switzerland 2016. All Rights Reserved
H.J. Scholl et al. (Eds.): EGOV 2016, LNCS 9820, pp. 61–73, 2016.
DOI: 10.1007/978-3-319-44421-5_5

been lately announced in various e-government journals (Government Information Quarterly, Social Science Computer Review, Journal of Organizational Computing and Electronic Commerce). This contributes to the growth of national and international research communities and networks in the field of open data (e.g. Open Data Research Network[1]).

In the Nordic countries open data research has been taking root as well in the past years. These countries have already made considerable progress in open data publication and use according to existing open data benchmarks. For instance, currently the Nordic countries are ranked in the top 25 globally by the Open Data Barometer survey[2].

However, no systematic overview exists yet of the open data research conducted in these countries or of the emerging research community. This paper therefore aims to fill this gap by conducting a comprehensive literature review. The objective of the literature review is to describe the body of knowledge focusing on open data and originating from this region. Zooming in on the Nordic region is motivated by the fact that historically Information Systems research from this region has managed to develop a distinct identity on the international research arena (Iivari and Lyytinen 1999). Hence the expectation is that also in the context of open data there exists room for unique contribution of Nordic researchers. Is such a contribution taking shape yet? This literature review thus aims to answer the following research question: *What progress is made in research to understand open data in the Nordic context?* This question will be answered by focusing on the following aspects: (1) which perspectives and topics are examined in the studies and (2) which empirical settings and methods are applied in the studies. Finding answers to these questions will enable us to propose a future research agenda and thereby stimulate debate in the Nordic open data research community. With this study we aim to open a discussion of (a) whether there is an emerging Nordic contribution to the international open data research and (b) to what extent such a contribution can and does build on the Scandinavian school of Information Systems research.

2   Open Data Research and the Scandinavian Tradition

Internationally open data research has seen rapid development in the past several years. Although it is an emerging field, important first steps have been taken to lay the conceptual foundations and explore the empirical evidence of open data benefits and impacts. Only a few attempts have yet been undertaken at literature reviews in the field of open data, but even those few offer valuable lessons.

The review by Zuiderwijk et al. (2014) found that the body of literature on open data consisted of 143 articles globally (as of October 2013). They were mainly conceptual articles, descriptions of empirical cases, or descriptions of design of systems and technologies (ibid). Only a handful of articles in that sample (19 articles)

---

[1] http://www.opendataresearch.org/.

[2] http://opendatabarometer.org/data-explorer/?_year=2015&indicator=ODB.

mentioned, used, or extended some theory, which points to the need for theory development in the open data field. Furthermore, there are topical gaps where future research is needed such as open data policies, process innovation, innovation resulting from open data, and stimulating open data use (ibid). In sum, open data is a nascent yet thriving research field where many future research directions exist.

Historically, some research directions have been in focus of the Nordic Information Systems (IS) research to a larger extent than others. The so-called Scandinavian School of IS can be summarized in the "grassroot" perspective on IS development (Iivari 2003) with close collaboration with relevant stakeholders (Mathiassen and Nielsen 2008). According to Iivari (2003), the Scandinavian school has emphasized four elements: IS evolution, user participation, alternative IS development models, and a search for a variety of theoretical IS foundations. In the Scandinavian tradition information systems are not necessarily aligned with organizations through deliberate one-time design decisions but rather through continuous alignment processes. This is due to organizations becoming less formal and more socially complex, as well as technology becoming more flexible. From the user participation perspective, the Scandinavian school has favored close collaboration with users to understand the work practices that information systems should support and to tap into the tacit requirements of users. In terms of IS development models, the Scandinavian school has favored prototyping, as well as incremental and cooperative approaches. Moreover, the Scandinavian school has used a variety of theoretical foundations including activity theory, structuration theory, and class theory while at the same time neglecting organization theory as a reference discipline (ibid.).

Considering this, there is much potential for capitalizing on these four elements of the grassroots approach in the Scandinavian school of IS for the benefit of open data research in these countries. Our literature review aims to shed some light on the state of the art of Nordic open data research and hence build the first bridge towards aligning it with the Scandinavian IS tradition.

In this paper we use the term "Scandinavian" in reference to the Scandinavian school of IS and the term "Nordic" in reference to the geographic region we focus on, i.e. Sweden, Norway, Denmark, Finland, Iceland and their territories. In the literature describing the school of approaches to IS development from these countries the term "Scandinavian" has been more common.

3 Method

The literature review proceeded according to the guidelines of Webster and Watson (2002). The literature search was conducted using keyword search in Scopus. This is arguably the most comprehensive database listing the majority of journals and conference proceedings in Information Systems. Prior literature reviews of open data (Zuiderwijk et al. 2014) referred to this database as the primary source of literature in the field.

The first search parameter was keywords 'open data', 'open government data', and 'open government' searched against the categories of keywords, title, and/or abstract. The second search parameter was the country of researcher affiliation; the selection criterion was that at least one of the co-authors was affiliated with a Nordic country (Sweden, Norway, Finland, Denmark, or Iceland). The review considered the time period up until the date of the search (16 November 2015).

The keyword search yielded 158 results in total. The search results were refined by document type to include only articles, conference papers, and book chapters and by subject area to include only results in the subject areas of Computer Science and Social Sciences (113 papers were selected). These two subject areas included the majority of found articles.

The relevance of the articles was determined by reading the abstracts. Only papers written by authors with an academic affiliation were considered. Only papers positioned in the Information Systems discipline were included in the review. Papers describing rather technical issues, such as e.g. data format conversion, data cubes, or data assimilation frameworks, were omitted. This might be seen as a limitation of this study, but our primary objective is to examine how IS and e-government researchers approach open data rather than to investigate cross-domain research.

Consequently, out of the 113 found articles 44 were selected for in-depth analysis based on the aforesaid criteria. The distribution per country was as follows: 8 papers from Denmark (out of 24 found), 15 papers from Finland (out of 39 found), and 21 papers from Sweden (out of 35 found). No relevant papers were identified from Norway, those found (20 papers) predominantly focused on technical issues. No relevant papers were identified originating from Icelandic researchers.

4   Results

The 44 articles included in the review are listed in the Appendix. The earliest articles in the list were dated year 2012. A number of different research institutions per country are involved in open data research. The author affiliations show that there is a fair degree of collaboration in the open data community, as the majority of papers (25) were coauthored with another researcher(s) either nationally (10), from another Nordic country (1), or abroad (14). Cross-border Nordic collaboration in open data research has so far been limited, since in our review we found just one article (37. Vogel et al. 2014) coauthored by researchers from two Nordic countries (Sweden and Finland). The lowest degree of collaboration is found in open data research from Denmark with all papers included in the review being authored by a single institution, with one exception (1. Henriksen 2015) with a double affiliation.

4.1   Perspectives and Topics

Examining which perspectives and topics are used in the papers can reveal what lies in focus of open data researchers from this region. This knowledge can help identify the niche for the Nordic contribution to international open data research.

Table 1 below classifies the reviewed articles by the topics examined in them. The topics were identified by screening the keywords provided by the authors and by reading the abstracts. Many articles examined several concepts in connection with one another and therefore were placed in several categories in Table 1.

Table 1. Topics of Nordic open data research

Concepts	Reference number
Open innovation	11, 41, 31, 33, 35, 23, 39, 40, 42
Innovation contests	31, 33, 35, 22, 40, 17, 16, 10, 43, 41, 42
Service innovation	31, 39, 41, 35, 23, 20, 21
Open data adoption	24, 25, 27, 28, 31
Open data entrepreneurship	24, 12, 13, 31, 33, 41, 35, 39
Open data evaluation	26, 28, 42
Open data applications	30, 22, 38, 37
Open data stakeholders	11, 28
Open data value	2, 3, 13, 4, 6, 21
Open data marketplace	9, 31, 20
Open data business models	12, 13
Open data barriers	14, 15, 35, 41
Open data benefits	18, 5
Open data discourse	29, 44, 7, 8, 43, 32
Open government	29
Open data research	1, 34, 36

Table 2 which follows below provides an overview of the perspectives adopted in the surveyed articles. In our analysis we applied the perspectives suggested by Zuiderwijk et al. (2014): social, economical, institutional, operational, technical, legal and political. The perspectives were identified by reading the abstracts.

Table 2. Perspectives adopted in Nordic open data research

Perspective	Reference number
Social	40, 35, 28, 41, 33, 31, 11, 1, 20, 30, 38, 15, 10, 16, 17, 24, 27, 34, 25, 44
Economical	12, 42, 9, 39, 13, 21, 4, 6
Institutional	43
Operational	
Technical	7, 37, 14
Legal	19, 36
Political	29, 8
Multiple	5, 22, 23, 18, 3, 2, 26
Discourse	32

From Table 2 we conclude that the social and economical perspectives are domi-nating. Some authors adopt multiple perspectives, primarily a combination of the social and economical ones. No author takes an operational perspective; while the paper comparing the discourses of open data and modern archiving (32. Borglund and Engvall 2014) did not fit any of the listed perspectives and was labeled as 'Discourse'. It should be noted that, since we deliberately excluded papers from our sample focusing predominantly on technical issues, this has had an effect on the number of papers in the technical perspective. It was also found that authors focus on different actor roles: in the social perspective the actor roles are shared between user, developer, supplier and intermediary (e.g. open data consultant or innovation contest); while in the economical perspective the focus is on the actor role of developer.

More specifically, as evidenced in Table 1, Nordic open data research focuses on a wide range of issues, however, certain aspects of open data have been highlighted to a greater extent. It appears that the stronghold of Nordic open data research so far has been the innovation-related topics. The most widely discussed topics in the reviewed articles were open innovation, open data entrepreneurship, service innovation, innovation contests. The authors focusing on innovation issues agree that, whereas there is much potential for businesses to generate value from open data (2. Jetzek et al. 2014; 39. Lakomaa and Kallberg 2013; 13. Lindman et al. 2014), many barriers to realizing this potential remain (35. Hjalmarsson et al. 2014; 24. Susha et al. 2015).

Another observation we can make is that, contrary to the global trend in open data research of being supply- and publication-focused, Nordic open data research (in this case exclusively from Sweden) has paid more attention to open data adoption. In this category studies focused on such issues as motivation of open data users (33. Juell-Skielse et al. 2014), measures to stimulate open data adoption (27. Susha et al. 2015), expectations and perceptions regarding open data use (25. Hellberg and Hedström 2015), among others.

As open data is an emerging research domain, the community of active researchers is quite small. Considering this, we observe that in different countries and institutions different core expertise concerning open data has been accumulating. For instance, research at Copenhagen Business School (Denmark) has prominently focused on open data value; research at Stockholm University and University of Borås (Sweden) has extensively studied innovation contests; research at Hanken School of Economics (Finland) offers expertise on open data market and business models. This provides an opportunity for learning from one another and combining expertise to undertake more holistic studies.

The aforesaid paints a picture of research gaps as well. There seems to be a lack of studies which focus explicitly on the democracy perspective of open data. Only one paper (29. Hansson et al. 2015) was identified which investigated open data in the context of open government and democracy principles. Another finding is that there is ample room for research on the effect of open data on public services including e-government services. The paper examining the use of open data in the e-government service process (30. Johansson et al. 2015) is a starting point in this respect.

4.2   Empirical Settings and Methods

Analyzing the empirical settings and methods applied in the papers is intended to reveal (1) on which level (international, national, or regional/local) open data issues are examined by Nordic researchers and (2) which methods are in use by this open data research community. This knowledge provides an insight into how researchers in the Nordic region choose to approach research problems in the open data field. Table 3 below provides an overview of the empirical settings examined in the selected papers.

Theoretical papers (reference numbers 3, 7, 8, 17, 23, 29) are not listed in the overview of empirical settings.

As follows from Table 3, open data research produced by Nordic researchers is not only focused on the Nordic country contexts but extends beyond the borders of the region. An important factor in this respect is the fact that other countries (in particular the US and UK) have advanced much further in open data, thereby presenting an opportunity for researching cutting edge issues and problems empirically. Nonetheless, there is also emerging knowledge about regional and local open data activities (in particular in Sweden) which may be utilized for cross-border knowledge transfer between Nordic researchers.

Table 3. Empirical settings examined in the articles

Country	International	National	Regional or local
Denmark	4, 2	1, 5, 6	
Finland	11, 16, 18, 9, 19	12, 13, 14, 15, 20, 21	10, 22
Sweden	24, 27, 26, 28, 31, 34, 36, 37	42, 41, 32, 33, 35, 38, 39	25, 30, 43, 44, 40

Table 4 below lists the methods which are used in the papers in our sample. It includes both empirical and conceptual papers. Papers without any mentioning of any particular method used (reference numbers 8, 14, 18, 36) are not listed in the table.

Table 4. Methods applied in the articles

Methods	Reference number
Empirical	
Case study	11, 25, 27, 28, 2, 44, 4, 43, 22, 38, 19
Interviews	12, 13
Survey	24, 39
Stakeholder analysis	34
Mixed	1, 41, 15, 31, 32, 33, 35, 21
Design science	30, 37, 40, 42, 20
Regression analysis	6
Goal modelling	10, 16, 17
Conceptual	
Literature review	29, 23, 9
Meta-analysis	26
Theory building	3, 7

From Table 4 it follows that case study is the most widely used research method to study open data issues. This can be explained by the fact that open data is an emerging practical development receiving varying levels of attention of different organizations.

There is hardly any systematic evidence or uniform implementation, especially at the subnational level. A case study is thus a well-suited method for studying emerging initiatives.

Nordic open data research has not only investigated ongoing open data applications (such as e.g. use of open data in decision support systems in the maritime industry, use of open data for smart cities) but also includes research in the design science tradition. Namely, Aaltonen et al. (20. Aaltonen et al. 2013) in their paper developed a proof-of-concept implementation of a mash-up system built on wellness data and Ayele et al. (42. Ayele et al. 2015) developed a measurement model for open digital innovation contests. Furthermore, the work of Johansson et al. (30. Johansson et al. 2015) resulted in a digital prototype allowing citizens to generate and acquire open data, as well as develop and publish their own e-services. Design science research is however less represented than descriptive and analytical work in the review sample.

Another observation is that the majority of papers used qualitative research methods, although mixed research designs were also well represented. There is a notable exception (6. Jetzek et al. 2013) in which the authors used regression analysis (Partial Least Squares method) to test their open data value framework using open secondary data sources.

5 Discussion and Conclusions

Based on the findings of this literature review we hereby propose an agenda for future research. This agenda highlights the research gaps identified in the previous section and aims to help advance the field forward. Our point of departure in this discussion is that such a research agenda must also be aligned with some of the key developments in practice in these countries.

In our review we established that some *topics* received more attention of Nordic researchers than others, namely the innovation-related topics were better represented than the democracy-related ones. At the same time in Denmark and Finland there is limited evidence of political and social impact of open data compared to the economic impact (Open Data Barometer 2015). This therefore calls for research into how and to what extent open data has an impact on political and social aspects, such as trust in government, citizen empowerment, quality of public services, improvement of public policies etc.

Furthermore, our analysis found that Nordic open data research focusing on *perspectives* other than economical and social is limited, hence a more nuanced approach also including legal, operational, institutional, political, and technical perspectives could provide a fruitful way forward. More specifically, based on our analysis we find that there is a lack of research on open data policies and process management, as well as on infrastructures for open data. We also believe that the work already done on the topic of open data adoption and citizen participation in the Nordic countries could be further strengthened, for example in the direction of user participation. So far in our sample we only found some seeds of the emerging focus on user participation which traditionally characterizes the Scandinavian IS school.

In terms of *empirical settings*, our review concluded that different levels (international, national regional/local) are represented in the sample of articles. However, the number of contributions focusing on regional or local open data contexts are much smaller (only 7 articles). This finding may be seen as surprising considering the prevalent focus of the Scandinavian Information Systems research tradition on small scale development (the grassroots approach). We envisage that a stronger emphasis on regional and local open data initiatives and on the benefits they create for the communities on the ground provides good opportunities for future contributions.

Finally, as regards the *methods* used in Nordic open data research, we find that there is a lack of theory building research, while case studies prevail. Thus, there is room for more theoretical work in the field which can examine the utility of existing IS theories for the studies of open data. As mentioned in Sect. 2, traditionally Scandinavian IS research is characterized by a variety of theoretical foundations. These are yet to be reflected on in the context of Nordic open data research.

To conclude, when we compare our results with the future research directions proposed by Zuiderwijk et al. (2014), we find that the Nordic researchers have made a most prominent contribution towards the research direction of open data innovation and use. The contribution is mainly concerned with open innovation, digital service innovation, innovation contests and the stimulation of use in terms of open data markets, adoption, benefits, and business models. In our future research we aim to continue our survey of the Nordic open data research in order to identify specific opportunities to further strengthen the Nordic contribution towards the global open data research community based on the legacy of the Scandinavian School of IS.

Acknowledgements. The authors thank the reviewers at the Scandinavian Workshop on E-government and the Electronic Government conference for their feedback. We appreciate the input of Åke Grönlund on the early version of this paper.

Appendix. Articles Included in Literature Review

Nbr	Reference
Denmark	
1	Henriksen, H. Z. (2015) Scrutinizing open government data to understand patterns in eGovernment uptake. *Vol. 9248. Lecture Notes in Computer Science*, pp. 144–155.
2	Jetzek, T., Avital, M., & Bjorn-Andersen, N. (2014). Data-driven innovation through open government data. *Journal of Theoretical and Applied Electronic Commerce Research, 9*(2), 100–120. doi:10.4067/S0718-18762014000200008
3	Jetzek, T., Avital, M., & Bjorn-Andersen, N. (2014) Generating sustainable value from open data in a sharing society. *Vol. 429. IFIP Advances in Information and Communication Technology* (pp. 62–82).

(Continued)

(Continued)

Nbr	Reference
4	J Jetzek, T., Avital, M., & Bjorn-Andersen, N. (2013). *Generating value from open government data.* Paper presented at the International Conference on Information Systems (ICIS 2013): Reshaping Society Through Information Systems Design.
5	Hansen, H Hansen, H. S., Hvingel, L., & Schrøder, L. (2013) Open government data - A key element in the digital society. *Vol. 8061 LNCS, Lecture Notes in Computer Science,* pp. 167–180).
6	Jetzek, T., Avital, M., & Bjorn-Andersen, N. (2013). *The Generative Mechanisms Of Open Government Data.* Paper presented at the ECIS.
7	Marton, A., Avital, M., & Jensen, T. B. (2013). *Reframing Open Big Data.* Paper presented at the ECIS.
8	Andersen, C. U., & Pold, S. B. (2012). *Occupation of the 'open city'.* Paper presented at the ACM International Conference Proceeding Series.
Finland	
9	Lindman, J., & Kuk, G. (2015). *From open access to open data markets: Increasing the subtractability of open data.* Paper presented at the Proceedings of the Annual Hawaii International Conference on System Sciences.
10	Shiramatsu, S., Tossavainen, T., Ozono, T., & Shintani, T. (2015) Towards continuous collaboration on civic tech projects: Use cases of a goal sharing system based on linked open data. *Vol. 9249. Lecture Notes in* Computer *Science* (pp. 81–92).
11	Perkmann, M., & Schildt, H. (2015). Open data partnerships between firms and universities: The role of boundary organizations. *Research Policy, 44*(5), 1133–1143. doi:10.1016/j.respol.2014.12.006
12	Lindman, J. (2014). Similarities of open data and open source: Impacts on business. *Journal of Theoretical and Applied Electronic Commerce Research, 9*(3), 59–70.
13	Lindman, J., Kinnari, T., & Rossi, M. (2014). *Industrial open data: Case studies of early open data entrepreneurs.* Paper presented at the Annual Hawaii International Conference on System Sciences (HICSS).
14	Jaakkola, H., Mäkinen, T., & Eteläaho, A. (2014). *Open data - Opportunities and challenges.* Paper presented at the ACM International Conference Proceeding Series.
15	Rohunen, A., Markkula, J., Heikkilä, M., & Heikkilä, J. (2014). Open traffic data for future service innovation - Addressing the privacy challenges of driving data. *Journal of Theoretical and Applied Electronic Commerce Research, 9*(3), 71–89. doi:10.4067/S0718-18762014000300007
16	Shiramatsu, S., Tossavainen, T., Ozono, T., & Shintani, T. (2014) A Goal matching service for facilitating public collaboration using linked open data. *Vol. 8654. Lecture Notes in Computer Science,* pp. 114–127.
17	Tossavainen, T., Shiramatsu, S., Ozono, T., & Shintani, T. (2014) Implementing a system enabling open innovation by sharing public goals based on linked open data. *Vol. 8482 LNAI. Lecture Notes in Computer Science,* pp. 98–108.
18	Jaakkola, H., Mäkinen, T., Henno, J., & Mäkelä, J. (2014). *Openn.* Paper presented at the 2014 37th International Convention on Information and Communication Technology, Electronics and Microelectronics, MIPRO 2014 - Proceedings.

(Continued)

(Continued)

Nbr	Reference
10	Palmirani, M., Martoni, M., & Girardi, D. (2014) Open government data beyond transparency. *Vol. 8650 LNCS. Lecture Notes in Computer Science* (pp. 275–291).
20	Aaltonen, T., Mikkonen, T., Peltola, H., & Salminen, A. (2013). *From mashup applications to open data ecosystems.* Paper presented at the Proceedings of the 10th International Symposium on Open Collaboration, OpenSym 2014.
21	Tammisto, Y., & Lindman, J. (2012) Definition of open data services in software business. *Vol. 114 LNBIP. Lecture Notes in Business Information Processing* (pp. 297–303).
22	Hielkema, H., & Hongisto, P. (2013). Developing the Helsinki Smart City: The Role of Competitions for Open Data Applications. *Journal of the Knowledge Economy, 4* (2), 190–204. doi:10.1007/s13132-012-0087-6
23	Lindman, J., Rossi, M., & Tuunainen, V. K. (2013, 7–10 Jan. 2013). *Open Data Services: Research Agenda.* Paper presented at the 2013 46th Hawaii International Conference on System Sciences (HICSS).
Sweden	
24	Susha, I., Grönlund, A., & Janssen, M. (2015). Driving factors of service innovation using open government data: An exploratory study of entrepreneurs in two countries. *Information Polity, 20*(1), 19–34. doi:10.3233/IP-150353
25	Hellberg, A. S., & Hedström, K. (2015). The story of the sixth myth of open data and open government. *Transforming Government: People, Process and Policy, 9*(1), 35–51. doi:10.1108/TG-04-2014-0013
26	Susha, I., Zuiderwijk, A., Janssen, M., & Grönlund, Å. (2015). Benchmarks for Evaluating the Progress of Open Data Adoption: Usage, Limitations, and Lessons Learned. *Social Science Computer Review, 33*(5), 613–630. doi:10.1177/0894439314560852
27	Susha, I., Grönlund, Å., & Janssen, M. (2015b). Organizational measures to stimulate user engagement with open data. *Transforming Government: People, Process and Policy, 9*(2), 181–206.
28	Hjalmarsson, A., Johansson, N., & Rudmark, D. (2015). *Mind the gap: Exploring stakeholders' value with open data assessment.* Paper presented at the Annual Hawaii International Conference on System Sciences (HICSS).
29	Hansson, K., Belkacem, K., & Ekenberg, L. (2015). Open Government and Democracy: A Research Review. *Social Science Computer Review, 33*(5), 540–555. doi:10.1177/0894439314560847
30	Johansson, D., Lassinantti, J., & Wiberg, M. (2015) Mobile e-services and open data in e-government processes-concept and design. *Vol. 9228. Lecture Notes in Computer Science* (pp. 149–160).
31	Juell-Skielse, G., Hjalmarsson, A., Juell-Skielse, E., Johannesson, P., & Rudmark, D. (2014). Contests as innovation intermediaries in open data markets. *Information Polity, 19*(3-4), 247–262. doi:10.3233/IP-140346
32	Borglund, E., & Engvall, T. (2014). Open data? Data, information, document or record? *Records Management Journal, 24*(2), 163–180. doi:10.1108/RMJ-01-2014-0012

(Continued)

(Continued)

Nbr	Reference
33	Juell-Skielse, G., Hjalmarsson, A., Johannesson, P., & Rudmark, D. (2014) Is the public motivated to engage in open data innovation?: *Vol. 8653 LNCS. Lecture Notes in Computer Science* (pp. 277–288).
34	Linde, P., Noorman, M., Wessels, B. A., & Sveinsdottir, T. (2014). How can libraries and other academic stakeholders engage in making data open? *Information Services and Use, 34*(3-4), 211–219. doi:10.3233/ISU-140741
35	Hjalmarsson, A., Johannesson, P., Juell-Skielse, G., & Rudmark, D. (2014). *Beyond innovation contests: A framework of barriers to open innovation of digital services.* Paper presented at the ECIS 2014 Proceedings - 22nd European Conference on Information Systems.
36	Sveinsdottir, T., Wessels, B. A., Smallwood, R., Linde, P., Kala, V., Tsoukala, V., & Sondervan, J. (2014). Policy recommendations for Open Access to research data in Europe-Stakeholder values and ecosystems. *Information Services and Use, 34*(3-4), 331–333. doi:10.3233/ISU-140756
37	Vogel, B., Kurti, A., Mikkonen, T., & Milrad, M. (2014). *From architectural requirements towards an open architecture for web and mobile societal applications.* Paper presented at the 1st International Workshop on Inclusive Web Programming - Programming on the Web with Open Data for Societal Applications, IWP 2014 - Proceedings.
38	Kazemi, S., Abghari, S., Lavesson, N., Johnson, H., & Ryman, P. (2013). Open data for anomaly detection in maritime surveillance. *Expert Systems with Applications, 40* (14), 5719–5729. doi:10.1016/j.eswa.2013.04.029
39	Lakomaa, E., & Kallberg, J. (2013). Open data as a foundation for innovation: The enabling effect of free public sector information for entrepreneurs. *IEEE Access, 1*, 558–563. doi:10.1109/ACCESS.2013.2279164
40	Hjalmarsson, A., & Rudmark, D. (2012) Designing digital innovation contests. *Vol. 7286 LNCS. Lecture Notes in Computer Science* (pp. 9–27).
41	Hjalmarsson, A., Juell-Skielse, G., Ayele, W., Johannesson, P., and Rudmark, D. (2015). From Contest to Market Entry: A Longitudinal Survey of Innovation Barriers Constraining Open Data Service Development. Proceedings of the 23rd European Conference on Information Systems (ECIS), Muenster, Germany.
42	Ayele, W., Juell-Skielse, G., Hjalmarsson, A., Johannesson, P., and Rudmark, D. (2015). Evaluating Open Data Innovation: A Measurement Model for Digital Innovation Contests. Pacific Asia Conference on Information Systems (PACIS), Singapore.
43	Hellberg, A. S., & Hedström, K. (2015). The story of the sixth myth of open data and open government. Transforming Government: People, Process and Policy, 9(1), 35–51.
44	Lassinantti, J., Bergvall-Kåreborn, B., & Ståhlbröst, A. (2014). Shaping local open data initiatives: politics and implications. Journal of theoretical and applied electronic commerce research, 9(2), 17–33.

References

Iivari, J., Lyytinen, K.: Research on information systems development in Scandinavia. In: Currie W. Galliers, B. (eds.) Rethinking Management Information Systems, pp. 57–102. OUP, Oxford (1999)

Iivari, J.: Is Scandinavian information system development becoming passé? History in Nordic Computing, pp. 339–356. Springer, US (2003)

Mathiassen, L., Nielsen, P.A.: Engaged scholarship in IS research. Scand. J. Inf. Syst. **20**(2), 3–20 (2008)

Open Data Barometer. Open Data Barometer 2nd edn. (2015). http://www.opendatabarometer. org/report/analysis/impact.html

Open Data Handbook. (n.d.). Glossary: open data. http://opendatahandbook.org/glossary/en/ terms/open-data/

Webster, J., Watson, R.T.: Analyzing the past to prepare for the future: writing a literature review. Manag. Inf. Syst. Q. **26**(2), 13–23 (2002)

Zuiderwijk, A., Janssen, M., Gil-García, J., Helbig, N.: Innovation through open data: a review of the state-of-the-art and an emerging research agenda. J. Theor. Appl. Electron. Commer. Res. **9**(2), 258–268 (2014)

Open Government Data Ecosystems: Linking Transparency for Innovation with Transparency for Participation and Accountability

Luigi Reggi[1](✉) and Sharon Dawes[2]

[1] Rockefeller College of Public Affairs and Policy,
University at Albany, Albany, USA
luigi.reggi@gmail.com
[2] Rockefeller College of Public Affairs and Policy and Center
for Technology in Government, University at Albany, Albany, USA
sdawes@ctg.albany.edu

Abstract. The rhetoric of open government data (OGD) promises that data transparency will lead to multiple public benefits: economic and social innovation, civic participation, public-private collaboration, and public accountability. In reality much less has been accomplished in practice than advocates have hoped. OGD research to address this gap tends to fall into two streams – one that focuses on data publication and re-use for purposes of innovation, and one that views publication as a stimulus for civic participation and government accountability - with little attention to whether or how these two views interact. In this paper we use an ecosystem perspective to explore this question. Through an exploratory case study we show how two related cycles of influences can flow from open data publication. The first addresses transparency for innovation goals, the second addresses larger issues of data use for public engagement and greater government accountability. Together they help explain the potential and also the barriers to reaching both kinds of goals.

Keywords: Open government data · Ecosystems · Transparency · Innovation · Participation · Accountability

1 Introduction

The open government philosophy has stimulated a global transparency movement with goals of innovation, participation, and accountability. National and subnational governments in every part of the world are adopting open data programs with the expectation that free and open publication of government data will lead naturally to an array of economic, social, and political benefits. Yet, Yu and Robinson [1] suggest that the vagueness of the label "Open Government" does not help distinguish between openness of government data in terms of technical access and reusability for service innovation and the use of open data for civic participation and accountability purposes. Data publication and re-use by private actors can and does support innovative

H.J. Scholl et al. (Eds.): EGOV 2016, LNCS 9820, pp. 74–86, 2016.
DOI: 10.1007/978-3-319-44421-5_6

applications that reflect the interests and skills of technical experts. But publication by itself does not necessarily lead to greater collaboration between government and ordinary citizens nor to greater accountability by government for policies and programs. For example, Shkabatur [2] contends that the US Open Government directive fosters "transparency without accountability", by allowing public agencies excessive discretion over which datasets are of "high value" and thus chosen to be published. Consequently, much of the data disclosed in discretionary OGD portals such as Data. gov can be irrelevant for purposes of accountability. Lourenço [3] draws similar conclusions from a systematic analysis of seven national open data portals. Even in places where all data is required to be published, there is no guarantee that civic collaboration or greater accountability will result [4].

While the rhetoric of open government data promises that data transparency will lead simultaneously to innovation, collaboration, and accountability, most research falls into one of two streams – one that focuses on data publication and re-use for purposes of innovation, and one that looks at data publication as a stimulus for civic participation and government accountability. Few attempts have been made to understand empirically whether and how these streams interact. In this paper we begin with a recent ecosystem model that draws on the first stream of work [4] and extend it through the use of an exploratory national case study to also encompass the second. In particular our research aim is to demonstrate conceptually and empirically the crucial connections that allow these two streams of effects to be understood as a complex and integrated ecosystem with attendant barriers and enablers.

2 Literature Review

Since the release of the Open Government directive in the United States in 2009 and the long process of revision of the European Directive on Public Sector Information concluded in 2013, public rhetoric has promised a trio of potential benefits: data-driven product and service innovation, greater public participation in policy making, and more government accountability. Researchers have generally followed two divergent paths – one group focusing on the innovation theme, the other on participation and accountability.

In the first group, authors have focused their attention on the economic benefits of re-use of OGD to foster innovation [5]. At the core of these works is the idea that the continuous release of easily accessible, machine-processable and possibly real-time government data can act "as a platform" for the creation of new applications and services [6], including "civic innovation" initiatives by NGOs and civic technology communities. To this end, Sieber and Johnson [7] identify two proactive strategies that governments can adopt to increase co-production of new services. In the *code exchange* model, governments actively support the use of OGD through app contests based on explicit public needs. In the *participatory open data* model, governments create feedback loops about data quality and structure, with the aim of initiating an "on-going co-creation of raw data between both governments and governed". A very similar view is presented in the *open data for engagement* framework [8], where users participate in the improvement of governmental datasets by offering feedback and creating new data resources.

For example, platforms for open data publication have been developed that integrate the collection of user feedback on the data released through Web 2.0 functionalities [9]. Related work has focused on data quality and management practices, and OGD program design and operation [10, 11].

Other scholars have highlighted the potential benefits of analyzing and visualizing government information to better understand public problems and make better decisions [12]. This literature also considers the contribution of OGD to more general Open Government objectives of increased availability of government information, improved civic participation and collaboration, and greater accountability of governmental activities. Peixoto [13] considers civic participation as a key contributor to "unlocking the potential for open data to produce better government decisions and policies". Janssen et al. [14] list political and social benefits including not only increased transparency, but also accountability, citizen empowerment, trust in government, and improvement of the policy making process. Published data can also be a powerful tool against corruption [15] in transparency initiatives that emphasize disclosure of public budgets, agency performance, and contracts.

However, whether focused on innovation or on participation and accountability, current OGD practices suffer from substantial legal, political, social, institutional, economic, operational and technical challenges [16], leading to what have been called the "myths" of open data [13]. These include the belief that opening data leads automatically to more open and inclusive government. Political challenges include the lack of institutional motivation and political will to publish relevant datasets. Additional challenges emerge when considering the actual use of OGD. On the supply side, OGD programs are often designed not for citizens but for technical experts and intermediaries [17]. On the demand side, the lack of incentives, interpretive tools, and contextual and technical knowledge among users can prevent meaningful data use [18]. Finally, lack of institutional processes for dialogue prevents integration of public feedback into existing strategies and programs [14].

Recently researchers have begun to use an ecosystem metaphor to model the complex dynamics among these different actors and concerns [4, 19]. In particular, Dawes et al. [4] draw from evidence in two empirical cases in different settings – New York City and St. Petersburg – to explore OGD programs as ecosystems of interconnected organizations and individuals working within a shared social context. Briefly, they identified a cycle of influences regarding the ways in which ecosystem factors shape publication, use, and feedback about the data itself. According to the model, OGD providers can influence data use by designing OGD strategies and publication practices that encourage use. In turn, the users, such as transparency advocates and civic technologists take advantage of the data by using it directly or by developing new applications that can reach a broader audience of beneficiaries, therefore acting as OGD intermediaries [17]. The resulting economic and societal benefits can influence further advocacy and interaction with providers to improve the quality of OGD data, strategies and practices.

In the next section we describe the case of OpenCoesione in which data publication is augmented by both government and intermediaries to become information usable by civic groups and individuals attempting to hold the government accountable for development projects in Italy. We then use the case data to suggest an extension of the

Dawes et al. [4] model to better integrate participation and accountability elements and discuss how the transparency inherent in OGD data publication programs can stimulate both innovation and participation and accountability.

3 An Exploratory Case Study

In this section we present preliminary results of a case study of an OGD initiative in Italy from 2014 to the present that aims to improve citizen engagement and accountability, and the related ecosystem of data intermediaries and users.

The data comprise participant observations and a review of three complementary open government applications (an OGD portal and a Massive Online Open Course developed by the Italian government and a civic technology application from civil society). In order to collect data on the perspectives of governmental and non-governmental actors with different roles in the ecosystem, key stakeholders with knowledge and direct experience in these programs were identified through purposive sampling and interviewed between January and March 2016. They include practitioners with different roles in the Italian government (one project manager and three analysts), two members of the steering committee of the civil society initiative *Monithon*, one representative of a local community in Southern Italy, and two researchers at two different Italian research institutions. The semi-structured interviews were focused on their perspectives on the enablers and barriers to an effective and sustainable OGD ecosystem. Three published program reviews [20–22] served as additional sources of information. The integrated conceptual model developed from the case was sent to the respondents for comment and validation.

3.1 Context

European Structural and Investment Funds (ESIFs) represent the main investment policy tool of the European Union (EU), with a total budget of €454 billion or 43 % of the total EU budget. The funds co-finance a wide range of national and local development policies, from the support of new businesses to the development of infrastructures in areas such as broadband, renewable energies, and water supplies, with a strong focus on reducing disparities among European regions and countries.

The economic literature has shown mixed results in assessing the real impact of European investment funding on economic growth [23], and these programs face challenges in terms of efficiency, effectiveness and the complexity of evaluating the performance and impact of millions of different projects funded across Europe.

Furthermore, concerns have been raised about the limited opportunities for bottom-up inclusiveness and participation in the policy process, from programming to implementation to evaluation of results. A much more inclusive participatory process has been suggested as a way to improve efficiency, effectiveness and accountability of the policy, with stakeholders, civil society and final beneficiaries to be substantively involved [24, 25].

Starting in 2014, new regulations were adopted to increase transparency and participation of relevant stakeholders. First, a set of mandatory information must be disclosed in the form of OGD through development of program-specific national OGD portals, increasing the number of mandatory fields from 3 to 11, thus forcing administrations to release more detailed information on each funded project and its recipients [26]. Second, the national portals must provide "information to all operational programs in that Member State, including information about the timing of implementation… and any related public consultation processes". Third, a code of conduct on partnership encourages broader engagement of local stakeholders.

3.2   ESIF in Italy: OpenCoesione, Monithon and A Scuola di OpenCoesione

Italy is the second largest recipient of ESIF among the EU countries, with an allocation of €42.7 billion for 2014–2020. The total budget for these policies is even higher – about €123 billion – thanks to national and regional co-financing and additional funds for regional development. These resources represent the main source of investments in Southern Italy, where about 80 % of the funding is to be spent.

3.2.1   OpenCoesione

All these financial resources are tracked on the national OGD portal OpenCoesione. gov.it, which acts as the national transparency portal under the new regulations. OpenCoesione was created in 2012 by the Ministry of Economic Development to publish information about every project carried out in the 2007–13 period. The portal makes use of a large set of administrative data from the national monitoring system managed by the Ministry of the Economy. The system is a federated information network that interoperates with dozens of local applications collecting information from the recipients of the funding, with a complex multi-level governance organization.

In March 2016, OpenCoesione was publishing data on almost 950.000 projects with a total investment of €51.2 billion. The projects range from the construction of large infrastructures worth billions of Euros to individual grants to students. For each project, users can access a webpage with information about the amount and sources of funding, approximate location, actors involved, and implementation timeframes. They can download raw data, use the Application Program Interfaces (APIs) to analyze the data or develop an application, or browse through interactive diagrams.

OpenCoesione also launched different initiatives to stimulate the use and re-use of the datasets, including publication of articles with news, analysis and infographics; maps and interactive visualizations; webinars; a data journalism school; and workshops and seminars at numerous research institutions. Interactive tools are available on the portal to receive comments and suggestions directly from the recipients and final beneficiaries. However, having insufficient resources for directly managing citizen engagement activities, OpenCoesione representatives also participated in hackathons organized by both national and local civic technology communities to stimulate new initiatives and applications and to collect feedback both on the data released and on the results of the projects included in OpenCoesione.

3.2.2   Monithon

During one of these hackathons in 2013, the OpenCoesione team organized a *Monithon*, that is a "civic monitoring marathon" of local eu-funded projects. based on the project-level OGD on OpenCoesione, a group of journalists, analysts, developers and individual citizens collected further information about five projects on the renovation of school buildings in Bologna by conducting interviews with people in charge of implementation and gathering evidence such as videos and photographs documenting progress and results. They soon realized that further investigations were needed since the OGD on the portal provided no clues about crucial questions such as: What are the policy motives and decisions that led to finance the project? Who is responsible within each governance actor? who are the contractors and subcontractors and how have their expenditures been tracked? Most Importantly, basic narratives about the projects' objectives and activities, performance data, and output indicators were all missing.

This first experiment then evolved into a nationwide, civil society initiative named Monithon.it, that in two years of activity drew dozens of local communities - some formed on purpose and others based on existing associations - and more than 3,000 people into civic monitoring activities. Both national and local communities are involved, such as Action Aid Italy or the main Italian anti-mafia association Libera. However, Monithon.it is not a formally funded organization; it relies mainly on volunteer effort. Although the costs of developing and maintaining the technical platform are partly covered by grants received thanks to partnerships with NGOs, Monithon.it faces a persistent problem of economic sustainability [20]. Effective engagement and coordination of local communities depends heavily on the work of the three volunteers who comprise the central staff.

Civic monitoring is organized as a group activity in which interdisciplinary competences are employed to carry out qualitative investigations to assess project performance. These include the project history, the underlying policy motives, and the network of governance actors and implementers responsible for programming or implementation. The purpose of this activity is not only to enrich the information in the publicly available datasets and collect feedback on data quality, but also to collect feedback on the ground about project results and suggestions for improvement from the perspective of the final beneficiaries. All the new information acquired is collected through a standard methodology (questionnaire, interview guide, guidelines for data analysis and fieldwork organization), and then represented in a map on the Monithon.it platform [21].

In March 2014, after one year of activity, 55 "citizen monitoring reports" were published on Monithon.it, covering different policy areas such as transportation, cultural heritage, urban policy, education, and social inclusion [21]. By July 2015, 98 reports had been uploaded. About 40 % contain basic information about the project, plus some evidence about the progress and the result, such as photographs. The remaining 60 % can be characterized as in-depth investigations with detailed descriptions of project history and motives, displaying photos, videos and links to project or policy documentation.

The information collected is published on the Monithon.it platform as OGD and can be used by administrations and local governments, journalists, researchers and NGOs to influence the implementation of the ESIFs and the programming of future policy actions. In some cases, citizen monitoring reports received the attention of local newspapers, especially during special events such as Open Data Day, generating public debate about the use of public funding. In other cases, new collaborations were created between local communities and administrations. For example, the group *Monithon Piemonte* in Torino initiated a dialogue with the director of the Egyptian Museum to improve a renovation project funded by ESIFs. In Bari, the results of civic monitoring of social innovation projects were used by the Ministry of Research to program future actions in this field. In other instances, the lobbying activity of NGOs like Libera has helped channel feedback to the attention of policy makers. In these cases, citizen feedback influenced the way national and local administrators made decisions, in both the monitoring and in the policy creation phases of the policy cycle.

However, in many cases the feedback is shared only within the community and fails to be addressed to or by policy makers. While OpenCoesione collects citizen feedback both on the data itself and on policy performance it does not directly bring feedback to the attention of policy makers, but instead points the users in the right direction by giving information about the agencies responsible for specific projects and programs. But, since no legal mechanisms are in place that force administrations to consider feedback from individual citizens and informal groups, the Monithon communities need to persuade local decision makers to listen and collaborate [20]. When it reaches local administrations, often it is not taken into account to make actual decisions. In addition, administrations have raised concerns about the representativeness of feedback collected.

A major challenge for sustainability, then, is creating enduring local groups with sufficient motivation and specific, interdisciplinary expertise to do this kind of work. While basic crowdsourcing activities such as collecting photos and videos documenting the progress of public works can be relatively easy to conduct, more sophisticated investigations require specific knowledge about ESIFs policy mechanisms, national and local administrative procedures, data analysis and visualization, fieldwork, data collection, and communication of findings. To this end, a partnership with Action Aid Italy was created to support local volunteers in developing new skills such as understanding financial data, via free workshops and laboratory sessions. In one case, a project financed by the European Commission will ensure three years of financial support to this kind of activity in Sibari (Calabria).

3.2.3   A Scuola di OpenCoesione

Partly in response to these problems, in September 2013 OpenCoesione in partnership with the Representation Office of the European Commission in Italy launched *a Scuola di OpenCoesione* (or OpenCoesione School), an educational challenge for high school students and a Massive Online Open Course (MOOC), in order to stimulate data use, civic engagement and awareness. The Ministry of Education also partnered in this initiative with the goal of increasing data literacy and ICT use among students and teachers. A Scuola di OpenCoesione Uses the Monithon tools and methodology to organize civic monitoring activities. The students learn not only how to analyze policy and administrative sources and conduct field investigations, but also how to use complex datasets regarding real-life civic issues to develop and present multimedia content.

In the 2015–16 edition, 120 schools and 2,800 students from all Italian regions enrolled. Each school chose a project to analyze based on OGD from OpenCoesione.

As the students organized events to disseminate their results, they created further opportunities to raise civic awareness and to strengthen the dialogue with NGOs and local representatives of the European Commission (the "Europe Direct" network) from which they received support. All of the events are public and represent a sort of "accountability forum" in which the students interact with the local community and political leaders and administrators responsible for implementing the projects, asking questions and suggesting solutions. These events produced mixed results. In some cases, they stimulated an evidence-based public debate. In others, especially when the results of the citizen monitoring were mainly negative, local politicians did not respond to issues raised or simply did not get involved. When events were organized in municipalities where courts have appointed administrators to replace elected officials implicated in mafia crimes, public institutions did not attend at all [20].

4 Discussion: Toward an Integrated Open Government Ecosystem

Drawing from the evidence in the case, we propose an extension of Dawes, et al. ecosystem model [4] to show how a related second cycle of influences can flow from open data publication. While the first cycle addresses transparency mainly for purposes of innovation, the second addresses issues of collaboration and engagement around government policies and toward greater accountability for policy performance.

As shown in Fig. 1, a government's *OGD Policies and Strategies* and *Data Publication* practices, such as choices about the format and granularity of the datasets, strongly shape the realm of possible *Data Uses and Apps*. In particular, OGD use in civic applications like Monithon.it not only stimulates civic awareness and social capital among local communities *(Socio-economic benefits)*, but also enables the systematic *Collection of citizen feedback* on government performance, spending and policy results from the perspective of the actual beneficiaries. This feedback can be directly addressed to policy makers, or can be conveyed through the work of intermediaries such as the media, NGOs or other relevant stakeholders. In the first case, feedback can be conveyed through engagement tools and channels developed by the government. In the second case, *Intermediaries* can influence policy decisions by stimulating public debate or lobbying for specific goals. Intermediaries can also press for better data increasing the level of *Advocacy and interaction* with data providers, with consequent influence on *OGD Policies and Strategies*. The realization of more participatory forms of *Policy Making* can enable evidence-based decision making with the desired effect of improving accountability, efficiency and effectiveness of the policy. These perceived benefits, in turn, can potentially lead not only to better policy making practices and choices but also to improved OGD programs. Our case shows that all these influences are possible, although the last few related to evidence-based policy making and public accountability tend to be weak and infrequent. Thus we indicate them in Fig. 1 with dotted arrows.

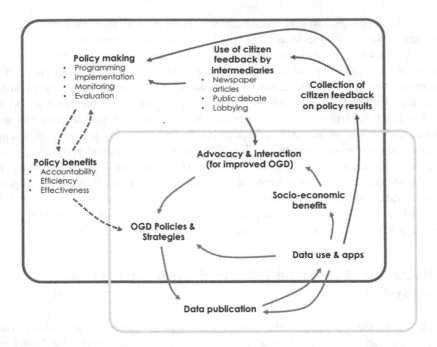

Fig. 1. Integrated OGD ecosystem for innovation, collaboration and accountability

The case shows how a combination of government and civic actions can stimulate a cycle of collaboration and accountability (the darker box in Fig. 1) that is linked to the more data-oriented innovation cycle (the lighter box) proposed by Dawes et al. [4]. According to our case, an OGD provider (*OpenCoesione*) published data with high granularity about significant European and national public investments, in ways that could prove useful for individual citizens and communities [27] for diverse uses. Civil society actors such as *Monithon.it* leveraged this data to develop civic technology tools and methodologies to foster civic engagement for systematic collection of citizen feedback on project results. The government-sponsored *A Scuola di OpenCoesione* created civic awareness, social capital and new skills for participation [28] based in public schools, while NGOs such as Action Aid Italy and Libera fostered both skills and use of the data for important public issues. These practices helped overcome some of the typical limitations of OGD programs, which tend to offer engagement only about the data itself, and then mainly with a restricted group of technical experts and data intermediaries.

Feedback collected from these communities on data content – that is on how public investment projects are progressing and what results they are achieving – shows the potential to influence not only existing OGD strategies and practices, but also the policy decisions about programming and implementation. The examples from the case show that new forms of direct engagement between communities and governments can be triggered by civic monitoring activities. In addition, indirect public influence for more evidence-based public debate can be enabled the intermediation of the media and

NGOs through news reporting, advocacy, and lobbying. These interactions set the stage for greater policy accountability, project efficiency and effectiveness, better policy decisions, and improved OGD strategies – although making these final connections to accountability and policy making are seldom fully achieved.

The case also highlights important enablers and barriers to substantial realization of an integrated OGD ecosystem. Enablers include at least two key elements. First, when the data content and characteristics match the interests of the user community, engagement seems more feasible and more productive. In the case, citizens and intermediaries were interested in understanding and giving feedback about specific local projects. Aggregated information about government spending, for example, would hardly be useful for meaningful analyses that could be directly used by policy makers to improve implementation or future programming of these specific public investments. The fact that OpenCoesione is dedicated to publishing data about development projects also helped the staff support efforts to collect feedback about them. All-purpose OGD portals seem too diffuse to offer this kind of support.

Second, proactive government strategies for stimulating use and re-use of OGD appear to improve both data quality and public engagement. Interaction between publishers and users stimulates interest in the content and quality of the data. In particular, involvement of communities and NGOs appears to stimulate local ecosystems of governmental and non-governmental actors working with the data. This involvement can enable new forms of collaboration, as the cases of Monithon and A Scuola di OpenCoesione demonstrate. In addition, active involvement of NGOs, associations and other stakeholders in monitoring activities is crucial to stimulate participation, especially when the realization of their own objectives also depends on the effectiveness of the public policies being monitored.

We also identified three main barriers. First, citizen feedback is greatly hampered by the absence of specific data and supplementary contextual information. For this case, information about project objectives and activities, underlying policy motives, decisions, contractors, results and output indicators – the elements of process transparency [2] - were missing. The available data did not allow users to fully understand the chain of responsibilities among these diverse actors and therefore was simply not legible for local communities [29]. This problem makes citizen investigations more difficult and less likely because specific skills and expertise are required not only to understand the published data, but also to retrieve additional information to put it in context. Consequently, effective civic monitoring seems to require expert support to obtain meaningful results. Without this kind of expertise, policy accountability and broad citizen participation and collaboration all suffer.

Second, the health of the ecosystem appears to depend heavily on the tenuous sustainability of civic technology initiatives and organizations acting as OGD intermediaries. In the case, intermediaries were sometimes supported by government or by NGOs created for other purposes. However, there were few such entities and their long-term economic prospects were usually dim. These infomediaries play a critical role in representing citizen interests or helping citizens represent themselves, therefore sustainable business models for this function, including a role for government, seem necessary [17].

Third, and perhaps most important, is the absence of real public accountability mechanisms between government and citizens. This absence is a powerful barrier to systematic integration of citizen feedback in the policy cycle. In the case, neither the ESIFs regulations nor the national legal framework provided these mechanisms. Specific internal government processes to encourage and process feedback from the bottom-up were weak, infrequent, and often completely missing. While the rest of the ecosystem may be robust, this gap at the end of the policy process may be the greatest barrier to achieving the collaboration and accountability benefits promised by OGD.

5 Conclusion

The objectives of OGD programs include not only fostering innovation but also encouraging greater government accountability and civic participation in policy making. In this paper we used an exploratory case study of OpenCoesione in Italy to try to understand whether and how all of these purposes can be served by open government data programs. We presented the results in a preliminary integrated open data ecosystem model that comprises two interrelated cycles of influence that flow from OGD publication. One cycle addresses the innovation potential of OGD, the other addresses how OGD might support democratic values of participation and accountability. Our case analysis showed actors inside and outside government interacting in a complex open data ecosystem to pursue these diverse goals. The case study emphasized the importance of intermediaries who represent a crucial link between data providers and the ultimate beneficiaries of OGD products. In the case of innovation, intermediaries seek to provide information-based services to interested consumers. In the case of participation and accountability, intermediaries provide expertise in analysis and a variety of other domains that puts data in context for ordinary citizens and helps them communicate their views to policy makers and administrators. We also found that the weakest link in the ecosystem is a lack of effective mechanisms that channel citizen feedback into the policy process.

This work is only a first effort to understand the interdependencies among the multiple goals of open data initiatives. In future research, we intend (a) to expand the Italian case study to include perspectives from other data intermediaries and users such as local authorities and NGOs, the media, teachers and students involved in the civic monitoring activities and (b) to apply the model in additional case studies (such as different EU countries in the same policy context) to improve its usefulness and generalizability.

References

1. Yu, H., Robinson, D.G.: The New Ambiguity of 'Open Government'. UCLA Law Review Discourse, p. 178 (2012)
2. Shkabatur, J.: Transparency with (out) accountability: open government in the United States. Yale Law Policy Rev. **31**(1), 79–140 (2012)

3. Lourenço, R.P.: An analysis of open government portals: a perspective of transparency for accountability. Gov. Inf. Q. **32**(3), 323–332 (2015)
4. Dawes, S.S., Vidiasova, L., Parkhimovich, O.: Planning and designing open government data programs: an ecosystem approach. Gov. Inf. Q. **33**(1), 15–27 (2016)
5. Ferro, E., Osella, M.: Eight business model archetypes for PSI Re-Use. In: Open Data on the Web Workshop, Google Campus, Shoreditch, London (2013)
6. O'Reilly, T.: Government as a platform. Innovations **6**(1), 13–40 (2011)
7. Sieber, R.E., Johnson, P.A.: Civic open data at a crossroads: dominant models and current challenges. Gov. Inf. Q. **32**(3), 308–315 (2015)
8. Davies, T.: Supporting open data use through active engagement. In: Using Open Data: Policy Modeling, Citizen Empowerment, Data Journalism (PMOD 2012), pp. 1–5 (2012)
9. Alexopoulos, C., Loukis, E., Charalabidis, Y.: A platform for closing the open data feedback loop based on Web2.0 functionality. JeDEM **6**(1), 62–68 (2014)
10. Zuiderwijk, A., Janssen, M.: Open data policies, their implementation and impact: a framework for comparison. Gov. Inf. Q. **31**(1), 17–29 (2014)
11. Dawes, S.S., Pardo, T.A., Cresswell, A.M.: Designing electronic government information access programs: a holistic approach. Gov. Inf. Q. **21**(1), 3–23 (2004)
12. Fung, A., Graham, M., Weil, D.: Full Disclosure: The Perils and Promise of Transparency. Cambridge University Press, Cambridge (2007)
13. Peixoto, T.: The Uncertain Relationship Between Open Data and Accountability: A Response to Yu and Robinson's 'The New Ambiguity of Open Government' (2013)
14. Janssen, M., Charalabidis, Y., Zuiderwijk, A.: Benefits, adoption barriers and myths of open data and open government. Inf. Syst. Manag. **29**(4), 258–268 (2012)
15. Bertot, J.C., Jaeger, P.T., Grimes, J.M.: Using ICTs to create a culture of transparency: E-government and social media as openness and anti-corruption tools for societies. Gov. Inf. Q. **27**(3), 264–271 (2010)
16. Zuiderwijk, A., et al.: Special issue on innovation through open data: guest editors' introduction. J. Theor. Appl. Electron. Commer. Res. **9**, i–xiii (2014)
17. Janssen, M., Zuiderwijk, A.: Infomediary business models for connecting open data providers and users. Soc. Sci. Comput. Rev. **32**(5), 694–711 (2014)
18. Barry, E., Bannister, F.: Barriers to open data release: a view from the top. Inf. Polity **19**(1, 2), 129–152 (2014)
19. Pollock, R.: Building the (Open) Data Ecosystem. Open Knowledge Blog (2011)
20. Zola, D., Naletto, G., Andreis, S.: How to do (good) things with data. In: Civil Society Data-Driven Engagement for Societal Progress and Innovation, Web-COSI "Web COmmunities for Statistics for Social Innovation", Rome, Italy (2015)
21. Buttiglione, P.L., Reggi, L.: Il monitoraggio civico delle politiche di coesione e lo sviluppo di comunità civiche. PRISMA Economia-Società-Lavoro (2015)
22. Ciociola, C., Reggi, L.: A Scuola di OpenCoesione: from open data to civic engagement. In: Atenas, J., Havemann, L. (eds.) Open Data as Open Educational Resources, pp. 26–37. Open Knowledge, Open Education Working Group, London (2015)
23. Rodriguez-Pose, A., Fratesi, U.: Between development and social policies: the impact of European structural funds in objective 1 regions. Reg. Stud. **38**(1), 97–113 (2004)
24. Rodríguez-Pose, A.: Do institutions matter for regional development? Reg. Stud. **47**(7), 1034–1047 (2013)
25. Barca, F.: An Agenda for a reformed cohesion policy: a place-based approach to meeting European union challenges and expectations. 2009, Independent Report Prepared at the Request of the European Commissioner for Regional Policy, Danuta Hübner. European Commission, Brussels (2009)

26. Reggi, L., Ricci, C.A.: Information strategies for open government in Europe: EU regions opening up the data on structural funds. In: Janssen, M., Scholl, H.J., Wimmer, M.A., Tan, Y.-H. (eds.) EGOV 2011. LNCS, vol. 6846, pp. 173–184. Springer, Heidelberg (2011)
27. Dawes, S.S.: Stewardship and usefulness: policy principles for information-based transparency. Gov. Inf. Q. **27**(4), 377–383 (2010)
28. Zuckerman, E.: New media, new civics? Policy Internet **6**(2), 151–168 (2014)
29. Picci, L.: Reputation-based governance and making states "legible" to their citizens. In: Masum, H., Tovey, M., Newmark, C. (eds.) The Reputation Society: How Online Opinions are Reshaping the Offline World. MIT Press, Cambridge (2012)

Open Government Policies: Untangling the Differences and Similarities Between the US and the EU Approach

Rui Pedro Lourenço[1,2](✉)

[1] INESC Coimbra, Coimbra, Portugal
ruiloure@fe.uc.pt
[2] Faculty of Economics, University of Coimbra, Coimbra, Portugal

Abstract. The purpose of this work is to explore the main differences and similarities between open government policies developed since 2009 by the US and
the EU, two major powerhouses in what concerns eGovernment-related policies.
For that purpose, the authors analyzed the information on webpages and main
policy documents as available to any ordinary citizen. The results show that both
the US and EU policy share the same core concepts and goals. However, while
the US opted to formulate an autonomous policy under a unifying 'open government' umbrella term, the EU choose to incorporate the goals and principles into
an already existing eGovernment development effort, emphasizing 'public services innovation' instead. As a consequence, in the US case it is easier to identify
and understand the policy main goals, and to find policy-related information
online. Furthermore, the US policy seems to have had a bigger external impact
and recognition.

Keywords: Open government · Policy · Assessment

1 Introduction

In 2003 the OECD published a report entitled "Open Government: fostering dialogue
with civil society" [1], based on a conference held in 2002. In this report, the concept
of an 'open government' was still mainly related with policy-making openness, with an
emphasis on information, consultation and public participation, the hallmarks of
eDemocracy and eParticipation [2]. Later on, Linders and Wilson [3] analyzed the
United States (US) Memorandum on Transparency and Open Government [4] and
further confirmed that the main ideas and concepts behind it were not entirely new. In
fact, they identified four main perspectives ("lenses") which influenced the Memorandum, namely with ideas from transparency advocates, technology savvies ("the futu-
rists"), civil society eParticipation promoters, and bureaucrats worried about compliance
to mandates and standards.

Nevertheless, 2009 seems to be a landmark year as both the US and the EU launched
their open government related policy framework. Despite the organizational differences
between the two 'blocks', federal state (US) and country union (EU), they are both highly
influential worldwide in what concerns eGovernment-related progress. Therefore it is

Published by Springer International Publishing Switzerland 2016. All Rights Reserved
H.J. Scholl et al. (Eds.): EGOV 2016, LNCS 9820, pp. 87–98, 2016.
DOI: 10.1007/978-3-319-44421-5_7

appropriate and relevant to jointly analyze the process by which both 'blocks' have defined and are currently implementing their open government related policies.

However, at this point, it does not seem straightforward, from an ordinary citizen (someone not directly involved in the open government policy-formulation process as a public official) point of view, to fully understand the key concepts and supporting documents of both the US and the EU open government policy. The long list of EU reports at the end of this paper (references section), and the apparent proliferation of related websites, portals and dedicated webpages, for instance, illustrates this difficulty.

Therefore, the first objective of this paper is to untangle the open government policy framework in both 'blocks' (US and EU), and shed some light on it from an ordinary citizen point of view. For this purpose, an exploratory research effort was conducted based on content analyses of websites and key policy documents[1]. More specifically, the following issues were addressed:

- How easy is it to find information, and to navigate through the different official documents, in order to have a clear picture about US and EU open government policy?
- What are the main distinctive characteristics between their open government policy, including concepts, development process, and assessment?
- Overall, what can we learn from the way both policies were defined and implemented?

This work did not aim to provide definitive answers but the main finding from this exploratory research effort indicate that the option to define an autonomous open government policy by the US may have contributed to an increased simplicity, clearness and (external) visibility when compared with the EU choice to embed its open government policy on pre-existing eGovernment development. Ultimately, the EU approach may render it more difficult to an ordinary citizen to understand the policy, its implications and impact.

The remainder of this paper is structured around four specific perspectives from which both open government policy framework were analyzed, ending with an overall discussion and conclusions.

2   Finding Information on Open Government Policy

To start untangling the differences and similarities between the US and the EU approach we need to consider how easy it is to find relevant information concerning the open government policy in both cases. An ordinary citizen point of view was adopted that assumes such information should be available on the Internet, and that some initial reference (starting point) would exist in the White House and the European Commission homepages respectively.

---

[1] All online content was last accessed in January–March 2015.

2.1 The US Case

No direct reference to 'open government' was found in the White House homepage[2], including in the Initiatives section, so it was necessary to perform an internet search. Using the expression 'Open Government USA' on Google yielded an 'Open Government Initiative I The White House' link[3], which pointed to the Open Government homepage. From this homepage, within different sections, it is possible to access:

- A description of the general aspects related to the Open Government initiative, including a link to the Directive and Memorandum documents;
- Direct links to some federal flagship initiatives on Transparency (such as data.gov, recovery.gov, USASpending.gov, IT.usaspending.gov, or foreignassistance.gov), Participation (such as 'We the People' or the 'Open Government Discussion Group') and Collaboration (such as 'Challenge.gov');
- A link to "The Obama Administration's Commitment to Open Government Status Report" [5];
- Links to a dedicated 'Open Government Partnership' webpage[4] and external 'Open Government Partnership' website[5]. Also made available here is:
  - A list of all Open Government National Action Plans, developed in the 'Open Government Partnership' context, including a link to the US Third (latest) Open Government National Action Plan [6];
  - The Open Government Partnership Government Self-assessment Report [7][6];
- Information concerning the Interagency Open Government Working Group, with a specific webpage[7] which lists and links to each agency Open Government program specific homepage. Another memorandum [8] is also available to "assist agencies as they prepare to launch their 2014 Open Government Plans".

The content and organization of this homepage not only reflects the major concepts of the US policy framework, but it also provides access in a single point to the most relevant initiatives and policy documents.

2.2 The EU Case

There was also no direct reference on the European Commission homepage[8] to 'Open Government'. As in the US case, it was necessary to perform an internet search to find the applicable information. Using the expression 'Open Government European Union' on Google yielded an 'Open government I Digital Agenda for Europe'[9]. The analysis of the webpage navigation path ('European Commission> Digital Agenda for Europe>

---

[2] https://www.whitehouse.gov.
[3] https://www.whitehouse.gov/open.
[4] https://www.whitehouse.gov/open/partnership.
[5] http://www.opengovpartnership.org/.
[6] Assesses the First National Action Plan.
[7] https://www.whitehouse.gov/open/about/working-group.
[8] http://ec.europa.eu/index_en.htm.
[9] https://ec.europa.eu/digital-agenda/en/open-government.

Open government') reflects an 'Open government' topic under the more broad 'Digital Agenda for Europe' subject.

In the navigation bar, the topic 'Open Government' is presented in a hierarchical tree structure under 'Public Services' and 'Digital Society' (top level), alongside with 'Action plan 2011–2015', 'Cross-border solutions' and 'eGovernment studies'. Still in the navigation bar, three topics are grouped under 'Open Government', each one linking to specific webpages which detail its associated content:

- 'eParticipation', which is considered a pillar of open government [3];
- 'Cloud of Public Services', a mostly technical aspect concerning digital public services infra-structure, with no clear relation with the 'open government' concept;
- 'Horizon2020', the EU Framework Programme for Research and Innovation.

Within the webpage content it is also possible to find three external links:

- 'Open data'[10], which links to a dedicated webpage and provides access to several legislative and non-legislative measures as well as a list of several Member State's and EU open data portals;
- 'ICT-enabled public sector innovation'[11], which links to the same content as the 'Horizon2020' topic in the navigation bar;
- 'Vision for public services', which links to another webpage and a specific policy document [9].

This webpage is somewhat hidden within and alongside several other eGovernment thematic pages without a clear and direct relation to open government. The way the navigation path and navigation bar are structured further contribute to create a fuzzy image about the EU open government policy. The actual content of this webpage does generically refer to some of the same components and principles also present in the US Directive, such as transparency, citizen participation and engagement, and "collaboration for the design, production and delivery of public service". However, the emphasis seems to be on 'public service innovation' and general eGovernment development.

3   Initial Landmark Event Information

Once an initial source of online information was found, the analysis proceeded to identify the initial landmark event which kick-started the open government policy.

3.1   The US Case

In the US case, a detailed description of the initial policy documents (Directive and Memorandum) is clearly available, including the documents themselves, in the White House open government homepage.

---

[10] https://ec.europa.eu/digital-agenda/en/open-data.
[11] https://ec.europa.eu/digital-agenda/en/ict-enabled-public-sector-innovation-horizon-2020.

Despite previous efforts to increase/adopt transparency, participation and collaboration principles in the US Administration, the Memorandum on Transparency and Open Government issued by President Obama in 2009 is considered the landmark event that initiated the systematic development of the US policy.

As a first consequence of the Obama Memorandum, Peter Orszag, Director of the Office of Management and Budget (OMB), issued an Open Government Directive [10]. The Directive[12] required "executive departments and agencies to take … steps toward the goal of creating a more open government" by publishing government information online and improving its quality, creating a policy framework and establishing a culture of open government.

The Directive also established several deadlines to implement specific actions ("Within 45 days, each agency, …") and guidelines on how these agencies should formulate and publish their individual plans, including the obligation to rely on "extensive public and employee engagement while formulating their open government plans. Apart from identifying the three original main areas covered by these plans, *transparency*, *participation*, and *collaboration*, federal agencies were also required to describe at least one "Flagship Initiative" in one of those areas.

In sum, it is easy to identify and access the initial US open government policy documents which, in turn, contain a clear and concise description of the main policy guidelines and implementation path.

3.2 The EU Case

Contrary to the US, in the EU case it is necessary to navigate through the 'ICT-enabled public sector innovation' link or the 'Horizon2020' topic in the navigation bar to access a description of its policy origin.

In a similar way to the US Directive, the Malmö Ministerial Conference on eGovernment, which also took place in 2009, seems to have provided the main initial political impulse to open government efforts in the EU. In fact, in the "ICT-enabled public sector innovation in Horizon 2020" webpage[13] there is a mention to the 2009 Malmö Ministerial Conference on eGovernment [11] as the moment when the vision to "make European public administrations open, flexible and collaborative in their relations with citizens and businesses" was laid out. According to the same webpage, this vision was afterwards translated "into several concrete actions through the open government concept, in the European eGovernment Action Plan 2011–2015" (this document was published in December 2010).

Although the Malmö Ministerial Conference Declaration does not specifically refer to 'open government' (there is no single mention of this particular term), it does refer generally to the need for "governments to be more open, flexible and collaborative in their delivery of public services".

The Declaration also addresses general concerns (such as reducing the carbon footprint) and traditional eGovernment themes such as the need to develop "user-centric

---

[12] https://www.whitehouse.gov/open/documents/open-government-directive.
[13] https://ec.europa.eu/digital-agenda/en/ict-enabled-public-sector-innovation-horizon-2020.

services", "multi-channel strategies", and to "apply information and communication technologies in order to increase efficiency and effectiveness".

Additionally, the Declaration does refer to some specific open government related shared objectives and policy priorities such as *transparency for accountability* ("Strengthen transparency of administrative processes. ... Transparency promotes accountability and trust in government"), *transparency for data re-use* ("Increase availability of public sector information for reuse.... encourage the reuse of public data by third parties"), *participation* ("Involve stakeholders in public policy processes. ... effective, useful and better ways for businesses and citizens to participate in the policy processes") and *collaborative service delivery* ("eGovernment services ... developed in collaboration with third parties") and the equivalent to *inter-agency partnering* in the European context ("seamless cross-border eGovernment services ... interoperability of eGovernment services and systems in the Single Market").

In the EU case, it was not easy to identify the Malmö Ministerial Conference Declaration as the policy kick-starter, namely because 'open government' does not appear to have been used as an umbrella term to describe the goals (policy priorities). Nevertheless, the Declaration does refer to specific implementation and monitoring actions and milestones, although the actual responsibility for its implementation is somewhat fuzzy.

4   Implementation Path and Impact

This section analyses the implementation paths followed once the initial policy documents were approved, and its impact both internally and externally.

4.1   The US Case

The Obama Memorandum charged the Chief Technology Officer to develop an Open Government Directive with instructions to "executive departments and agencies to take specific actions implementing the principles set forth" in the memorandum.

In the same year (December) the Directive instructed those departments and agencies to take specific actions, such as improving the quality of government information and publishing it online by taking a proactive approach to FOIA, publishing at least three high-value data sets on Data.gov, and creating its own Open Government Webpage with a specified URL structure.

Agencies were also required to develop their own Open Government Plan, to be revised every two years. The Directive contained general guidelines about the main plan domains (transparency, participation, collaboration), required them to describe at least one specific new flagship initiative in one of these main domains, and provided guidelines on how the general public and agency employees should be included in the formulation process. The Directive also required each plan to be disclosed in the agency webpage. Some of these instructions came with a defined deadline for implementation.

Furthermore, the Directive planned the creation of an Open Government Dashboard "designed to provide an assessment of the state of open government". Although it was not possible to find this specific dashboard within the White House Open Government homepage[14], the 'Open Government Working Group' webpage does provide a list of all agencies' dedicated open government homepages.

The analysis of the US Department of Justice general homepage, for instance, also revealed a direct link to its dedicated open government homepage[15] where all policy related information is available, including the Department's plans, actions and progress assessment.

With the exception of the requirements directed at federal agencies, and as far as the information available on the US open government homepage is concerned, no reference was found concerning the implementation of open government principles in the State and Local government.

Apart from this internal (federal) implementation path, the US also developed several Open Government National Action Plans to comply with the requirements of the Open Government Partnership (OGP). These plans were bound to "outline specific and measurable open government commitments ... made within five "grand challenge" topic areas"[16], and participating countries were required to assess and revise their own plans every two years. The OGP, launched in 2011 and currently involving 69 countries (including some EU Member States), may itself be considered as an example of the external impact of the US open government policy[17].

The most prominent open data US portal, Data.gov, may also be considered as an example of the external influence of the US policy as it established the 'data.gov. <country>' URL structure standard for this type of portal as the list of more than 300 similar portals around the world[18] illustrates. A quick search on Google Scholar also found several references which address Data.gov, thus showing its relevance as a study case for academia.

4.2   The EU Case

The Malmö Declaration is clear about developing an eGovernment action plan which consider the policy priorities outlined. However, it clearly stated that these objectives were "proposed ways", "entirely without prejudice to the competencies exercised at European, national or sub-national level".

The second eGovernment Action Plan [12] does indeed state that it "aims to realise the ambitious vision contained in the Declaration made at the 5th Ministerial eGovernment Conference (the 'Malmö Declaration')". Once again, there is no mention of the

---

[14] Wilson and Linders [14] do refer to a White House scorecard available at http://www.white-house.gov/open/around, but it was not available anymore in this location and it could not be found elsewhere.

[15] http://www.justice.gov/open.

[16] "Improving Public Services, Increasing Public Integrity, More Effectively Managing Public Resources, Creating Safer Communities, Increasing Corporate Accountability" https://www.whitehouse.gov/open/partnership/national-action-plans.

[17] "President Obama launched the Open Government Partnership (OGP) in 2011 at the U.N. General Assembly meeting with seven other heads of state and an equal number of leaders from civil society." https://www.whitehouse.gov/open/partnership.

[18] http://www.data.gov/open-gov/.

expression 'open government' in the plan. Instead, the Action Plan aims to support "the transition from current eGovernment to a new generation of open, flexible and collaborative seamless eGovernment services", that is, the terminology used emphasises 'Open eGovernment Services' rather than broad 'Open Government'.

In this Action Plan there seems to be no reference to specific actions to be further developed or implemented by EU Directorate-Generals as is the case of the US Administration Federal Agencies. Instead, the EU Commission recognizes "the central role of national governments in the implementation" of the action plan, and defines the Commission's main responsibility being "to improve the conditions for development of cross-border eGovernment services ... establishing pre-conditions, such as interoperability, eSignatures and eIdentification" [12, p. 5].

The Action Plan also urged all Member States to incorporate the "political priorities of the Malmö Declaration in their national strategies" by 2013, and required "all Member States to inform the Commission and the High-Level Expert Group how the political priorities of the Malmö Declaration have been achieved" by 2015 [12, p. 15].

The structure of the Action Plan reflects four political priorities, including one termed "User Empowerment" which contains four sub-political priorities easily identified with the US Directive open government objectives: "Collaborative Production of Services", "Re-use of Public Sector Information"; "Improvement of Transparency"; "Involvement of citizens and businesses in policy-making processes". The remaining (sub-) political priorities could be more easily associated with traditional eGovernment development.

It was not possible to find any specific individual impact of the EU open government policy in the different European Commission Directorates-General, considered here as the equivalent to US Federal Agencies. In the case of the European Commission Directorate-General for Justice and Consumers, for instance, no reference to 'open government' was found on its homepage[19], although a 'Transparency' area exists where it is possible to access a list of meetings held by the Director-General and Secretary-General (date, location, entities met, subject). Contrary to the US Department of Justice, searching for 'open government' in the Directorate-General search engine did not yield any significant result.

In what concerns the EU external policy impact, apart from the recommendations for its implementation by Member States, the EU current eGovernment benchmark exercise [13] also involves European Free Trade Association (EFTA) countries (thus being referred to as EU28+).

From the 'Open Data' section in the EU open government homepage it was possible to identify at least two EU level open data portals:

- The European Union Open Data Portal[20] (Open Data Portal of the EU institutions), currently holding 8017 datasets;
- The European Data Portal[21], currently holding 386,027 datasets harvested from national (Member States) public data portals.

---

[19] http://ec.europa.eu/justice/index_en.htm.
[20] https://open-data.europa.eu/en/data.
[21] http://www.europeandataportal.eu/ ("currently available in beta mode since November 2015").

Although both portals were said to "target relevant user audience, offering tailored content" it was not clear why there were two different portals at the EU level. A quick search on Google Scholar found no relevant references to any of these portals, which may be considered as an indicator of its relatively low impact in the academia.

5   Monitoring and Assessment

Apart from the implementation path, both the US and the EU open government policy frameworks call for several monitoring and assessment actions.

5.1   The US Case

In the US case, monitoring and assessment comprises two dimensions: one directed at federal agencies compliance with the Memorandum and Directive; the other, with a national scope, assesses the OGP commitments fulfillment.

Federal agencies and departments are responsible for the development, revision, and monitoring the progress of their own open government plans. Such plans and progress assessment should be available at their open government specific homepages, as listed in the Interagency Open Government Working Group section of the White House open government homepage (see Sect. 2).

For instance, to assess the current status of the open government policy implementation in the US Department of Justice, it is possible to find in its homepage an "Open Government Progress Report"[22].

From a global perspective, Wilson and Linders [14, p. 390] referred to a "White House's post-implementation" scorecard which could not be found. Instead, a status report from 2011 [5] is available at the White House open government homepage (see Sect. 2), where the US National Action Plan and Self-Assessment Report are also accessible.

Furthermore, within the OGP website it is possible to find National Actions Plans, Self-Assessment Reports, Progress Reports and other documents, organized by country in a common site structure, depending on whether or not each country choose to submit it.

5.2   The EU Case

The EU has been performing regular eGovernment benchmarking exercises since 2001 [15]. In the latest benchmarking report [13] there is no mention to the Malmö Declaration and just one use of the term 'open government' was found:

"The results for user centric government (52 %) and transparency (48 %) make clear that the envisaged modern and open public sector, delivering public services in an open government setting (enabled by ICT), is far from reality." [13, p. 23].

---

[22] https://www.justice.gov/open/department-justice-open-government-progress-report-december-2015.

In a different document, the Midterm Evaluation of the eGovernment Action Plan 2011–2015 [16], it is indeed possible to find direct references to the Malmö Declaration and the term 'open government' (there is even a dedicated section called "Towards Open government"). This report "aims to provide a first measurement of the progresses that the European Commission and the Member States are making with respect to the vision stated in the Malmö Declaration" [16, p. 1]. As part of the assessment process, an eGovernment Action Plan-evaluation website[23] was created to allow Member States to submit information on their progress. This website, which could not be found while browsing the Commission website, does indeed contain detailed data about each Member State self-assessment as well as two overall dashboards.

Overall, there seems to be a two path assessment effort (assessing the Action Plan implementation; eGovernment maturity benchmarking), something which is recognized in the Midterm Evaluation report:

"The European eGovernment 'Benchmarking' framework should be aligned with the eGovernment Action Plan and measure the outcomes." [16, p. 4]

In 2011 an eGovernment Benchmark Pilot on Open Government and Transparency was performed [17] and the results were incorporated in the new 2012–2015 benchmark framework [18]. Efforts to develop a new eGovernment Action Plan 2016–2020 are already underway, this time under the banner of The Digital Single Market (DSM) Strategy for Europe [19].

6 Discussion

There are similarities between the US and the EU open government policy frameworks: they were both initiated in 2009 and, most importantly, they share the same core principles and goals. But even if the core concepts are common, the EU open government policy documents and webpage content and structure directly emphasize its relation to public services innovation, while the US policy seems to have a broader scope and it is organized around three clear principles: transparency, participation and collaboration.

Furthermore, the analysis seems to confirm that there is a major difference: while the US policy was designed and presented as a standalone framework, clearly formulated and implemented under a single umbrella term ('open government'), in the EU the option was to embed the same principles in an already existing eGovernment framework. As a result, in the US case the information is provided with greater visibility and simplicity in what concerns policy goals, implementation path and monitoring. In the EU case, the lack of usage of an autonomous umbrella term makes it more difficult from an outsider (ordinary citizen) point-of-view to find specific open government related policy information and to understand it. In a sense, it is more difficult to untangle the EU open government policy. This lack of an autonomous open government policy may also have contributed to a lesser external impact both in academia and other ('third-party') countries. For instance, the Obama Administration Memorandum and Directive is more recognizable as the origin of the US open government policy than the Malmö Declaration

---

[23] http://www.egovap-evaluation.eu/.

in the EU case, and the OGP creation is a good example of the US policy influence outside the US itself. Particularly in academia, the US Data.gov open data portal seems to have drawn much more attention than the two existing EU-level open data portals.

Another striking policy difference may be a result of the differences between a federal country (US) and an association of Member States (EU). In the US case, the policy implementation and assessment is directed at federal departments and agencies. Each agency has an obligation to elaborate its own plan, to assess and revise it periodically, and to disclose all the related information in a clearly identified online location. In the EU case, there seems to be no direct requirement for Directorates-General to develop and implement specific open government plans in their area, and Member States are simply "urged" to incorporate the Malmö Declaration policy principles into their individual national eGovernment strategies. As a consequence, progress in the EU case seems to be mainly assessed as part of the regular (from 2001) eGovernment maturity benchmarking exercises.

7   Conclusion

Since the US and the EU are two important policy development 'blocks' with influence in many countries worldwide, it is relevant to consider how they both defined and implemented their open government policy. The analysis results may provide guidance for other countries defining their open government policies, as well as for new policy-making processes.

In what concerns the issues listed in the Introduction, and despite the differences in nature between the US and the EU, the analysis found that it was more difficult to find information (online) concerning the EU process. Furthermore, as the list of references to EU reports in this paper may illustrate, it is not easy to form a clear picture of the whole EU policy framework. The way online information about open government is organized and structured, bundled with other apparently unrelated information, does not help either. On the contrary, the US defined a clear and simple process to implement and assess the policy, as well as a clear online structure (one webpage for each department or agency) to disclose policy-related information.

Although the core concepts and goals underlying both the US and EU open government policy were broadly the same, the US opted to define and maintain an autonomous open government policy, around well-defined principles, and always using the umbrella 'open government' term. This fundamental difference may have contributed decisively to a policy process that was easy to understand and follow, particularly from an ordinary citizen point-of-view. As a practical implication, we may conclude that new policy processes benefit from autonomy, simplicity and transparency, not only in the formulation stage, but also in what concerns its implementation and monitoring.

Acknowledgements. This work has been partially supported by the Fundação para a Ciência e a Tecnologia (FCT) under project grant UID/MULTI/00308/2013.

References

1. OECD. Open Government. OECD Publishing, Paris (2003)
2. OECD. Citizens as Partners - OECD Handbook on Information, Consultation and Public Participation in Policy-Making. OECD, Paris (2001)
3. Linders, D., Wilson, S.C.: What is open government? one year after the directive. In: 12th Annual International Conference on Digital Government Research (Dg.o 2011), pp. 262–271 (2011)
4. Obama, B.: Transparency and open government. Memorandum for the heads of executive departments and agencies (2009)
5. White House. The Obama Administration's Commitment to Open Government Status Report (2011)
6. White House. The Open Government Partnership: Third Open Government National Action Plan for the United States of America. (2015)
7. White House. The Open Government Partnership: Government Self-assessment Report for the United States of America (2013)
8. White House. Memorandum for the Heads of Executive Departments and Agencies (2014)
9. European Commission. A vision for public services (draft version dated 13/06/2013), Brussels (2013)
10. Orszag, P.: Open government directive. Memorandum for the Heads of Executive Departments and Agencies (2009). http://www.whitehouse.gov/open/documents/open-government-directive
11. European Commission. Ministerial declaration on eGovernment. In: 5th Ministerial eGovernment Conference Teaming up for the eUnion of the Swedish Presidency, 18 November 2009
12. European Commission. The European eGovernment action plan 2011–2015: harnessing ICT to promote smart, sustainable and innovative government. European Comission, Brussels (2010)
13. European Commission. Delivering the European advantage? How European governments can and should benefit from innovative public services (eGovernment Benchmark Final Background Report - May 2014), Brussels (2014)
14. Wilson, S.C., Linders, D.: The open government directive: a preliminary assessment. In: iConference 2011, pp. 387–394 (2011)
15. European Commission. Summary Report: Web-Based Survey on Electronic Public Services (Results of the First Measurement: October 2001) (2001)
16. European Commission. Midterm Evaluation of the eGovernment Action Plan 2011–2015, Brussels (2015)
17. European Commission. eGovernment Benchmark Pilot on Open Government and Transparency: Measuring the potential of eGovernment to foster Open Government and Transparency in Europe. European Commission, Brussels (2011)
18. European Commission. eGovernment Benchmark Framework 2012–2015: Method Paper, Directorate General for Information Society and Media (2012)
19. European Commission. eGovernment Action Plan 2016–2020 Roadmap, Brussels (2015)

Towards Effective and Efficient Open Government in Parliaments with Situational Awareness-Based Information Services

Elena Sánchez-Nielsen[1(✉)] and Francisco Chávez-Gutiérrez[1,2]

[1] Departamento Ingeniería Informática y de Sistemas, Universidad de La Laguna,
38271 San Cristóbal de La Laguna, Spain
enielsen@ull.edu.es
[2] Parlamento de Canarias, 382002 Santa Cruz de Tenerife, Spain

Abstract. Open Government poses broad challenges to contemporary parliaments with its emphasis not just on openness and transparency but also on participation and collaboration. The situational awareness obtained from citizen-sourcing and the advances in information and communications technology are key enablers for effective and efficient Open Government in parliamentary institutions. Citizen-sourcing, on one hand, may help parliaments be more sensible and effective because citizens are able to improve parliaments' situational awareness and then influence direction and outcomes for policy making process. On the other hand, exploiting the opportunities created by the emerging ICT paradigms allows parliaments to put Open Government into practice in an efficient way. This paper presents a situational awareness process model to support effective decision-making with citizens' insights. Based on this model, an architecture for situational awareness-based information services is presented. This architecture makes use of the opportunities that cloud computing paradigm, social media applications and semantic enrichment offer to provide an efficient implementation of Open Government in parliaments. A motivating scenario of the proposed architecture is illustrated to show a use case of a situational awareness-based information service, which has the potential to function as a new mechanism of relationship between a parliament and its citizens to enable collective knowledge in order to enhance the passage of a draft bill.

1 Introduction

The Open Government (OG) action plan commitments provide a new space for openness, transparency, participation and collaboration between parliaments and their citizens. Before the emergent OG movement, parliaments have traditionally provided a one-way interaction: from parliaments to citizens. As a representative example of this interaction is the way to pass a bill as a proposal for a new law. It is based basically on introducing the bill for a first reading by Members of the Parliament (MPs), debating the main principles and purposes of the bill by MPs, consideration of amendments and, a final debate on the bill. However, driven by policy impacts from the OG

H.J. Scholl et al. (Eds.): EGOV 2016, LNCS 9820, pp. 99–112, 2016.
DOI: 10.1007/978-3-319-44421-5_8

Directive [2], parliaments' roles have shifted [3], allowing parliaments to become consumers to whom citizens provide information via the citizen-sourcing mechanism [4]. This mechanism allows the design and configuration of a new relationship between a parliament and its citizens to enable collective knowledge and expertise of the public in order to improve the policy making process. Therefore, the importance of incorporating citizens performing role of partners rather than customers, together advances in information and communications technology (ICT) are our premises to deploy OG in parliaments in an effective and efficient way. Citizen-sourcing, on one hand, may help parliaments be more sensible and effective because citizens are able to improve parliaments' situational awareness (SA) and then influence direction and outcomes for policy making process. On the other hand, exploiting the opportunities created by the emerging ICT paradigms allows parliaments to put OG into practice in an efficient way.

Citizen-sourcing as a new mode of parliaments' operation in the OG movement faces two significant challenges. Firstly, identifying the process model to support SA from citizen-sourcing for OG. Secondly, defining what technologies and emerging ICT paradigms are available to implement OG information services that integrate SA from citizen-sourcing with linked parliamentary information. With these challenges in mind, the contributions of this paper are:

- The development of a conceptual map of OG for parliaments with an emphasis on citizen-sourcing.
- The development of a SA process model to make sense of how the parliaments' perspective on the public can be changed from an understanding of citizens as "users and choosers" of legislative deliberations to "makers and shapers" of laws under consideration.
- The development of a layered-architecture to provide useful information through delivered services for OG. The architecture combines analysis and visualization of SA achieved from citizen-sourcing with linked parliamentary information. Social analysis (e.g. sentiment analysis) and semantic enrichment (e.g. ontology-based data models) are used to perform information integration. To provide an efficient technological approach, the architecture exploits the potential that cloud-based ICT paradigm and social media applications offer.
- A user scenario that shows the benefits of incorporating SA from citizen-sourcing for the deployment of OG information services.

The remainder of this paper is organized as follows. Section 2 reviews the background and state of the art of OG in parliaments, the SA concept, and the technologies that are necessary in the development of the work presented in this paper. Section 3 describes our conceptual model to support OG in parliaments. Section 4 introduces our SA process model to address citizen-sourcing. Section 5 presents our architecture to support OG services for parliaments that integrates SA from citizen-sourcing with linked parliamentary information. Section 6 shows a user scenario for the architecture presented in previous section, illustrating how the integration of SA from citizen-sourcing and parliamentary data is transformed into useful information delivered through cloud-based services. Section 7 highlights the conclusions and future work.

2 Background and Related Work

2.1 Open Government in Parliaments

The Open Government movement in parliaments was initiated in 2012, when the parliamentary monitoring organizations (PMOs) issued a Declaration on Parliamentary Openness to ensure making parliamentary information more accessible to citizens, strengthening the capacity of citizens to participate in parliamentary processes, and improving parliamentary accountability [1]. Further, a Legislative Openness Working Group was created by the Open Government Partnership (OGP) Steering Committee with the intention of deepening the exchange of knowledge across governments, parliaments, civil society and international institutions on the opportunities and challenges associated with opening the legislative process [5]. The crucial challenges that permeate the OG concept in the scope of the parliamentary context are:

- Promote a culture of openness.
- Making parliamentary information transparent.
- Easing access to parliamentary information.
- Enabling electronic communication of parliamentary information to facilitate participation and collaboration, as opportunities to influence the political dialogue and policy making process.

To date, the current trends in OG using ICT for parliaments have been essentially focused on opening legislative data and some e-participation initiatives [3, 23].

2.2 Situational Awareness (SA)

SA is the understanding of the environment critical to decision-makers in complex and critical areas. This awareness is usually defined in terms of what information is important for a particular goal or job [6]. Although, diverse frameworks have been widely used and validated in different domains (e.g. surveillance services, software development, and collaborative platforms in science), little is known about the research and application to the OG domain in the parliamentary context to fulfil policy-making on input from public.

Different theoretical models have been proposed for SA. Of these models, Endsley's model [6, 7] is the most relevant one for our research issue of achieving SA from citizen-sourcing for OG. This model involves being aware of what is happening in the vicinity to understand how information, events, and one's own actions will impact goals and objectives, both immediately and in the near future. SA is achieved in three progressive stages as a chain of activities and outputs that occur in the context of decision-making and action. In *Level 1 SA (perception)*, relevant information is perceived about the environment (or "situation"), given information requirements for the proposed goals. When *Level 2 SA (comprehension)* is achieved, the incoming information's intrinsic meaning is understood. *Level 3 SA (projection)* occurs when the implications of things perceived within the environment can be extrapolated to predict what will happen.

2.3 Social Media Applications

Social media applications have become useful information and communication channels in governments in the last years [8, 9]. They are operated outside the information and communication infrastructure of government on third-party platforms. Twitter is currently the most popular microblogging service used to communicate with parliaments [10]. This tool has been traditionally used in one-way from parliaments to citizens [11]. Little attention and research has been paid to create meaningful citizen-parliament participation and collaboration through Twitter in order to exploit the potential capabilities that this tool offers such as instant information gathering and sharing, potential for networking, knowledge co-creation, and interactivity [12]. To date, government adopters have not taken the full advantages of the potential that this tool facilitates and thus meaningful citizen participation and engagement has not been achieved successfully [13, 14]. The emerging research has used sentiment analysis techniques to evaluate how the polarity of Twitter posts (positive, neutral or negative) from local government influences citizen involvement on Twitter [15].

2.4 Cloud Computing

The cloud computing paradigm offer a model for enabling ubiquitous and on-demand access to shared and configurable computing resources (e.g. servers, networks, storage, applications and services) with cost saving [16]. This cloud model promotes three delivery models. In SaaS model, Cloud Service Providers (CSP) run and maintain computing resources, operating system and applications software. While in PaaS model, CSP is responsible for providing, running and maintaining system software and computing resources. Finally, in IaaS model, CSP provides a set of virtualized computing resources to the customer who runs and maintains the operating system and the software applications using the virtual resources. All these services can be deployed through one of the four different deployment models: public, private, hybrid and/or community model.

Since 2009, the cloud computing paradigm has been investigated in the context of e-government [17]. Most of these studies have been focused on reviewing the e-government challenges, and benefits and barriers of e-government on the cloud; however, little is known about conceptual frameworks, architectures and implementation scenarios for the development and implementation of OG.

2.5 Semantics: Providing Machine "Understandable" Information

The semantic web technologies allow semantic enrichment by means of the use of ontologies to accurately describe contents in a machine-readable way. Ontologies define common, shareable and reusable views of a domain, and they give meaning to information structures that are exchanged by information systems [18]. The World Wide Web Consortium offers different standards to support semantics: the Resource Description Framework (RDF) [19] for representing data about resources. The RDF Vocabulary Description Language, also called RDF Schema (RDFS) [20], and the Web Ontology

Language (OWL) [21] are used to describe the terms, classes, properties and relationships used in a RDF model. An RDF store can be queried via the SPARQL Query Language for RDF datasets [22] through a SPARQL endpoint.

3 Conceptual Model of Open Government

In this section, a conceptual map of OG is introduced to identify the issues related to the different dimensions of OG in the parliamentary context in order to provide, on one hand, the support for the development of a SA process model to address citizen-sourcing and; on the other hand, a layered-architecture to supply SA-based information services for OG's dimensions. Figure 2 illustrates the conceptual model built on the dimensions of transparency, participation and collaboration.

Transparency is classified into three levels. The first level, *reactive transparency*, refers to the public right of access to public information generated by parliamentary institutions, and that lets the knowledge of parliament's affairs, public oversight and accountability. Accessible mechanisms and channels to request available information must be provided by parliaments to theirs citizens; the second level, *proactive transparency* means that information on parliament's operations, procedures and tasks such as parliament's roles, members of parliament, parliamentary agenda, draft legislation, records of plenary proceedings must be published in a proactive way, which means publishing the information without the need to be previously requested and; the third level, *collaborative transparency*, under this model the problem is not on the access to parliamentary information. The challenge is how to process, analyse, transform, and innovate in the use of the information. It can be deployed by open data portals and civic apps.

Participation aims including citizens to help parliaments to be more responsive and effective. Parliaments hold primary responsibility, but citizens influence direction and outcomes, and improve the parliament's SA for draft legislation and deliberative dialogue (Fig. 1).

Collaboration is aimed at more responsive decision-making based on the collaborative work to achieve specific tasks and outcomes. Collaboration enables involvement of all stakeholders in parliament operations and decision-making. There are different types of collaboration in parliaments: external collaboration between parliaments and the citizens (*P2C* – parliament to citizens), internal collaboration within the parliaments (*P2P* – parliament to parliament), and intra-collaboration between parliaments and non-profit organizations and the private sector (*P2B* – parliament to business).

4 Situational Awareness Process Model

The motivation behind developing a SA process model for OG in the parliamentary context is to enable policy-making on input from public. Citizens are increasingly aware of what happening in the vicinity, what are the facts and issues related to draft legislation, what are the needs and, how the goals and objectives of draft bills would be able to

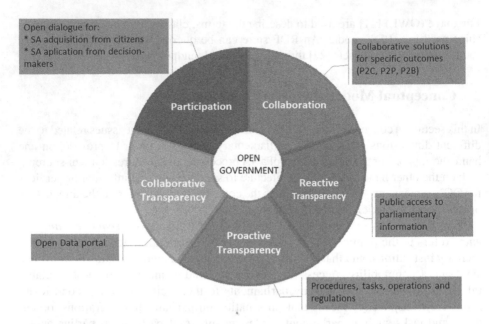

Fig. 1. Conceptual model of Open Government for parliaments

impact their lives. This collective knowledge and experience may help decision-makers to influence the direction and outcomes of draft legislation and legislative deliberations.

Endsley's SA model [6, 7] provides a sound foundation for the understanding of the environment critical to decision-makers. We adapt this model and extend it to support the SA from citizens as a new mode for policy-making. The model is extended, on one hand, by including SA acquisition from citizens not just as individuals, but as whole. On the other hand, by incorporating decision-makers as customers who apply the SA acquired from public. As a result, citizen-sourcing is related to SA making prior to decision-making while decision-makers are linked to SA application. A representative example is the passage of a draft bill, where citizens with their awareness are able to increase the quality of the final policy, decisions or documents. Figure 2 shows the SA process model for OG in parliaments as a chain of ten different outputs, where stages 1 and 6, 2 and 7, and; 3 and 8 correspond respectively to Level 1 (perception), 2 (comprehension) and 3 (projection) of the SA Endsley's model. The goals and objectives of decision-makers determine the initial requirements. These requirements guide data collection and analysis. They are transformed to specific questions to citizens in order to collect innovative ideas and data on topics that are addressed within the draft period of a bill. The goals and objectives provide the context by which situational elements are requested – determining what needs and facts should be perceived by public. The progressive stages for SA acquisition on the citizens' side are:

- *Collect and aggregate information from public:* during the collection stage, situational element state data are gathered according to the requirements established by

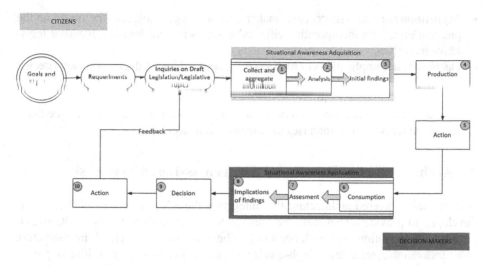

Fig. 2. Situational awareness process model for Open Government in parliaments

the goals and objectives on draft legislation and/or legislative topics for policy-making. In this stage, citizens are able to provide their knowledge and expertise about facts and issues related to the draft legislation and/or specific topics related to legis-lative deliberations. The use of an appreciative inquiry model to build appreciative inquiries [23] is essential to foster and vitalize the active engagement of citizens in this stage.

- *Analysis and findings:* data gathered in the previous stage are processed and analysed using science data methods in order to achieve situation comprehension. The analysis stage is also expected to be able to anticipate the implications of a situation's current status, and its likely future state.
- *Production:* findings achieved in the previous stage are combined with linked parliamentary information to obtain citizens' insights together related parliamen-tary information.
- *Action:* the outcomes obtained in the previous stage is provided as useful information through delivered services for OG (e.g. e-transparency, e-participation and e-collab-oration services).

The stages of the SA process model for SA application on the decision-makers' side are:

- *Consumption:* decision-makers acquire the findings achieved from the collective knowledge and expertise of citizens on specific topics related to draft legislation and/or legislative deliberations.
- *Assessment:* decision-makers evaluate the findings provided by citizens to gain insights on how to proceed in draft legislation and legislative initiatives. The findings achieved allow decision-makers be able to detect events, signals in a timely manner, to react to them properly, as well as, innovative ideas that can be incorporated in the policy making process.

- *Implications of findings:* decision-makers, in this stage, project to the future on the possible effects on incorporating citizens' insights in draft legislation and/or legislative initiatives.
- *Decision:* once implications of findings have been achieved, decision-makers decide on how to incorporate citizens' insights.
- *Action:* decision-makers inform about their decision. The two action lines are: (1) inform about the decisions adopted on citizens' contributions and (2) feedback request in terms of new inquiries to citizens if it is necessary.

5   Architecture for Situational Awareness-Based Services

A cloud-based layered architecture that integrates the SA process model (Sect. 4) is developed to provide information services for the different dimensions of OG (transparency, participation and collaboration). The adoption of a cloud infrastructure provides available, reliable and high-quality services with cost-saving to citizens, parliaments, government and business. Figure 3 shows the architecture and it consists of five horizontal and two vertical layers.

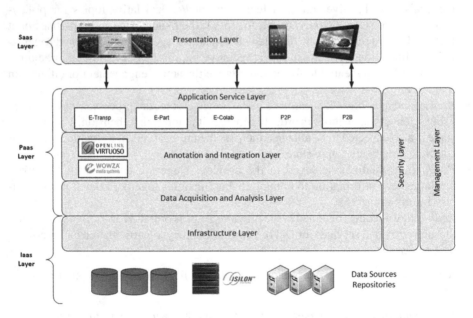

Fig. 3. Architecture for situational-awareness Open Government information services

5.1   Infrastructure Layer

This layer includes communication networks and IT infrastructures like servers and storage. It is based on a hybrid and community cloud environment. Public cloud is used for the services delivered on a network that is open for public use while private cloud is allocated for the parliamentary organization. The community cloud shares resources and services between parliaments and government with similar concerns and requirements.

5.2 Data Acquisition and Analysis Layer

This layer corresponds to *stages 1* and *2* on the citizens' side of the SA process model. Therefore, this layer is first devoted to the generation of SA from citizens and, further the computation of social data analysis to obtain initial findings. The generation of SA about a given topic proposed by decision-makers is based on content created by citizens through social media applications. Twitter is adopted as candidate application for bi-directional interaction and active networking with the public given Twitter is the communication tool most used between parliaments and citizens. Specifically, facilitating individual twitter posts on appreciative inquiries (provided by decision-makers) about draft legislation enable citizens to communicate personal opinions, concerns, preferences, facts and situational data on the topics that are addressed during the draft period of a bill. The initial findings can be processed using sentiment analysis techniques [15] on twitter posts and mapping geo-referenced micro-posts. The results of sentiment analysis application help decision-makers and citizens to know if the polarity of posts tends towards positive, negative or neutral. On the other hand, mapping geo-referenced micro-posts gives a geographical image to allow decision-makers and citizens to obtain an overview of target sources of twitter posts.

5.3 Semantic Enrichment and Integration Layer

This layer corresponds to *stage 4* on the citizens' side and *stage 9* on the decision-makers' side of the SA process model. This layer is devoted to integrate SA obtained from citizens and initial findings with linked parliamentary information (e.g. polarity of public posts on a draft bill combined with type of bill, proponent, current status, procedural actions undertaken to date, related initiatives and decision-making adopted to date). To address the integration layer challenge, an ontology that models the different entities and relationships that exists for the parliamentary activity domain related to: members of the parliament, structure of legislative initiatives and, activity taking place in plenary sessions need to be developed in order to annotate all the content. In the SA context, the content related to the parliamentary activity in plenary sessions involves not only to annotate decision-makers' decisions, but also the annotation of public opinion as twitters posts and the results of its analysis to achieve initial findings. Furthermore, to provide transparent information services which offer public opinion related to specific video fragments on the draft bill being debated, the ontology must be able to relate each separate activity to precise parliamentary video fragments. According to W3C standards, data on public opinion, social data analysis, legislative initiatives and related parliamentary information have to be available as RDF standard. Having available data into RDF standard enable them to be queried through a SPARQL query engine.

The Virtuoso universal server[1] is the tool that can be used as RDF storage while Wowza[2] can be used as streaming server on-demand.

5.4 Application Service Layer

This layer corresponds to *stage 5* on the citizens' side and *stage 10* on the decision-makers' side of the SA process model. Public opinion and initial findings, combined with related parliamentary information and, decision-makers' feedback is transformed to explicit information services. Three different services are proposed: (1) *E-transp*, this service provides information according to the three levels of transparency: reactive, proactive and collaborative; (2) *E-part*, this service enables citizen participation through content on twitter posts and; (3) *E-colab*, this service enables citizens and stakeholders to collaborate to produce specific outcomes for parliaments. This service corresponds to *P2C* service described in Sect. 3; while *P2P* and *P2B* corresponds respectively to collaboration between parliaments and government and, parliaments and business to produce specific outcomes.

5.5 Presentation Layer

This layer corresponds to the user interface and it visualizes the information services corresponding to the application layer according to users' information needs. Different visualizations are provided depending on requested services.

- *E-Transp service:* this layer visualizes information according to three information levels of this service. *Reactive level* provides access to public information generated by parliamentary institutions by means of online forms. *Proactive level* publishes information on parliament's operations, procedures and tasks. This information can be searched via search mechanisms. *Collaborative level* provides information via open data portals.
- *E-Part service:* this service distinguishes two different sides. On one hand, *participation side*, by which users give their contributions as twitter posts to topics addressed during the draft period of a bill. On the other hand, *visualization side*, by which users are able to visualize all users' contributions combined with social data analysis and linked parliamentary information.
- *E-Colab service:* like *E-Part* service, this service differentiates two different sides: collaboration and visualization side. The *collaboration side* involves users to provide specific data on explicit issues for the passage of a bill draft (e.g. a request on the number of assistance dogs that public have seen in their neighborhood in the last year in order to pass a draft bill on assistance dogs for people with disabilities); *visualization side* provides users all users' contributions and social analysis linked with the related parliamentary information on the draft bill such as the MPs who present the bill.

---

[1] https://www.semantic-web.at/virtuoso-universal-server.
[2] https://www.wowza.com/products/streaming-engine.

5.6 Security and Management Layer

The security layer ensures the necessary authentication and authorization for the use of data and services by legitimate users. *P2P* and *P2B* services are supported on a community cloud while remaining services are supported on a public cloud. The management layer addresses users' profiles, provides service alerts, and supplies a single point access to all information services.

6 User Scenario

In this section we present a motivating-scenario for the provision of situational-awareness based information services. Our premise rests on the importance of considering citizens not as mere consumers of draft bills but we highlight their inclusive role by acting as "makers and influencers" of laws under consideration. We show how our SA process model (see Sect. 4) and a layered cloud infrastructure (see Sect. 5) to support it is well placed to address the provision of situational-awareness based information services. To present our user scenario we consider a bill draft on "Assistance Dogs for People with Disabilities" (9L/PPL-0001)[3] published in the parliamentary session of The Canary Islands Parliament, Spain, and held on 10th November, 2015. The aim of this draft bill is the regulation of the rights and obligations of persons with disabilities who require an assistance dog. In the following, for our user scenario, we describe the different functionalities provided from each layer of the proposed architecture in order to show: (1) how SA is obtained from citizen-sourcing, (2) how it is applied by decision-makers and, (3) a specific example on how it can be deployed as an *E-Part* service.

Data Acquisition and Analysis Layer: Through the presentation layer of the *E-Part* service, users are informed about the aim of the draft bill. Decision-makers formulate the questions on the different topics that are addressed within the draft period of the bill under consideration (initial stage of the SA process model) before decision-making. Examples of questions that can be formulated by decision-makers to citizens on the essential topics addressed in the draft bill are: (1) Would you like to promote assistance dogs in working places?, (2) Would you like to coexist with assistance dogs in a public space?, (3) Would you like to increase the access of assistance dogs in any public or private place?, (4) Would you like to increase the simultaneous number of assistance dogs?, (5) What situations do you think should be included for obtaining the recognition of assistance dogs?, (6) Is there any dog that should not get the recognition as assistance dog? and, (7) Would you increase the economic sanctions devoted to infractions?

Twitter is adopted as social media platform to formulate these questions. Subsequently, citizens' answers are processed with social media analysis techniques, and initial findings are produced. These findings (e.g. 75 % of users think that assistance dogs should be promoted in working places and 70 % of users would like to coexist with

---

[3] http://www.parcan.es/iniciativas/tramites.py?id_iniciativa=9L/PPL-0001.

assistance dogs in a public state) are acquired by decision-makers to help them to increase the quality of final decisions in the draft bill.

Annotation and Integration Layer: This layer annotates semantically all the content: initial findings and parliamentary activity. This layer also annotates the implications of findings corresponding to public SA, once these implications have been evaluated by decision-makers, and they have decided how to incorporate these insights in the draft bill and, if new feedback is required through the formulation of new questions. The semantic annotation of all the content allows delivering through the presentation layer of the *E-part* service specific information on the draft bill according users' information needs.

Application Service Layer: The services at this layer build upon the data and annotated content in the lower layers. Services related to transparency, participation and collaboration are delivered through this layer.

Presentation Layer: This layer corresponds to the user interface. It includes a single point access to all services for citizens (*E-Transp*, *E-Part* and *E-Colab* services) and, a parliament internal point access for other parliaments, government and business (*P2P* and *P2B* services). For *E-Part* service, this interface allows users to post their contributions to questions formulated by decision-makers and, to access to all the citizens' contributions and linked parliamentary information. Customized visualization of content delivery can be provided as video fragments on demand about the debate of the specific draft bill in the parliamentary session with public SA and, accurate and well-timed parliamentary information. An example of the content that can be provided by the *E-part* service is the request by users on the exact parliamentary video fragment (e.g. a five-minute fragment within a four-hour video) which displays the public opinion from twitter posts related to the draft bill; initial findings expressed as the percentage of twitter posts whose polarity tends to be positive, negative or neutral; public opinion geolocalization; procedural actions undertaken to date related to SA obtained from citizens; background information related to the proponent of the draft bill being debated in the video fragment; current status of the draft bill, voting related information and, transcription documents.

Manager Layer: Through this layer users give their profiles and they are able to receive alert services about the processing of the draft bill (e.g. an amendment related to economic sanctions has been incorporated given public SA feedback agrees with it).

7 Conclusions and Future Work

This paper addresses how to deploy an effective and efficient OG in parliaments. Citizen-sourcing, on one hand, allows parliaments to enable citizens to engage more effectively in the policy making process by providing their SA. On the other hand, the emerging ICT paradigms are able to provide essential tools and support to foster a bi-directional interaction between citizens and parliaments. To that end, a SA process model is developed as a chain of different stages and outcomes to acquire SA making from citizens related to the topics that are addressed within the draft period of a bill prior decision-making, by further allowing decision-makers apply this knowledge to decision-making. The SA data presents useful information from citizens to decision-makers based on situational evidences about draft legislation, such as, what facts and issues are related to the context of the draft bill, what are the needs for this draft bill and, the benefits and concerns on how this draft bill would be able to influence daily life. In order to support the SA process model, a cloud based situational-awareness services architecture has been proposed. This architecture has the potential to provide the necessary infrastructure and storage to parliaments and rapid high-quality information services to citizens, business and, other parliaments and government institutions with cost-saving. The layers of this architecture enable to acquire and analyze SA making from citizens and, integrate and visualize it with linked parliamentary content, after all the content has been previously annotated in a semantic way. This architecture provides specific information services related to transparency, participation and collaboration to visualize the information corresponding to each OG dimension. A user scenario related to the passage of a specific draft bill describes how the SA making from citizens may help decision-makers in the policy making process and how citizens can see their feedback has contributed to policy-making. Our future work aims to incorporate contextual information to strength the SA process model and apply it through the development of participatory and collaborative e-services using smart phones.

Acknowledgement. The work has been funded in part by the Spanish Government by project TIN 2011-24598.

References

1. Declaration on Parliamentary Openness. OpeningParliament.org (2012). http://www.openingparliament.org/declaration
2. White House. Memorandum on transparency and open government. White House, Washington, DC. https://www.gpo.gov/fdsys/pkg/FR-2009-01-26/pdf/E9-1777.pdf
3. Linders, D.: From e-government to we-government: defining a typology for citizen coproduction in the age of social media. Gov. Inf. Q. **29**, 446–454 (2012)
4. Nam, T.: Suggesting frameworks of citizen-sourcing via Government 2.0. Gov. Inf. Q. J. **29**, 12–20 (2012)
5. Legislative Openness Working Group. Open Government Partnership. http://www.opengovpartnership.org/groups/legislative
6. Endsley, M.R., Jones, D.G.: Designing for Situation Awareness: An Approach to User-Centric Design. CRC Press, London (2011)
7. Endsley, M.R.: Design and evaluation for situation awareness enhancement. In: Proceedings of the Human Factors and Ergonomics Society 32nd Annual Meeting, pp. 97–101, Santa Monica, California (1988)
8. Mergel, I.: Social media adoption and resulting tactics in the U.S federal government. Gov. Inf. Q. **30**, 123–130 (2013)
9. Mergel, I.: A framework for interpreting social media interactions in the public sector. Gov. Inf. Q. **30**, 327–334 (2013)

10. Bertot, J., Jaeger, P., Grimes, M.: Using ICTs to create a culture of transparency: e-government and social media as openness and anti-corruption tools for societies. Gov. Inf. Q. **27**, 264–271 (2010)
11. Global Centre for ICT in Parliament United Nations Department of Economic and Social Affairs. World e-Parliament Report 2012. In Inter-Parliamentary Union Press, by the Division for Public Administration and Development Management of the United Nations
12. Bryer, T.A., Zavattaro, S.M.: Social media and public administration. Adm. Theory Prax. **33**(3), 325–340 (2011)
13. Zavattaro, S., Sementelli, A.: A critical examination of social media adoption in government: introducing omnipresence. Gov. Inf. Q. **31**(2), 257–264 (2014)
14. Brainard, L.A., Derrick-Mills, T.: Electronic commons, community policing and communication: on-line police – citizen discussion groups in Washington D.C. Adm. Prax. **33**(3), 383–410
15. Zavattaro, S.M., EdwardFrench, P., Mohanty, S.D.: A sentiment analysis of U.S. local government tweets: the connection between tone and citizen involvement. Gov. Inf. Q. **32**, 333–341 (2015)
16. Mell, P., Grance, T.: The NIST definition of cloud computing. NIST Spec. Publ. **800**(145), 7 (2011)
17. Mohammed, F., Ibrahim, O.: Models of adopting cloud computing in the e-government context: a review. Teknologi **73**(2), 51–59 (2015)
18. Studer, R., Benjamins, R., Fensel, D.: Knowledge engineering: principles and methods. IEEE Trans. Data Knowl. Eng. **25**(1–2), 161–197 (1998)
19. W3C: W3C Semantic Web. Activity Resource Description Framework 1.1 (RDF) http://www.w3.org/RDF/
20. W3C: W3C Semantic Web activity. RDF Schema 1.1. http://www.w3.org/TR/rdf-schema/
21. W3C Web Ontology Language. http://www.w3.org/TR/owl-features/
22. W3C Semantic Web Activity. SPARQL query language for RDF. http://www.w3.org/TR/rdf-sparql-query/
23. Sánchez-Nielsen, E., Lee, D., Panopoulou, E., Delakorda, S., Takács, G.: Engaging citizens in policy issues: multidimensional approach, evidence and lessons learned. In: Tambouris, E., Macintosh, A., Bannister, F. (eds.) ePart 2014. LNCS, vol. 8654, pp. 102–113. Springer, Heidelberg (2014)

E-government Services and Governance

Coordinating Decision-Making in Data Management Activities: A Systematic Review of Data Governance Principles

Paul Brous[1(✉)], Marijn Janssen[1], and Riikka Vilminko-Heikkinen[2]

[1] Delft University of Technology, Delft, The Netherlands
{P.A.Brous,M.F.W.H.A.Janssen}@tudelft.nl
[2] Tampere University of Technology, Tampere, Finland
Riikka.Vilminko-Heikkinen@iki.fi

Abstract. More and more data is becoming available and is being combined which results in a need for data governance - the exercise of authority, control, and shared decision making over the management of data assets. Data governance provides organizations with the ability to ensure that data and information are managed appropriately, providing the right people with the right information at the right time. Despite its importance for achieving data quality, data governance has received scant attention by the scientific community. Research has focused on data governance structures and there has been only limited attention given to the underlying principles. This paper fills this gap and advances the knowledge base of data governance through a systematic review of literature and derives four principles for data governance that can be used by researchers to focus on important data governance issues, and by practitioners to develop an effective data governance strategy and approach.

Keywords: Data · Governance · e-Government · Data governance · Data quality · Data management

1 Introduction

Many public organizations routinely store large volumes of data. The storage and analysis of this data should benefit society, as it can enable organizations to improve their decisions. Members of the public often assume that the authorities are well equipped to handle data, but, as Thompson et al. [41] illustrate, this is not always the case. Thompson et al. explain that these issues often do not arise from existing business rules or the technology itself, but from a lack of sound data governance. The objective of this article is to derive principles for data governance for developing effective data governance strategies and approaches.

Many academic sources follow the information governance definition of Weill and Ross [46] and define data governance as specifying the framework for decision rights and accountabilities to encourage desirable behavior in the use of data [18, 28, 49]. Practitioners such as the Data Management Association (DAMA) tend to disagree with

© IFIP International Federation for Information Processing 2016
Published by Springer International Publishing Switzerland 2016. All Rights Reserved
H.J. Scholl et al. (Eds.): EGOV 2016, LNCS 9820, pp. 115–125, 2016.
DOI: 10.1007/978-3-319-44421-5_9

this generalization believing that data governance is more than only the specification of a framework, but can also be practiced. According to Otto [25], important formal goals of data governance for public organizations are: 1. to enable better decision making, 2. to ensure compliance, 3. To increase business efficiency and effectiveness, 4. to support business integration [25].

Data governance provides both direct and indirect benefits [20]. Direct benefits of data governance for business processes can be linked to efficiency improvements [13, 15, 20, 35], an increase in revenue and market share [3, 4, 7], reduced risk [25, 28, 49] and a reduction in costs incurred [22, 26, 27, 29]. Reductions in risk can be found in reducing privacy violations [39, 41, 42], increasing data security [18, 29, 41], and reducing the risk of civil and regulatory liability [26, 39]. Indirect benefits of data governance can be found in improving the perception of how information initiatives perform [13, 20, 43], improving the acceptance of spending on information management projects [29, 39, 41], and improving trust in information products [27, 28, 49].

Although scant attention has been paid to this topic by the scientific community, there have been several calls within the scientific community for more systematic research into data governance and its impact on the information capabilities of organizations [25, 28, 49]. Little evidence has been produced so far indicating what actually has to be organized by data governance and what data governance processes may entail [25]. Most research into data governance till now has focused on structuring or organizing data governance. Evidence is scant as to which data governance processes should be implemented, what data governance should be coordinating or how data governance could be coordinated [49]. By means of a systematic review of literature, the principles of data governance we present here attempt to fill this gap. This article is in line with Wende's [49] call for further analysis of the guidelines and policy aspect of data governance.

2   Research Methods

According to Webster and Watson [45], a methodological review of past literature is important for any academic research, and they criticize the Information Systems (IS) field for having very few theories and outlets for quality literature review. A lack of proper literature reviews can and has hindered theoretical and conceptual progress in IS research [21, 45]. This article follows the method proposed by Webster & Watson and Levy & Ellis and attempts to methodologically analyze and synthesize literature and as such provide a firm foundation to data governance and advance the knowledge base of data governance by providing number of principles for data governance that can be used by researchers to focus on important data governance issues, and by practitioners to develop an effective data governance strategy and approach. There is only limited research on data governance [25, 49] and an elaborate analysis of the interaction of roles and responsibilities, and the principles of data governance is missing. For our research, we therefore also incorporate data governance sources from practitioners (e.g., [9, 13, 20, 35, 37, 38, 43]).

In November, 2015, the keywords: "data governance", and "principles", returned 17 hits within the databases Scopus, Web of Science, IEEE explore, and JSTOR. 8 hits were journal articles, 6 were conference papers, 2 were books and 1 hit was an article in the press. OF these articles, only 1 article, [41], was directly related to e-governance. The query [all abstract "data governance" "principles"] searching between 2000 and 2015 returned 1710 hits in Google Scholar. We found a great deal of these articles covered data governance in general, but few articles included an explicit list of principles for data governance. We then filtered these results and performed a forward and backward search to select relevant articles based on the criteria that they included a theoretical discussion on what data governance is or does. Based on this forward and backward search, 35 journal articles, conference proceedings and books were selected and relevant principles from these sources were listed. Practical sources were only used when the authors provided factual evidence for their assertions.

As the review is concept-centric, the sources were grouped according to concept proposed by Webster and Watson [45]. Webster and Watson recommend the compilation of a concept matrix as each article is read (Table 1). The next step recommended by Webster and Watson is to develop a logical approach to grouping and presenting the key concepts that have been uncovered (Table 2) and synthesize the literature by discussing each identified concept.

Table 1. Long list of data governance key concepts

Data governance key concepts			
Accountability [1, 2, 6, 11, 19, 41, 49];	Meeting business needs [2, 8];	Compliance [1, 2, 35, 41];	Shared data commons [1, 7, 26, 27, 39];
Decision rights [25, 35, 41, 49];	Aligning business and IT [29];	Policy enforcement [30, 39, 42];	Use of standards [27, 41];
Balanced roles [1, 15, 35];	Developing data strategy [18, 22, 27, 30, 39, 49, 50];	Due diligence [6, 15, 35];	Metadata management [18, 27];
Stewardship [8, 15, 18, 33, 41, 49];	Defining data quality [2, 15, 19, 27, 35, 43, 49];	Privacy [1, 7, 11, 15, 18, 19];	Standardized data models [27, 41];
Ownership [13, 41, 43];		Openness [11, 19];	Standardized operations [27, 41];
Separation of duties [22];	Reducing error of use [7, 26, 49];	Security [1, 6, 7, 11, 12, 15, 18, 19, 24, 30, 39, 42];	Facilitates communication [22, 27, 39]
Separation of concern [22];	Effective policies and procedures [13, 15, 35, 48]	Measuring data quality [15, 18, 19, 27, 35, 43, 48]	
Improved coordination of decision making [27, 35, 39]			

Following the recommendations of Bharosa and Janssen for principle generation, the long list of concepts seen in Table 1 was reduced to a short list as seen below in Table 2. The articles were categorized based on the types of variables examined, a scheme that helps to define the topic area. Principles constrain the design which ultimately seeks to attain the required business goals. By focusing on the formal goals of data governance which contribute to e-governance (enable better decision making, ensure compliance, increase business efficiency and effectiveness, and to support business integration), which we identified as independent variables, we were able to identify the dependent variables (long list of concepts, Table 1) contributing to these goals and grouped them according to intervening variables (short list of principles, Table 2), which appear in more complex causal relationships. Intervening variables come between the independent and dependent variables and shows the link or mechanism between them. Four concepts related to the goals of data governance were identified in the literature (Table 2). At this stage in our research no unit of analysis is included in the matrix, as the unit of analysis currently used is the organization. Future research can focus on identifying which principles are applicable to the varying units of analysis (organizational, group, or individual).

Table 2. Concept matrix showing the concepts in relation to the authors

Concepts			
Organization	Alignment	Compliance	Common understanding
[1, 3, 8–10, 13, 15, 18, 22, 23, 25–27, 31, 33, 35, 38, 39, 41, 43, 47, 49, 50]	[1–3, 6–15, 18–20, 22, 23, 25–27, 29, 30, 35, 38, 39, 41, 43, 49, 50]	[1–3, 5–7, 9–12, 18–20, 22–27, 29–31, 33, 35, 38, 39, 41–43, 47, 49, 50],	[1, 3, 7, 9, 10, 18, 22, 23, 25–27, 38, 39, 41, 43, 50]

3   Foundation and Boundaries

Principles are particularly useful when it comes to solving ill-structured or "complex" problems, which cannot be formulated in explicit and quantitative terms, and which cannot be solved by known and feasible computational techniques [34]. Principles are a set of statements that describe the basic doctrines of data governance [9]. This paper follows the definition of Bharosa and Janssen who define principles as "normative, reusable and directive guidelines, formulated towards taking action by the information system architects" p. 472. In their Architecture Framework (TOGAF), the Open Group [40] lists five criteria that distinguish a good set of architecture principles: understandable, robust, complete, consistent and stable. Van Bommel et al. [4] believe that the underlying tenets should be quickly understood by individuals throughout the organization and according to Khatri and Brown [18], principles should be supported by a rationale and a set of implications. A robust principle should enable good quality decisions to be made, and enforceable policies and standards to be created.

   There is much confusion about what 'data' really is. Data is a set of characters, which have no meaning unless seen in the context of usage. The context and the usage provide a meaning to the data that constitute information [1]. Most scientific sources use the terms "information" and "data" interchangeably. This generalization has led academic sources to follow the information governance definition of Weill and Ross [46] and define data governance as specifying the framework for decision rights and accountabilities to encourage desirable behavior in the use of data [18, 28, 49]. Practitioners tend to disagree with this generalization as whilst the scope of data governance may include information as well as data, the two are different. The term, "data" is often distinguished from "information" by referring to data as simple facts and to information as data put in a context or data that has been processed [16, 32]. Also, many practitioners prefer to define data governance as a business function, [for example, Forrester research defines data governance as being "a strategic business program that determines and prioritizes the financial benefit data brings to organizations as well as mitigates the business risk of poor data practices and quality" [51, p. 1]. DMBOK [17], defines data governance as, "The exercise of authority, control, and shared decision making (planning, monitoring and enforcement) over the management of data assets" p. 37. As such, in the eye of the practitioner, data governance is more than only the specification of a framework, but can also be practiced. Data governance ensures that data and information are managed appropriately. Theoretically, data governance describes the processes, and defines responsibilities. Data managers then work within this framework.

4 Principles of Data Governance

Four principles were identified from the basis of the literature review. These principles are presented individually in detail in the following sections.

4.1 Organization

Most researchers agree that data governance has an organizational dimension [18, 26, 49]. For example, Wende and Otto [49] believe that data governance specifies the framework for decision rights and accountabilities to encourage desirable behavior in the use of data. The first organizational dimension of Otto (2013) relates to an organization's goals. Formal goals measure an organization's performance and relate to maintaining or raising the value of a company's data assets [26]. Functional goals refer to the tasks an organization has to fulfil and are represented by the decision rights defined such as the definition of data quality metrics, the specification of metadata, or the design of a data architecture and a data lifecycle [44]. Otto's second organizational dimension is the organizational form, such as the structure in which responsibilities are specified and assigned, and the process organization. Issues are addressed within corporate structures [49]. The data governance model is comprised of roles, decision areas, main activities, and responsibilities [49]. However, the organization of data governance should not be seen as a "one size fits all" approach [49]. Decision-making bodies need to be identified for each organization, and data governance must be institutionalized through a formal organizational structure that fits with a specific organization [22]. Decision rights indicate who arbitrates and who makes those decisions [9]. According to Dawes [8], "stewardship" focuses on assuring accuracy, validity, security, management, and preservation of information holdings. Otto's [26] third organizational dimension consists of a transformation process on the one hand and organizational change measures on the other. Malik [22] indicates the need to establish clear communications and patterns that would aid in handling policies for quick resolution of issues [22], and Thompson et al.

[41] show that coordination of decision making in data governance structures may be seen as a hierarchical arrangement in which superiors delegate and communicate their wishes to their subordinates, who in turn delegate their control.

4.2 Alignment

Data governance should ensure that data meets the needs of the business [29]. A data governance program must be able to demonstrate business value, or it may not get the executive sponsorship and funding it needs to move forward [35]. Describing the business uses of data establishes the extent to which specific policies are appropriate for data management. According to Panian [29], if used correctly, data can be a reusable asset as data is a virtual representation of an organization's activities and transactions and its outcomes and results. Data governance should ensure that data is "useful" [8]. According to Dawes, information should be helpful to its intended users, or should support the usefulness of other disseminated information. While government organizations may want to achieve the goals of data governance in theory, they often have difficulty justifying the effort unless it has a practical, concrete impact on the business [29]. Data governance also provides the framework for addressing complex issues such as improving data quality or developing a single view of the customer at an enterprise level [29]. Wende and Otto [49] believe that a data quality strategy is therefore required to ensure that data management activities are in line with the overall business strategy. The strategy should include the strategic objectives which are pursued by data quality management and how it is aligned with the company's strategic business goals and overall functional scope. Data quality is considered by many researchers to be an important metric for the performance of data governance [18, 27, 49].

4.3 Compliance

Data governance includes a clearly defined authority to create and enforce data policies and procedures [50]. Panian [29] states that establishing and enforcing policies and processes around the management data is the foundation of an effective data governance practice. Delineating the business uses of data, data principles establish the extent to which data is an enterprise wide asset, and thus what specific policies are appropriate [18]. According to Malik [22], determination of policies for governance is typically done in a collaborative manner with IT and business teams coming together to agree on a framework of policies which are applicable across the whole organization [22]. Tallon [39] regards data governance practices as having a social and, in some cases, legal responsibility to safeguard personal data through processes such as "privacy by design", whilst Trope and Power [30] suggest that risks and threats to data and privacy require diligent attention from organizations to prevent "bad things happening to good companies and good personnel" [30] p. 471. Mechanisms need to be established to ensure organizations are held accountable for these obligations through a combination of incentives and penalties [1] as, according to Felici et al. [11], governance is the process by which accountability is implemented. In such a manner, accountability can unlock further potential by addressing relevant problems of data stewardship and data protection in emerging in data ecosystems.

4.4 Common Understanding

According to Smith [36], governing data appropriately is only possible if it is properly understood what the data to be managed means, and why it is important to the organization. Data understanding is essential to any application development, data warehousing or services-oriented-architecture effort. Misunderstood data or incomplete data requirements can affect the successful outcome of any IT project [36]. Smith believes that the best way to avoid problems created by misunderstanding the data, is to create an enterprise data model (EDM) and that creating and developing an EDM should be one of the basic activities of data governance. Attention to business areas and enterprise entities should be the responsibility of the appropriate data stewards who will have the entity-level knowledge necessary for development of the entities under their stewardship [36]. To ensure that the data is interpretable, metadata should be standardized to provide the ability to effectively use and track information [18]. This is because the way an organization conducts business, and its data, changes as the environment for a business changes. As such, Khatri and Brown [18] believe that there is a need to manage changes in metadata as well. Data governance principles should therefore reflect and preserve the value to society from the sharing and analysis of anonymized datasets as a collective resource [1].

5 Discussion

Data governance is a topic that is attracting growing attention, both within the practitioners' community and among Information Systems researchers, due to growth of the amount of data. But data governance is a complex undertaking, and data governance projects in government organizations have often failed in the past. There is not one, single, "one size fits all" approach to the organization of data governance. Decision-making bodies need to be identified for each individual organization, and data governance should have a formal organizational structure that fits with a specific organization [22]. An organization outlines its individual data governance configuration by defining roles, decision areas and responsibilities, with a unique configuration, and specialized people need to be hired, trained, nurtured, and integrated into the organization. Researchers have proposed initial frameworks for data governance [18, 27] and have analyzed influencing factors [44] as well as the morphology of data governance [25]. A number of data governance principles have emerged out of this research. These principles are depicted in Fig. 1 below. From the Long list of principles, four principles of data governance for public organizations were distilled. These principles are: 1. Organization, 2. Alignment, 3. Compliance Monitoring and Enforcement, 4. Common Understanding. Data Governance should ensure that data is aligned with the needs of the business. This includes aligning the quality of the data with the quality required by the business. Data quality is often related to "fitness for use" and data governance demands binding guidelines and rules for data quality management [27].

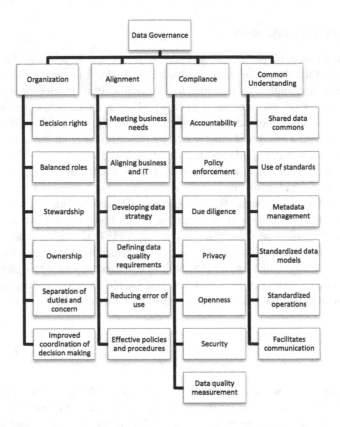

Fig. 1. Long list of key concepts and principles of data governance

Governing data also includes ensuring compliance to the strategic, tactical and operational policies which the data management organization needs to follow. While use of data has significant potential, many policy-related issues must be addressed before their full value can be realized. These include the need for widely agreed-on data stewardship principles and effective data management approaches [15]. Public organizations need to be able to create and share information in a way that is specifically customized for that organization to ensure a common understanding of the data.

6   Conclusions

Data governance is a complex undertaking and many data governance initiatives in public organizations have failed in the past. Principles of data governance include organization of data management, ensuring alignment with business needs, ensuring compliance, and ensuring a common understanding of data. However, the organization of data governance should not be seen as a "one size fits all" approach and data governance must be institutionalized through a formal organizational structure that fits with a specific organization. Data governance should also ensure that data is aligned with the needs of the business. This includes ensuring that data meets the necessary quality requirements. Ensuring alignment can take the form of defining, monitoring and enforcing data policies (internal and external) throughout the organization. Establishing and enforcing policies regarding the management of data is important for an effective data governance practice. But governing data appropriately is only possible if it is properly understood what the data to be managed means, and why it is important to the organization.

References

1. Al-Khouri, A.M.: Data ownership: who owns "my data". Int. J. Manag. Inf. Technol. **2**, 1–8 (2012)
2. Alofaysan, S. et al.: The significance of data governance in healthcare: a case study in a tertiary care hospital. In: HEALTHINF 2014 - 7th International Conference on Health Informatics, Proceedings; Part of 7th International Joint Conference on Biomedical Engineering Systems and Technologies, BIOSTEC 2014 (2014)
3. Begg, C., Caira, T.: Data governance in practice: the SME quandary reflections on the reality of data governance in the small to medium enterprise (SME) sector. In: Proceedings of 5th European Conference on Management Information and Evaluation System, pp. 75–83 (2011)
4. van Bommel, P., Hoppenbrouwers, S.J.B.A., Proper, H., van der Weide, T.: Giving meaning to enterprise architectures: architecture principles with ORM and ORC. In: Meersman, R., Tari, Z., Herrero, P. (eds.) OTM 2006 Workshops. LNCS, vol. 4278, pp. 1138–1147. Springer, Heidelberg (2006)
5. Breaux, T.D., Alspaugh, T.A.: Governance and accountability in the new data ecology. In: 2011 Fourth International Workshop on Requirements Engineering and Law (RELAW), pp. 5–14 (2011)
6. Bruening, P.J., Waterman, K.K.: Data tagging for new information governance models. IEEE Secur. Priv. **8**, 5 (2010)
7. Coleman, D.W., et al.: The role of data governance to relieve information sharing impairments in the federal government. In: 2009 WRI World Congress on Computer Science and Information Engineering, pp. 267–271 (2009)
8. Dawes, S.S.: Stewardship and usefulness: policy principles for information-based transparency. Gov. Inf. Q. **27**(4), 377–383 (2010)
9. Dyché, J.: A Data Governance Manifesto: Designing and Deploying Sustainable Data Governance (2007). http://searchsoftwarequality.bitpipe.com/detail/RES/1183551857_231.html
10. Egelstaff, R., Wells, M.: Data governance frameworks and change management. Stud. Health Technol. Inform. **193**, 108–119 (2013)
11. Felici, M., Jaatun, M.G., Kosta, E., Wainwright, N.: Bringing accountability to the cloud: addressing emerging threats and legal perspectives. In: Felici, M. (ed.) CSP EU FORUM 2013. CCIS, vol. 182, pp. 28–40. Springer, Heidelberg (2013)
12. Felici, M., Pearson, S.: Accountability for data governance in the cloud. In: Felici, M., Fernández-Gago, C. (eds.) A4Cloud 2014. LNCS, vol. 8937, pp. 3–42. Springer, Heidelberg (2015)
13. Griffin, J.: Action record - four critical principles of data governance success. J. Pediatr. Matern. Fam. Health-Chiropr. **20**(1), 29 (2010)

14. Haider, A.: Asset lifecycle data governance framework. In: Lee, W.B., Choi, B., Ma, L., Mathew, J. (eds.) Proceedings of the 7th World Congress on Engineering Asset Management (WCEAM 2012), pp. 287–296. Springer, Heidelberg (2015)

15. Hripcsak, G., et al.: Health data use, stewardship, and governance: ongoing gaps and challenges: a report from AMIA's 2012 Health Policy Meeting. J. Am. Med. Inform. Assoc. 21(2), 204–211 (2014)

16. Huang, K.-T., et al.: Quality Information and Knowledge. Prentice Hall PTR, Upper Saddle River (1999)

17. International, D.: The Dama Guide to the Data Management Body of Knowledge. Technics Publications, LLC, Bradley Beach (2009)

18. Khatri, V., Brown, C.V.: Designing data governance. Commun. ACM 53(1), 148–152 (2010)

19. Kim, K.K., et al.: Data governance requirements for distributed clinical research networks: triangulating perspectives of diverse stakeholders. J. Am. Med. Inform. Assoc. 21(4), 714–719 (2014)

20. Ladley, J.: Data Governance: How to Design, Deploy and Sustain an Effective Data Governance Program. Newnes, Boston (2012)

21. Levy, Y., Ellis, T.J.: A systems approach to conduct an effective literature review in support of information systems research. Inf. Sci. Int. J. Emerg. Transdiscipl. 9, 181–212 (2006)

22. Malik, P.: Governing big data: principles and practices. IBM J. Res. Dev. 57(3–4), 1–13 (2013)

23. Morabito, V.: Big data governance. In: Morabito, V. (ed.) Big Data and Analytics, pp. 83–104. Springer, Heidelberg (2015)

24. Murtagh, M.J., et al.: Navigating the perfect [data] storm. Nor. Epidemiol. 21, 2 (2012)

25. Otto, B.: A morphology of the organisation of data governance. In: ECIS, p. 1 (2011)

26. Otto, B.: On the evolution of data governance in firms: the case of Johnson & Johnson consumer products North America. In: Sadiq, S. (ed.) Handbook of Data Quality, pp. 93–118. Springer, Heidelberg (2013)

27. Otto, B.: Organizing data governance: findings from the telecommunications industry and consequences for large service providers. Commun. Assoc. Inf. Syst. 29(1), 45–66 (2011)

28. Otto, B., Weber, K.: Data governance. In: Hildebrand, K., Gebauer, M., Hinrichs, H., Mielke, K.M. (eds.) Daten-und Informationsqualität, pp. 277–295. Springer, Heidelberg (2011)

29. Panian, Z.: Some practical experiences in data governance. World Acad. Sci. Eng. Technol. 38, 150–157 (2010)

30. Power, E.M., Trope, R.L.: The 2006 survey of legal developments in data management, privacy, and information security: the continuing evolution of data governance. Bus. Lawyer 62(1), 251–294 (2006)

31. Prasetyo, H.N., Surendro, K.: Designing a data governance model based on soft system methodology (SSM) in organization. J. Theoret. Appl. Inf. Technol. 78(1), 46–52 (2015)

32. Price, R., Shanks, G.: A semiotic information quality framework. J. Inf. Technol. 2005(20), 88–102 (2005)

33. Rosenbaum, S.: Data governance and stewardship: designing data stewardship entities and advancing data access. Health. Serv. Res. 45(5p2), 1442–1455 (2010)

34. Simon, H.A.: The Sciences of the Artificial. MIT Press, Cambridge (1996)

35. Smallwood, R.F.: Information governance, IT governance, data governance: what's the difference? In: Information Governance: Concepts, Strategies, and Best Practices. Wiley (2014)

36. Smith, A.: Data governance and enterprise data modeling – don't do one without the other! Enterprise Information Management Institute. http://www.eiminstitute.org/library/eimi-archives/volume-1-issue-2-april-2007-edition/data-governance-and-enterprise-data-modeling-dont-do-one-without-the-other

37. Soares, S.: The IBM Data Governance Unified Process: Driving Business Value with IBM Software and Best Practices. MC Press, LLC, Woolham (2010)

38. Sweden, E.: Data Governance – Managing Information as an Enterprise Asset Part I – An Introduction (2008). http://www.nascio.org/publications/documents/NASCIO-DataGovernance-Part1.pdf

39. Tallon, P.P.: Corporate governance of big data: perspectives on value, risk, and cost. Computer 46(6), 32–38 (2013)

40. The Open Group: TOGAF® 9.1. http://pubs.opengroup.org/architecture/togaf9-doc/arch/

41. Thompson, N., et al.: Government data does not mean data governance: lessons learned from a public sector application audit. Gov. Inf. Q. 32(3), 316–322 (2015)

42. Trope, R.L., et al.: A coherent strategy for data security through data governance. IEEE Secur. Priv. 5(3), 32–39 (2007)

43. Tupper, C.D.: Understanding architectural principles. In: Tupper, C.D. (ed.) Data Architecture, pp. 3–22. Morgan Kaufmann, Boston (2011)

44. Weber, K., et al.: One size does not fit all—a contingency approach to data governance. J. Data Inf. Qual. 1(1), 1:1–1:27 (2009)

45. Webster, J., Watson, R.T.: Analyzing the past to prepare for the future: writing a literature review. MIS Q. 26(2), 13–23 (2002)

46. Weill, P., Ross, J.W.: IT Governance: How Top Performers Manage It Decision Rights for Superior Results. Harvard Business Press, Boston (2004)

47. Weller, A.: Data governance: supporting datacentric risk management. J. Secur. Oper. Custody. 1(3), 250–262 (2008)

48. Wende, K.: A model for data governance – organising accountabilities for data quality management. In: Australasian Conference on Information Systems, Toowoomba, Australia, 5 December 2007

49. Wende, K., Otto, B.: A contingency approach to data governance. In: International Conference on Information Quality, Cambridge, USA, 11 October 2007

50. Wilbanks, D., Lehman, K.: Data governance for SoS. Int. J. Syst. Syst. Eng. 3(3–4), 337–346 (2012)

51. Michele Goetz' Blog. http://blogs.forrester.com/michele_goetz/15-09-11-data_governance_and_data_management_are_not_interchangeable

Determinants of Clarity of Roles and Responsibilities in Interagency Information Integration and Sharing (IIS)

Djoko Sigit Sayogo[1,4(✉)], J. Ramon Gil-Garcia[1,2], and Felippe Cronemberger[3]

[1] Center for Technology in Government, University at Albany, State University of New York,
1400 Washington Avenue, Albany, NY 12222, USA
{dsayogo,jgil-garcia}@ctg.albany.edu
[2] Department of Public Administration and Policy, University at Albany,
State University of New York, 1400 Washington Avenue, Albany, NY 12222, USA
[3] Department of Informatics, University at Albany, State University of New York,
1400 Washington Avenue, Albany, NY 12222, USA
fcronemberger@albany.edu
[4] University of Muhammadiyah at Malang, Jl. Raya Tlogomas No. 246, Malang, Indonesia

Abstract. Interagency information sharing (IIS) has been identified as a powerful strategy to improve information and services in the public sector. In order to accomplish effective information sharing across organizational boundaries, the definition and clarity of roles and responsibilities are very important, particularly when the number and diversity of the agencies involved is high. However, there are very few studies that analyze the variables that affect this clarity in interagency information sharing efforts. Based on a review of current literature and a national survey conducted in the US, this paper quantitatively explores the determinants of clarity of roles and responsibilities. Consistent with existing literature, we found a significant and positive influence of diversity of participating organizations, the use of boundary objects, and communication skills on the use and emergence of need for clarity of roles and responsibilities in IIS project. Our findings open avenues for future research about the role of clarity of roles and responsibilities, its determinants, and other variables may play in mediating or directly explaining IIS success.

Keywords: Interagency information sharing · Role clarity · IIS · Boundary object

1 Introduction

Information integration and sharing (IIS) are the foundation of government efforts to develop and execute public policies that are smart, efficient and more responsive to nowadays social problems. IIS often involves collaboration of participants across various domains and beyond the boundary of individuals, units and organizations [2].

Track: General e-Government Track – Ongoing Research.

© IFIP International Federation for Information Processing 2016
Published by Springer International Publishing Switzerland 2016. All Rights Reserved
H.J. Scholl et al. (Eds.): EGOV 2016, LNCS 9820, pp. 126–134, 2016.
DOI: 10.1007/978-3-319-44421-5_10

Working on an IIS initiative within such a collaborative setting might pose challenges for government officials, who were unaccustomed to working collaboratively across their respective agency's boundary [2]. The government officials might be more accustomed to the "need to know" as compare to "need to share" culture [3].

Clear roles and responsibilities enable the building of trust among members of IIS initiatives [15]. Having clarity on roles and responsibilities in collaborative efforts precipitate the formation of mutual expectations; a clear understanding of what are expected from them and from other participants [19].

While research has demonstrated the importance of clarity of roles and responsibilities (CRR) in IIS initiatives [15], very few or even not one have attempted to systematically test the determinants of CRR using quantitative analysis. We adopt Pardo et al. [15] three determinants of CRR and add three other determinants based on our review of existing studies. The objective of this paper is to examine the determinants of clarity of roles and responsibilities in IIS project using data from the National Survey conducted by the Center for Technology in Government. We tested whether three determinants of CRR identified in Pardo et al. [15] and other three determinants from the literature truly influence the use or emergence of CRR in IIS project. Hence, this paper addresses the following research question, what are the determinants of clarity of roles and responsibilities in interagency IIS.

The rest of the paper is organized in 5 sections, including the foregoing introduction. Section 2 highlights studies evaluating the influence of clarity of roles and responsibilities on organizational and inter-organizational information sharing and performance. Section 2 also presents the main hypothesis and the preliminary model used for this study. Section three describes our research methodology, including the data distribution, variable measurement and analysis technique. Section 4 discusses the results from the statistical analysis. Finally, Sect. 5 offers some concluding remarks and suggests areas for future research about this topic.

2   Determinants of Clarity of Roles and Responsibilities

Clarity of roles can be defined as "…the presence [or absence] of adequate role-relevant information due either to restriction of this information or to variations of the quality of the information … [or] the subjective feeling of having as much [or not as much] roler-elevant information as the person would like to have [12, p. 100]". Consequently, role ambiguity arises when a person is not aware of what the expectations of such role are [9] or from poor communication practices [16].

Studies have found the great importance of clarity of roles and responsibilities in an interorganizational setting where several organizations or agencies must interact with each other. Lack of clarity regarding roles and responsibilities hinder interagency collaboration [13, 17] and hamper an effective communication in interagency collaboration [4, 7]. On the other hand, clarity of roles and responsibilities could positively affect the success of collaboration in multi-agencies setting such as IIS project [15].

Having clear sense of what should be done for achieving common goals through collaborative effort gives ideas to participants about what they need to do and what they can expect from other participants [19].

Clarity of roles and responsibilities are crucial in multi-organizational collaborations because individuals who accustomed to work within their respective boundaries have to traverse the border and interacts with other boundaries. These "people at the boundary" often feel that they "sort of belong and sort of don't" in between the boundaries [18]. Thus, having clarity of roles and responsibilities alleviate the burden for the "people at boundary" in interactive circumstances.

Despite the positive effect of clarity of roles, a systematic assessment of the determinants of clarity of roles and responsibilities is not so well understood, particularly in IIS setting. An initial proposition of the determinants of clarity of roles and responsibilities was suggested by Pardo et al. [15]. They propose a three determinants of clarity of roles and responsibilities in interagency information sharing, namely: past experiences, diversity of participating organizations and exercise of formal authority. Past experiences in the collaboration provides indication of the participant's expectations about collaboration [8]. Acknowledging and acting on the differences among the participants facilitate the creation of clarity of roles and responsibilities in the IIS project [15]. Sensitivity to the different interests of the participating organizations help the project leaders to delineate roles and responsibilities that minimize potential conflicts. Similarly, interagency collaboration entail variety and distributed power and authority relationships. Given the diversity of the agencies involved, agency had no authority to mandate the roles and responsibilities of other agencies. As such, ensuring efficient collaboration necessitate a judicious way to exercise formal authority [15].

In addition to the three determinants proposed by Pardo et al. [15], studies have identify three other determinants of clarity of roles and responsibilities and inter-organizational information sharing: (1) extent of boundary object use [10, 14], (2) degree of respect for autonomy of participating organizations [19] and (3) collaboration, coordination, and communication skills [1, 5, 11]. Due to the crossing of boundaries, the use of boundary object is key to generate shared understanding and commonalities [19]. Boundary objects are necessary to establish and maintain clear roles and responsibilities [10] and by doing so, it becomes critical for the success of interorganizational information system [14].

Fear of losing agency identity and autonomy create a major barrier for interagency cooperation [6]. Thus, the participating agencies will strive to protect their interest and to maintain their identity [6]. Presumably, respect to the autonomy of the participating agencies induce willingness to cooperate which can lead to success in IIS collaboration. Finally, collaboration and communication skills are important in generating clarity of roles and responsibilities and lead to success of IIS. Communication and collaboration skills are paramount because learning each other's objectives, roles and constraints constitutes the first starting point in inter-organizational initiatives [11]. Clarifying and achieving the agreed upon roles and responsibilities can be achieved through intensive conversations among the participants in the collaboration process [5]. Subsequently, the agreed upon roles and responsibilities must be communicated and coordinated to avoid ensuing ambiguity [1]. Based on the review of the literature, we proposed a model in

Fig. 1 above connecting the determinants of clarity of roles and responsibilities to the success of IIS project. Likewise, based on extant studies, we propose the hypotheses as follows.

H_1: Past experiences significantly influence the clarity of roles and responsibilities in IIS initiatives.

H_2: Boundary object use significantly influences the clarity of roles and responsibilities in IIS initiatives.

H_3: Collaboration and communication skills significantly influence the clarity of roles and responsibilities in IIS initiatives.

H_4: Diversity of participating organizations significantly influences the clarity of roles and responsibilities in IIS initiatives.

H_5: Exercise of formal authority significantly influences the clarity of roles and responsibilities in IIS initiatives.

H_6: Respect of autonomy significantly influences the clarity of roles and responsibilities in IIS initiatives.

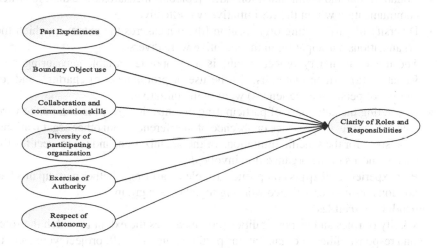

Fig. 1. Research model

3   Research Methodology

3.1   Data and Data Collection

This study analyzes data from a national survey conducted by the Center for Technology in Government (CTG) in April 2008. The use of older data should not be a problem considering that this study aims to test theory, hence it is expected that the relationship among the variables is generalizable and stable over time. The original random-sampled dataset consists of 171 responses. After data cleaning, the regression analysis was based on 158–160 responses, with about 7–8 % of the responses being dropped from the analysis due to missing values.

3.2   Variables and Measurement

In this study, all variables or sub-variables were derived from extensive review of literature from information science, information system and public administration and policy
studies. We use Boolean search by combining keywords of interagency information
Sharing and role clarity to search academic databases such as Academic Search
Complete, Scopus or Web of Science. We use variations of synonyms for the keyword
role clarity to include clarity of roles and clarity of responsibilities.

All variables or sub-variables in this study were measured in a 7- point Likert scale,
ranging from "Not at all (1)" to "To a great extent (7)" Due to the variation in 7-point
scale, we regarded the variable as continuous variable. The summary of data is provided
in Table 1 and the description and measurement of each variable is provided below:

a. **Independent Variables**
   - Exercise of formal authority [auth] measure whether leaders and/or participants
     misused the power of their official positions.
   - Collaboration and communication skills [colcom] measures the extent to which
     communication within the IIS initiative was effective.
   - Diversity of participating organization [dive] measures the extent to which the
     organizations participating in the initiative were diverse.
   - The use of boundary object [boun] is a composite variable measuring how
     valuable: (a) written materials, (b) the use of prototypes, (c) charters, and (d)
     stories (of personal experiences) were in the initiative.
   - Respecting the autonomy of participating organization [resp] is composite vari-
     able measuring: (a) presence or absence of interference from other organizations,
     (b) respect for the specific limitations of the organization, and (c) respect for the
     specific needs of the organization involved.
   - Past experiences [exp] is composite variable measuring whether participants had
     previous positive experience working together as a group.

b. **Dependent Variables**
   a. Clarity of roles and responsibilities [crr] measures the extent to which the roles
      and responsibilities of organizations participating in the IIS project were clear to
      the participants.

Table 1. Means and Chronbach's alpha

Variables	Abb	μ	Std dev	ii-cor[a]	α
Clarity of roles and responsibilities	Crr	0.012	1.2821	1.011	0.8070
The use of boundary object	Boun	0.004	1.5597	1.798	0.7798
Respecting the autonomy of participating organizations	Resp	0.003	1.5437	1.408	0.8617
Previous experience	Exp	−0.007	1.3089	2.211	0.8199
Exercise of authority	Auth	1.563	1.2157	1.563	–
Diversity of participating organizations	Dive	5.552	1.6281	5.552	–
Communication and collaboration skill	Colcom	0.016	1.5956	0.016	–

[a]ii-cor refers to the average of interrelation correlation for composite variables

The reliability of the resulting variables was examined using Chronbach's alpha values (Table 1). As mentioned previously, all the Chronbach's alpha values were above 0.70, representing acceptable levels of reliability. We ran multivariate regression analysis to test the causal relationship of the determinants to the clarity of roles and responsibilities variable. We used robust regression to account for the possible heterogeneity issue.

4 Results: Testing the Determinants of Clarity of Roles and Responsibilities

Building from the case studies on the Public Health and the Criminal Justice information sharing network, Pardo et al. [15] posit three determinants of clarity of roles and responsibilities in a cross-boundary information sharing initiative. We add additional three determinants based on our review of the literature. Our first analysis was to evaluate the extent to which these six determinants influence the clarity of roles and responsibilities in a IIS initiative.

Table 2 shows that three variables emerge as significant and positive predictors of clarity of roles and responsibilities. The results indicate that the use of boundary object is positively and statistically significant in influencing the clarity of roles and responsibilities in an IIS project ($t_{value} = 3.20$; $p_{value} = 0,002$). The coefficient for the use of boundary object is 0.1919. Because the use of boundary object is a composite variable, we have to interpret it in terms of increase or decrease in standard deviation. The predicted effects of the use of boundary object is an increase of $1.5597 * 0.1919 = 0.299$. An increase of one standard deviation in the use of boundary object will increase clarity of roles and responsibility in IIS project by 0.2335 standard deviation (0.299/1.282). The standard deviation of the use of boundary object (1.5597) and clarity of roles (1.282) was derive from the descriptive statistics in Table 1.

Table 2. Regression result for clarity of roles and responsibilities

Variables	Abb	Coeff	Beta	SE
The use of boundary object	Boun	0.1919	0.2263	0.0600**
Previous experience	Exp	0.0525	0.0053	0.0688
Communication and collaboration skills	Colcom	0.3270	0.3986	0.0822**
Diversity of participating organizations	Dive	0.1459	0.1812	0.5017**
Exercise of authority	Auth	−0.0684	−0.0626	0.0956
Respecting autonomy of participating organizations	Resp	0.0462	0.0556	0.0688
Constant		−0.7041		0.3362
N				159
R2				0.367
F(6,152)				13.86

*** Significant at 0.05*

The same transformation was used for interpreting the rest of the composite variables. The collaboration, coordination and communication skills [colcom] was also found to be a significant predictor of clarity of roles and responsibilities in IIS project with ($t_{value} = 3.98$; $p_{value} = 0,000$). One standard deviation increase in the collaboration and communication skills will bring clarity on roles and responsibilities in IIS project up by 0.4069 standard deviation. The influence of diversity of participating organizations is positive and significant for bringing clarity of roles and responsibilities in IIS project. If diversity of organizations participating in the initiative increases by one standard deviation, the likelihood of fostering clarity of roles and responsibilities among the participants increases by 0.1853 standard deviation. This result indicates that the participants gauge the needs for clarity on roles and responsibilities of the project based on the numbers and diversity of the participants in the IIS project collaboration.

Comparing the three significant variables, the results in Table 2 (see beta column) indicate that collaboration and communication skills are the most dominant predictors with beta value of 0.3986, followed by the use of boundary object (0.2263) and the diversity of participating organization (0.1812). Based on the beta results in Table 2, the other three non-significant variables have a very low magnitude of beta coefficient. The results further authenticate the significance of the three variables – use of boundary object, coordination and communication skills, and diversity of participating organizations – to predict the need to have clarity on roles and responsibilities in the IIS project.

5   Concluding Remarks and Implications

5.1   Concluding Remarks

Our analysis results strengthen the importance of the use of boundary object, communication and collaboration skills, and diversity of participating organization for the use and emergence of need for clarity of roles and responsibilities in IIS project. Our results demonstrate the strong influence of using boundary object to determine the use and need for clarity of roles and responsibility. The findings suggest that the use of boundary object in the IIS project influences the participant need to have clarity in roles and responsibilities. The use of boundary object facilitate the creation of shared understanding among the participants. As such, the use of boundary object is very instrumental in bringing about clarity and acceptance among the organizations involved in the IIS project.

Our regression results suggest that the likelihood of framing clarity of roles and responsibilities among the participants increases with an increase in the diversity of organizations participating in IIS project. Thus, we posit that participants judge when and how much clarity of roles and responsibilities are needed early in the collaboration from their assessment on the diversity of organizations participating in IIS project. Presumably, during the process of framing and setting of the IIS project's goals, the participants gauge and correlate the numbers and diversity of participants with the likelihood of success. Based on their evaluation, the participants assess the needs for clarity of roles and responsibilities to help them achieved the IIS project's goals. Further research is needed to ascertain the connection between diversity of participants, clarity of roles and success of IIS project.

Our findings also strengthened the importance of communication and collaboration skills in bringing clarity of roles and responsibilities in the IIS project. The intensity of communication is crucial so that the diverse perspective and interests of the participants can be accommodated and the agreed upon roles and responsibilities is communicated and coordinated to avoid ensuing ambiguity [1].

5.2   Research and Practical Implications

The main finding of this study implies implications for future research as follows.

1. Our findings indicate that clarity of roles and responsibilities as variable possess unique characteristics. Clarity of roles can emerge as independent predictor as well as mediating variables in a relationship. For that, it is necessary re-evaluate the significance of clarity of roles and its determinants by considering other variables such as leadership, communication, organizational capacity to the model. Future research could test the relationships using non-linear methods such as structural equation modelling or partial least square.
2. Our findings also point to the possible connection between clarity of roles and its determinants to the likelihood of achieving success of IIS project. For instance, in effort to correlate between the diversity of participating organizations with the likelihood of IIS success, the participants might decide on the need to have clarity of roles. Such research thus could ascertain whether the effect of clarity of roles is mediated by other variables in determining success for IIS projects.
3. Our result also signifies the importance of diversity of participating organizations which presumably affect the likelihood of IIS project success. Public managers could use this knowledge to evaluate when and how deep role clarity is needed for IIS project through the assessment of the numbers and diversity of the participants.

Acknowledgements.   This work was partially supported by the National Science Foundation under Grant No. ITR-0205152. Any opinions, findings, and conclusions or recommendations expressed in this material are those of the authors and do not necessarily reflect the views of the National Science Foundation.

References

1. Casey, M.: Partnership – success factors of interorganizational relationships. J. Nurs. Manag. **16**(1), 72–83 (2008)
2. Dawes, S.S.: Interagency information sharing: expected benefits, manageable risks. J. Policy Anal. Manag. **15**(3), 377–394 (1996)
3. Dawes, S.S., Cresswell, A.M., Pardo, T.A.: From "need to know" to "need to share": tangled problems, information boundaries, and the building of public sector knowledge networks. Publ. Adm. Rev. **69**(3), 392–402 (2009)

4. Dickerson, J.G., Collins-Camargo, C., Martin-Galijatovic, R.: How collaborative the collaboration? Assessing interagency collaboration within a juvenile court diversion program. Juvenile Fam. Court J. **63**(3), 21–35 (2012). http://doi.org/10.1111/j.1755-6988.2012.01078.x

5. Hardy, C., Lawrence, T.B., Grant, D.: Discourse and collaboration: the role of conversations and collective identity. Acad. Manag. Rev. **30**(1), 58–77 (2005). http://doi.org/10.5465/AMR. 2005.15281426

6. Hoban, T.J.: Barriers to interagency cooperation. J. Appl. Sociol. **4**, 13–29 (1987)

7. Hocevar, S.P., Thomas, G.F., Jansen, E.: Building collaborative capacity: an innovative strategy for homeland security preparedness. In: Innovation through Collaboration, vol. 12, pp. 255–274. Emerald Group Publishing Limited (2006)

8. Jonker, J., Nijhof, A.: Looking through the eyes of others: assessing mutual expectations and experiences in order to shape dialogue and collaboration between business and NGOs with respect to CSR. Corp. Gov. Int. Rev. **14**(5), 456–466 (2006)

9. Kahn, R.L., Wolfe, D.M., Quinn, R.P., Diedrick, J., Rosenthal, R.A.: Organizational Stress: Studies in Role Conflict and Ambiguity, vol. xii. Wiley, Oxford (1964)

10. Kegerise, K.E.: Keys to Successful Collaboration, pp. 1–4. University of Pittsburgh Office of Child Development, Pittsburgh (1999)

11. Luna-Reyes, L.F., Black, L.J., Cresswell, A.M., Pardo, T.A.: Knowledge sharing and trust in collaborative requirements analysis. Syst. Dyn. Rev. **24**(3), 265–297 (2008). http://doi.org/ 10.1002/sdr.404

12. Lyons, T.F.: Role clarity, need for clarity, satisfaction, tension, and withdrawal. Organ. Behav. Hum. Perform. **6**(1), 99–110 (1971)

13. Meyer, S., Mazerolle, L.: Police-led partnership responses to high risk youths and their families: challenges associated with forming successful and sustainable partnerships. Policing Soc. **24**(2), 242–260 (2014)

14. Nidumolu, S.R.: Interorganizational information systems and the structure and climate of seller-buyer relationships. Inf. Manag. **28**(2), 89–105 (1995). http://doi.org/ 10.1016/0378-7206(95)94020-D

15. Pardo, T.A., Burke, B., Gil-Garcia, J.R., Guler, A.: Clarity of roles and responsibilities in government cross-boundary information sharing initiatives: identifying the determinants. In: Proceedings of 5th International Conference on e-Government, pp. 148–155 (2009)

16. Schaubroeck, J., Ganster, D.C., Sime, W.E., Ditman, D.: A field experiment testing supervisory role clarification. Pers. Psychol. **46**(1), 1–25 (1993). http://doi.org/10.1111/j. 1744-6570.1993.tb00865.x

17. Sloper, P.: Facilitators and barriers for co-ordinated multi-agency services. Child Care Health Dev. **30**(6), 571–580 (2004)

18. Tanggaard, L.: Learning at trade vocational school and learning at work: boundary crossing in apprentices' everyday life. J. Educ. Work **20**(5), 453–466 (2007). http://doi.org/ 10.1080/13639080701814414

19. Thompson, A.M., Perry, J.L.: Collaboration processes: inside the black box. Pub. Adm. Rev. **66**, 20–32 (2006)

Requirements for an Architecture Framework for Pan-European E-Government Services

Ansgar Mondorf[✉] and Maria A. Wimmer

Institute for IS Research, University of Koblenz-Landau,
Universitätsstr. 1, 56070 Koblenz, Germany
{mondorf,wimmer}@uni-koblenz.de

Abstract. Interoperability is a major challenge in providing pan-European e-government services (PEGS) across Member State (MS) borders. Improving interoperability in PEGS is expected to increase collaboration and efficiency across public administrations. Yet, a comprehensive approach to develop interoperable PEGS is still missing. Enterprise architecture (EA) is a concept used in the private sector to deal with organisational complexity, interoperability and the multifaceted challenges of information systems. We argue that EA can be used in a similar manner to foster interoperability in PEGS. This paper elicits requirements for constructing an EA framework for PEGS. The requirements are used to argue the suitability of existing EA frameworks and to propose areas of further research to build a customised architecture framework for ensuring interoperability in the design and implementation of PEGS.

Keywords: Interoperability · E-government · Requirements · Architecture framework · Pan-European e-government services

1 Introduction

The European Commission refers to PEGS as a means to realize public service delivery across MS borders. PEGS are provided by different levels of public administration in the MS. They embark on modular, loosely coupled service components and infrastructure services [1].

Complexity, coordination and long term planning processes make it difficult for actors in e-government to create PEGS that are sustainable. Janssen et al. argue that organizations aiming to collaborate and work across institutional boundaries have to rethink and reshape existing strategies, structures, processes, infrastructures and business models. They claim that there is no consensus about the shape and elements of a government EA framework supporting the development of PEGS [2, 3].

An EA framework is used to develop an enterprise architecture (EA) [4]. An EA framework helps to establish customized conventions, principles and practices within an organization leading to shared perspectives regarding information and communication technology (ICT) related strategies, investments, designs and implementations [5]. The resulting EA helps decision makers to proactively and comprehensively identify and analyse the execution of changes towards a desired vision and outcomes [4].

© IFIP International Federation for Information Processing 2016
Published by Springer International Publishing Switzerland 2016. All Rights Reserved
H.J. Scholl et al. (Eds.): EGOV 2016, LNCS 9820, pp. 135–150, 2016.
DOI: 10.1007/978-3-319-44421-5_11

An EA framework for PEGS should adopt a holistic view, where interoperability is examined beyond technical connectivity, that is, considering social, political, cultural and legal factors as well [2, 6, 7]. The holistic view on ICT provided by EA frameworks is seen as a vehicle and means to overcome interoperability challenges [2]. However, even though EAs are successfully used in the private sector, they are not yet appropriately adopted in government contexts [2, 6]. Successful EA adoption depends on appropriate institutional forces and transformation processes [3]. The use and effectiveness of EA is determined by the acceptance, coherence and governance of the architecture approach within the organizational context [8].

Hjort-Madsen and Pries-Heje argue that governmental EA is a means to improve efficiency of public services [3]. Governmental EAs are based on different frameworks which vary in scope and specialization [4, 9–14]. A governmental EA may refer to an organization, it can emerge as a result of implementing individual projects or it may be directly specified on the basis of national/domain reference architectures. Thus, a governmental EA may relate to government as a whole, to a particular domain or to an organizational context. Hence, the abstract types of architectures provide plenty of guidance and references to generate more specific architectures [15]. Thus, EA can support governments to integrate relevant programs and projects and it provides elements such as standards, principles, technologies, services and building blocks [2].

To effectively support PEGS design and implementation, key components of governmental EA need to be identified and their relationships discussed. Current efforts in Europe are directed towards the establishment of a European Interoperability Reference Architecture (EIRA)[1] and to initiate PEGS through a number of large-scale pilot projects (LSPs)[2]. LSPs run in different areas such as eHealth, eProcurement and eJustice. The e-SENS (Electronic Simple European Networked Services)[3] project is an overarching LSP which creates a European Interoperability Architecture (EIA). E-SENS follows an architecture approach which is based on EIRA and other European interoperability policies. The major goal of e-SENS is to consolidate, improve, extend and sustain the results of previous LSP projects by identifying and sustaining building blocks (BB).

This paper aims to elicit architecture requirements that guide the construction of an EA framework for PEGS. The architecture requirements are derived from a systematic review of e-government and interoperability literature. The comparison of these requirements with established EA theories, concepts and frameworks helps to scope and to identify core components of an EA framework for PEGS. The analysis discloses gaps and determines areas of future research and therewith can be used to check the completeness of approaches like EIRA.

The paper is organised as follows: Sect. 2 provides an overview about research related to interoperability frameworks and EA frameworks. Section 3 introduces the research design for the subsequent requirements elicitation. Section 4 presents the architecture requirements guiding the examination of EA components. Major EA components along the architecture requirements are summarized in Sect. 5. Section 6

---

[1] EIRA: https://joinup.ec.europa.eu/node/99464.

[2] LSPs: https://ec.europa.eu/digital-agenda/en/large-scale-pilot-projects.

[3] E-SENS: http://www.esens.eu/.

investigates, which architecture requirements are fulfilled by existing EA frameworks and the components they provide. The final section (7) concludes the work and discusses limitations and implications for further research.

2 Review of Interoperability Frameworks and EA Architectures

Since the publication of the European Interoperability Strategy (EIS) and European Interoperability Framework (EIF) in 2004, interoperability has been increasingly in focus of e-government [1]. The EIF has stimulated the adoption of government interoperability frameworks (GIF) in the different MS [16, 17]. GIFs are strategic by nature. They provide guidance on what to consider when establishing interactions among public administrations. The catalogue of policies, specifications, and standards provided by GIFs outlines a desired profile for e-government services [16, 18]. GIFs like the EIF emphasize on technical, semantic and organizational aspects of interoperability. However, they neglect methodological support for projects and initiatives [1, 19]. Due to missing methodological support, GIFs only provide a limited assistance to interoperability initiatives and projects [20].

Complementary to GIFs, EA frameworks offer assistance through methodological support in translating business visions and strategies into effective services [4]. EA frameworks provide a multidimensional approach [9, 16–19]. They further detail the how, where, who, when and why next to the what which is addressed by GIFs [20]. EA frameworks can support a broader range of objectives and influence decision making on different levels. However, any EA adoption depends on an architectural governance process. A governance-centric approach ensures long-term sustainability and stakeholder acceptance [2, 7, 19, 21]. EA needs to respond to social interdependencies [15]. Thus, EA can be a successful tool, but it has to be adjusted to the strategic, social and technological context in which the architecture is embedded [22].

Before adopting an EA framework in a given context, the varying goals of EA frameworks are assessed: The Zachman framework is an analytical EA framework, which is used to describe ICT from different perspectives while lacking details on the design methods. Hence, it provides less support to adopters [9]. The Open Group's Architecture Framework (TOGAF) is a sophisticated architecture framework with a very detailed level of organizational support. Due to its large scope, TOGAF requires serious customization before being applied [10]. FEAF (Federal Enterprise Architecture Framework) may fit better with the idea of PEGS because it aims to improve interoperability among federal government agencies in the United States. However, the scope of FEAF is larger than the objective of PEGS because it promotes effective IT investment processes and consistent architectures among federal agencies [11, 23]. EAP (Enterprise Architecture Planning) and EITA (Enterprise IT Architecture) are planning oriented EA frameworks. They follow a pragmatic approach and structure. While EAP provides a set of well-defined steps to support the establishment, implementation, and ongoing maintenance of an EA program [14], EITA aims to handle, manage and integrate multiple systems [4, 12, 13]. Even though none of these EA frameworks perfectly fits the demands of PEGS, each one may contribute to interoperability needs.

Interoperability needs are captured by the European interoperability policy, which is realized by a series of initiatives and instruments. The strategic alignment of an EA framework for PEGS can be ensured by integrating previous achievements of the European interoperability policy [1, 18, 20, 24, 25]. The European interoperability policy helps to reach a consensus, to identify interoperability needs and to promote cross-border developments. It is structured into four phases: The first phase (awareness building) relates to the establishment of the EIS and the EIF. The EIS and EIF provide guidance for the creation of EIRA in phase two (establishment). The third phase (operation) initiates the use of this EIRA in different domains. Phase four (value adding) uses established domain architectures to improve the value of public services [1, 18, 20, 25]. Since approx. a decade, the European interoperability policy and the transition from GIFs to governmental EAs has been analysed in literature. Ray et al. compare various GIFs along the analytical dimensions context, content and process, and present a set of recommendations for new interoperability initiatives [17]. Charalabidis et al. compare GIFs and architectures in different countries in order to indicate the similarities and differences and to provide recommendations for the advancement of GIFs [16]. Guijarro investigates GIFs and EAs in Europe and the United States with a view on the methodological support of these frameworks and derive a two-phased interoperability roadmap consisting of an enabling phase and an alignment phase [18]. Gøtze et al. assess national EA programs and show how these programs serve as precursors for cross-border collaborations. The analysis points to major obstacles and drivers for cross-border collaborations [20]. Kubicek et al. review important GIFs, develop a four-layer framework and provide guidance for their re-conceptualization [26]. The findings of these reviews strongly contribute to the identification of requirements for an EA framework for PEGS, which is the main objective of this paper.

3 Research Design

This paper is part of a larger research effort which follows a qualitative approach using exploratory research for theory development. Design science research is used to derive the EA framework for PEGS. The architecture requirements presented in this paper provide a ground to that research effort by synthesizing and integrating research in the fields of e-government, EA and information systems. They are used to develop and justify theories that explain how EA frameworks can be used to overcome interoperability challenges. In IS research, design science is concerned with the design, specification and evaluation of design products. By choosing design-science research, the overall research methodology follows a proactive approach. The danger of design science research is a missing theory base, which results in well-designed but useless artefacts. Hence, requirements analysis is used to overcome this limitation. The requirements express a need for design products, which is derived from an extensive literature review in the fields of interoperability and EA research [27].

In order to propose sufficient design products or components of an EA framework for PEGS, it is required to generate a problem space and to incorporate a search process to detect appropriate solutions. The architecture requirements scope the problem space, in which the envisioned EA framework shall operate. Hence, these requirements also guide the search process by providing a set of defined criteria to determine, assess and customize appropriate EA components. The identified EA components are thoroughly evaluated by conducting literature reviews in the fields of EA research, EA standards and EA frameworks. The analysis is carried out in three steps: A static analysis helps to examine the structure of EA components and their qualities. The fit of EA components is studied during the architecture analysis. Finally, the optimal properties of EA components are elaborated during an optimization process [27].

The hypothesis for the review of EA framework components against the architecture requirements for PEGS is as follows: While some PEGS architecture requirements are adequately addressed by one or more EA framework components, other architecture requirements are not or only partially addressed. Differences between requirements and EA components are defined as a gap. The identified gaps are further consolidated and structured into areas of further research. All results are linked to an analytical structure in order to construct a taxonomy, which is divided into three organizing themes: *context*, *contents* and *processes*, a typical approach of system analysis [17, 28]. The organizing themes enrich the qualitative research design and support the study of the socio-technical phenomena of the EA framework for PEGS [29].

4   Requirements of an EA Framework for PEGS

The literature review in the field of governmental interoperability brought forward thirty architecture requirements. The requirements have been structured into the following six categories: project management (PM), stakeholder management (ST), service development (SD), interoperability layers and architecture viewpoints (LV), building blocks (BB), and collaboration agreements (CA). The categories are used to arrange the requirements in Sect. 4. Existing EA components are assessed in Sect. 5 against the fulfilment of these requirements. The requirement indications in the running text provide a unique numbering reference to each of the requirements.

4.1   Requirements Related to the Management of Interoperability Projects (PM)

E-government interoperability cannot be achieved by focusing on technical issues alone [16–18]. Nevertheless, it is important to share a common framework of technical standards, to follow general technological paradigms and to make use of best practice guidelines PM03 [16]. An EA framework for PEGS should adopt and promote high-level policies on interoperability [17]. It should provide means to ensure sufficient top-level management and political support, which is a critical factor when realizing cross-national collaborations PM05 [20]. Interoperability projects need to manage complexity and risks. They need to put attention to variables and factors beyond the technological view, such as availability of resources, legal and jurisdictional constraints, information security, governmental incentives, market forces, knowledge etc. PM04 [30].

Strategies to achieve interoperability do not automatically transform to the operational level. While top-down approaches often result in reduced legitimacy and acceptance of the planned collaboration solution, bottom-up approaches often result in technology-driven approaches. When realizing PEGS, contextual strategies may be better than control-seeking strategies. They are useful to address a critical thread on the path to interoperability, enabling a top-down approach PM01 without losing the link between the strategic and the operational level PM02 [16, 20, 22].

4.2   Requirements Related to the Management of Stakeholders (ST)

The EA framework for PEGS has to ensure appropriate management and governance of stakeholders and their concerns ST01 including cross-organizational relationships ST02 [15]. Janssen et al. as well as Flak and Rose note that techniques that describe how to practically specify, implement and govern relationships and the information exchange between different actors and their IT systems are missing ST03 [2, 21].

4.3   Requirements Related to Service Development (SD)

Interoperability should help to realize business transformation and service innovation processes by combining infrastructures services, business services, people and work processes SD03 [1]. Several authors mention that it is important to encourage openness, to follow business-driven needs SD01 and to rethink organizations and processes SD02 in order to enable business transformation processes and change of infrastructure and business (models) SD04 [1, 2, 16]. Service development should rather concentrate on business-driven needs than to lay its focus on technology or advancement-driven opportunities SD01 [16, 22]. Business requirements identify the scope of reform and help to find commonalities among agencies [17]. Implementations may be realized in several ways because interoperability shall encourage openness and a variety of solutions in the software industry SD05 [1].

4.4   Requirements Related to Interoperability Layers and Architecture Viewpoints (LV)

While EA frameworks provide detailed guidelines on how to use EA viewpoints, interoperability frameworks classify system concerns using interoperability layers. Thus, an EA framework for PEGS should provide guidance on how to use the interoperability layers systematically LV03 [20]. While the EIF focuses on semantic interoperability as a means to inter-link different systems, EA frameworks emphasize on application viewpoints and application integration as a means to achieve interoperability. Following EIF recommendations, EA frameworks for PEGS should emphasize on common organizational and semantic specifications LV02 [1, 16–18].

The EA framework for PEGS should make clear how to use interoperability layers and architecture viewpoints to address different stakeholder needs and views LV04 [17, 20, 22]. Layers and viewpoints support the analysis of business related concepts as well as the alignment of IT systems and collaboration towards a shared vision [17, 20]. Thus, interoperability layers and architecture viewpoints follow a similar approach with different intentions. A link between them should be provided LV01.

4.5   Requirements Related to the Management of Building Blocks (BB)

The EIF emphasizes on service orientation, a component-based service model and the reusability of BBs BB01. An EA framework for PEGS should provide guidance on how to create BBs and how to enable a systematic (de)composition BB03 [1, 22]. Aggregate public services are typically constructed by grouping several service components into a coherent whole BB02 [1, 22]. The management of architecture and solutions BBs is a critical threat for interoperability projects. Interoperability projects need to embrace existing artefacts and repositories should provide access to them BB05. Architecture guidelines should offer the necessary guidance on how to assemble and implement aggregate public services BB04 [17, 22]. The integrated use of repositories in combination with adequate modelling tools and collaboration tools has the potential to increase the provision, acceptance and adoption of BBs BB06 [16].

4.6   Requirements Related to the Provision of Collaboration Agreements (CA)

Collaboration agreements ensure a successful interaction and are preferred means to achieve interoperability [1, 6]. Interoperability requires the publication of agreements (methods, specifications, standards) that describe the ways of interoperation CA02 [6]. Collaboration agreements are often restricted to the syntactical level of the data exchange. An EA framework for PEGS should provide guidelines, rules and principles that show how to use them on a semantic and organisational level CA 03 [2].

There are problems related to the uptake of collaboration agreements, their evolution and how to ensure trust across multiple organizations. Life-cycle management of collaboration agreements can be used to improve governance and compliance mechanism. Collaboration agreements have to be suitable for designing and standardizing the next generation of interfaces CA05 [17, 22]. Next to a good cooperation ability [17], it is important to share principles for service development such as scalability, reusability, flexibility, preference for open standards, preference for open standards and security in order to establish trust among organizations CA01 [16]. Maturity levels and compliance levels should be used to measure the compliance of specifications and implementations with the defined principles and business requirements CA06. Thus, a methodology to assess and select technologies, standards and implementations (e.g. quality measurement, conformance testing, requirements based incorporation/ withdrawal of standards etc.) should be considered CA04 [16, 20].

5 EA Components Addressing the Architecture Requirements

The previous section outlined 30 architecture requirements of an EA framework for PEGS. In this section, important EA components and their capabilities are studied and assessed in regards to whether they fulfil the identified architecture requirements. The analysis is structured along the three organizing (cf. Sect. 3). A requirement may be linked to one or more EA components. The relationship is described through two types of indicators: A requirement ID is indicated as *resolved* with the indicator [RES] (14 requirements, cf. Table 1 in Sect. 5.4); the indicator [OPN] points to a contribution of an EA component to resolve a requirement, while the requirement itself remains *open* for further research (16 requirements). The 16 open requirements are consolidated into areas of future research in the concluding Sect. 6.

5.1 Contextual EA Components

The use of baseline architecture and target architecture in EA frameworks provides a basis for increasing maturity and enabling business standardization over time [OPN-CA06] [8, 10, 11]. Levels of architecture scope (e.g. national, sector, local) describe the types of organizational complexity, which are addressed by an EA. They promote comparability and consistent use of architecture outputs for certain usage levels [11]. According to the EIF, European-wide and sector-specific architecture solutions are the envisioned levels of scope for PEGS [OPN-PM04] [1]. The concept of primary outcomes represents areas of an EA framework where a direct, positive impact can be made [11]. The primary outcomes of an EA framework for PEGS are service delivery, cooperation, information exchange, sharing and reuse and reduction of costs [1]. A defined set of primary outcomes offers principle guidance when developing PEGS [OPN-BB03].

EA frameworks comprise basic elements such as principles, methods, tools and standards [10, 11, 31]. Basic elements ensure that EA programs and EA projects are complete and effective in developing service components and building blocks [OPN-PM04]. They can be used as a basis for projects to define a project-specific architecture approach, to establish a standards framework and technological paradigm and to adopt best practice guidelines [RES-PM03] [11, 31].

Architecture documentation shall be created along a set of core artefacts. The TOGAF content framework determines various types of analysis, modelling techniques and artefacts for each architecture viewpoint [OPN-LV03]. It structures architectural contents and clarifies the relationships between building blocks, artefacts and deliverables and therewith provides guidance for the composition of aggregate public services. The TOGAF enterprise continuum operates on a higher level of abstraction. It clarifies how foundation architectures, reusable service components and building blocks can be adapted to certain contexts in order to create specific architectures and solutions. Both, TOGAF Enterprise Continuum and the TOGAF content framework provide a powerful way for allocating, classifying and combining artefacts on various levels [RES-BB04] [10].

Architecture meta-models clarify various EA concerns. While the Zachman framework puts forward different perspectives on information systems, enterprise analysis and modelling [9], ISO/IEC/IEEE std. 42010:2011 addresses the management of architectures through the use of architecture descriptions. The ISO/IEC/IEEE meta-model is a generic approach related to the creation of architecture descriptions RES-BB05. It separates between architecture viewpoints and views OPN-LV04 enabling partitioning of system concerns according to stakeholder needs OPN-ST01 [32]. The definition of model fragments along architecture viewpoints supports the process to create architecture models and BBs. Pattern-based approaches are helpful when aiming to create reusable, modular and loosely coupled service components and building blocks OPN-BB01 [33].

5.2 Content-Related EA Components

Architecture viewpoints offer the possibility to follow a top-down approach by providing links between business and technical viewpoints. This approach increases legitimacy and acceptance of outputs. The use of a strategy viewpoint in an EA viewpoint model helps to find a common agreement upon the desired outputs. The strategy viewpoint drives the developments done along other architecture viewpoints RES-PM01 [5]. Links to the operational level can be best established through requirements management, a central activity of the EA life-cycle (cf. Sect. 5.3) OPN-SD01 [10].

EA viewpoints can be easily mapped to interoperability layers as shown in [20] RES-LV01. A reorganization process leads to changed foci of architecture development. Less emphasis is put on intentions related to an application architecture, while more emphasis is put on semantic, organizational and legal interoperability layers by integrating them into the information architecture, business architecture and strategy viewpoint RES-LV02. The understanding and scope of architecture viewpoints may vary from one community to another. ArchiMate is an architecture description language which aims to systemize the creation of architecture models along architecture viewpoints. Thereby, ArchiMate offers the possibility to separate between the different service concerns imposed by an architecture RES-BB02. The separation allows for example to change a business service without affecting the services defined on the technical or infrastructure level RES-SD04. ArchiMate also specifies model fragments for each architecture viewpoint. It therewith provides guidance on the systematic use of architecture viewpoints OPN-LV03. The use of ArchiMate therewith offers the possibility to provide a consistent way to describe business processes, organizational structures, information flows, IT systems, and technical infrastructures RES-BB06 [34, 35].

5.3 Process-Related EA Components

EA life-cycle models (LCM) define a number of activities to enable structured, comprehensive and systematic architecture development. The phases identified by major EA frameworks (cf. Sect. 2) are the analysis phase, the design phase, the transition and the implementation phase. We propose an adaptation of TOGAF's Architecture Development Method (ADM).

The EA LCM distinguishes between six sequential (A-F) and six central (G-L) phases. By combining sequential and central phases, top-down processing of architecture issues is ensured [RES-PM 02]. The proposed EA life-cycle model for PEGS adopts the structure of TOGAF architecture development method and integrates components from other EA life-cycle models (Fig. 1). The first two phases, A. *Planning & Initialization* and B. *Architecture Vision*, are well documented by all frameworks. Thus, sufficient methodologies to adopt best practices, to define project architecture, standard framework and technological paradigm are offered [RES-PM03]. The next two phases aim to define C. *Baseline Architecture* and D. *Target Architecture* (cf. Sect. 5.1) using the different architecture viewpoints as an underlying structure (cf. Sect. 5.2). The distinction between baseline and target helps to systematically develop issues related to the information system exchange [OPN-ST 03] [10, 12, 14]. The phases E. *Architecture Transition* and F. *Architecture Governance* realize business transformation and change processes through iterative planning. Detailed guidelines for architecture transition and architecture governance are provided by many EA frameworks (e.g. TOGAF guideline on Business Transformation & Readiness Assessment) [OPN-SD03] [10, 13, 14].

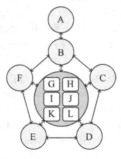

Fig. 1. EA LCM for PEGS adapted from [10]

The central phase J. *Requirements Management* enables the alignment of architecture outputs with business-driven needs. Requirements driven approach is used to increase legitimacy and acceptance of outputs [OPN-SD 01] [10]. The TOGAF guideline for Business Scenarios helps to elicit business requirements and business goals [OPN-SD01]. Acceptance of outputs is controlled via G. *Stakeholder Management* phase, which offers the possibility to establish collaboration agreements on the basis of formalized stakeholder approval and change processes [RES-CA02]. TOGAF deliverables like stakeholder contract, change request, request for architecture work are supportive to many types of stakeholder concerns. The TOGAF guideline on Interoperability Requirements offers a means to formalize cross-organizational relationships [RES-ST02]. Stakeholder Management ensures the safeguarding of stakeholder support, a critical threat in many interoperability projects. TOGAF provides a detailed guideline and various techniques for Stakeholder Management [RES-PM05] [10, 12]. Requirements driven selection of standards and technology is part of the phase I. *Standards &*

Technology Management. The phase ensures adequate management of specifications and technologies in order to establish, select and validate adequate architecture foundations according to a technology strategy [10], [12]. Maturity models and levels help to measure the state of technology and help to visualize how standards and technologies pass through stages (e.g. trial, active, phasing out) [RFC-CA05] [10, 12]. Phase *I. Repository Management* acknowledges the need for managing artefacts across the architecture landscape. The TOGAF approach to Repository Management provides a mature repository structure which helps to organize, access and manage different outputs [RES-BB05] [10, 14]. The phases *H. Risk Management* and *K. Project Management* acknowledge risks and complexities accompanied with interoperability projects and efforts. TOGAF and other EA frameworks provide guidelines on Risk Management, which include methodologies for risk mitigation [OPN-PM04] [10, 12, 14].

5.4   Fulfilment of Requirements Through EA Components

In the previous sub-sections, several EA components were identified, examined and re-arranged. Table 1 shows how the architecture requirements identified in Sect. 4 are resolved through above EA components. Major contextual EA components are the levels of architecture scope, primary outcomes and basic elements of an architecture framework. Architecture principles provide a ground and can be used to guide system development and identify directions to be taken in interoperability programs and projects. EA frameworks distinguish between baseline and target architecture in order to reach a desired vision and to identify necessary modifications. Architecture outputs can be systemized using std. 42010:2011 [32], TOGAF content framework or TOGAF enterprise continuum [10].

EA viewpoint components describe architecture contents that range from strategic to technical concepts. EA viewpoints which are harmonized with interoperability layers build a cornerstone of an EA framework for PEGS. Each architecture viewpoint can be described through a range of model fragments and techniques that support the development of architecture content. The use of an architecture description language helps to systemize the model fragment use [35].

EA life cycle components describe how an EA evolves over time (i.e. the development process). EA management is an important function. It describes how EA is established and it addresses the management of contents, technologies, standards, requirements, stakeholders, complexities and risks. The phased approach of architecture development integrates the architecture viewpoints and shows how architecture transition and architecture governance is executed.

The architecture requirements, which are declared to be open, are structured into areas of further research in the concluding section.

Table 1. Fulfilment of architecture requirements through EA components

Area	EA component description	NR
Contextual EA components	Primary outcomes, levels of scope and basic elements (principles, methods, tools, patterns and standards) ensure that EA programs are complete and effective	PM03
	TOGAF Deliverables: Stakeholder Contract, Change Request, Request for Architecture Work and Communication Plan	ST02
	TOGAF content framework structures architectural content and shows how to compose aggregate public services. TOGAF enterprise continuum provides method how to adapt architectures and solutions to certain contexts	BB04
	ISO/IEC/IEEE std. 42010: 2011 clarifies how to create, analyse & sustain architectures using architecture descriptions	BB05
EA content components (viewpoints)	Use of strategy viewpoint to drive architecture development	PM01
	Inclusion of strategy viewpoint	PM02
	ArchiMate distinguishes between different types of services. Each service type can be defined and changed independently	SD04 BB02
	Establishment of links between interoperability layers and architecture viewpoints	LV01
	Integrating semantic, organizational and legal aspects of interoperability layers into the information architecture, business architecture and strategy viewpoint	LV02
	ArchiMate models provide capabilities to collaborate and agree on service components	BB06
EA process components (life-cycle)	Sequential phases of ADM ensure top-down processing	PM01
	Combination of sequential and central phases. Requirements Management provides bridge between strategy and operation	PM02
	Planning & Initialization and Architecture Vision phase clarify how to initialize interoperability projects	PM03
	Stakeholder Management phase and TOGAF guideline and techniques on Stakeholder Management help to manage various concerns	PM05
	TOGAF guideline on Interoperability Requirements can be used to visualize cross-organizational relationships	ST02

(*Continued*)

Table 1. (*Continued*)

Area	EA component description	NR
	Repository Management Phase and TOGAF Architecture Repository help to organize architectures outcomes	BB05
	Stakeholder Management phase offers possibility to introduce formalized stakeholder approval and change processes	CA02
	Standard & Technology Management phase clarifies when to establish, select and validate standards and technologies and how to use them as architecture foundations	CA05

6 Conclusions

An efficient EA framework for the design, implementation and maintenance of interoperable PEGS should combine generic EA components with concepts, methods and solutions from e-government and interoperability research. In this contribution, we investigated requirements for the design and implementation of interoperable PEGS and we studied how well these architecture requirements are already fulfilled by existing EA frameworks and components. The study has certain limitations. The completeness of the architecture requirements was not approved in a separate process and only five EA frameworks and one standard were investigated (beside important contributions in EA research and practice). The measurement of fulfilment did not follow a formal evaluation process but relied on reviews carried out by the authors. This may result in a limited traceability of results.

We conclude that EA is a helpful means to realize interoperable PEGS. The investigation has shown that approx. half of the 30 architecture requirements identified throughout the study are adequately addressed by existing EA frameworks and EA components. However, not all architecture requirements identified throughout this paper are successfully implemented in existing EA frameworks or they are only partially addressed. These issues point to areas of further research, summarized in the following ten research needs, which are stated per analytical dimension (cf. Sect. 3).

The contextual design of an EA framework for PEGS can be strengthened by integrating a number of aspects. There are many common interoperability challenges when establishing PEGS. (1) Critical success factors to overcome these challenges should be identified and integrated in order to provide a general guidance for interoperability projects. (2) An EA framework for PEGS should be built upon widely accepted principles and strategies (e.g. outlined by the EIF and EIS). Additionally it should (3) comprise architecture design principles and guidelines to reason about alternative design strategies. In order to facilitate stakeholder management, an EA framework for PEGS should (4) refer to abstract stakeholder classes and roles in interoperability projects and determine drivers for their engagement.

The creation of contents within an EA framework for PEGS can be improved through the following aspects and methods: (5) Development of a requirements management methodology that supports the capturing of requirements from business-driven needs, policy implementation processes and other strategic aspects in order to establish common path and to increase the acceptance of architecture outputs among stakeholders. (6) Another methodology should describe how to define interoperability specifications on semantic and organizational level, which can be used as a basis for collaboration agreements. (7) A detailed design of each architecture viewpoint should be outlined. Such detailed design should identify relevant model fragments and should be based on a commonly agreed architecture description language [35].

The processes of architecture development can be improved as follows: (8) There are missing guidelines and methods that describe how to transition and to govern architectures in multi-stakeholder environments. Several independent implementations of PEGS have to be coordinated, extended and sustained over time. (9) An EA framework for PEGS should integrate appropriate assessment methodologies that can be used at different phases of architecture development. Assessment methodologies can be used to measure the current state of specifications and the compliance of solutions with the underlying collaboration agreements. (10) Other assessment methodologies can help to determine the level of business standardizations in a domain and to appraise the maturity of market solutions in order to detect appropriate ways forward.

The ten research needs identified before are subject of ongoing investigations towards the development of a comprehensive EA framework for PEGS.

References

1. European Commission. European Interoperability Framework (EIF) for European public services. COM(2010) 744 final, European Commission, Brussels, p. 40 (2010)
2. Janssen, M., Charalabibis, Y., Kuk, G., Cresswell, T.: Guest editors' introduction: e-government interoperability, infrastructure and architecture: state-of-the-art and challenges. J. Theor. Appl. Electron. Commer. Res. 6(1), I–VIII (2011)
3. Hjort-Madsen, K., Pries-Heje, J.: Enterprise architecture in government: fad or future? In: 42nd Hawaii International Conference on System Sciences (HICSS-42), Waikoloa, Big Island, Hawaii, p. 132 (1–10) (2009)
4. Armour, F.J., Kaisler, S.H., Liu, S.Y.: A big-picture look at enterprise architectures. IEEE IT Prof. 1(1), 35–42 (1999)
5. Winter, R., Fischer, R.: Essential layers, artifacts, and dependencies of enterprise architecture. J. Enterp. Archit. 3(2), 7–18 (2007)
6. Scholl, H.J., Klischewski, R.: E-government integration and interoperability: framing the research agenda. Int. J. Publ. Adm. 30(8–9), 889–920 (2007)
7. Scholl, H.J., Kubicek, H., Cimander, R.: Interoperability, enterprise architectures, and it governance in government. In: Janssen, M., Scholl, H.J., Wimmer, M.A., Tan, Y.-H. (eds.) EGOV 2011. LNCS, vol. 6846, pp. 345–354. Springer, Heidelberg (2011)
8. Janssen, M.: Framing enterprise architecture: a meta-framework for analyzing architectural efforts in organizations. In: Doucet, G., Gøtze, J., Saha, P., Bernard, S. (eds.) Coherency Management-Architecting the Enterprise for Alignment, Agility and Assurance, pp. 99–119. AuthorHouse, Bloomington (2009)

9. Zachman, J.A.: A framework for information systems architecture. IBM Syst. J. **26**(3), 276–292 (1987)
10. The Open Group. TOGAF Version 9.1 (2011). http://pubs.opengroup.org/architecture/togaf9-doc/arch/. Accessed 30 Mar 2015
11. US Office of Management & Budget. Federal Enterprise Architecture Framework - Version 2. The White House, pp. 1–434 (2013)
12. Armour, F.J., Kaisler, S.H., Liu, S.Y.: Building an enterprise architecture step by step. IEEE IT Prof. **1**(4), 31–39 (1999)
13. Armour, F.J., Kaisler, S.H.: Enterprise architecture: agile transition and implementation. IT Prof. **3**(6), 30–37 (2001)
14. Spewak, S., Tiemann, M.: Updating the enterprise architecture planning model. J. Enterp. Archit. **2**(May), 11–19 (2006)
15. Janssen, M.: Sociopolitical aspects of interoperability and enterprise architecture in e-government. Soc. Sci. Comput. Rev. **30**(1), 24–36 (2012)
16. Charalabidis, Y., Lampathaki, F., Askounis, D.: A comparative analysis of national interoperability frameworks. In: 15th Americas Conference on Information Systems (AMCIS 2009), vol. Paper 694, pp. 1–10. AIS, San Francisco (2009)
17. Ray, D., Gulla, U., Dash, S.S., Gupta, M.P.: A critical survey of selected government interoperability frameworks. Transform. Gov. People Process Policy **5**(2), 114–142 (2011)
18. Guijarro, L.: Interoperability frameworks and enterprise architectures in e-government initiatives in Europe and the United States. Gov. Inf. Q. **24**(1), 89–101 (2007)
19. Kubicek, H., Cimander, R.: Three dimensions of organizational interoperability: insights from recent studies for improving interoperability frameworks. Eur. J. ePractice **6**, 3–14 (2009)
20. Gøtze, J., Christiansen, P.E., Mortensen, R.K., Paszkowski, S.: Cross-national interoperability and enterprise architecture. Informatica **20**(3), 369–396 (2009)
21. Flak, L.S., Rose, J.: Stakeholder governance: adapting stakeholder theory to e-government. Commun. Assoc. Inf. Syst. **16**, 642–664 (2005)
22. Klischewski, R.: Architectures for tinkering? Contextual strategies towards interoperability in e-government. J. Theor. Appl. Electron. Commer. Res. **6**(1), 26–42 (2011)
23. US Office of Management and Budget. The Common Approach to Federal Enterprise Architecture. Office of Management and Budget. The White House, p. 52 (2012)
24. European Commission. European Interoperability Strategy (EIS) for European public services. European Commission, Brussels, pp. 1–8 (2010)
25. Criado, J.I.: Interoperability of eGovernment for building intergovernmental integration in the European Union. Soc. Sci. Comput. Rev. **30**(1), 37–60 (2012)
26. Kubicek, H., Cimander, R., Scholl, H.J.: Organizational Interoperability in E-Government - Lessons from 77 European Good-Practice Cases. Springer, Berlin (2011)
27. Hevner, A.R., March, S.T., Park, J., Ram, S.: Design science in information systems research. MIS Q. **28**(1), 75–105 (2004)
28. Attride-Stirling, J.: Thematic networks: an analytic tool for qualitative research. Qual. Res. **1**(3), 385–405 (2001)
29. Hjort-Madsen, K.: Enterprise architecture implementation and management: a case study on interoperability. In: 39th Hawaii International Conference on System Sciences (HICSS-39). Computer Socientry Press, Kauai, p. 71c (1–10) (2006)
30. dos Santos, E.M., Reinhard, N.: Barriers to government interoperability frameworks adoption. In: 16th Americas Conference on Information Systems (AMCIS 2010), pp. 1–10 (2010)

31. Janssen, M., Flak, L.S., Sæbø, Ø.: Government architecture: concepts, use and impact. In: Wimmer, M.A., Janssen, M., Scholl, H.J. (eds.) EGOV 2013. LNCS, vol. 8074, pp. 135–147. Springer, Heidelberg (2013)
32. ISO/IEC/IEEE. Systems and software engineering - Architecture Description (ISO/IEC/IEEE 42010), vol. 2011, p. 46. ISO/IEC/IEEE (2011)
33. Buckl, S., Ernst, A.M., Lankes, J., Matthes, F., Schweda, C.M.: Enterprise architecture management patterns – exemplifying the approach. In: 12th International IEEE Enterprise Distributed Object Computing Conference (EDOC 2008), pp. 393–402 (2008)
34. Lankhorst, M.M., Proper, H.A., Jonkers, H.: The architecture of the ArchiMate language. In: Halpin, T., Krogstie, J., Nurcan, S., Proper, E., Schmidt, R., Soffer, P., Ukor, R. (eds.) Enterprise, Business-Process and Information Systems Modeling. LNBIP, vol. 29, pp. 367–380. Springer, Heidelberg (2009)
35. The Open Group. ArchiMate 2.1 Specification. The Open Group, Berkshire, p. 181 (2013)

Integrating Digital Migrants: Solutions for Cross-Border Identification from E-Residency to eIDAS. A Case Study from Estonia

Gerli Aavik[✉] and Robert Krimmer

Ragnar Nurkse School of Innovation and Governance,
Tallinn University of Technology, Tallinn, Estonia
aavikgerli@gmail.com, robert.krimmer@ttu.ee

Abstract. The electronic identification and trust service regulation (eIDAS) was adopted in 2014 to create a digital common market in the European Union (EU). As the world is becoming more and more digital, countries need to develop ways to integrate digital migrants. While the EU does not currently have a digital common market, several EU countries already have working systems for cross-border digital cooperation. The principal focus of this article was to address whether eIDAS can be implemented in these countries, without challenging the local initiatives. The Estonian e-government system (EES) was chosen as an exemplary case. Here we analyzed whether the eIDAS complements or challenges the national e-government initiatives, such as Estonia's e-residency project, and whether it is in the interest of member states to contribute to the fast implementation of the eIDAS as the most effective measure for achieving cross-border use of e-services. To address these questions, a content, context and process (CCP) analysis framework was used. Based on our findings, we concluded that, although the eIDAS creates some additional obligations, the regulation supports national e-government goals and domestic cross-border initiatives. Also, without supranational interference, it is highly unlikely that digital open borders could be created among 28 member states. Thus, it is in the interest of the member states to contribute to a fast implementation of the eIDAS.

Keywords: E-government · Case study · Cross-border e-services

1 Introduction

The mobility of European Union (EU) citizens and open borders have created an increasing need for a secure and digital common market. To guarantee the four basic freedoms of the EU, digital services will be required. Since 1999, the digital services of EU member states have been derived from a common legal framework[1], however, in reality the digital identities of the citizens of other member states have not been acknowledged. As the world is becoming more and more digital, countries need to develop ways

---

[1] The basis has been Directive 99/93/EC.

© IFIP International Federation for Information Processing 2016
Published by Springer International Publishing Switzerland 2016. All Rights Reserved
H.J. Scholl et al. (Eds.): EGOV 2016, LNCS 9820, pp. 151–163, 2016.
DOI: 10.1007/978-3-319-44421-5_12

to integrate digital migrants[2]. Thus, the electronic identification and trust service regulation (eIDAS) was adopted in July 2014 and a framework to develop the digital common market in the EU was created. [2].

Although the eIDAS could provide digital services across the EU, alternative systems also exist. Various EU countries have different initiatives aimed at decreasing digital fragmentation, so it is important to evaluate how the eIDAS could be implemented in a way that is compatible with local initiatives. Estonia has been a pioneer in cross-border cooperation [3], being a source for cross-border electronic initiatives such as SignWise, the e-residency and bilateral cross-border mutual recognition agreements[3]. In December 2015, Estonia's e-residency program celebrated its first birthday by 3-fold exceeding its initial annual goal, having enrolled 7,000 members from 119 countries. Estonian Prime Minister Taavi Rõivas called the program "a pioneering move to open up our efficient digital services to anyone in the world" [4]. Here we investigate whether the EIDAS supports or undermines national measures, using the Estonian case as an example. The following research questions will be answered:

- Do the changes introduced by the eIDAS complement or challenge the domestic goals and e-government initiatives of Member States?
- Should Member States contribute to the fast implementation of the eIDAS as the most effective measure for achieving cross-border use of e-services?

To answer these questions, the key aspects of the EES, local cross-border initiatives and the eIDAS are mapped and the compatibility of the eIDAS with an existing e-government systems (ES) is evaluated. In addition to giving insight to the compatibility of the eIDAS with the local initiative, the article also aims to strengthen the theoretical knowledge with a new case study.

2   Theoretical Framework: Context, Content and Process (CCP)

Information systems (IS) are essential part of e-governing and IS theories are often used for evaluating ES and e-services. Trends in public administration are forcing governments to reengineer the administration processes and to set higher requirements on accountability of ICT-based systems [5]. Systems theory, organizational rationalism, social theory of structuration and critical theory are the most commonly employed theories in IS research [6]. Although these theories and frameworks offer a variety of analysis options, because e-government analyses encompass multiple spheres of research, a more complex, multi-faceted approach is needed [7]. CCP analysis creates **linkages between context, content and process** and enables the researcher to ask questions both from the perspective of technology and people engaged [8], ensuring that important variables are not overlooked [9]. CCP analysis is used in different research areas, such as education [10], psychology and psychotherapy [11], biology [12] and management [13], but was

---

[2] For us (in contrast to definitions such as by Prensky [1]) we mean citizens with no legal residence in the country, but wanting to engage digitally with its public services.

[3] The concepts of SignWise, e-residency and bilateral cross-border agreements are introduced in Sect. 4.2.

first introduced in IS research by Symons [14]. The CCP framework offers a high level of structure [8], by breaking processes into a number of elements – **purpose** (*why*), **subject** (*what*), **timeframe** (*when*), **methodologies** (*how*) and **people** (*who*) – thus allowing the researcher to recognize a wide scope of interrelated factors [15]. This also allows the researcher to ask the correct questions and explore a wide range of influences, by inherently including social, political, cultural and economic factors [8].

Here, the CCP framework is used to assess whether it is in the interests of EU member states with existing e-government systems (e.g., the EES) to contribute to the fast implementation of eIDAS. CCP framefork allows to evaluate changes through measures such as effectiveness, efficiency and understanding of the context [16], making it possible to assess whether the changes are compatible with the contexts they are implemented in. To assess the compatibility of the EES and eIDAS, the contextual dimensions introduced by Heeks [17] are used. The principal arguments of CCP framework are that changes are most likely to be accepted when the core values of organizations are not impacted [18], there are little or no substantial mismatches between contextual dimensions [17], acceptance among stakeholder is gained, there is thorough communication [9] and the timing is right [19]. The focus of the article is empirical, so the theoretical framework is not elaborated in more detail. The main purpose of the framework is to determine how to structure and analyse the data [20].

3   Methodology

To analyze the compatibility of the eIDAS in an existing e-government system, we applied a deductive approach, moving from a general theory to an explorative single case study [21]. Qualitative research design was used to analyze **linkages between causally relevant factors** and map causal paths in a given situation [22]. Although case studies can involve multiple cases, here we focus on the EES as the center of a single case analysis. Case studies focus on understanding the dynamics within a single setting [23], while also creating a basis for generalization of these results [24]. Although it can be argued that generalizability is limited when using a single case study, using a single case design highlights the contrast between case studies and clear statistical analyses [25]. Here, CCP analysis was used, including key aspects of the observed case, creating clear causal paths and explaining how the conclusions were reached.

It was important to ensure that key causal relationships would not be missed [22] and expert interviews had a substantial impact to prevent that [26]. In addition to the legal documents, reports, impact analyses, written expert opinions, notes from presentations, news and academic articles, six semi-structured expert interviews were carried out with leading experts from the Estonian e-government department. As the network of the EES is small and integrated, these six interviewees represent the main stakeholder viewpoints from the Estonian governmental sector, the private sector and e-government critics. The case of the EES is introduced in the following sections.

4   Case Study: The Estonian E-Government System (EES)

As Estonia has a working ES with remarkably high usage, the Estonian case was chosen for analysis [27]. For a small state, Estonia has managed to create a remarkable image of an e-state [3, 28, 29]. In strong cooperation with the private sector [28], the principal idea has been to create a single system that could be used for all e-services, enabling the creation of low cost usable e-services. The X-road solution[4], electronic ID cards[5] and data protection acts are seen as the solid building blocks of the system [3]. It is important to note that the innovative services and the image of an e-state do not hold a high value in itself, unless it is visible to citizens and the services needed by citizens are actually delivered. Services such as an e-tax office and e-banking have significantly improved the convenience of Estonian citizens [27], and are used on a daily bases. According to the 2014 UN e-government survey, Estonia is ranked 15th in the list of world e-government leaders and 8th among European countries, being one of the 25 countries ranked as having a very-high-EGDI[6]. Estonia is also among the top 20 countries in online service delivery, being one of the six European countries in that list, and among the top 25 performers in e-participation [33].

4.1   The EIDAS Regulation as the Content of Change

The content dimension allows researchers to see the substance of a planned change [13]. Here, the eIDAS is considered as that content. The current e-Signature Directive [34] has been in use for over 15 years. As the directive has substantial gaps, such as undefined obligations for the national supervision of service providers, and legal and technical cross-border interoperability issues [35], a new framework was needed and, after thorough discussions, new regulations were adopted. The new legislative solution was proposed in 2012 and adopted in 2014 [36]. The European Commission has conducted Large scale pilots (LSP) in the past, such as STORK, E-CODEX, SPOCS and E-SENS, with the aim to test the interoperability and the legality of this new framework [37]. Based on the previously held discussions and conducted pilot projects, new regulations were introduced to develop mutual recognition of electronic identification, cross-border electronic trust services and cross-border electronic documents [38]. Some of the main ideas introduced with the eIDAS include: enhancing trust in electronic transactions by

---

[4] X-road is the most important environment in the Estonian e-government system, connecting different public and private e-service databases, and making the services interoperable [30] . The end user is identified with an ID card or through online banking. Public and private sector enterprises and institutions can connect their own electronic environment with x-road, and make data exchange more effective [31].

[5] Electronic ID card is a smart card, which can be used for authentication of the card holder and for giving digital signatures and encrypt documents. Digital IDs are issued to citizens and residents of Estonia [32].

[6] E-government development index (EGDI) is an index, which aims to view e-government development and reflect relative knowledge of best practices by analysing three dimensions of e-government – provision of online services, telecommunication connectivity and human capacity [33].

providing a common foundation for secure cross-border electronic actions; providing key enablers across borders (such as electronic IDs, documents, signatures and delivery services); creating public key infrastructure at pan-European level; identifying different assurance levels to characterize the degree of confidence of a party being identified; and establishing a general legal framework for the use of trust services. It is important to emphasize that the regulation is technology-neutral and does not seek to interfere with the electronic ID management systems and related infrastructures, which are established in member states [36].

4.2 EES as the Content That is Changed. Possibilities for Cross-Border Digital Cooperation

Estonia is unquestionably a pioneer of e-services [3, 28, 29]. Based on the EES, four possible models for cross-border cooperation can be described, which are introduced in following sections.

The first option (Fig. 1) is forming **bilateral agreements between member states** to cooperate digitally across national borders. An example here would be the cooperation agreement between the tax offices of Finland and Estonia [31], which began in 2013 with the first digitally signed intergovernmental contract [39].

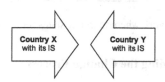

Fig. 1. Forming bilateral agreements.

The Estonian e-residency project, which enables non-residents to access the same electronic benefits as the residents of Estonia, can be seen as the second option (Fig. 2). Estonian aimed to be the first country to start issuing e-residency, as it was believed that the accessibility of digital services should not be dependent on the person's residency or citizenship. With digital residency, new e-residents (both from the EU and outside) receive a digital ID with a smart card identical to an Estonian electronic ID certificate, which can be used in the digital environment to identify a person and give digital signatures, using the same software as citizens do with their ID-cards [40].

The third option is offering **cross-border services through a neutral non-governmental body** (Fig. 3). This has been done by a private sector initiative, SignWise, which is a cloud-based digital identification service, enabling people and businesses to digitally sign documents across borders by providing trusted and secure cross-border infrastructure for authentication and validation [41].

Fig. 3. Enabling people and companies to digitally sign documents across borders by providing secure infrastructure.

The fourth option is **a supranational framework** (Fig. 4) where, based on a principle of subsidiarity, transnational interference is seen as the most effective and efficient solution. The example here is the eIDAS, which aims to create a system of mutual recognition of Member States' national identification systems, by creating a comprehensive legal framework for both the electronic identification and authentication services [42].

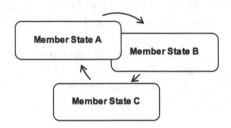

Fig. 4. Supranational framework where member states recognize each other's digital IDs.

4.3   The Context Surrounding the Change Processes

E-government applications are often seen as isolated technical artefacts, but it is important to understand that their contents are always used in certain contexts [17]. In the following sections, the reasons behind the adoption of new regulation and the involved stakeholders are analyzed through the questions why and who.

Stakeholders. In the case of Estonia, a small circle of people deal directly with IS in the EES. The EES is built on a bottom-up system, with each minister being responsible for the ICT system and e-services of their field. Ministers consult public and private sector stakeholders, and based on the collected information, proposals are then presented

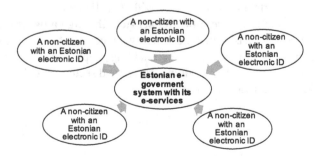

Fig. 2. Enabling non-citizens to access the national e-state and use e-services.

at the national central level. [3] As the eIDAS requirements are set by the EU, the bottom-up system cannot be applied and the responsible network here is formed by the Ministry of Interior, the Estonian Information System Authority, the Ministry of Economic Affairs and Communications and the Certification Centre [3, 29]. Also, close coopera-tion with the private sector needs to be emphasized: electronic identity was developed clearly on the initiative of banks and telecommunication companies [28, 43], certifica-tion services are provided solely by the private-owned SC, and most ICT services are bought in from the private sector [28].

As the networks are rather small, personal opinions and characteristics of individuals have been very important. Ideologies are often carried on from one individual to another, forming a symbiosis between personal opinions and organizational views [3]. (I6) From early on, there were pioneers who wanted to develop cross-border e-cooperation, which meant that when the discussions about the eIDAS started, the question was not whether to do it, but how [3, 29]. Charismatic leadership can be helpful for supporting a clear vision and mission, but critics [44, 45] bring out that this can also lead to people following ideas blindly, as they do not actually understand the technical part of these solutions. Thus, the more extensive involvement of ICT people and critics could be beneficial [45].

Reasons for the New Regulation and for Accepting or Repulsing the Change. When adopting and implementing changes, it should be made clear why these changes are needed in the given contexts and why are they accepted or repulsed [46]. IS serves a purpose to simplify the work, enabling organizations to work better [14]. In the public services, IS are used to provide for citizens faster, more conveniently and to reduce costs [47]. In the Estonian case, efficiency has been the core driver of adopting IS [3]. Estonia has had paperless decision-making in the government cabinet since 2000, and most of the public sector services are available digitally [30]. Using digital signatures domesti-cally has helped save 2 % of GDP and governmental stakeholders believe that this number could be higher once digital IDs are acknowledged throughout the EU [3]. Although Estonia does already have a cross-border digital initiative, this does not neces-sarily mean that the eIDAS would be seen as a competing concept. It is clear that the Estonian initiatives could not create open borders within the 28 Member States and a two-speed Europe would not be the most desirable option. eIDAS sets the minimal requirements for cooperation but does not limit greater cooperation between strategi-cally important counterparts [3]. Also, aligning after European principles could signif-icantly strengthen the EES, as there are stronger requirements on security, privacy, openness and data protection at the EU level [45]. Thus, the question in Estonia regarding the development of cross-border e-services has not been whether to do it, rather how best to do it [3, 28, 29].

Categorizing Contextual Dimensions. Contextual divisions (information, tech-nology, processes, objectives and values, staffing and skills, management and structures and other resources) introduced by Heeks [17] are used here to map and compare the EES and requirements introduced with the eIDAS. These divisions enable better comprehension of the scope of changes for the EES.

As mentioned before, the goals of the eIDAS coincide with the objectives and values of Estonian digital policies [3, 28, 29], thus, although some additional obligations are surely created for the EES [29], there are no substantial mismatches in the objectives and values. Regarding the technology and processes dimensions, some changes are needed. As the eIDAS aims to be technology-neutral [36] and Estonia participated in the pilot project STORK, it is believed that existing Estonian technical solutions and processes would not require significant change [3]. However, it should be noted that the current systems were created and secured for the internal market and, when the number of users multiples, these systems would need to be rebuilt accordingly. Some auditing functions would also be required to strengthen the e-governing process [29]. At the same time, these development would also support the local cross-border initiatives [3], and critics hope that implementing the eIDAS would motivate further strengthening of the technical content [44].

More substantial changes would be needed in the divisions of information, staffing and skills and management systems and structures. The eIDAS sets several new requirements for data exchange, such as exchanging information about supervision activities and best practice [36]. Also, requirements are set on the preservation of information for electronic signatures and seals [36] and EU privacy measures are more strict [3, 45]. As Estonia is a small state, the lack of specific resources is seen as a significant barrier [3, 28, 29]. The main issue here is having too few people, but the technical and legal competencies of the existing people would also need to be developed to fulfil the eIDAS requirements [29, 45]. The lack of resources also influences the division of management systems and structures. While the EES is flexible and receptive towards change [3], the resources are lacking and the mental willingness might be insufficient [29]. Implementing eIDAS certainly creates additional tasks and financial obligations [3], but the key issue here is in the effective use of resources [29]. Also, the EU provides financial support, which should ameliorate resources insufficiencies [28].

4.4 Process of Change and Factors of Timing

For the EES, it was clear that the directive was not working [29] and most stakeholders agreed that in order to develop cross-border cooperation, a new regulation was needed [3]. It is believed that Estonia has had more influence on the European digital policies than it would be assumed based on the size of the country [3, 29]. The same is considered true in the chance process for the EES, where Estonia managed to defend its interests well while the content of regulation was worked out. The goal was that the change in Estonian domestic systems would be minimal [29]. If more had to be changed, the resistance against the eIDAS due to large investment needs would likely have been greater [43].

It has been an Estonian ambition to achieve cross-border identification measures and cross-border e-services as fast as possible, but it is clear that comprehensive changes, such as digital open borders, do not happen instantly. It is believed that the timing of the eIDAS has been good [3, 48]. Implementation of the eIDAS and the e-residency project are happening simultaneously, which makes it is easier for Estonia to use its resources reasonably [3]. Simultaneous processes also create a better platform for communication, especially since the stakeholders in Estonia overlap greatly [48]. At the same time, it should be remembered that the older the systems become, the more difficult it will be to implement changes [28]. Thus, had the eIDAS been implemented earlier, there would likely have been greater flexibility [29].

Another important aspect of the change process is communication, often determining the end result [8]. As the majority of people do not understand the technical processes behind electronic services and digital identification means, trust is essential, as are communication and branding [44]. In the case of the EES, branding has been mainly been targeted outwards, to create a global e-state image [3]. Although a lack of domestic communication has drawn criticism [45], the wider communication is planned for the period of implementation [3]. The influence of the communication of the change process cannot be evaluated at this point.

5 Discussion

By analyzing the Estonian case, we aimed to answer two research questions: (1) whether the changes introduced by the eIDAS are complementary to or challenge the domestic goals and e-government initiatives of Member States; and (2) whether Member States should contribute to the fast implementation of the eIDAS, as the most effective measure for achieving cross-border use of e-services [49]. The CCP framework was used here to map and analyze the key aspects of the chosen case. In the following sections, the research questions are answered based on the theoretical framework and empirical findings.

5.1 Do the Changes Introduced by the EIDAS Complement or Challenges the Domestic Goals and E-Government Initiatives of Member States?

The CCP framework allowed us to analyze, based on the EES, whether the eIDAS complements or challenges the existing e-government solutions. It is important to note that the content of change influences the attitudes towards the change, meaning that when the core of the system is not affected, there is less resistance [18]. Also, mismatches between contextual features can cause extensive instability [49], so that comparing contextual dimensions is often key to evaluations of compatibility. If the contexts do not match, contents should be changed [17]. However, in this case, the content under observation is directly applicable. This means that any mismatches not negotiated in the development phase, will require domestic systems (contents) to be changed later. In the case of the EES, most of the identified mismatches were minor. Although there were more requirements for substantial change in the divisions of information, staffing, skills, management systems and structures, we expect that when the necessity of these changes is accepted [3, 29, 45], major resistance will be unlikely.

The second aspect under investigation was the compatibility of the eIDAS with the domestic e-government initiatives. The Estonian case shows that the eIDAS can be compatible with local initiatives. However, it should be noted that resources can be scarce (especially within a small state context), making it important to prioritize. In the Estonian case, the changes introduced by the eIDAS also supported the domestic needs and goals (e.g., the development of e-residency) [3, 28, 29]. Thus, it can be reasoned that, although the eIDAS was enforced to fulfil wider goals of the EU, by creating an open system, it also supports the development of local initiatives [3, 28, 29]. As the content does not conflict significantly with the EES, local initiatives can be developed simultaneously with the eIDAS.

5.2 Should Member States Contribute to the Fast Implementation of the EIDAS as the Most Effective Measure for Achieving Cross-Border Use of E-Services?

As Directive 99/93/EC has proved to have substantial gaps, the eIDAS was introduced to develop secure mutual recognition of cross-border electronic identification, electronic trust services and electronic documents [38]. Developing cross-border e-services should be in the interest of Member States. However, it should be evaluated whether Member States should contribute to the fast development of the eIDAS as the most effective solution. In the Estonian public sector, efficiency is a priority and digital solutions are seen as a way to achieve it. On the domestic level, around 2 % of GDP has been saved due to the use of digital signatures. It is predicted that, if digital IDs were acknowledged across borders, yet further improvements in efficiency could be made [3]. It is clear that none of the domestic solutions have so far managed to create a common digital market, so the eIDAS can certainly support efficiency by doing so.

In any successful change, maximum output should be achieved with minimum input [14]. It could be argued that, for countries that already have usable cross-border solutions, developing new system might be an unnecessary additional use of resources. At the same time, even Estonian e-governance visionaries agree [3, 28, 48] that a digital single market including 28 Member States would be impossible without the eIDAS, thus justifying the use of additional resources [3].

With a supranational framework, impact can be greater, as the partners of the EU are also influenced [29]. For example, when Directive 1999/93/EC was implemented, many of the neighbouring countries were guided by it while developing their digital signature acts. For example, Estonia passed its Digital Signature Act based on the directive, while still outside of the EU [28]. As businesses are keen to cooperate with the EU, the building of a successful digital common market should create the possibility of expanding internationally. Thus giving the EU an opportunity to create something innovative, giving stakeholders (e.g., the EES) the chance of reaching a significantly bigger market. Theoretically, the eIDAS could create a system where countries can use the best available e-services (e.g., the tax system created by one country, a pension system by another and a health register by a third) making e-governing remarkably more effective and cost-efficient. [29].

6 Conclusion

By analyzing the dimensions of content, context and process, we concluded that, despite some additional obligations imposed by the eIDAS, the regulation supports the national e-government's goals and domestic cross-border initiatives. Also, as the creation of digital open borders among 28 member states would be unlikely without supranational interference, we propose that it is in the interest of the member states to contribute to the fast implementation of the eIDAS. Still, as only the Estonian case was analysed, we cannot say that this would be the case in all member states. In future research, more cases need to be covered to make comprehensive conclusions.

Acknowledgements. The work of Gerli Aavik has been supported in parts by TUT Project B42. The work of Robert Krimmer has been supported in parts by TUT Project B42 and ETAG IUT19-13.

References

1. Prensky, M.: Digital natives, digital immigrants part 1. On the Horizon **9**, 1–6 (2001)
2. European Commission: Impact Assessment Accompanying the Proposal for A Regulation of the European Parliament and of the Council on Electronic Identification and Trust Services for Electronic Transactions in the Internal Market, Brussels (2012)
3. Sikkut, S.: Interview on 2015-04-13 (2015)
4. Estonian Investment Agency: e-Residency Celebrated Its First Birthday (2015)
5. Bernroider, E., Koch, S., Stix, V.: A comprehensive framework approach using content, context process views to combine methods from operations research for it assessments. Inf. Syst. Manag. **30**, 75–88 (2013)
6. Avgerou, C.: information systems: what sort of science is it? Omega **28**(5), 567–579 (2000)
7. Hardy, C.A., Williams, S.P.: Assembling e-government research designs: a transdisciplinary view and interactive. Public Adm. Rev. **71**, 405–413 (2011)
8. Stockdale, R., Standing, C.: An interpretive approach to evaluating information systems: a content, context, process framework. Eur. J. Oper. Res. **173**, 1090–1102 (2006)
9. Self, D., Armenakis, A., Schraeder, M.: Organisational change content, process, and context: a simultaneous analysis of employee reactions. J. Change Manag. **7**, 211–229 (2007)
10. Begler, E.: Wheels and straw: balancing content, process, and context in global teacher education. Theory Pract. **32**, 14–20 (1993)
11. Vaughan, F.: Transpersonal psychotherapy: context, content and process. J. Transpers. Psychol. **11**, 101–110 (1979)
12. Primm, S.A., Clark, T.W.: Making sense of the policy process for carnivore conservation. Conserv. Biol. **10**, 1036–1045 (1996)
13. Ketchen, J.D., Thomas, J., McDaniel, J.R.: Process, content and context: synergistic effects on organisational performance. J. Manag. **22**, 231–257 (1996)
14. Symons, V.J.: A review of information systems evaluation: content, context and process. Eur. J. Inf. Syst. **1**, 205–212 (1991)
15. Song, X., Letch, N.: Research on IT/IS evaluation: a 25 year review. Electron. J. Inf. Syst. Eval. **15**, 276–287 (2012)
16. Miller, D., Droge, C., Toulouse, J.-M.: Strategic process and content as mediators between organisational context and structure. Acad. Manag. J. **31**, 5 (1988)

17. Heeks, R.: E-government as a carrier of context. J. Publ. Pol. **25**, 51–74 (2005)
18. Devos, G., Buelens, M., Bouckenooghe, D.: Contribution of content, context, and process to understanding openness to organisational change: two experimental simulation studies. J. Soc. Psychol. **147**, 607–630 (2007)
19. Ongaro, E.: Explaining contextual influences on the dynamics of public management reforms: reflections on some ways forward. In: Retirement Workshop for Professor Christopher Pollitt, 29–30 March 2012, Catholic University of Leuven (K.U. Leuven) (2012)
20. Yin, R.K.: Applications of Case Study Research, 2nd edn. Sage Publications, Thousand Oaks (2003)
21. Yin, R.K.: Case Study Research: Design and Methods, 3rd edn. Sage Publications, Thousand Oaks (2003)
22. Mahoney, J., Goertz, G.: A tale of two cultures: contrasting quantitative and qualitative research. Polit. Anal. **14**, 227–249 (2006)
23. Eisenhardt, K.M.: Building theories from case study research. Acad. Manag. Rev. **14**, 532–550 (1989)
24. Flyvbjerg, B.: Five misunderstandings about case-study research. Qual. Inq. **12**, 219–245 (2006)
25. Mariotto, F., Zanni, P., De Moraes, G.: What is the use of a single-case study in management research? RAE: Revista De Administração De Empresas **54**, 358–369 (2004)
26. Rubin, H.J., Rubin, I.S.: Topical interviewing. In: Qualitative Interviewing: The Art of Hearing Data, pp. 196–225. Sage Publications, Thousand Oaks (1999)
27. Reinsalu, K.: Is Estonian local e-government responsive to citizens' needs? The case study of Tartu. Inf. Polity: Int. J. Gov. Democr. Inf. Age **11**, 255–272 (2006)
28. Pedak, M.: Interview on 2015-04-29 (2015)
29. Pihl, K.: Interview on 2015-04-24 (2015)
30. E-Estonia: E-Cabinet
31. Republic of Estonia Information Systems Authority. Finland to create a data exchange layer (2013)
32. C. Center: What is Digi-ID, How Can I Get it and What Can I Do With it (2015)
33. United Nations: E-Government Survey 2014. E-Government for the Future We Want (2014)
34. EP: Directive 1999/93/EC on a Community framework for electronic signatures (1999)
35. European Commission: European Interoperability Framework for European Public Services (2012)
36. European Parliament: Regulation No 910/2014 (2014
37. Galler, G.: Proposal for a Regulation on Electronic Identification and Trust Services for Electronic Transactions in the Internal Market (eIDAS). Progress of the Legislative Process (2013)
38. Servida, A.: IAS Study 2 - Stakeholders Workshop (2015)
39. Estonian Government Communication Unit: Estonian PM and Finnish PM Signed the World's First Digitally Signed International Agreement. Press release (2013)
40. Parliament of Estonia: Mitteresidentide digitaalse isikutunnistuse väljaandmine: e-residentsuse loomine. Kontseptsioon. Isikut tõendavate dokumentide seaduse ja riigilõivuseaduse muutmise seaduse eelnõu seletuskirja lisa 1 (2014)
41. SignWise: About SignWise. https://www.signwise.me/EE/et/p/about/about
42. Stibbe: The New Regulation on Electronic Identification and Trust Services – eIDAS (2014)
43. Kirsipuu, M.: Interview on 2015-04-20 (2015)
44. Vaarik, D.: Eesti kui Rajaleidja (2014)
45. Põder, M.: Interview on 2015-04-15 (2015)

46. Mahmood, M., Becker, J.: Effect of organisational maturity on end-users' satisfaction with information systems. J. Manag. Inf. Syst. **2**, 37–64 (1985)
47. Miyata, M.: Measuring impacts of e-government support in least developed countries: case study of the vehicle registration service in Bhutan. IT Dev. **17**, 133–152 (2011)
48. Korjus, K.: Interview on 2015-04-24 (2015)
49. Pollit, C.: Public management reform: reliable knowledge and international experience. OECD J. Budg. **3**, 121–136 (2003)

IS Acquisition Characteristics
in the Public Sector

Paula Mäki-Lohiluoma, Pasi Hellsten[✉], and Samuli Pekkola

Department of Information Management and Logistics,
Tampere University of Technology, Tampere, Finland
{Paula.makilohiluoma,
Pasi.Hellsten,Samuli.Pekkola}@tut.fi

1 Introduction

Public sector organizations aim to acquire the best possible information systems (IS) and, at the same time, comply with public procurement regulations [4]. Evidently, this task is not easy [5] as the success rate remains low [6]. This lack of success has made the public procurement of IS, its challenges, and different features an increasingly popular research topic [1–3].

These failures are often associated with the project's size [6], policies, and legislation [2], in addition to common reasons for failed IS projects [7]. However, these reasons are usually reported as project specific. Therefore, their applicability or broader understanding is debatable. A generic list of IS acquisition characteristics would provide better understanding and, thus, explain why some acquisitions fail and others succeed. This need and potential motivate our research.

Moe [2] argued that the lack of know-how in the acquisition process hinders to successful IS acquisition. This lack of expertise has several causes and consequences. For example, the vendor might not be aware of what the customer or user really wants and/or needs while the user may mistrust the vendor as the company is offering strange features and solutions [1]. Incompetent, inexperienced, and careless preparation and construction of the requirements are likely to result inauspicious tendering and procurement [8].

However, studies on the different characteristics of public IS procurement and their influence on acquisition projects are rare. This lack of research emphasizes two research needs: acquisition characteristics and their impacts. In this paper, we focus on the former. We seek answers to the question, "What are the key characteristics of a public sector IS acquisition?" To construct a taxonomy for public sector IS acquisition, we explore four public sector IS acquisition cases and classify their characteristics.

The paper is organized as follows: Sect. 2 provides the theoretical background. The following section introduces the research settings and methods. Then we briefly present our findings. The discussion section summarizes the results, and the conclusion places the paper in a broader context.

H.J. Scholl et al. (Eds.): EGOV 2016, LNCS 9820, pp. 164–175, 2016.
DOI: 10.1007/978-3-319-44421-5_13

2   Theoretical Background

Public procurement refers to the process of acquiring goods or services for a government or public organization through buying or purchasing [9]. The procurement process can be divided into five phases: specifying the requirements, tendering, selecting the vendor, contracting, and implementing and completing the process [2]. An important difference between public and private sector organizations is the question of ownership. Individuals in a society 'own' public organizations while private businesses are owned by a limited number of shareholders or entrepreneurs [10]. Furthermore, the funding for public acquisitions is based mainly on taxation. In addition, in the public sector there are fewer market-related disturbances than in the private sector [11]. The control mechanisms for the public sector are imposed by political factors and specific legislation instead of only economic factors. However, public sector organizations rarely have direct competition offering the same services [10]. These factors lay the foundation for the characteristics of all public sector organizations, but the way the characteristics occur in IS acquisitions is rarely studied.

Procuring IS differs significantly from more standardized goods or services [5]. The actual need may sometimes be challenging to recognize or articulate. The alternative solutions for needs may not always be comparable without careful analysis and operationalization. This issue applies to assessing different options and their significances [1].

A standardized, off-the-shelf information system seldom fulfills the needs of any organization without target-specific configurations. This also applies in the public sector. Therefore, fulfilling an organization's needs require customization. This often leads to outsourcing the development. As public sector organizations tend to decrease their IS departments, intensive cooperation and communication with external stakeholders are emphasized; outside vendors are seldom sufficiently familiar with the context and the operations [12]. This also applies to internal parties. An IT department in a public sector organization rarely knows or understands the use context of social services, for example. This means that when decisions about the requirement specifications and the scope must be made, the appropriate content may remain vague [13].

The procurement process itself, with its legislative restrictions and payment model and standard government contracts has several obstructions and limitations. If, for example, the call for tenders is poorly prepared, it will narrow the vendors' willingness to participate in the tendering process and to engage in the project. This will limit competition and provide fewer alternatives for the customer organization. To put it in other words, this will hinder the organization from getting the best solution or price [4, 14].

Another relevant stream of literature is IT investments. Xue et al. [15] argued that IT investments are influenced by the characteristics of the investment (scope, requirements), the external environment (competitive pressures, institutional forces, external resources), and the internal context (centralization, the IT unit's power). Premkumar and King [16] similarly emphasized organizational size, industry, planning time horizon, resources, and organizational capabilities and resources. Jones and Hughes [17] stated that the size of the IS investment has an impact on the evaluation and success of the investment. The IT investment literature thus emphasizes the role of generic characteristics in investments. However, the literature does not accentuate or differentiate the characteristics in the public sector context.

All this indicates that several characteristics frame the acquisition. However, a comprehensive list is not available, and some characteristics may actually be derived from other features. In other words, the vagueness in the requirement specification phase may originate from the organizational structures, culture, and system characteristics. Consequently, the literature, even when combined, does not comprehensively describe IS acquisition characteristics, as the research premises are derived from various perspectives and approaches in individual studies.

3   Research Setting

3.1   Research Methods

This study follows a qualitative collective case study [18] approach in which the cases might "be similar or dissimilar, redundancy and variety [are] each important. They are chosen because it is believed that understanding them will lead to better understanding, perhaps better theorizing, about a still larger collection of cases" [19, p. 437]. Four cases were selected according to their type (public sector IS acquisition) and appropriate project phase (the acquisition activities had ended and the system implementation had either just been completed or was ongoing). Two cases appeared to be successful IS acquisitions while two cases faced major problems. The unit of analysis is a case.

The data was collected by interviewing every key person in each project in a semi-structured interview. The list of cases and interviewees is presented in Table 1. The interviewees were chosen by snowball sampling [20, pp. 816–817]. The first interviewee was selected by our contact, after which we deliberately asked the interviewees about other stakeholders to interview later. The interviews, approximately an hour each, were conducted in spring 2014 face-to-face at the interviewees' premises. The interviews followed the thematic open interview approach in which a general frame was modified according to the interviewees' state and status. We wanted to gain an in-depth understanding of how the project proceeded and its details.

The cases were analyzed by utilizing grounded theory [21] as the coding method. This means that the data was coded several times. In this paper, we do not intend to develop a theory, as is often the case with grounded theory [22]. Instead, we investigate a collection of open and axial codes as characteristics of IS acquisition. This means that two authors analyzed the data by first identifying distinct characteristics of each case (open coding) and then revised the codes several times until they were harmonized. Finally, similar codes were grouped into larger groups and labeled with appropriate names (axial coding). These groups, with representative examples, are presented in the discussion.

3.2   The Cases

The four public sector IS acquisition cases are briefly described in Table 1.

Table 1. Descriptions of the cases

	Case A	Case B	Case C	Case D
Acquisition organization	Maternity Ward in a Hospital District	Municipal Dental Care	Municipal Social Welfare Sector, Home Care Unit	Municipal Social Services, Income Support Division
Participating parties	10 Hospital districts' maternity wards and IT departments, Commonly owned ICT Provider, third-party Consultant	Ministry, National Institute for Health and Welfare, IT department, Dental Care	Municipal IT department, Procurement department	Municipal IT department, Income Support Division
Acquisition object	New maternity care IS to cover non-institutional and specialized healthcare	New dental patient system including connection to a national database as a national pilot project	Two systems: one including door opening application and mobile devices and the other for organizing and optimizing work	Vendor's offered electronic application handling component of an existing system
Number of interviews	5	5	10	4
Interviewees according to organization	**Hospital district:** CIO, Chief Medical Officer **ICT provider:** Project Manager **Vendor:** Product Manager Salesperson	**Dental Care:** Chief Dental Officer **IT department:** Project Coordinator **The National Institute for Health and Welfare:** Supervisor **Vendor:** Product Manager, Salesperson	**Home Care Unit:** Project Manager, Supervisor, Supervisor, Care person, Labor Organizer **IT department:** Agreement Specialist, Project Coordinator **Social Welfare Sector:** Process Manager **Vendor:** Project Manager	**Income support division:** Division's Director, Superior **IT department:** Project Manager **ICT Provider:** Person in Charge

The Case A acquisition was initiated by one hospital district, but the acquisition was broadened to cover multiple hospital districts in the end. The interviewees were selected from the initial hospital district. The Case B acquisition had strong political supervision as the acquisition was initiated by the Ministry of Social Affairs and Health. The ministry stated that all public dental care systems had to be connected to the national database. This project was coordinated by the National Institute for Health and Welfare that launched a call for piloting projects. The case municipality applied for the pilot project and received guidance and funding from the institute. The Case C acquisition was complex with multiple components. The acquisition encountered severe challenges when the losing vendors sued the municipality in market court. The market court, to which disputed public sector case parties may appeal, ruled the tendering process had been unlawful, derived from the ambiguous terms used in the requirement specification. Case D was the least problematic acquisition, as the income support division had just purchased a complete IS. Cases A and C had to be tendered by legislation, while Cases B and D were not tendered.

4 Empirical Findings

The data analysis depicted 19 recurring characteristics in the public sector IS acquisitions. These characteristics were present in all cases, although, because of space limitations, only an example from one case illustrates each characteristic.

Assuming Uniformity. In all cases, the stakeholders assumed that equivalent services, provided by public sector organizations, would have identical processes elsewhere. It was thus assumed that an IS utilized in one public sector organization could be easily copied and replicated elsewhere. For example, in Case A, the project manager stated, "As a whole, the processes are relatively similar." The chief information officer (CIO) stated, "In the beginning, we agreed on conducting a specification project, in which we describe the process, general requirements, and architecture to a maternity care system. We stated that there are ten hospital districts; it would be good to get them all involved in this." As the project included two isolated departments, with separate IS, inside the hospital districts, the chief medical officer stated, "The idea was to deliberately achieve non-institutional and specialized healthcare under the same model." These assumptions created challenges for the vendor, as the municipalities participating in the joint acquisition had diverse needs. "We cannot start always carrying out the requests. He says so. We do it. The next one says no, we want it in this way" (Case A, Product Manager).

Creating a Consortium. In Case A, the CIO and the chief medical officer saw the opportunity to create a consortium with multiple hospital districts to leverage their bargaining power with the vendor. "Our aim was a joint acquisition with economies of scale. We wanted to get the vendor to bend for better conditions and thus gain work of better quality" (Case A, CIO). "The idea was that we would have had a national project, and we would have been big enough a counter-power to these companies in negotiation positions" (Case A, Chief Medical Officer). Thus, the acquisition was a joint acquisition for multiple hospital districts.

In other cases, the acquisitions were not jointly conducted, but they had features of similar consortium acquisitions. For example, in Case D, the IS was developed by the customer group with members from multiple municipalities using the same system. "They had a working group, which met every now and then. Municipalities presented requests to the vendor and disclosed in what direction they are moving" (Case D, Division Director).

IS Acquisition Complexity. Single IS acquisitions are connected to multiple divisions or even municipalities. In Case A, the new IS covered two maternity wards' departments in multiple hospital districts. The bases, needs, and processes differed in the municipalities. "Every hospital district could, in their own time, in their own schedule, take the tendered system into use" (the CIO). The diversity between the clients increases the complexity of the IS.

Divided Decision Making. In Case A, in which the acquisition was carried out by a consortium, decision making was divided among multiple hospital districts. "It actually ended so that because every district had an equal decision-maker, we did not achieve a common mindset" (Case A, CIO).

Steering and Working Groups. Every case had multiple stakeholder groups: steering and planning groups and project groups. In addition, Case C had working groups for different specialties, e.g., security and telecommunication. In Case B, there were isolated user, steering, project, and testing groups. This created problems although the groups made decisions, gave statements, and provided information. The project manager (Case B) stated, "I do not know who makes the final decision about the acquisition; there has to be probably a kind of steering group which has made the decision."

Initial Idea Derived from Operations. In three cases, the acquisition idea was initiated by a non-IT employee. "The need arises always from the substance, I mean from the labor and delivery room, child health center, and hospital wards" (Case A, Product Manager).

Idea Is Carried Out by IT Department. In all cases, IT departments conveyed the idea forward. "Business units usually tell their own IT departments their needs because budgeting is their responsibility. They always have the budget" (Case A, Product Manager). The IT department is then assumed to gain approval for the acquisitions. "A proposal was written to IT department [...], and then [they] launched the acquisition as they should" (Case C, Project Manager).

Political Forces. In Case B, the initial idea was not launched by the business unit but by a ministry. The acquisition topic was going to be mandatory sooner or later. "This IS acquisition has been like 'implement it or else..'" (Case B, Project Coordinator). Political forces thus strongly influenced the case. Similarly, in Case D, legislation and the municipality's council directed the acquisition. In the public sector, political aspects and agendas affect decision making as the voices of various task forces and teams must be heard before decisions about specific points are made. Political forces were thus evident.

Detailed Requirement Specification. In Cases B and D, the requirements were not specified by the organizations doing the acquisition. Instead, the requirements were either steered by national requirements (Case B) or set by a superficially configured product (Case D). Legislation required no tendering. In Case A, the hospital district employed a commonly and publicly owned ICT provider to lead and coordinate the IS acquisition. In addition, the provider employed a consultant to help specify the requirements: "We actually had multiple user groups: doctors, midwives, non-institutional side, nurses, secretaries, everyone defining how this system should be used. All of this was written down, and then we negotiated multiple times and refined the specification" (Case A, Chief Medical Officer). The time-consuming phase resulted in the requirement specification being partly indefinite and partly a detailed trade-off of diverse needs. Case C was similar as legislation necessitated formal tendering. Detailed and thorough requirement specification steered the tendering process and vendor selection. Specifying the requirements was equally time-consuming.

Burden of Existing Systems. In all cases, the organizational IS had a long history. In Cases A, B, and D, the acquisition was an update or an add-on to existing systems. In Case C, the system was meant to be built from the scratch, although the organization had a similar system. In all cases, the interfaces with existing systems caused significant problems. "We don't practically have any other options than [vendor's name], because we use their systems" (Case D, Division's Director). Consequently, existing legacy systems were burdens.

Only a Few Potential Vendors in the Market. Existing systems and closed interfaces led to situations in which the organization had only a few potential vendors or only one in Cases B and D. In addition, the size of the acquisitions in Cases A and C reduced the number of potential vendors. In contrast, the smaller acquisitions in Cases B and D were updates and add-ons, which made the current vendor an obvious candidate. Although the interfaces did not bind the client to the vendor, the customers relied on a well-known vendor if tendering was not required, as in Case B. "Our experts have been strongly participating in [existing patient system] with [vendor's name], and we know it inside out, its pros and cons. We know how to use it, and we have stated that it is workable. It is possible that we didn't want to take the risk to end up in something worse" (Case B, Project Coordinator).

Seeking Preliminary Information. All acquisition organizations sought information before the acquisition. In Case D, a business unit representative was assigned to explore customer needs. "His task was to carry out a customer survey and explore customers' willingness patronize electronically and their technical premises, possible support needs" (Case D, Division's Director). In Case C, the "IT department purchased a preliminary report, and in the report, they collected the current situation of home care. They had various workshops and interviews for different user groups" (Project Manager). The acquisition organization also requested information from possible vendors about technical solutions to specify the requirements.

Mapping Processes. In all cases, the processes that would be connected to the upcoming IS were mapped and described. The mindset was to get a system to support the processes, not vice versa. "I understand that we have to change the age-old healthcare processes and bend them to certain limit according to the IS, but we have some core processes, which we won't bend; the IS has to bend" (Case A, Chief Medical Officer). This task was executed internally, although different parties participated.

Lack of Resources in the IT Department. A person from the IT department acted as the project manager or coordinator in every acquisition. However, the role was taken on in addition to other projects and tasks. "I acted as the project manager in addition to my own job" (Case D, Project Manager). The IT department and project sizes and competencies varied. "We have, in the IT department, one technical person, who is me, and then I have four people, nurses and social workers, on a team" (Case A, CIO). The lack of resources became visible to other parties.

Innovation Is Derived from Individuals. The initial ideas were launched or highlighted by individuals. For example, in Case A: "As we know, all good ideas derive from a bar encounter. So did this, so we had many years ago, a hospital's chief medical officer's meeting, and later in the evening, we sat with the boys and a couple of ladies at the bar. We stated that we had a common factor, and it is this IS. We noted that it was reaching its end, and we needed a new one" (Chief Medical Officer). Individuals' personal formal and informal contributions seem to be remarkable factors in hatching and launching ideas. Only in Case B was the idea launched and driven by political bodies. However, there was an individual at the function who took the idea forward.

Competency. Acquisition competence was distributed to multiple organizations and departments. This is displayed vividly in Case C: "Home care people do the practical specifications. Then the specifications go to the IT department, because the users know only how to say 'I don't want the hatch to open,' so the IT department knows how to define it in requirement form—and then we have dialogue about all the requirements. We have a work distribution so that we [the procurement department] provide after that all the economic conditions for the tendering" (Case C, Procurement Specialist).

Dedicated Procurement Organization. Cases A and C had a dedicated procurement organization for the tendering phase. In Case A, the organization was an external information and communications technology (ICT) provider and in Case C an internal procurement organization. Sometimes, this style caused problems as the business units did not understand tendering, and the procurement organization did not understand the business: "It was outside my expertise. I did the requirements. The tendering part did not interest me" (Case A, Chief Medical Officer). The procurement specialist (Case C) stated, "We do not know diddly-squat about home care."

IT Department Owns the Contract. The IT department always owned the contracts. It even seemed obvious. Other units did not seem to be interested in the contracts or were not allowed to participate in the contract phase. "Of course, the responsibility for the contracts is in the IT department" (Case C, Project Manager).

Distant Funding. Funding the acquisitions was not a question in the cases. Interviewees mentioned that the acquisition was budgeted for and approved by different steering groups. The main actors did not seem to worry about the funding, especially in the business units. "The costs were never actually a problem; I think they were no driver here. We're talking about tens of thousands of euros. When I think about the hospital's expenses, it equals a few hip surgeries" (Case A, Chief Medical Officer). The IT departments negotiated the prices although the funding was not discussed.

5 Discussion

Our findings indicate that all public sector organizations sought to collaborate as bigger units in the beginning of the IS acquisition [23]. However, the cases demonstrate that the advantages of volume did not materialize; instead, the opposite occurred as the complexity of the acquisition increased [24]. Volume created problems in Case A. For example, they received only three bids from the major actors in the national ICT field. This reduced the number of potential solutions significantly. In addition, although the municipalities provided seemingly similar services, the organizations and processes differed. Here, joint acquisition increased complexity as diverse needs, processes, and actors had to be considered. This complexity increased the number of non-decision-making groups whose opinions and statements were still valued, which caused time delays and overlap in conferring with the various parties. Then, as decision making was distributed among multiple equal parties, no one was in charge. Therefore, larger consortia seem to create more problems instead of providing the advantages of volume.

The IS acquisitions were initiated by business units and their senior managers. Then the idea was presented to the internal IT department. This is a bottom-up approach. Although in Case B the idea originated from political parties (the top-down approach), it was opportunistically adopted by the business unit and the IT department. Together, they presented the proposal to several steering groups for support and funding. The cases indicate that no matter where the idea for the acquisition originated, the role of individuals is emphasized.

Planning the acquisition depends on the need for tendering. In the cases in which tendering was required, the requirement specifications were done carefully: The processes were mapped and described in detail. In addition, different actors participated in specifying the requirements. However, although the requirements were accurate from the individual actors' viewpoints, no one considered the big picture (c.f. [1]). In cases where tendering was not required, the planning phase was not clear. The customer did not explore alternative vendors but simply acquired the system from a well-known vendor with which the customer had an existing relationship. Thus, the need to tender forced the acquisition organization to explore different solutions, map their processes, and commit the business personnel to create accurate requirement specifications.

The acquisition parties included the business unit, the IT department, and, in some cases, a separate procurement organization. An external procurement consultant is an ICT acquisition specialist while an internal consultant is in charge of all kinds of acquisitions. Thus, the parties' competences vary. In some cases, the acquisition was carried out by only the business unit and the IT department which had appropriate experience and competence. Then no tendering was required. The IT department took an active role, usually with an assigned technical project manager or coordinator. However, the employee often had multiple concurrent projects, lessening his or her commitment and participation. Sometimes, a business unit representative was also assigned to the project to provide an operational perspective. Although the participants might have the necessary knowledge and competence, they were divided into multiple units and working groups, and each group represented its own field. This makes information sharing difficult as understanding others and their specialties is not supported [1]. No one understands the big picture. Table 2 groups the characteristics of public sector IS acquisitions into six groups.

Table 2. Grouping of characteristics

Grouping	Characteristics
Size	Assuming uniformity
	Creating a consortium
	IS acquisition complexity
	Divided decision making
Dispersed groups	Steering and working groups
	Isolated procurement organization
	Competency
	Distant funding
Comprehensive preparation	Detailed requirement specification
	Seeking preliminary information
	Mapping processes
IT department's central role	Idea is promoted by the IT department
	Lack of resources in the IT department
	IT department owns the contract
Driving forces	Political forces
	Project is carried out by individuals
	Initial idea is derived from operations
Market/Locking in a vendor	Only a few possible vendors in the market
	The burden of existing systems

Although tendering was often carried out by a separate procurement organization, the business unit and the IT department evaluated the bids and selected the vendor. After the vendor was selected, the procurement organization withdrew from contracting and transferred the responsibility to the IT department. The lengthy contracting phase, including the negotiation of prices and conditions as the most challenging aspects, was carried out by the IT department. Surprisingly, no one worried about funding.

6   Conclusion

We have provided a list of public sector IS acquisition characteristics. Our analysis indicated 18 common characteristics: assuming the uniformity of municipalities and divisions, creating a consortium, IS acquisition complexity, divided decision making, steering and working groups, initial idea derived from operations, idea is carried out by the IT department, political forces, detailed requirement specification, locking in a vendor, seeking preliminary information, mapping processes, lack of resources in the IT department, innovation is derived from individuals, competency, isolated procurement organization, the IT department owns the contract, and distant funding. These characteristics were categorized into six groups: size, dispersed groups, comprehensive preparation, IT unit's central role, driving forces, and market/locking in a vendor.

Size seemed especially challenging. Joint tendered acquisitions seem to displace smaller vendors. This contradicts Moe's [2] need for the technologically best solutions. As tendering is costly and time-consuming, the public sector pays a higher price for the acquisition and then tenders it again. This is not necessarily in line with the need for the most economical alternative. All this reduces the public sector's bargaining power and even their know-how, allowing the major vendors to dominate the tendering and contracting phases. As non-tendered acquisitions are often made with a well-known vendor, the public sector organizations get locked in to vendors, increasing their monopoly.

Our findings provide an explanation of the IS acquisition characteristics in the public sector. This list helps researchers and practitioners understand the context and challenges. These characteristics also help organizations anticipate different emerging features in IS acquisitions. However, these characteristics should be further studied as we did not focus on influences and impacts.

One limitation is that the country in which the study took place is largely dominated by two to four vendors. Therefore, smaller, sometimes more innovative, vendors are often excluded from tendering. This exclusion may have implications for various characteristics. In addition, the selection of the cases may have caused limitations. The number of cases was small (4), and they are mainly in the health and social security sector. Whether the findings are generalizable to other areas of societal infrastructure, such as building and housing, or other acquisitions, remains debatable, and necessitates further research.

References

1. Alanne, A., Hellsten, P., Pekkola, S., Saarenpää, I.: Three positives make one negative: public sector IS procurement. In: Tambouris, E., et al. (eds.) EGOV 2015. LNCS, vol. 9248, pp. 321–333. Springer, Heidelberg (2015)
2. Moe, C.E.: Research on public procurement of information systems: the need for a process approach. Commun. Assoc. Inf. Syst. **34**(1), 78 (2014)
3. Pan, S.C.G., Mehta, M., Seow, P.S.: Information systems procurement process risk and control: insights from a public sector organization. Account. Bus Public Interest **11**, 123 (2012)
4. Moe, C.E., Risvand, A.C., Sein, M.K.: Limits of public procurement: information systems acquisition. In: Wimmer, M.A., Scholl, H.J., Grönlund, Å., Andersen, K.V. (eds.) EGOV 2006. LNCS, vol. 4084, pp. 281–292. Springer, Heidelberg (2006)
5. Moe, C.E., Päivärinta, T.: Challenges in information systems procurement in the public sector. Electron. J. E-Gov. **11**(1), 307–322 (2013)

6. Goldfinch, S.: Pessimism, computer failure, and information systems development in the public sector. Public Adm. Rev. **67**(5), 917–929 (2007)
7. Gauld, R.: Public sector information system project failures: lessons from a New Zealand hospital organization. Gov. Inf. Q. **24**(1), 102–114 (2007)
8. Johansson, B., Lahtinen, M.: Requirement specification in Government IT procurement. Procedia Technol. **5**, 369–377 (2012)
9. Hommen, L., Rolfstam, M.: Public procurement and innovation: towards a taxonomy. J. Public Procure. **9**(1), 17 (2009)
10. Boyne, G.: Public and private management: what's the difference? J. Manag. Stud. **39**, 97–122 (2002)
11. Flak, L.S., Rose, J.: Stakeholder governance: adapting stakeholder theory to e-government. Commun. Assoc. Inf. Syst. **16**(1), 31 (2005)
12. Alanne, A., Pekkola, S.: Riding for a fall in outsourced ISD: knowledge transfer challenges between the onshore vendor and the offshored unit. In: Proceedings of the 9th Global Sourcing Workshop, La Thuile, Italia (2015)
13. Saarinen, T., Vepsäläinen, A.P.: Procurement strategies for information systems. J. Manag. Inf. Syst. **11**, 187–208 (1994)
14. Doshi, B.: The new OGC guidance: the future roadmap for government IT procurement. Comput. Law Secur. Rev. **21**(4), 344–348 (2005)
15. Xue, Y., Liang, H., Boulton, W.R.: Information technology governance in information technology investment decision processes: the impact of investment characteristics, external environment, and internal context. MIS Q. **15**, 67–96 (2008)
16. Premkumar, G., King, W.R.: Organizational characteristics and information systems planning: an empirical study. Inf. Syst. Res. **5**(2), 75–109 (1994)
17. Jones, S., Hughes, J., et al.: Understanding IS evaluation as a complex social process: a case study of a UK local authority. Eur. J. Inf. Syst. **10**(4), 189–203 (2001)
18. Stake, R.E.: Multiple Case Study Analysis. Guilford Press, New York (2013)
19. Denzin, N.K., Lincoln, Y.S.: Handbook of Qualitative Research. Sage Publications Inc., London (1994)
20. Morgan, D.L.: The Sage encyclopedia of qualitative research methods (2008)
21. Corbin, J.M., Strauss, A.: Grounded theory research: procedures, canons, and evaluative criteria. Qual. Sociol. **13**(1), 3–21 (1990)
22. Urquhart, C.: Grounded Theory for Qualitative Research: A Practical Guide. Sage, London (2012)
23. Johnson, P.F., Leenders, M.R., McCue, C.: A comparison of purchasing's organizational roles and responsibilities in the public and private sector. J. Public Procure. **3**(1), 57 (2003)
24. Zollo, M., Singh, H.: Deliberate learning in corporate acquisitions: post-acquisition strategies and integration capability in U.S. bank mergers. Strateg. Manag. J. **25**(13), 1233–1256 (2004)

E-Government Challenges: Methods Supporting Qualitative and Quantitative Analysis

Catherine G. Mkude[1] and Maria A. Wimmer[2(✉)]

[1] Department of ICT, The Open University of Tanzania,
P.O. Box 23409, Dar es Salaam, Tanzania
catherine.mkude@out.ac.tz
[2] Institute for IS Research, University of Koblenz-Landau,
Universitätsstr. 1, 56070 Koblenz, Germany
wimmer@uni-koblenz.de

Abstract. To develop robust and achievable e-government strategies that build the grounds for sustainable solutions, decision makers need to have a good understanding of their country's socio-economic, political and legal contexts. Particularly, they need to be well aware about challenges that might hinder successful implementation of their strategy. To make valuable contributions in e-government strategy development, analysis of e-government challenges needs to be comprehensive and informative by including insights of qualitative and quantitative analysis. Although numerous studies in e-government challenges exist, they fail to do a systematic and structured qualitative analysis of the challenges in regards to interdependencies among challenges or to measure the wider impact of challenges. Methods to support such a comprehensive analysis are scarce. In this contribution, we propose a novel mix of three methods for qualitative and quantitative analysis of e-government challenges, combining the PESTELMO analysis method, DEMATEL and ANP. The results show that this mixed approach is suitable and significant to provide the complementarity needed for a comprehensive understanding of e-government challenges.

Keywords: E-government strategy planning · PESTELMO · DEMATEL · ANP · E-government challenges · Interdependencies · Qualitative/quantitative analysis

1 Introduction

Governments around the world strive for sustainable development of their economy, societies and welfare, and of their environments. The contributions of e-government to support governments in transforming towards better public service delivery, greater interaction between their citizens and government, and improving the efficiency of public organisations while saving taxpayers' money are well received [6, 7]. The new

© IFIP International Federation for Information Processing 2016
Published by Springer International Publishing Switzerland 2016. All Rights Reserved
H.J. Scholl et al. (Eds.): EGOV 2016, LNCS 9820, pp. 176–187, 2016.
DOI: 10.1007/978-3-319-44421-5_14

eGovernment Action Plan 2016-2020 of the EU commits the Member States to continue investments in e-government to modernise public administrations, to promote
open data and to enhance cross-border and cross-sector interoperability.[1] With this
Action Plan, the EU and the Member States continue to deploy innovative measures to
reduce administrative burdens to citizens and businesses. For administrative burdens
reduction, the Action Plan will include the implementation of the Once-Only principle,
and in turn generate saving at EU level of approx. 5 billion Euro per year by 2017.[2]
Hence, e-government is expected to help resolve the complex and multi-faceted
challenges embodied with achieving above ultimate goals.

To continue leveraging on the advantages of implementing e-government, governments in developed and developing countries make significant investments to
develop and implement e-government strategies. E-government strategy planning and
analysis form necessary and fundamental steps to ensure that the investments yield the
expected outcomes. Responsible authorities need to ensure they formulate
well-grounded, robust and achievable e-government strategies. To do this, the
responsible authorities need to be aware of their countries' context and, in particular,
about the challenges that might hinder realisation of the strategies.

Several studies on e-government challenges exist, which look into challenges
encountered at different levels of government in developed countries (see e.g. [1–3, 5,
26]) and in developing countries (see e.g. [11, 13, 14, 20]). Two important weaknesses
are observed in these studies (see detailed analysis of the studies in Sect. 2). The first
weakness is a lack of a systematic structuring of the challenges. This way of representing the challenges, i.e. without any systematic structuring, does not inform decision
makers about the challenges in depth. For example, some challenges are political and
others are economic, which need to be understood and dealt with differently. Some
challenges may be interdependent, such as the lack of available telecommunication
infrastructure may be based on a weak economy and the lack of financial resources.
Second, the existing studies in e-government challenges do not include a quantitative
analysis of the challenges. In lacking a quantitative analysis, the studies do not provide
insights into how the challenges could be measured in order to determine their weights
and importance (of the challenges).

From these weaknesses, we argue that it is not sufficient for decision makers to only
be aware of e-government challenges in their countries. The decision makers also need
to know about existing interdependencies among these challenges, which can be
identified through a systematic structuring of the challenges. Furthermore, the decision
makers need to be able to quantitatively evaluate the interdependencies among the
challenges. Therefore, the existing mere representation of the challenges needs to be
extended to include qualitative and quantitative analyses.

In this paper, we introduce a novel methodical mix of analysing e-government
challenges through qualitative and quantitative methods. By combining the two types
of empirical analyses, the decision makers' understanding of e-government challenges

---

[1] https://ec.europa.eu/digital-agenda/en/news/egovernment-action-plan-2016-2020-public-
consultation-faq [Last accessed on 22 February 2016].
[2] Ibid.

will be deepened, and this can enhance their decision making processes during strategy formulation. Additionally, the analyses will support decision makers in developing sustainable and better solutions for addressing the challenges through a better understanding of their interdependencies. In consequence, decision makers can make more informed and grounded decisions on what might or might not work in long term considering the existing challenges and, especially, the interdependencies among them. Accordingly, the contribution is directed towards e-government strategy planners and analysts to support them in making more informed decisions when formulating e-government strategies. The paper also demonstrates the value-add of using the different methods and the complementarity needed for a comprehensive understanding of e-government challenges. The paper is exploratory and it applies literature review and the lessons learned from previous research work to achieve its objectives.

The remainder of the paper is as follows: Sect. 2 sets the grounds of the research and provides insights into existing analysis of e-government challenges. Based on this, Sect. 2 elaborates the need for methods to support qualitative and quantitative analysis of e-government challenges. Section 3 presents the selected methods for qualitative and quantitative analysis of e-government challenges and explains their application and combination. The value-add of the presented methods is reflected in the discussion of the findings in Sect. 4. Section 4 also concludes the paper and provides directions for future research.

2   Setting the Grounds and Related Work

An e-government strategy defines a set of actions that are to be carried out in programmes and projects in order to realise the vision set by a government [12, 19, 22]. E-government strategy development involves processes through which decision makers derive strategic actions. For effective development of an e-government strategy, decision makers need to have a good understanding of their countries' context, i.e. of aspects such as politics and democracy, economy, culture, people, infrastructure etc. For example, the decision makers need to take into account the political sphere and existing democratic processes when developing an e-government strategy and its objectives. In analysing the context of their countries, the decision makers need to particularly identify and analyse e-government challenges that exist in their countries ([10] p. 123). Only then, it is possible to develop a strategy that is robust and achievable and to invest in e-government solutions that are sustainable.

Scanning the literature reveals that e-government challenges are either categorised in certain groups or mentioned without any categorisation. This section reviews and compares eleven studies in order to identify any pattern, in which e-government challenges are analysed. The aims are to provide insights into the existing analysis of e-government challenges in literature and to identify research gaps. From these gaps, the section emphasises the need for using different methods to support systematic qualitative and quantitative analyses of e-government challenges.

Table 1 presents the eleven studies that investigate e-government challenges in developed and developing countries and that are published in 2009 or later. Table 1 also provides insights into the number of challenges mentioned by each of the studies and whether any scheme has been applied to categorise the challenges. Six out of eleven studies mention less than ten challenges, and among them, the one by Belachew [4] has categorised the challenges. The other five studies list between eleven and thirty-two challenges. Among these, only Sæbø [15] does not provide a systematisation through categories.

Among the common categories shown in Table 1, the following occur at minimum 3 times: organisational (institutional), technological (infrastructure), social, political,

Table 1. Literature studies on e-government challenges with insights into the number of challenges mentioned and categorisation of the challenges

Literature sources (sorted alphabetically)	Year of publication	No. of key challenges mentioned	Are the challenges categorised? (Yes/No), and if Yes, what categories are used?	
Angelopoulos et al. [1]	2010	6	No	
Anthopoulos et al. [2]	2015	9	No	
Asogwa [3]	2012	8	No	
Belachew [4]	2010	7	Yes	Infrastructure; Human resources; Standards, guidelines and legal issues; Leadership commitment; Public-private partnership
Bhuiyan [5]	2010	7	No	
Mkude [10] (embarking on Yüksel's PESTEL method [25])[a]	2016	32	Yes	Political; Economic; Socio-cultural; Technological; Environmental; Legal; Managerial and organisational
Nkohkwo and Islam [13]	2013	20	Yes	Financial; Organisational; Political; Socio-economic; Human resources; Infrastructure
Rashid and Rahman [14]	2010	11	Yes	Institutional; Resource-related; Access-related; Legal
Sæbø [15]	2012	11	No	
Schuppan [20]	2009	20	Yes	Political; Social and demographic; Economy; Infrastructure; Institutional/organisational
Zhao et al. [26]	2012	4	No	

[a]An earlier version is published in Mkude and Wimmer [11], which is not yet including the category'managerial and organisational' challenges.

legal and economic. The results depict a lack of a common scheme for categorising the challenges. This gap is contributed by a lack of a systematic method to qualitatively analyse and structure e-government challenges.

In addition, the studies investigated in Table 1 do not investigate the interdependencies among the challenges, except the study of Mkude [10] (see also [11]). The investigation of the interdependencies among e-government challenges is a nascent subject in e-government literature, which is conceptualised in [10, 11] – embarking on Yüksel's PESTEL method [25] – and grounded in the mutual influence of challenges. In this regard, the authors also argue that a holistic analysis of e-government challenges is needed to enhance our understanding of the challenges. Through such an analysis, it is possible to assess whether the challenges influence each other and to measure the interdependencies. It is also possible to determine any causal relationships among the challenges. As a step forward towards addressing this weakness, the authors propose the use of PESTEL [11], which is amended with managerial and organisational challenges to PESTELMO ([10] p. 72), to analyse, identify and structure e-government challenges in a holistic way so to support the assessment of the interdependencies (cf. Sect. 3.1 for more details on the method).

A third weakness identified is that none of the studies investigated in Table 1 provides means to quantitatively analyse the challenges identified therein. None of the eleven studies indicates any metrics to evaluate and weigh the challenges in order to prioritise them in decision making. Accordingly, we identify the need to add quantitative aspects in the analysis of e-government challenges.

To tackle the identified weaknesses towards a comprehensive analysis of e-government challenges, we propose a mix of qualitative and quantitative analysis methods as introduced in the next section.

3   Methods Supporting Qualitative and Quantitative Analysis of E-Government Challenges

The analysis of e-government challenges forms a crucial part in e-government strategy planning and development (cf. Sect. 2). Decision makers need to go beyond being aware of existing political and legal challenges. They need to have a profound understanding, if such challenges influence one another, and what will be the impacts of any interdependencies among these challenges. To achieve such an understanding, we propose a mix of the PESTELMO (Political, Economic, Socio-cultural, Technological, Environmental, Legal, Managerial and Organisational) analysis method [10], DEMATEL (Decision Making Trial and Evaluation Laboratory) [21, 24, 25] and ANP (Analytic Network Process) [25]. This methodical mix supports in carrying out a comprehensive analysis of e-government challenges to better inform decision making in e-government strategy development. The rationale for this combination is driven by the research aim, which is to provide means for comprehensive and more meaningful analysis of e-government challenges (see Sects. 1 and 2).

Based on a literature review, insights from the authors' previous work (see [10, 11] and the objective of this research, the above three methods were identified as most appropriate to ensure the complementarity needed to achieve the aim of the research.

The methodical mix combines qualitative and quantitative analysis methods. Qualitative analysis involves a systematic identification and structuring of e-government challenges encountered in a country. We propose the PESTELMO analysis method for this as the first step of analysing e-government challenges. Then, the structured challenges are analysed quantitatively to investigate interdependencies and to weigh the challenges and interdependencies. First, the interdependencies among the challenges are analysed using the DEMATEL method. Second, the weights of the challenges and the interdependencies among them are calculated using the ANP. The methods DEMATEL and ANP are widely used to solve complicated problems in Multiple Criteria Decision Making (MCDM) [24, 25]. The methods allow decision makers to determine and measure the interrelations among different criteria/alternatives with respect to their effects in decision making. The methods have been used to solve many problems in different fields such as project selection, product planning, development of marketing strategies and safety problems [8, 9, 21, 24]). Subsequently, the objectives of the methods and their functions in the analysis of e-government challenges are described.

3.1 PESTELMO Analysis Method: Identifying and Structuring Challenges

To identify and structure e-government challenges in a systematic way, the PESTELMO analysis method is proposed. PESTELMO embarks on PESTEL [25] and extends the method with managerial and organisational categories (MO), therewith stressing the importance of these two aspects in holistic e-government strategy development and implementation. In relying on the PESTEL method, organisations and decision makers are supported in analysing their internal and external environments in which they operate [25] and in determining the context, in which the e-government strategy is expected to be implemented.

The steps for the application of the PESTELMO analysis method are as follows:

1. *Identify e-government challenges*. In this step, decision makers identify challenges that might hinder successful implementation of an e-government strategy. To identify the challenges, qualitative analysis methods such as interviews, surveys and desk research are used. In this step, the research can already be designed in line with the eight categories of PESTELMO (political, economic, socio-cultural, technological, environmental, legal, managerial and organisational).
2. *Categorise the challenges into PESTELMO* (if not yet categorised after step 1).
3. *Form a hierarchical model of PESTELMO* to depict the challenges in PESTELMO's categories as shows in Fig. 1. The first level of the model contains a title of the model (the decision makers specify in (N) the name of a country or an organisation). The second level of the model contains the main categories of PESTELMO. The third level contains the challenges identified in step 1. This level depicts the work done in step 2 graphically.

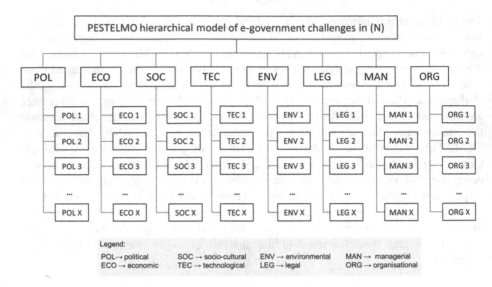

Fig. 1. PESTELMO hierarchical model of e-government challenges

Following these three steps, the decision makers will have a hierarchical model of systematically structured e-government challenges. These steps complete a qualitative analysis of the challenges.

Next, the quantitative analysis follows using DEMATEL and ANP in order to determine existing interdependencies among the identified challenges and to provide decision makers the priority values of the challenges and the interdependencies.

3.2 DEMATEL: Analysing Interdependencies Among E-Government Challenges

DEMATEL is a method to identify interdependencies and interrelations among the criteria/alternatives being studied through a causal diagram and to determine the degree of influence of the criteria [21, 24, 25]. DEMATEL supports in handling the inner dependencies within a set of criteria through a visual structural model [21, 23]. We propose DEMATEL to support a comprehensive assessment of the interrelations, interdependencies and causal relations among e-government challenges and to determine the degree of influence of the challenges. The method is widely used in different applications in MCDM (see e.g. [21, 23–25]). In e-government strategy development, the method supports decision makers to make more informed strategy decisions and to find sustainable solutions for the challenges to be resolved.

The proposed steps for using DEMATEL are as follows (cf. [21, 23–25]):

1. *Calculate the initial average matrix.* This step requires evaluation of the degree of direct influence between the identified e-government challenges by experts on a scale 0–4, where the higher value indicates greater influence. The results from each respondent then produces a matrix stated as $X^k = [X_{ij}^k]$, where k is the number of

experts involved in the study with $1 \leq k \leq H$, and i and j are different challenges. The average matrix is then produced through the mean of the same challenges in the various matrices of the experts. The average matrix A is represented as the following equation:

$$a_{ij} = \frac{1}{H} \sum_{k=1}^{H} x_{ij}^{k} \tag{1}$$

2. Calculate the normalised initial direct-relation matrix. The initial direct matrix D is normalised by D = AxS, where S is:

$$S = \frac{1}{\max\limits_{1 \leq i \leq n} \sum_{j=1}^{n} a_{ij}} \tag{2}$$

Where n is the total number of e-government challenges identified and each element in matrix D falls between 1 and 0.

3. *Derive the direct and indirect influence matrix T by $T = D(I-D)^{-1}$, where I is the* nxn identity matrix. In T, the sum of rows and the sum of columns are represented by vectors r and c, respectively. r_i denotes the row sum of the ith row of matrix T and shows the sum of direct and indirect effects of challenge i on the other challenges. Similarly, c_j denotes the column sum of the jth column of matrix T and shows the sum of direct and indirect effects that challenge j has received from the other challenges. When $i = j$, $(r_i + c_i)$ provides an index of the strength of influences given and received, that is $(r_i + c_i)$ shows the degree of the central role that challenge i plays in the problem. If $(r_i + c_i)$ is positive, then challenge i is affecting other challenges, and if $(r_i + c_i)$ is negative, then challenge i is being influenced by other challenges [1, 23–25].

4. *Set a threshold value to obtain a digraph.* Matrix T provides information on how one challenge affects another. Hence, a threshold value needs to be set to filter out negligible effects. Effects greater than the threshold value are chosen and shown in the digraph. The digraph can be acquired by mapping the dataset of $(r + c, r-c)$.

At the end of step 4, a structural visual model of interrelations and dependencies among the challenges will be developed through the digraph. The digraph shows the relations and inner dependencies among the challenges within the same category and across categories, and independency of one category of PESTELMO from the others.

DEMATEL does not support a quantitative assessment of the challenges and of the interdependencies among the challenges. As such, it becomes impossible for decision makers to better understand the potential impacts of the challenges and of the interdependencies during strategy development. Therefore, to complement DEMATEL, the use of ANP is proposed and introduced next.

3.3 ANP Method: Supporting Quantitative Evaluation of the Challenges and the Interdependencies Among the Challenges

In 1996, Saaty proposed the use of Analytical Network Processing (ANP) to overcome the restrictions of the AHP (Analytic Hierarchy Process) by including analysis of dependencies among different criteria/alternatives ([18] cited in [25]). AHP was developed by Saaty [16] to support MCDM [25]. In AHP, the general assumption is that the criteria exist in independence of each other and can be structured hierarchically; hence, lacking considerations of the interdependencies, which is added in ANP [17]. To complement the analysis of e-government challenges with PESTELMO and DEMA-TEL, we propose the use of ANP to quantitatively analyse the interrelations, independencies and interdependencies among e-government challenges.

The proposed steps for using ANP are proposed as follows, basing on Yüksel [25]:

1. *Determine the local weights of the independent PESTELMO categories by forming a pairwise comparison matrix.* Here, experts respond to questions such as "which challenge should be emphasized more in a macro environment, and how much more?" [25], and the responses are assessed using Saaty's 1–9 scale [18]. Then, the local weight vector *w1* is computed as follows:

$$A_{w1} = \lambda_{max}w1 \tag{3}$$

2. Where, λ_{max} is the largest eigenvalue of the pairwise comparison matrix A. The obtained vector is further normalized by dividing each value by its column total to represent the normalized local weight vector *w2* [25].
3. *Determine the inner dependence matrix* of PESTELMO's main categories based on the digraph derived using DEMATEL (see step 4). The inner dependence matrix of PESTELMO's main categories is then formed according to the weights of the inner dependence of the factors.
4. *Calculate the interdependent weights of the PESTELMO categories* by multiplying the local weights calculated in step 1 by the inner dependence matrix from step 2.
5. *Determine the weights of the PESTELMO challenges.* The weights are determined by forming a pairwise comparison matrix of the challenges, evaluating each matrix using the scale 1–9 (according to the evaluation provided by the experts in step 1), calculating local weights and determining consistent ratio. This step calculates the weight of each challenge in PESTELMO.
6. *Compute the global weights of the PESTELMO challenges* by multiplying the interdependent weights of the challenges from step 3 by the local weight of challenges obtained from step 4.

At the end of step 5, decision makers are provided with a quantitative evaluation and measurement of the PESTELMO challenges identified for a given context. They are informed about the interdependent weights of PESTELMO categories, and the local and global weights of the PESTELMO challenges. These insights inform decision makers about the extent of the interdependencies among the challenges and the weights of the challenges. Accordingly, decision makers will be able to make more informed and well-grounded decisions during strategy development and in finding solutions for the challenges.

The proposed methodical mix of PESTELMO, DEMATEL and ANP supports in comprehensively analysing e-government challenges. In the next section, we reflect on the proposed methodical mix of analysing e-government challenges and discuss the findings.

4 Reflection of Findings and Outlook for Further Research

E-government challenges are widely known and documented in literature. However, the challenges are only either listed or categorised following a certain scheme (cf. Table 1 in Sect. 2). These studies have left out key and valuable aspects that need to be included in analysis of e-government challenges. First, the studies do not take into account the interdependencies among the challenges. The assumption is that the challenges are independent, which is not the case in the real world. Second, they do not include methods to measure and evaluate the challenges and the interdependencies.

A combination of the PESTELMO analysis method, of DEMATEL and of ANP has been proposed in this study to analyse e-government challenges in a more comprehensive way to better inform decision makers in e-government strategy development and implementation. These methods are proposed to enhance the current research in which e-government challenges are investigated (cf. Table 1). Extending from a mere representation of e-government challenges that is found in most studies, this study goes a step further to include systematic qualitative and quantitative analyses of the challenges and their interdependencies.

To identify the challenges encountered in a country, the widely applied research methods such as interviews, surveys and desk research are used. From here, the identified challenges still need to be systematically represented and analysed in order to provide more valuable insights during strategy development. Particularly, the interdependencies among the challenges need to be identified and measured. For instance, if the legal challenges are highly influenced by the political challenges, then a more comprehensive approach is needed to tackle the legal challenges while taking into account the political ones. Even so, the possibility of tackling the political challenges first and assessing the resulting impacts on the legal challenges can also be examined. The research methods that are currently used to identify the challenges do not support such an analysis. Accordingly, the proposed combination of the three methods adds value to e-government research.

In a qualitative analysis, PESTELMO systematically categorizes e-government challenges. This holistic approach can also be used to highlight potential interrelations and interdependencies among the challenges as depicted in Fig. 1. Yet, PESTELMO does not construct the interrelations and interdependencies among the challenges in a structural and visual way. To complement PESTELMO in this regard, DEMATEL is proposed.

In quantitative analysis, first the DEMATEL method is used to identify and structure the potential interdependencies among the challenges through its four steps outlined in Sect. 3.2. DEMATEL identifies and structures the interdependencies among e-government challenges. Therewith, decision makers are better able to understand the complexity of e-government challenges in terms of existing interdependencies and how the challenges influence one another. However, for more comprehensive and accurate results, the interdependencies and the challenges need to be measured and evaluated with metrics. Accordingly, the ANP method is proposed to measure the local and global weights of the challenges (see steps 1, 4 and 5 in Sect. 3.3), to resolve the matrices resulting from DEMATEL (see step 2 in Sect. 3.3), and to measure the weight of the interdependencies (see step 3 in Sect. 3.3).

To sum up, the proposed combination of PESTELMO, DEMATEL and ANP is expected to provide valuable results that will deepen the decision makers' understanding of the challenges of a country's (or organisation's) context, in which an e-government strategy is to be defined and implemented. With this understanding, decision makers get help in developing more robust, achievable and sustainable e-government strategies.

The paper at hand proposes a methodical mix for qualitative and quantitative analysis of e-government challenges. It also explains the rationale for proposing the methods and their expected contributions in e-government strategy planning and development. However, future research will need to exemplify the methods in case study research. The lessons learned will help to streamline and improve the application of the methods. Moreover, it will be interesting to investigate how the decision makers benefit from case study results and how the results are fed into the decision making processes in e-government strategy development.

References

1. Angelopoulos, S., Kitsios, F., Kofakis, P., Papadopoulos, T.: Emerging barriers in E-government implementation. In: Wimmer, M.A., Chappelet, J.-L., Janssen, M., Scholl, H.J. (eds.) EGOV 2010. LNCS, vol. 6228, pp. 216–225. Springer, Heidelberg (2010)
2. Anthopoulos, L., Reddick, C., Giannakidou, I., Mavridis, N.: Why e-government projects fail? An analysis of the healthcare.gov website. Gov. Inf. Q. 33(1), 161–173 (2016). doi:10. 1016/j.giq.2015.07.003
3. Asogwa, B.: Electronic government as a paradigm shift for efficient public services: opportunities and challenges for Nigerian government. Libr. Hi Tech 31(1), 141–159 (2013)
4. Belachew, M.: E-government initiatives in Ethiopia. In: Davies, J., Janowski, T. (eds.) Proceedings of the 4th International Conference on Theory and Practice of Electronic Governance (ICEGOV 2010), pp. 49–54. ACM, New York (2010)
5. Bhuiyan, S.H.: E-government in Kazakhstan: challenges and its role in development. Public Organ. Rev. 10(1), 31–47 (2010)
6. Gauld, R., Goldfinch, S., Horsburgh, S.: Do they want it? Do they use it? The demand-side of e-government in Australia and New Zealand. Gov. Inf. Q. 27(2), 177–186 (2010)
7. Karunasena, K., Deng, H.: Critical factors for evaluating the public value of e-government in Sri Lanka. Gov. Inf. Q. 29(1), 76–84 (2012)
8. Lee, J.W., Kim, S.H.: Using analytic network process and goal programming for interdependent information system project selection. Comput. Oper. Res. 27(4), 367–382 (2000)
9. Meade, L.M., Presley, A.: R&D project selection using the analytic network process. IEEE Trans. Eng. Manag. 49(1), 59–66 (2002)

10. Mkude, C.G.: Framework for E-Government Systems Design and Implementation for Developing Countries. Fölbach Verlag, Koblenz (2016). ISBN: 9783956388002. Submitted for publication
11. Mkude, C.G., Wimmer, M.A.: Studying interdependencies of e-government challenges in Tanzania along a PESTEL analysis. In: Proceedings of ECIS 2015, Completed Research Paper, Digital Proceedings, Paper 135, AIS Electronic Library (2015)
12. Mkude, C.G., Wimmer, M.A.: Strategic framework for designing e-government in developing countries. In: Wimmer, M.A., Janssen, M., Scholl, H.J. (eds.) EGOV 2013. LNCS, vol. 8074, pp. 148–162. Springer, Heidelberg (2013)
13. Nkohkwo, Q.N., Islam, S.M.: Challenges to the successful implementation of e-government initiatives in Sub-Saharan Africa: a literature review. Electron. J. e-Gov. 11(2), 253–267 (2013)
14. Rashid, N., Rahman, S.: An investigation into critical determinants of e-government implementation in the context of a developing nation. In: Andersen, K.N., Francesconi, E., Grönlund, Å., van Engers, T.M. (eds.) EGOVIS 2010. LNCS, vol. 6267, pp. 9–21. Springer, Heidelberg (2010)
15. Sæbø, Ø.: E-government in Tanzania: current status and future challenges. In: Scholl, H.J., Janssen, M., Wimmer, M.A., Moe, C.E., Flak, L.S. (eds.) EGOV 2012. LNCS, vol. 7443, pp. 198–209. Springer, Heidelberg (2012)
16. Saaty, T.L.: The Analytic Hierarchy Process. McGraw-Hill, New York (1980)
17. Saaty, T.L., Takizawa, M.: Dependence and independence: from linear hierarchies to nonlinear networks. Eur. J. Oper. Res. 26(2), 229–237 (1986)
18. Saaty, T.L.: Decision Making with Dependence and Feedback: The Analytic Network Process. RWS Publications, Pittsburgh (1996)
19. Scherer, S., Schneider, C., Wimmer, M.A. Shaddock, J.: Studying eParticipation in government innovation programmes: lessons from a survey. In: Proceedings of 21st Bled eConference on eCollaboration: Overcoming Boundaries Through Multi-Channel Interaction, AIS Electronic Library, Paper 9 (2008)
20. Schuppan, T.: E-government in developing countries: experiences from Sub-Saharan Africa. Gov. Inf. Q. 26(1), 118–127 (2009)
21. Tzeng, G.H., Chiang, C.H., Li, C.W.: Evaluating intertwined effects in e-learning programs: a novel hybrid MCDM model based on factor analysis and DEMATEL. Expert Syst. Appl. 32(4), 1028–1044 (2007)
22. Wimmer, M.A.: A European perspective towards online one-stop government: the eGOV project. Electron. Commer. Res. Appl. 1(1), 92–103 (2002)
23. Wu, W.-W.: Choosing knowledge management strategies by using a combined ANP and DEMATEL approach. Expert Syst. Appl. 35(3), 828–835 (2008)
24. Yang, Y.P.O., Shieh, H.M., Leu, J.D., Tzeng, G.H.: A novel hybrid MCDM model combined with DEMATEL and ANP with applications. Int. J. Oper. Res. 5(3), 160–168 (2008)
25. Yüksel, I.: Developing a multi-criteria decision making model for PESTEL analysis. Int. J. Bus. Manag. 7(24), 52–66 (2012)
26. Zhao, F., Scavarda, A., Waxin, M.-F.: Key issues and challenges in e-government development: An integrative case study of the number one eCity in the Arab world. Inf. Technol. People 25(4), 395–422 (2012)

Techno-Government Networks: Actor-Network Theory in Electronic Government Research

Marcelo Fornazin[1(✉)] and Luiz Antonio Joia[2]

[1] Mathematics and Statistics Institute,
Rio de Janeiro State University, Rio de Janeiro, Brazil
fornazin@ime.uerj.br
[2] Brazilian School of Public and Business Administration,
Getulio Vargas Foundation, Rio de Janeiro, Brazil
luiz.joia@fgv.br

Abstract. The Actor-Network Theory (ANT) is a theoretical approach for the study of controversies associated with scientific discoveries and technological innovations through the networks of actors involved in such actions. This approach has generated studies in Information Systems (IS) since 1990, however few studies have examined the use of this approach in the e-government area. Thus, this paper aims to broaden the theoretical approaches on e-government, by presenting ANT as a theoretical framework for e-government studies via published empirical work. For this reason, the historical background of ANT is described, duly listing its theoretical and methodological premises. In addition to this, one presented ANT-based e-government works, in order to illustrate how ANT can be applied in empirical studies in this knowledge area.

Keywords: Electronic government · Methodology · Actor-Network Theory

1 Introduction

Studies in e-government have expanded and investigated the nuances of Information and Communication Technology (ICT) projects in government. Although the relevance of e-government has been confirmed in recent years through the growing academic and professional interest in this field, authors question the theoretical fragility of this area [1]. Thus, academics have defended broadening e-government theoretical frameworks, where there is "little use of frameworks of knowledge from governance," "dominance of positivist research approaches, alongside absence of statements on research philosophy," a "dominance of a-theoretical approaches that, simultaneously, often fail to provide any significant practical recommendations" [1, p. 260]. To a certain extent, these questions also arise within the IS community in general, where there is a demand for studies geared at looking beyond the efficiency of ICT in organizations [2–5].

Bearing in mind the importance of broadening the e-government theoretical framework, this theoretical essay seeks to strengthen the theoretical side of this

© IFIP International Federation for Information Processing 2016
Published by Springer International Publishing Switzerland 2016. All Rights Reserved
H.J. Scholl et al. (Eds.): EGOV 2016, LNCS 9820, pp. 188–199, 2016.
DOI: 10.1007/978-3-319-44421-5_15

knowledge area, by presenting the Actor-Network Theory (ANT) as a viable approach to the study of government ICT projects.

ANT consists of a theoretical and methodological framework for the study of scientific discoveries and technological innovation. As such, it encompasses different heterogeneous actors involved in scientific activities, from researchers and their equipment, to politicians, investors and social movements which are, in some way, related to technological undertakings [6].

As has occurred in other areas, ANT has been used in Information Systems research since the 1990s [7, 8] and with greater intensity since 2000 [9]. Studies based on ANT have also been undertaken on topics related to e-government [10, 11], such as tax systems [12–14], intellectual property [15], IT public policy [16], e-health [17, 18], and digital inclusion [19–21]. ANT is consequently considered to be a relevant theoretical approach to use for IS studies [7, 9, 22], as well as for e-government. This paper therefore aims to analyze how ANT has inspired studies in the e-government area, so as to better understand the possibilities of conducting ANT-based research in this realm.

For this, a bibliographic review was undertaken on ANT-based studies in the area of e-government, seeking to evaluate: (a) how the ANT-based approach has developed over the last thirty years; (b) the theoretical and methodological concepts proposed by the ANT approach, and (c) the way ANT-based research has contributed towards a better understanding of the socio-technical phenomena associated with e-government ventures. Finally, a discussion is presented regarding the limitations of this research approach, as well as the possibility of using other ANT-based concepts in research into e-government.

2   Actor-Network Theory (ANT)

2.1   ANT Background

The Actor-Network Theory emerged in the late 1970s in the context of Science and Technology Studies (STS), when Callon [23] and Latour [6] presented their preliminary concepts of ANT. This approach began to take shape in the early 1980s, when Callon and Latour [24] made use of the inscription and black boxes concepts to describe associations between heterogeneous actors. Such associations can be preceded by infighting and conflict but, once established, can conceal dissonant voices and become black boxes. These black boxes "contain that which no longer needs to be reconsidered, those things whose contents have become a matter of indifference" [24, p. 285]. Thus, Callon and Latour [24] argued that successive black boxes form the so-called social structure, challenging the existence of an underlying strength that governs society, ascribing that strength to the own history of men and artifacts.

A few years later, while studying the work of scientists involved in scallop farming in the south of France, Callon [4] explained the negotiation and consensus process between the different actors involved in that research, including scientists, fishermen, and the scallops per se. That work presented the concepts of translation, obligatory passage point (OPP) and generalized symmetry.

The translation widely used in ANT studies can be understood as the mobilization of actors around a common objective [4], called an obligatory passage point (OPP), which establishes the link between the network of actors [4].

In his study about the scallop researchers, Callon observed that the three researchers established an OPP and created identities for the fishermen, the scallops and the scientific community, thereby becoming the spokesman for these groups. Figure 1 shows examples of the OPP established – the scientists' research program – for which the different case actors altered their preferences.

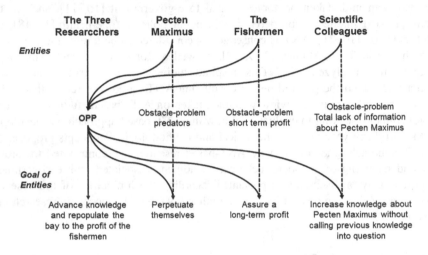

Fig. 1. Establishing an obligatory passage point. Source: Callon [4].

The translation is operationalized in four moments: problematization, interessement, enrollment, and mobilization. That is to say, the translation moments "are discerned in the attempts by these researchers to impose themselves and their definition of the situation on others" [4, p. 196]. Problematization involves identifying the actors and the OPP to which the actors should converge. Interessement is the stage involving the mapping of the identities, preferences and alliances of the actors and their possible relationships with the OPP. Enrollment involves the negotiations to alter the preferences of the actors towards the OPP. Finally, mobilization encompasses the actions of the actors to ensure that the objective is attained.

Furthermore, Callon explores the concept of generalized symmetry, since the same vocabulary is used to analyze negotiations with the natural and social world, so as "not to change registers when we move from the technical to the social aspects of the problem studied" [4, p. 199]. In other words, all actors are analyzed in the same way, without separating nature from society, or the technician from the lay person. Thus, the author argues that it is not possible to separate the technical from the social, and that these two categories should be analyzed within the same plan and by using a symmetrical approach.

2.2   Technoscience in Action

In 1987, Latour [6] published his book Science in Action, in which he presented the principles and methodological procedures of ANT-based research. Latour therefore proposed a methodological framework for the study of scientific discoveries and technological innovation.

Latour put forward a technoscience concept that involves "all the elements tied to scientific content, no matter how dirty, unexpected or strange they may appear" [6, p. 286]. That is to say, technoscience seeks to include all heterogeneous actors involved in scientific activities, from researchers and their equipment, to politicians, investors and society who are, in some way, related to scientific ventures. This is based on the six principles and seven methodological rules derived, as shown in Table 1.

Table 1. Methodological principles and rules for the study of Techno-science. Source: Latour [6].

Principles	Methodological rules
I. A scientific fact or a technological innovation is "what is collectively stabilized from the midst of controversies, when the activity [...] does not consist only of criticism or deformation but also of confirmation" (p. 42)	I. Study the technoscience under construction
II. Scientists and engineers "speak in the name of new allies that they have shaped and enrolled; representatives among other representatives, they add these unexpected resources to tip the balance of force in their favor." (p. 90)	II. "the fate of facts and machines is in the hands of later users" (p. 59)
III. "We are never confronted with science, technology and society, but with a gamut of weaker and stronger associations; thus, understanding what facts and machines are, is the same task as understanding who the people are" (p. 140–141)	III. "We can never use the outcome-Nature-to explain how and why a controversy has been settled" (p. 99)
	IV. "We cannot use society to explain how and why a controversy has been settled." (p. 258)
IV. "science and technology' is only a subset of technoscience" (p. 259)	V. "every time an inside/outside divide is built, we should study the two sides simultaneously and make the list, no matter how long and heterogeneous, of those who do the work" (p. 176)
V. No separation exists between scientists and lay persons.	VI. Consider the other person's point of view
VI. Major scientific discoveries & technological innovations are merely a succession of events	VII. Analyze the network to understand the behavior

The six principles presented in Table 1 form the ontology of ANT, whereas the seven methodological rules shown in Table 1 guide the work of a researcher who seeks to reconstruct the actor-networks that represent scientific discoveries and innovations. Thus, it may be observed that there are no differences between science, technology and society. That is to say, all of these are interlinked within the same world via actor-networks, which can consist of both humans as well as technical artifacts.

ANT does not assume the free will of individuals, nor the possibility of underlying structures that govern social relationships. As a counterpoint, it is based on the assumption that relationships between human beings are governed by long chains of actor-networks which have been inscribed by successive translation processes.

Finally, the work of scientists and engineers is not to make discoveries, but to enroll allies and establish actor-networks, which are inscribed by means of technical artifacts and scientific facts. Several studies have thus been developed based on these assumptions.

One of these studies, which is often cited in the area of e-government, is the research undertaken by Law and Callon [25] on the trajectory of a project to construct military aircraft in England. That study expanded the analysis of networks and actors by observing that: "the success and shape of a project, the TSR.2, depended crucially on the creation of two networks and on the exchange of intermediaries between these networks." [25, p. 41]. That is to say, it can be seen that, in addition to emphasizing only one local network, as elaborated by Callon [4] in his study on scallops, Law and Callon [25] study the interaction between two networks of actors, broadening their analysis to include, not only the technicians, but also the project sponsors.

Law and Callon [25] represented the trajectory of the TSR.2 project by means of a bi-dimensional chart (Fig. 2), "where x axis measures the degree of mobilization of local actors," and the "y axis measures the extent to which external actors are linked" [25, p. 47]. A project where the global network is highly cohesive and the local network is highly mobilized, that is to say, one that is placed in the top right hand quadrant, is a solid, indispensable project; the opposite, placed in the lower right hand quadrant, is a very weak and disaggregated project. This is how the different stages of the project were designed in the chart, indicating the degree of cohesion of the global network and the mobilization of the local network.

Another pertinent study was carried out by Akrich [26], who analyzed social technological projects developed in France and used in countries in Africa. According to Akrich [26, p. 208]: "A large part of the work of innovators is that of 'inscribing' this vision of (or prediction about) the world in the technical content of the new object. I will call the end product of this work a 'script' or a 'scenarium.'" Thus, technologies "represented a large set of technically delegated prescriptions addressed by the innovator to the user." [26, p. 211].

Akrich [26, pp. 208–209] states that: "we have to go back and forth continually between the designer and the user, between the designer's projected user and the real user, between the world inscribed in the object and the world described by its displacement." That is to say, Akrich defends an investigation of the controversies that exist between functions inscribed in technical artifacts and their use in the real environment. This concept has been widely used in IS research, where information systems inscribe specific visions and, when deployed, go through a series of negotiations with the users.

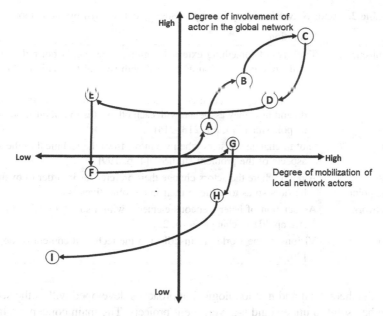

Fig. 2. Chart showing the trajectory of the TSR.2 project. Source: Law and Callon [26].

2.3   ANT Advances and Revisions

Later in the 1980s, John Law joined forces with Callon and Latour and this group began to foment an ANT-based research agenda. After this period of conceptual development, a debate began about the ANT approach in sociology in general [22]. It is worth remembering that studies undertaken in the decade between 1980 and 1990 were limited to the discussion of scientific discoveries. From 1990 onwards, ANT researchers began to defend this theory in a much broader and more complex space, such as economic sociology and political economy.

In 1999, Law and Hassard [5] edited a book called "Actor Network Theory and After," which resulted from a seminar with the main researchers engaged with ANT, to assess the implications of this approach up to that time. Over the following years, ANT-based research multiplied on various fronts, especially in the areas of communications [27], environment [28], economic sociology [29], and heterogeneous methods [30]. It is worth stressing that, in 2006, Latour [3], presented a review of ANT. That research work redeems the main concepts of ANT, providing a guide for social research based on this approach.

The concepts revised by Latour [3] were strongly influenced by the book Science in Action, published in 1987 [6] and presented in Sect. 2.2. The difference between these two is that, while Latour's work is limited to scientists and engineers [6], the most recent publication presents an outline for general social science research [3]. The recent work does not go into a lengthy discussion about such concepts, though the reader can obtain more in-depth information by studying the original work [3].

Table 2. Actor-Network Theory concepts. Source: constructed by the authors.

Concept	Definition
Fact establishment	Truth is not something external waiting to be caught but rather a collective construction associated with several translations [6]
Translation	"To translate is to displace [...] to translate is also to express in one's own language what others say and want, why they act in the way they do and how they associate with each other: it is to establish oneself as a spokesman" [4, pp. 213–214]
Symmetry	"not to change registers when we move from the technical to the social aspects of the problem studied" [4, p. 199]
Obligatory passage point	A point where the actors change their preferences in order to overcome barriers so as to achieve their initial objectives [4]
Actor-Network	Association of heterogeneous elements with a structure, which is susceptible to change [4, 6, 25]
Inscription	Visions of the world are inscribed in the technical content of objects [26]

Thus, the theoretical and methodological approaches developed within the scope of ANT can be useful to understand e-government projects. The main concepts related to these approaches are summarized in Table 2.

The following section therefore discusses how ANT has served to inspire studies in e-government.

3   Actor-Network Theory and Electronic Government Research

As mentioned in the introduction, Actor-Network Theory has served to inspire research into information systems since 1990. In relation to the area of e-government, such research has involved e-procurement [12], tax systems [13, 14, 31], the judicial system [32, 33], intellectual property [15], IT public policy [16], geo-processing [34, 35], e-health [17, 18, 36], e-governance [11, 37] and digital inclusion [19–21]. Some of the theoretical and methodological concepts outlined in this approach can be useful to understand e-government undertakings. In this respect, some of these elements may be highlighted.

Moments of translation [4] have been widely used in e-government research [13, 19, 21]. In these processes, systems of e-government are understood to be similar to an OPP, where the other actors tend to converge during the course of the translation. In this way, research seeks to understand how e-government projects involve a heterogeneous network of actors, since their success is closely linked to the occurrence of translations. This means that the purpose is not to find factors of success associated with the system, but to understand why e-government projects are a collective construction, in which different actors altered their preferences around an e-government system, by means of successive translations.

Furthermore, in ANT-inspired studies on e-government, a longitudinal approach is often observed [10, 13, 15, 19, 21], the aim of such research being to study the movement, formation of groups and translations, rather than collecting information about a specific moment.

The study related to the I'SII / IIIIIIIIft [23] has also become a benchmark in ANT-based e-government studies, which sought to understand the trajectory of projects by means of analyses based on global and local networks [13, 16, 19]. In several cases, the research transcends the formal dimensions of an organization. The empirical freedom of ANT enables researchers to understand the relationship that exists between politicians, technicians and professionals [17], between governments and international organs [13, 31] or, indeed, between citizens and social movements [38]. This complex scenario was revealed, for example, in the study into the computerization of the Brazilian judicial system, which investigated the country's courts of justice [32] and the cooperation between patent offices for the transfer of technology [15]. Analysis of the cases in a symmetric manner took into consideration the whole spectrum of actors involved in e-government projects. Thus, in addition to the professionals involved, it also included other actors – such as politicians, citizens, social movements, etc.

In this way, the studies analyzed complex environments involving multiple actors who often have markedly divergent preferences. By means of the translation concept, ANT provides a theoretical tool to analyze the points of convergence of these preferences and the studies are therefore able to illustrate the political dimensions involved in installing an e-government system. On this point, ANT-based studies reinforce the entreaties of the scientific community, who defend the importance of changing the focus from tools to management of IS projects in organizations, while also bearing in mind the economic, political and negotiation aspects of such systems [2].

Moreover, in ANT research, there is an age-old tradition of using graphs to explain phenomena. For this reason, several studies use them to unveil the dynamics of heterogeneous networks associated with IS and e-government development and implementation [11, 13, 16, 34, 37–40, 41, 42, 43, 44, 45]. Thus, ANT can also be used to depict the research context under analysis.

The flexibility shown by researchers in their approach to the field of e-government may also be observed. In accordance with ANT premises, micro or macro actors, simple or complex contexts, are not differentiated a priori, since such definitions are obtained during the empirical analysis. The proposal outlined by Latour [3], which is to follow the actors themselves, has contributed to revealing the issues that emerge from the actors themselves, rather than seeking responses based on pre-defined models. For instance, situations peculiar to developing countries, such as telecenters [20, 21], can provide a relevant contribution to the academic debate about e-government.

4 Discussion and Final Considerations

This theoretical essay reviewed the scientific literature to identify how the ANT approach has been used in e-government studies. Based on the historical trajectory in relation to ANT, it may be seen that an approach such as this, which began with studies in technological science, also came to discuss sociological and political issues in general. By and large, the empirical nature of ANT can contribute to the development of research directions that can take into consideration the nuances of e-government projects. That is to say, instead of starting with a pre-existing model from another area, researchers can dedicate themselves to understanding a practical situation and deliberate over this.

The proposal to avoid using previously-established theories has led to a certain amount of criticism about the essentially descriptive character of ANT; that is to say, ANT-based studies run the risk of becoming mere case descriptions [7, 9], without having to provide any explanations or indicators for social change. Latour [3] responded to these criticisms by suggesting that a description that requires an explanation is not a good description.

The idea of following the actors, and thereby avoid having to provide theories on the field, does not purport to serve as encouragement to researchers to produce studies devoid of theory, which are justifiably criticized by the academic community [39]. On the contrary, such a suggestion leaves open the possibility of deliberating over issues that emerge during the course of the research [39]. However, reporting on a study merely by means of a description can become an impossible task. Thus, some authors suggest an integration of ANT with other theoretical perspectives [9]. This matter is not a general consensus in academic debates, leaving room to the researcher to decide whether to follow only ANT premises, or to seek support in other research approaches as well.

Another criticism relates to the linearity of the translation process which, although focusing on the convergence of preferences, mimics a functionalist concept [35]. ANT does not presuppose the existence of previously-established social rules, nor does it exclude them, whereby various negotiations and exchanges between the actors are necessary to ensure that their preferences are made to converge to an OPP [4]. Thus, a translation is not everlasting, since the tensions between the actors can unravel a network that has been previously established. As noted by Callon [4], such tensions between the actors continue to be present, since the previously established network may disentangle as the result of a succession of unexpected events. That is to say, an initially established OPP may no longer be attractive to the actors, which results in the unraveling of the network.

In ANT-based e-government studies, attempts have been made to ensure that the implementation of systems matches the four moments of translation [13, 16, 19, 21]. However, it is important to take into consideration that, although a seminal study on ANT has proposed these four moments of translation, such moments may not necessarily appear in all situations, or they may even occur at once. While taking into consideration the empirical freedom of ANT and defending the exploration of new theoretical frontiers, Law [40] contends that ANT is a way of representing the world in different ways, going beyond Euclidean space. In other words, in the same way that representations of actor networks were constructed [4, 25], there is also room to explore other ways to represent heterogeneous relationships.

However, the latest ANT developments have still not been absorbed by the IS and e-government academic community. When criticizing the term ANT, Latour [40, p. 24] states that: "yes, I think there is life after ANT [...], thus abandoning what is so wrong with ANT, that is 'actor,' 'network,' 'theory' without forgetting the hyphen! – some other creature will emerge, light and beautiful, our future collective achievement." Basically, this provocation is actually an invitation to embark on a continual process of collective construction of a theoretical approach to the study of society.

This essay therefore provides an incentive for e-government researchers exploring new directions for ANT to go beyond the moments of translation, as well as bring new concepts to investigate this topic.

References

1. Heeks, R., Bailour, S.: Analyzing e-government research: perspectives, philosophies, theories, methods and practice. Gov. Inf. Q. **24**, 243–265 (2007)
2. Ives, B., et al.: What every business student needs to know about information systems. Commun. Assoc. Inf. Syst. **9**, 467–477 (2002)
3. Latour, B.: Reassembling the Social: An Introduction to Actor-Network Theory. Oxford University Press, Oxford (2005)
4. Callon, M.: Some elements of a sociology of translation: domestication of the scallops and the fisherman of St Brieuc Bay. In: Law, J. (ed.) Power Action and Belief a New Sociology of Knowledge, pp. 196–223. Routledge, London (1986)
5. Law, J., Hassard, J. (eds.): Actor-Network Theory and After. Blackwell, Oxford (1999)
6. Latour, B.: Science in Action: How to Follow Scientists and Engineers Through Society. Harvard University Press, Boston (1987)
7. Walsham, G.: Actor-network theory and current status and future prospects. In: Lee, A.S., Liebenau, J., DeGross, J.I. (eds.) Information Systems and Qualitative Research, pp. 466–480. Chapman Hall, London (1997)
8. Ciborra, C.U., Hanseth, O.: From tool to Gestell Agendas for managing the information infrastructure. Inf. Technol. People **11**(4), 305–327 (1998)
9. Mitev, N.N., Howcroft, D.: Post-structuralism, social shaping of technology, and actor-network theory: what can they bring to IS research? In: Galliers, R.D., Currie, W.L. (eds.) The Oxford Handbook of Management Information Systems, pp. 292–322. Oxford, Londres (2011)
10. Priyatma, J.E.: A critical review of the ontological assumptions of actor-network theory for representing e-government initiatives. Int. J. Actor-Netw. Theory Technol. Innov. **5**(3), 12–24 (2013)
11. Gao, P., Gunawong, P.: Understanding e-government failure from an actor-network perspective: the demise of the Thai smart ID card. In: iGovernment Working Paper Series, University of Manchester, Manchester (2014)
12. Hardy, C.A., Williams, S.P.: E-government policy and practice: a theoretical and empirical exploration of public e-procurement. Gov. Inf. Q. **25**, 155–180 (2007)
13. Heeks, R., Stanforth, C.: Understanding e-Government project trajectories from an actor-network perspective. Eur. J. Inf. Syst. **16**(2), 165–177 (2007)
14. Ayyad, M.: Using the actor-network theory to interpret e-Government implementation barriers. In: International Conference on Theory and Practice of Electronic Governance – ICEGOV, Bogota, Colombia (2009)
15. Cavalheiro, G.M., Joia, L.A.: Examining the implementation of a European patent management system in Brazil from an actor-network theory perspective. Information Technology for Development (2014)

16. Ramos, E.A.: Remontando a Política Pública: A Evolução da Política Nacional de Informática Analisada pela Ótica da Teoria do Ator-Rede. Getulio Vargas Foundation, Rio de Janeiro, Brazil (2009)

17. Braa, J., Monteiro, E., Sahay, S.: Networks of action sustainable health information systems across developing countries. MIS Q. **28**(3), 337–362 (2004)

18. Greenhalgh, T., Stones, R.: Theorising big IT programmes in healthcare: strong structuration theory meets actor-network theory. Soc. Sci. Med. **70**, 1285–1294 (2010)

19. Teles, A., Joia, L.A.: Assessment of digital inclusion via the actor-network theory the case of the Brazilian municipality of Piraí. Telemat. Inform. **28**, 191–203 (2011)

20. Soares, C.D.M., Joia, L.A.: LAN house implementation and sustainability in Brazil: an actor-network theory perspective. In: Janssen, M., Scholl, H.J., Wimmer, M.A., Bannister, F. (eds.) EGOV 2014. LNCS, vol. 8653, pp. 206–217. Springer, Heidelberg (2014)

21. Andrade, A.D., Urquhart, C.: The affordances of actor-network theory. ICT Dev. Res. **23**(4), 352–374 (2010)

22. Rao, R.A., De, R.: Technology assimilation through conjunctures – a look at IS use in retail. Inf. Syst. Front. **17**, 31–50 (2015)

23. Callon, M.: Struggles and negotiations to decide what is problematic and what is not: the socio-logics of translation. In: Krohn, K.K., Whitley, R. (eds.) The Social Process of Scientific Investigation, pp. 197–220. D. Reidel Publishing Company, Dordrecht (1980)

24. Callon, M., Latour, B.: Unscrewing the big leviathan; or how actors macrostructure reality, and how sociologists help them to do so? In: Knorr-Cetina, K., Cicourel, A. (eds.) Advances in Social Theory and Methodology, pp. 277–303. Routledge e Kegan Paul, London (1981)

25. Law, J., Callon, M.: The life and death of an aircraft: a network analysis of technical change. In: Bijker, W., Law, J. (eds.) Shaping Technology/Building Society, pp. 21–52. The MIT Press, Cambridge (1992)

26. Akrich, M.: The description of technical objects. In: Bijker, W., Law, J. (eds.) Shaping Technology/Building Society, pp. 205–224. The MIT Press, Cambridge (1992)

27. Latour, B.: What is iconoclash? Or is there a world beyond the image wars? In: Latour, B., Weibel, P. (eds.) Iconoclash: Beyond the Image Wars in Science, Religion and Art, pp. 15–40. Center for Art and Media, Karlsruhe (2002)

28. Latour, B.: Politiques de la nature. Comment faire entrer les sciences en démocratie. La Découverte, Paris (1999)

29. Callon, M. (ed.): The Laws of the Markets, p. 278. Blackwell, Oxford (1998)

30. Law, J.: Making a Mess with Method (2003)

31. Stanforth, C.: Using actor-network theory to analyse E-government implementation in developing countries. Inf. Technol. Int. Dev. **3**(3), 35–60 (2006)

32. Andrade, A.G.: Trajetórias do PROJUDI à Luz da Teoria Ator-Rede. Getulio Vargas Foundation, Rio de Janeiro, Brazil (2013)

33. Faik, I., Walsham, G.: Modernisation through ICTs: towards a network ontology of technological change. Inf. Syst. J. **23**, 351–370 (2013)

34. Silva, L.: Institutionalization does not occur by decree: institutional obstacles in implementing a land administration system in a developing country. Inf. Technol. Dev. **13**(1), 27–48 (2007)

35. Rajão, R.: The site of IT actor-network and practice theory as approaches for studying IT in organisations. In: Vilodov, S.O., et al. (eds.) Heterogeneities, Multiplicities and Complexities; Towards Subtler Understandings of Links Between Technology, Organisation and Society, pp. 92–105. UCD School of Business, Dublin (2008)

36. Silvis, E., Alexander, P.M.: A study using a graphical syntax for actor-network theory. Inf. Technol. People **27**(2), 110–128 (2013)

37. Ranerup, A.: The socio-material pragmatics of e-governance mobilization. Gov. Inf. Q. **29**, 413–423 (2012)
38. Heeks, R., Seo-Zindy, R.: ICTs and social movements under authoritarian regimes: an actor-network perspective. In: Working Paper Series, Center for Development Informatics, Manchester (2013)
39. Heeks, R.: Development studies research and actor-network theory. In: Working Paper Series, Center for Development Informatics, Manchester (2013)
40. Latour, B.: On recalling ANT. In: Law, J., Hassard, J. (eds.) Actor-Network Theory and After, pp. 15–25. Blackwell, Oxford (1999)

Smart Innovations

An Analytic Framework for Open Government Policy Design Processes

Alex Ingrams[✉]

School of Public Affairs and Administration, Rutgers University-Newark, Newark, USA
alex.ingrams@rutgers.edu

Abstract. This paper lays out an analytical framework for OG policy design processes. It uses a systematic review of (1) scholarly literature, and (2) real OG policies to corroborate existing definitions of OG and its sub-categories. The sub-categories are then used for an in-depth literature review of policy design research that is developed into a conceptual model of OG design processes. The model establishes the design considerations needed by policymakers and administrators of OG policies, and can be used as a framework for evaluating OG policy processes. The paper also clarifies design concepts and best practices in a growing e-government domain, and outlines a research agenda for studying OG within organizational theory in public administration.

Keywords: Open government · E-government · Policy design · ICT · Structuration

1 Introduction

The research developed here is an investigation of OG policy design. It addresses the research question of what design processes support the achievement of open government policies. OG is a broad descriptive label that encompasses a range of governmental policies and processes associated with the use of information and communications technology (ICT) to improve democracy, create transparency, accountability, and foster synergies between governmental and non-governmental actors [1, 2]. This range of policies includes, but is not limited to, transparency, freedom of information, public participation, and the pro-active publication and archiving of government data.

While there is a nascent OG research agenda in public administration, scholars frequently highlight the normative and practical limitations of existing theory (e.g., [3, 4]). The research in this paper probes two main puzzles in the theory of OG in particular. The first puzzle in OG theory is related to the coherency of the collection of practices that are conventionally grouped in the category of OG such as transparency, freedom of information, and citizen participation. OG is not synonymous with any one of these practices, but rather is interdependent with them as they are weaved together in open government reforms. However, it is unclear what OG and its sub-categories are and whether they have robust conceptual validity and coherency. The second puzzle, which is an extension of the first puzzle, is that it is unclear what

© IFIP International Federation for Information Processing 2016
Published by Springer International Publishing Switzerland 2016. All Rights Reserved
H.J. Scholl et al. (Eds.): EGOV 2016, LNCS 9820, pp. 203–214, 2016.
DOI: 10.1007/978-3-319-44421-5_16

exactly the policy design features of openness are that are common across these different sub-categories of OG practice. Without such a unified approach it becomes difficult to know how the policy design features of openness can be used for more effective OG policies.

If scholars of public administration and technology do not address the conceptual ambiguity and breadth of the term "open government" the concept becomes liable to be used as a rhetorical device in politics or to be offered as a panacea for an unrealistic range of political problems [5, 6]. Open government is a relatively new field of scholarship and it needs to have a clearer idea of its conceptual parameters and its best practices and methods for public administration. It remains to be shown that OG is a meaningful and distinctive perspective of public policy that can be approached and implemented within a coherent framework for organizational and administrative design processes.

Therefore, in seeking to advance an analytic framework for a policy design theory of OG and to address the aforementioned puzzles of OG, respectively, the following two research questions will be investigated: (1) what are the component sub-categories of OG policies? And (2) what policymaking processes support the design of open government across these sub-categories? The research steps used in the paper involve a systematic OG literature review and deductive content analysis to address the first question, and a broader literature review of OG, structuration theory, and policy design theory to address the second question. The themes developed to answer the second question are used to construct a conceptual model. The model is analyzed and explained using a hypothetical OG policy design example before the paper concludes with suggestions for future use of the model.

2   Literature Review and Definition of Open Government

In previous research, OG has been defined as a collection of governmental practices relating to transparency, public participation, collaboration, and use of ICT technology [2, 7]. However, in order to verify and more clearly define OG, I conducted a systematic survey of scholarly literature (Table 1) and OG initiatives in practice (Table 2) to identify sub-categories of open government.

Table 1 shows the frequency results of a keyword search of "open government" in titles and abstracts of articles in the Web of Science Library for the years 1980 to 2015. A total of 275 articles and conference papers were identified. Each article was then categorized according to its main topic. A total of 11 topics were identified, but there are five most frequently studied topics that are clearly dominant: open data (41 %), general open government (15 %), transparency (14 %), citizen participation (11 %), and access to information (9 %).

In order to make sure that these topics were cross-referenced with actual practice in the open government field, the 11 topics were used deductively to perform a frequency analysis of the OG initiatives in the largest known database of OG initiatives from the

OGP national action plans[1]. There were 433 individual OG initiatives in the database across a two year period (2011-2013) in 33 countries. Table 2 shows the results of the OGP database frequency analysis. The most frequently used policy topics of open government are (1) open data; (2) transparency; (3) citizen participation; and (4) access to information. Apart from the general topic of 'open government' (which is removed because it would obviously be tautological to include as a sub-category of open government) these four topics match precisely with the four in Table 1. This match answers

Table 1. Topics of open government in scholarly literature (1980–2015)

Open government topic	Frequency	Percentage
Open Data	115	41
General open government	42	15
Transparency	38	14
Citizen participation	31	11
Access to information	24	9
Open innovation	8	3
Budget openness	8	3
Geographic information systems	5	2
Open education	2	1
Open science	1	0.5
Intergovernmental collaboration	1	0.5
Total	275	100

Table 2. Topics of open government in national action plans (2011–2013)

Open government topic	Frequency	Percentage
Open data	106	11
Transparency	93	10
Citizen participation	86	9
Access to information	57	6
Budget openness	54	6
General open government	12	1
Intergovernmental collaboration	7	0.7
Open innovation	6	0.6
Open education	4	0.4
Open science	3	0.3
Geographic information systems	1	0.1
Total	433	100

---

[1] Open Government Partnership. "OGP IRM Database". Last accessed on 06/05/2016 from www.opengovernmentpartnership.org/irm/ogp-irm-database-12.

the first puzzle and demonstrates a strong set of core sub-categories within the study and practice of OG.

The systematic review of the main sub-categories of OG gives better definition and finds empirical support for the OG typologies already used by scholars (e.g., [2, 7]). If these sub-categories are all part of OG reforms they must be related in the policy design process. However, the policy design characteristics that link the sub-categories under the umbrella of OG have not been set out by public administration scholars. This point addresses the second theoretical puzzle discussed above, and will be the focus of the remaining sections of the paper.

Already, some prior work has begun to take OG theory to a more fundamental level of organizational practice. In one conceptual framework for the related OG topic of transparency, Meijer [8] proposed three core interpretative lenses for understanding the practice of transparency: cognitive, strategic, and institutional. Dawes et al. [9] have proposed an ecosystem model of open government data (OGD) that can accommodate the complex range of strategies and barriers. In approaching the theory of OG policy design it is necessary to understand these complex factors that underlie the policy processes within OG reforms across the four sub-categories.

3   Theoretical Framework and Conceptual Model of OG Policy Design

Policy design theory is a core topic in public administration scholarship. Previous scholars have studied design because government policies have important outcomes for democratic performance and public values such as health, education, public safety, and social equity [10].

The definition of design processes adopted here is the one used by Davenport [11] to describe approaches to organizational process using IT: "a structured, measured set of activities designed to produce a specific output" (p. 5). Davenport's is a basic definition of process and is especially relevant to OG policies that often rely on process involving ICT innovations.

3.1   A Structurational Approach to OG Policy Design Processes

Policy design theorists, such as Beierle and Konisky [12], frequently describe a policy design process in terms of two main ingredients: a context and a process. The former comprises the fixed social and institutional variables, which can also be referred to as the *structure* of the organization. On the other hand, the process includes the design and participant variables that are controlled during the design development, which can also be referred to as the *agency* of the organization.

According to Giddens' [13] original formulation of structuration theory, organizational structures are continually enacted by the actions of members of organizations and the characteristics of their institutions. Structuration theory can be used as a micro-foundation for policy design approaches in combination with macro-level institutional processes [14]. Orlikowski [15] says that "[d]rawing on the ideas of social shaping and inscription, structurational models have posited that technology is developed through a social political process which results in structures (rules and resources) being embedded within the technology" (p. 405). This concept of decision-making has been adapted in Fig. 1 with 'open government policy' taking the place of the 'technology' outcome in Orlikowski's original formulation of a structuration process

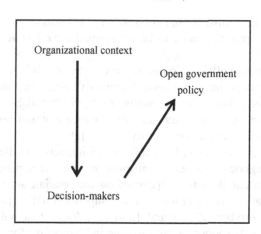

Organizational context

Open government
policy

Decision-makers

Fig. 1. Strategic choice model. Adapted from Orlikowski [16]

In the following theoretical framework, I examine the agentic and structural factors that contribute to OG program processes and use them to propose a unified conceptual model of OG design. To select the literature on policy design for the framework, I used the core sub-categories of OG derived from the frequency analysis of OG literature (open data, access to information, citizen participation, and transparency) as keywords in conjunction with the keywords "policy design" and "organizational design". In order to supplement my literature review, I also expanded on this initial set of results to draw on important works on policy design theory from outside of OG research. I grouped the findings into five themes (managerial skills, institutions, technology, environment, and organizational ambiguity) and then corroborated and developed these themes using related conceptual models in Sect. 4.

Managerial Skills and Strategies. Previous literature has addressed the role of managerial skills in the micro-level design factors and leadership planning of government programs [17, 18]. For example, the micro-level design of effective program objectives should involve a coherent strategy with clear goals and specific and measurable outcomes [19], accountable leadership [20], and, in the context of OG, management of a culture of publicizing open data, inter-organizational collaboration, and focusing on the impact of policies [21].

In the area of open data, previous literature also finds that an incremental and experimental approach by managers of open data is better than just releasing data for its own sake [22]. Open data usually fails in the goal of informing citizens of how they can make objective and intelligent decisions about policy if it does not have a mechanism for conveying context as well as content of data [23]. Bertot et al. [24] say that managerial measurement of open government initiatives must include knowledge of wider impacts as well as understanding of the route to compliance. Similarly, the level of professionalism of managers, their perception of the political environment, and their attitude towards citizen input strongly shapes the use of citizen participation in budgeting processes [25].

Institutions. The role of institutional environments in terms of governance structures, policies, and legal approaches need to be understood for effective use of ICT for e-governance [26, 27].

Institutions underpin collaboration that is necessary for OG. A strong institutional integration agenda is important in successful interactive e-government initiatives so that design challenges and tensions can be managed [28]. Such collaboration effectiveness is determined by "process, structural and governance components, constraints and contingencies, outcomes, and accountability issues" [29].

But institutional processes can have differential impacts on different areas of OG. For the OG sub-categories of access to information and citizen participation, political institutions are important. Berliner [30] carried out multivariate analysis of antecedents of access to information laws and found that competition within political institutions was the strongest correlate. Zhang and Liao [31] found that political competition increased the likelihood of adopting participative and interactive forms of e-government tools, while institutions that mandate citizen participation have better performance of citizen participation initiatives [32].

Technology. Open government policies rely heavily on ICT, but empirical research shows numerous examples that contextual variables of trust, self-efficacy, and level of digital literacy are key determinants of digital government performance (e.g., [33, 34]). Bailard [33] in a multi-country study of e-governance, civic engagement, and trust found that higher levels of internet use increased frustration with e-government in undemocratic countries but increased satisfaction with e-government in democratic countries. In understanding these structural components of technology, Meijer [35] says that there are three areas of barriers in e-government performance: government, citizen, and structural-cultural.

From the perspective of structuration theory, technologies are not fixed parts of the organizational environment but are enacted through agentic and structural processes [15, 36]. The theory of technology enactment thus has special relevance to the policy design process of OG, where both environmental shifts in ICT capacity and the specific tools of ICT in individual OG policies and programs are vital.

Environmental Factors. Environmental factors in terms of social, political, geopolitical, and economic forces have been found to play a strong role in shaping effectiveness of policymaking in the OG arena. Freedom of information reforms, for example, have repeatedly been found to be driven by improved information flow resulting from gradual social, political, and economic changes [37].

Policy reform such as OG is an essentially tension- and conflict-laden organizational process because new policy fashions threaten the stability of existing policy communities [38, 39]. The political leadership involved in OG is important because, as von Furstenberg [40] says, "without a change in power and political will, externally imposed transparency codes and standards will forever be chasing an elusive target" (p. 115). The leadership of Barack Obama was a primary motivation behind open government initiatives in the United States [1].

Finally, research on OG and related areas such as ICT use and e-government has firmly established that the citizen environment is indispensable to policy design. Citizen demands for e-government strongly determine e-government level [41, 42]. Larger population, higher growth, lower unemployment, and larger population density is associated with higher e-government adoption [43].

Organizational Ambiguity. The theory of organizational ambiguity was originally developed by James March and Johan Olsen [44], but, for the present work, even more pertinent research on the topic of OG can be found in the work of Nils Brunsson [45], who understood well that the public character of government increases political-administrative tension. This tension inevitably leads to organizational de-coupling and hypocrisy, a natural state of organizations that is heightened in OG.

According to Brunsson [45] public organizations are *meta-organizations*. Meta-organizations are characterized by significant collaboration challenges and points of conflict, which are proliferated by OG processes that spread policy-making processes widely over a range of organizations and organizational environments. Scholars of OG have begun to elucidate the specific forms of ambiguity that are created by open, meta-organized forms of policy design. Yu and Robinson [6] refer to a kind of ambiguity where openness of data is conflated with transparency of government operations. There are also the trade-offs in OG between transparency and national security interests [46], accountability [47], and participation [36].

Another common area of open government ambiguity is the conflation of collaborative ICT platforms such as social media or wikis with open government [48]. Many government open data and transparency initiatives ostensibly enable governments to be more participative and responsive with citizens, but are ambiguously operating mainly as one-way information pathways [49].

4 Policy Process Design and Open Government: A Conceptual Model

At this point in the paper, I have validated the concept of OG and its four sub-categories, addressed the literature on the three theoretical perspectives of this paper – open government, structuration theory, and policy design theory – and presented five themes for a theoretical framework of the supporting factors of OG policy design. In this section a conceptual model of open government processes is first proposed starting with a corroboration of the themes (factors) proposed in Sect. 3. Secondly, the conceptual model is tested using e-participation as a hypothetical example of an OG policy.

4.1   A Conceptual Model of Open Government Policy Design Processes

Prior literature on the role of public administrators in design of open government-related program areas has started to propose similar conceptual models (e.g., [9, 50, 51]) and have identified a similar range of factors such as managerial, bureaucratic, technological, and political, but none of these has addressed OG as a common area of policy design processes in organizational theory. Therefore, the themes are likely to have overlap but not to be identical. Gonzalez-Zapata and Heeks [51] found that OGD takes on four main stakeholder processes; bureaucratic, political, technological, and economic.

In another of the existing conceptual models, by Gil-García and Pardo [50], the processes involved in successful e-government programs can be categorized as environmental or institutional, legal and regulatory, organizational and managerial, information technology, and information and data. Gil-García and Pardo [50] address both the environmental (external) processes and the managerial and technology (internal) processes that contribute to the context of complex governance.

The conceptual model here also has a dualistic approach in keeping with structuration theory. In Fig. 2 the institution factors sit directly at the intersection of the agentic enactment process of management strategy and technology, while environment, which is a broader socio-political structurational factor, is less directly involved. On the agency side, the factors are technology and management skills. The arrows joining the agentic components of the structuration process from t_1 to t_2 represent a structuration enactment process connecting to the structural variables of environment and institution. However, as discussed above the organizational environment is an area of organizational ambiguity and so the structuration process encounters ambiguity during the process of change between t_1 and t_2 (the shaded area).

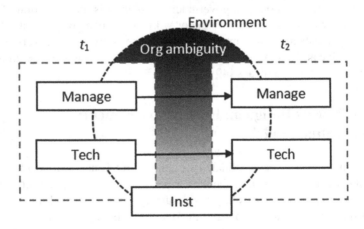

Fig. 2. Conceptual model of the open government policy design process

4.2 Analysis of the Conceptual Model Using a Hypothetical Example of E-Participation

The management skills and the technology factors play similar roles in the structura-tional process. These are other aspects interact with the institutional factors and are on the same circular plane moving from t_1 to t_2 in Fig. 2. For example, in the design of an e-participation platform, structural enactment takes place in the decision to attain a certain level of citizen accessibility (management skill) and the enactment of the tech-nological knowledge and resources in the organization from previous e-participation efforts or new technology hardware or software (technology). Both these things interact with the structure of rules, regulations, and culture of the organization (institutional factors), which in the example of e-participation, pertain to legal disclosure and data privacy standards, competition with other jurisdictions, policy mandates, and organiza-tional attitudes around the value of citizen participation.

Organizational ambiguity shown in Fig. 2 in the space inside the structuration process of management, technology, and institutional factors is not continuous within any of the structuration planes. However, it is bounded by the institutional plane symbolizing that ambiguity is a unique product of the particular organization. Note that the institutional plane also divides organizational ambiguity and the environment because, while neither are structurally continuous, they are, respectively, undetermined internal and external properties impacting the organization. In e-participation policy, a broad array of envi-ronmental factors have an impact such as economic level, stability of the political situa-tion, and public services infrastructure. These determine how many and what kinds of people participate as well as the quality of their interaction. Organizational ambiguity relates to the clarity (or lack thereof) of purpose for which the participation takes place such budgetary outcomes, legislation decision-making, or mere process participation with no target outcome. Organizational ambiguity could also pertain to the level of accountability or authority given to participants such as whether it is informative, consultative, delegative, etc.

5   Conclusion

This paper initially empirically derived a typology of OG and its core sub-categories using a systematic literature review and a multicountry categorization of OG policies. Secondly, a theoretical framework organized previous empirical findings regarding the policy design processes associated with the growing body of research on the design of OG initiatives and its sub-categories. The work of Nils Brunsson was used to frame organizational ambiguities associated with OG. It was argued that the multidimensional characteristic of OG calls for a model that combines agency and structural components of policy design in a structuration process. A conceptual model was developed along these theoretical lines and it was tested using a hypothetical example of e-participation.

The conceptual model of OG policy design process can be empirically tested in future research by operationalizing the relationships as measurable hypotheses. It can also be used as an analytic framework for evaluating the effectiveness of OG policy design processes. This paper has focused on the 'process' side of policy design and says very little about the 'outcomes' or 'impacts' side, which are also important. I expect that the conceptual model will help identify and analyze heightened effects of organizational ambiguity within OG policy design outcomes as well as ambiguities in the processes. OG 'success', referred to only in passing here, should be unpacked and studied in order to establish exactly how the OG design process relates to different kinds of outcomes for society. A related area for further research is to see if these relationships between processes and outcomes are different among the sub-categories of OG.

The objective of this paper was to address two puzzles of OG: firstly, relating to its conceptual coherency and, secondly, to the unified character of the design processes that enables public administrators to address more effective management and technological approaches. The paper shows that research on OG does suggest unique kinds of design processes and barriers in the form of ambiguities. Further understanding the OG specific design processes and barriers will be necessary to aid policymakers and public administrators in designing OG policies and programs that are likely to be more effective in meeting their goals.

References

1. Jaeger, P.T., Bertot, J.C.: Transparency and technological change: ensuring equal and sustained public access to government information. Gov. Inf. Q. 27(4), 371–376 (2010)
2. Linders, D., Wilson, S.C.: What is open government? One year after the directive. In: 12th Annual International Conference on Digital Government Research (Dg.o 2011), pp. 262–271 (2011)
3. Meijer, A.J., Curtin, D., Hillebrandt, M.: Open government: connecting vision and voice. Int. Rev. Admin. Sci. 78(1), 10–29 (2012)
4. Trivellato, B., Boselli, R., Cavenago, D.: Design and implementation of open-government initiatives at the sub-national level: lessons from Italian cases. In: Gascó-Hernández, M. (ed.) Open Government, pp. 65–84. Springer, New York (2014)
5. Grimmelikhuijsen, S.: A good man but a bad wizard. About the limits and future of transparency of democratic governments. Inf. Polit. 17(3), 293–302 (2012)
6. Yu, H., Robinson, D.: The new ambiguity of 'open government'. UCLA Law Rev. Discl. 59, 178–208 (2012)
7. McDermott, P.: Building open government. Gov. Inf. Q. 27(4), 401–413 (2010)
8. Meijer, A.: Understanding the complex dynamics of transparency. Publ. Adm. Rev. 73(3), 429–439 (2013)
9. Dawes, S.S., Vidiasova, L., Parkhimovich, O.: Planning and designing open government data programs: an ecosystem approach. Gov. Inf. Q. 33, 15–27 (2016)
10. Bouckaert, S.G., Peters, B.G.: Performance measurement and management: the Achilles' Heel in administrative modernization. Publ. Perform. Manag. Rev. 25(4), 359–362 (2002)
11. Davenport, T.H.: Process Innovation: Reengineering Work Through Information Technology. Harvard Business Press, Cambridge (2013)
12. Beierle, T.C., Konisky, D.M.: Values, conflict, and trust in participatory environmental planning. J. Policy Anal. Manag. 19(4), 587–602 (2000)
13. Giddens, A.: The Constitution of Society: Outline of the Theory of Structuration. University of California Press, Berkeley (1984)
14. Cooney, K.: Fields, organizations, and agency toward a multilevel theory of institutionalization in action. Adm. Soc. 39(6), 687–718 (2007)

15. Orlikowski, W.J.: Using technology and constituting structures: a practice lens for studying technology in organizations. Organ. Sci. **11**(4), 404–428 (2000)
16. Orlikowski, W.J.: The duality of technology: rethinking the concept of technology in organizations. Organ. Sci. **3**(3), 398–427 (1992)
17. May, P.J., Winter, S.C.: Collaborative service arrangements: patterns, bases, and perceived consequences. Publ. Manag. Rev. **9**(4), 479–502 (2007)
18. Sørensen, E., Torfing, J.: Making governance networks effective and democratic through metagovernance. Publ. Adm. **87**(2), 234–258 (2009)
19. de Lancer Julnes, P., Holzer, M.: Promoting the utilization of performance measures in public organizations: an empirical study of factors affecting adoption and implementation. Publ. Adm. Rev. **61**(6), 693–708 (2001)
20. Brudney, J.L., Hebert, F.T., Wright, T.S.: Reinventing government in the American states: measuring and explaining administrative reform. Publ. Adm. Rev. **59**(1), 19–30 (1999)
21. Zuiderwijk, A., Janssen, M.: Open data policies, their implementation and impact: a framework for comparison. Gov. Inf. Q. **31**(1), 17–29 (2014)
22. Conradie, P., Choenni, S.: On the barriers for local government releasing open data. Gov. Inf. Q. **31**, S10–S17 (2014)
23. Zhang, J., Puron-Cid, G., Gil-Garcia, J.R.: Creating public value through open government: perspectives, experiences and applications. Inf. Polit. **20**(2), 97–101 (2015)
24. Bertot, J.C., McDermott, P., Smith, T.: Measurement of open government: metrics and process. In: 2012 45th Hawaii International Conference on System Science (HICSS), pp. 2491–2499. IEEE (2012)
25. Zhang, Y., Yang, K.: Citizen participation in the budget process: the effect of city managers. J. Publ. Budg. Acc. Financ. Manag. **21**(2), 289 (2009)
26. Lee, C., Chang, K., Berry, F.S.: Testing the development and diffusion of e-government and e-democracy: a global perspective. Publ. Adm. Rev. **71**(3), 444–454 (2011)
27. Nasi, G., Frosini, F., Cristofoli, D.: Online service provision: are municipalities really innovative? The case of larger municipalities in Italy. Publ. Adm. **89**(3), 821–839 (2011)
28. Sun, P., Ku, C., Shih, D.: An implementation framework for e-government 2.0. Telemat. Inform. **32**(3), 504–520 (2015)
29. Bryson, J.M., Crosby, B.C., Stone, M.M.: The design and implementation of cross-sector collaborations: propositions from the literature. Publ. Adm. Rev. **66**(s1), 44–55 (2006)
30. Berliner, D.: The political origins of transparency. J. Polit. **76**(2), 479–491 (2014)
31. Zhang, Y., Liao, Y.: Participatory budgeting in local government: evidence from New Jersey municipalities. Publ. Perform. Manag. Rev. **35**(2), 281–302 (2011)
32. Martins, M.R.: Size of municipalities, efficiency, and citizen participation: a cross-European perspective. Environ. Plan. C: Gov. Policy **13**(4), 441–458 (1995)
33. Bailard, C.S.: Democracy's Double-Edged Sword: How Internet Use Changes Citizens' Views of Their Government. JHU Press, Baltimore (2014)
34. West, D.M.: Digital Government: Technology and Public Sector Performance. Princeton University Press, Princeton (2005)
35. Meijer, A.: E-governance innovation: barriers and strategies. Gov. Inf. Q. **32**(2), 198–206 (2015)
36. Fountain, J.E.: Building the Virtual State: Information Technology and Institutional Change. Brookings Institution Press, Washington (2001)
37. Xiao, W.: Freedom of information reform in China: information flow analysis. Int. Rev. Adm. Sci. **79**(4), 790–808 (2013)
38. Richardson, J.: Government, interest groups and policy change. Polit. Stud. **48**(5), 1006–1025 (2000)

39. Schaffers, H., Komninos, N., Pallot, M., Trousse, B., Nilsson, M., Oliveira, A.: Smart cities and the future internet: towards cooperation frameworks for open innovation. Future Internet Assem. **6656**(31), 431–446 (2011)

40. Von Furstenberg, G.M.: Hopes and delusions of transparency. North Am. J. Econ. Financ. **12**(1), 105–120 (2001)

41. Ahn, M.J.: Adoption of E-communication applications in US municipalities: the role of political environment, bureaucratic structure, and the nature of applications. Am. Rev. Publ. Adm. **41**(4), 428–452 (2010)

42. Li, M., Feeney, M.K.: Adoption of electronic technologies in local US governments distinguishing between E-services and communication technologies. Am. Rev. Publ. Adm. **44**(1), 75–91 (2014)

43. Nelson, K.L., Svara, J.H.: The roles of local government managers in theory and practice: a centennial perspective. Publ. Adm. Rev. **75**(1), 49–61 (2015)

44. March, J.G., Olsen, J.P.: Ambiguity and Choice in Organisations, vol. 37. Universitetsforlaget, Bergen (1976)

45. Brunsson, N.: The Organization of Hypocrisy: Talk, Decisions and Actions in Organizations. Copenhagen Business School Press, Copenhagen (1999)

46. Roberts, A.: Blacked Out: Government Secrecy in the Information Age. Cambridge University Press, Cambridge (2006)

47. Fox, J.: The uncertain relationship between transparency and accountability. Dev. Pract. **17**(4–5), 663–671 (2007)

48. Lourenço, R.P., Piotrowski, S., Ingrams, A.: Public accountability ICT support: a detailed account of public accountability process and tasks. In: Tambouris, E., Janssen, M., Scholl, H.J., Wimmer, M.A., Tarabanis, K., Gascó, M., Klievink, B., Lindgren, I., Parycek, P. (eds.) EGOV 2015. LNCS, vol. 9248, pp. 105–117. Springer, Heidelberg (2015)

49. Layne, K., Lee, J.: Developing fully functional e-government: a four stage model. Gov. Inf. Q. **18**(2), 122–136 (2001)

50. Gil-García, J.R., Pardo, T.A.: E-government success factors: mapping practical tools to theoretical foundations. Gov. Inf. Q. **22**(2), 187–216 (2005)

51. Gonzalez-Zapata, F., Heeks, R.: The multiple meanings of open government data: understanding different stakeholders and their perspectives. Gov. Inf. Q. **32**(1), 441–452 (2015)

In Search of ICT in Smart Cities – Policy Documents as Idea Carriers in Urban Development

Karin Axelsson[✉], Ulf Melin, and Malin Granath

Department of Management and Engineering, Information Systems,
Linköping University, Linköping, Sweden
{karin.axelsson,ulf.melin,malin.granath}@liu.se

Abstract. This paper explores how policy documents carry and institutionalize smart city ideas from high policy level to concrete policy level in an urban development context. We analyze the national urban development vision for Sweden and documents in a local urban development project in a Swedish city, in order to explore what kind of roles and expectations ICT is given in these documents. We contrast this with views of how social and environmental aspects are discussed in the studied documents. In order to understand and analyze the result we apply the concept of institutional carriers from institutional theory to our findings. Our analysis shows that as carriers of how ICT can contribute to increased sustainability in urban development, the policy documents do not function very well. ICT aspects are not put forth by any policy-making actor, neither on national nor on local level. The notion of institutional carriers helped us understand that without a responsible actor focusing on ICT's role in smart cities, it is easy to forget or lose sight of technology.

Keywords: Smart city · Urban development · Policy · Institutional theory · Institutional carriers

1 Introduction

The smart city concept is often used to emphasize how modern urban planning initiatives use information and communication technology (ICT) to fulfil the goals in sustainable development [1, 2, 10]. Strategic policy documents and visionary programs are formulated both on international (e.g. in EU), national and local levels. Previous research shows that these kind of smart city policies seem to both black-box ICT and, at the same time, take it for granted [9]. This may result in a situation where a city misses to develop and use innovative ICT solutions and, thus, becomes less smart. It might not be explicitly mentioned what kind of ICT that is envisioned in plans for a future smart city, but it is concurrently spoken of in a way as if the ICT solution already was in place and ready to use. In reality the situation often is the opposite. Visionary programs do not go into detail about specific ICT solutions, but express positive notions of technology in general terms [e.g. 6]. When the visions are realized in urban development projects other issues which impact sustainability are focused and ICT is reduced to e.g.

Published by Springer International Publishing Switzerland 2016. All Rights Reserved
H.J. Scholl et al. (Eds.): EGOV 2016, LNCS 9820, pp. 215–227, 2016.
DOI: 10.1007/978-3-319-44421-5_17

smart electricity meters or smart alarms. The innovative potential of ICT in urban development is, thus, not fully taken advantage of. In general information systems (IS) literature this problem has been discussed for a long time; "The IT artifact itself tends to disappear from view, be taken for granted, or is presumed to be unproblematic once it is built and installed." [14, p. 121]. As a response to this there is a call to highlight and investigate ICT as an artefact more thoroughly in development and use (ibid.). The smart city context is no exception in this case; a main challenge here is to thoroughly understand ICT in order to find out how humans can utilize it in innovative ways that support participation, interaction, and empowerment in the city [7, 10, 12]. Only then we can claim that the city is "smart" in this context.

In this paper we aim to analyze and compare policy documents on two levels; the national urban development vision for Sweden and documents in a local urban development project in a Swedish city. We do this in order to explore what kind of roles and expectations ICT is given in these documents. We contrast this with views of how social and environmental aspects are expressed in the studied documents. The purpose of the paper is to explore how policy documents carry and institutionalize smart city ideas from high policy level to concrete policy level in an urban development project. In order to understand and analyze this we apply the concept of institutional carriers from institutional theory to our findings.

After this introduction, the paper is organized in the following way: In Sect. 2 we discuss previous research on this paper's two theoretical foundations; smart city initiatives and institutional theory. The research approach is reported in Sect. 3. The findings from our analysis of policy documents are presented in Sect. 4. In Sect. 5 the findings are discussed in the light of institutional theory. The paper is concluded in Sect. 6, in which we also make some suggestions about the need for further research efforts in this area.

2 Theoretical Foundations

This paper focuses on how policy documents carry and institutionalize smart city ideas from national visions to concrete plans in a local urban development project. In this section we discuss previous research on smart city initiatives in order to show societal challenges such urban development projects intend to address. We then give a brief overview of institutional theory, especially focusing on institutional carriers.

2.1 Smart City Initiatives

We are experiencing a time with several intertwined mega-trends that impact our lives [6]. Climate changes and emission of greenhouse gases are important reasons for taking the climate threats seriously and striving for environmental-friendly solutions in urban development [cf. 18]. The globalization has been on-going for a long time and includes an intense interchange of information, goods and trade, tight links between different parts of the world and interdependent economies [6]. Increasing urbanization is another trend; in 2030 the prognosis says that more than half of the world's population will live in cities [23]. Many cities thus grow rapidly which make construction activities and good planning important ways to deal with the increasingly dense cities. The fourth trend, which impacts on smart city development, is digitization [3, 26]. Digitization is discussed in terms of an intensive information flow, communication speed, integration, and digital meetings as complement to, or alternative to physical meetings. The need for a robust and accessible communication infrastructure as a precondition for creating smart cities is highlighted [12].

Facing all challenges that these mega-trends comprise, the city has been assigned an important role in achieving sustainability [11]. The concept of smart cities has been defined as an inclusive framework to "mitigate and remedy current urban problems" [1, p. 40], by focusing on several dimensions of city development such as economy, governance, people, natural environment, and infrastructure [13]. Caragliu et al. [5, p. 70] argue that a city is smart "when investments in human and social capital and traditional (transport) and modern (ICT) communication infrastructure fuel sustainable economic growth and a high quality of life, with a wise management of natural resources, through participatory governance". It is obvious in both research and policy-making that hope is put on smart cities to solve the above-mentioned problems [6].

Several researchers have discussed what constitutes a smart city. Hollands [10] argues that in order to be successful a smart city must focus on humans and understand how they interact, instead of just hoping that ICT by itself will transform and improve cities. A similar argument is found in Nam and Pardo [12] who emphasize the need of a socio-technical view of the smart city. They pinpoint a smart city's main components as technology factors, human factors, and institutional factors. In order to understand smart city development we need to understand the relation between technology, people and policy, and how these interact with outer factors such as governance, economy, built infrastructure, and natural environment [1]. Building on this notion of several interacting aspects that together define a smart city, we will focus on social, environmental and ICT aspects when analyzing policy documents in urban development, below.

2.2 Institutional Theory and Institutional Carriers

Institutional theory, or new institutionalism [17], in institutions and organizations [e.g. 20] is powerful when studying the complex nature of ICT, institutional forms, its embeddedness in contexts and understanding change [19]. The smart city is an example of a context where we find this kind of complexity [12]. Institutions are structural arrangements that guide and restrict actors' behaviour [4]. Important dimensions in institutionalism can be expressed as three pillars both representing and supporting institutions; regulative, normative, and cultural-cognitive [20, 22].

Studying ICT within an institutional framework can be motivated by the fact that ICT have a directive power within institutions and institutionalization that can be traced back to the cognitive and normative elements embedded in ICT artefacts [8]. The three pillars above can be summarized as follows. The regulative pillar contains the constraints and regulation of behaviour; setting and formulating rules, monitoring and sanctioning such activities (e.g. to arrange rules, to follow or monitor rule compliance, rewards or even punishments). The normative pillar contains values and norms. This includes what is preferred or desirable and the assessment of such aspects. Norms express how things should be done and is the core of legitimacy and the means to reach certain objectives [22]. The cultural-cognitive element as the third pillar rests heavily on sociology and organizational studies. Symbols are important and expressed in terms of signs, gestures, and words shaping collective and individual understanding in institutions (ibid.).

The pillars and elements above are carried in institutions by different vehicles [21]. Carriers are tightly linked to every aspect of the pillars and can be understood and analyzed for example in terms of symbolic systems carrying: regulative elements (e.g. rules in smart city development regarding buildings and infrastructures), normative elements (e.g. values and expectations of ICT in a smart city on a conceptual level), and cultural-cognitive elements (e.g. categories and typifications of ICT or smartness in policy documents). Relational systems can also carry regulative elements (e.g. governance structures and power systems), normative elements, and cultural-cognitive ditto. Activities as a third type of carrier are also a vehicle for regulative, normative, and cultural-cognitive elements. Last but not least, artefacts (like ICT) can have a role as vehicles for all three types of elements. All carriers are non-neutral and carry the values, preferences, and social constructions given to or implemented in them.

3   Research Approach

We have followed and studied a Swedish local urban development project in a qualitative and interpretative case study [25] for almost two years and have, thus, gained detailed understanding of the early phases of the project (from its launch to the municipality's local plan decision). In this paper we focus on the qualitative and discursive analysis [15, 16, 27] of policy documents on different levels; a national vision of sustainable urban development as well as several policy documents that are important in the studied development project. By analyzing how social, environmental, and ICT aspects are expressed and formulated in the documents we illustrate how smart city ideas and ideals are transferred and "flow" between documents representing different phases in a development project – from a strategic and overall level to a more operative and local level. At the same time we acknowledge the deliberate and network-oriented perspective on policy-making and policy processes as being more "messy" and less linear than they usually appear on a strategic level, and also carried by human actors. As information systems and e-government researchers we focus extra on how ICT is described because of the identified risk that ICT is taken for granted and not problematized, as discussed above, in previous studies.

The studied urban development project was launched in late 2011. We have studied the project during the phases of architect competition, exhibition, planning, exploitation, procurement, and local plan decision (see Fig. 1 below). The project aims to build a new district and organize a home and urban construction expo in parallel. Social and ecologic sustainability are two dimensions that are much emphasized in the project. The project shows typical characteristics of the aim of a smart city which makes it suitable to use as an empirical case in this paper.

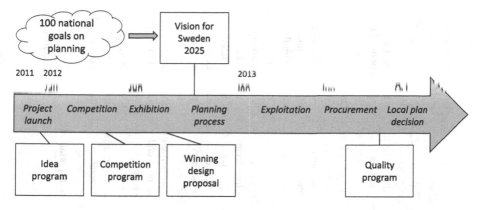

Fig. 1. Project development process and related policy documents

We have collected data about the project through several methods; we have attended internal project meetings and external stakeholder workshops, interviewed stakeholders, and studied documents, such as policy documents, project information material, and project web information. Altogether we have gained rich empirical data about the early phases of the project through different kinds of sources and interventions. In this paper we have a certain focus on policy analysis and other data collected in the project serves, thus, as background information. Here the qualitative data analysis of the policy documents is guided by institutional theory, as we use the concept of institutional carrier as a theoretical lens [24]. However, our data analysis is also inductive in terms of being sensitive towards the empirical material when identifying and acknowledging interpretations of the overall view from the policy documents and the urban development project.

4   Analyzing Policy Documents

Five policy documents on different abstraction levels are analyzed below, in order to illustrate how social, environmental and ICT aspects are expressed on different policy levels and possibly transferred between levels (Table 1). The documents are: (1) Vision for Sweden 2025, (2) the idea program of the studied local urban development project, (3) the competition program, (4) the winning design proposal, and (5) the quality program including the local plans.

4.1   Studied Policy Documents

In 2012, Sweden's National Board of Housing, Building and Planning conducted a strategic analysis, based on existing global analyses, which is reported in *"Vision for Sweden 2025"* (translated to English in 2014). The purpose of the vision is to present holistic objectives for Sweden's future based on 100 national goals that relate to physical and social planning in different ways. The document has a long term planning perspective and puts physical planning in the foreground; other related issues like

Table 1. Policy documents' expressions of social, environmental, and ICT aspects

	Vision for Sweden	Idea program	Competition program	Winning design proposal	Quality program incl. local plans
Social aspects	Social development and a good life are promoted Physical spaces that fit people Social integration	A place for everyone to meet, work, live and learn Citizen involvement in planning process Parks for recreation	A resource efficient, beautiful and human-friendly district	Neighbours share winter gardens Community houses where people can meet and interact	A community house and a green house in every block Demands for outdoor lightening, access to nature, and health-friendly materials
Environ-mental aspects	A sustainable environment with "places fit for people", decreased motor traffic in cities and an overall resource-saving lifestyle Efficient transport infrastructures	Innovations in energy effective buildings, locally produced electricity, and sustainable construction material	Easy for the individual to act climate smart Bicycle and public transportation instead of cars A dynamic and robust environment, sustainable and easy to adjust to new demands	Densified, close living increases energy efficiency Public transportation Car pool and charging stations Locally grown vegetables decreases transportation	Walking, biking and public transportation Car pools, no parking by the houses Smart meters installed in all houses Electricity surplus possible to deliver to the power grid

(Continued)

Table 1. (*Continued*)

	Vision for Sweden	Idea program	Competition program	Winning design proposal	Quality program incl. local plans
ICT aspects	Communication infrastructure, a precondition for services and information flows E-services – connecting e.g. citizens and public sector agencies Mobile devices for communica-tion in cities	Smart and innovative ICT solutions to decrease consumption of natural resources and increase availability, service and social presence	Mobile solutions to enable people to work at home, in cafés and public places Smart grid technology	CO_2 neutral district 2025 Smart grid technology enables both energy production and consumption	"Climate smart" is mentioned, but no technology or ICT aspects are explicitly discussed

social sustainability are in the background and included only if related to the physical social structure. A sustainable society is the major long term objective; i.e. building for environmental care. The document is: "Intended to be used as a conceptual foundation when preparing strategies for sustainable development at different levels." (p. 51) and should be used as inspiration for: "[…] promoting sustainable social development at all levels from national to local" (p. 51). The target group for the vision is politicians and public officials at all levels: from national to local, from central to local agencies and different organizations and private stakeholders.

The *idea program* describes the purpose of the project in order to guide the future work. It rests on three pillars; knowledge, social sustainability, and creativity which should permeate the future local district. The idea program is written by municipality officers and is targeted to anyone interested in the project. The program states the project's visions of future front edge urban development based on citizen dialogue.

The *competition program* is based on the idea program and communicates the visions of the future district in order to inspire architects to come up with design proposals for how to realize the project. The view that is conveyed to the architects is the one of a varied district where nature, culture and social activities are in focus. The competition program is written by officers from the municipality in collaboration with representatives from a university, a local energy company, and a housing company.

The *winning design proposal* was chosen by a jury examining the 27 proposals sent in to the competition. The design proposal explains the architect firm's idea of how to realize the visions of the local district, both in text and illustrations.

The *quality program* contains the local plans which are developed based on the winning proposal. The program is written to support coordination and design of the district. By expressing the desired character of the district a holistic approach is aimed for. The quality program also stipulates demands, recommendations, and responsibilities concerning sustainability that must be met by the building companies that take part in the project. The document is written by the Environment and Planning Administration in the municipality and it is directed to the building companies as a base for their participation in the land allocation process.

4.2   Expressions of Social, Environmental, and ICT Aspects

Social aspects could of course include many different issues, but in the vision for physical and social planning in Sweden the main emphasis is put on social development and how to achieve a good life. The expression "places fit for people" is used to describe a future where urban districts include everything needed to work and live there. Such urban districts are described as hubs for development. Extensive public transportation networks and green areas for recreation are two examples of how human needs are focused. Everything should be close by and easy to access, no cars are needed and people should be able to choose a resource-saving lifestyle. Opportunities for social integration and distance-learning are included in this vision. In the idea program these ideas are transferred into "a place for everyone to meet, work, live, and learn". Parks and gardens are also highlighted as places for recreation. The importance of citizen involvement in the planning process is highlighted as a consequence of a main emphasis on achieving social sustainability through this urban development project. In the competition program social aspects are found in the objective to develop a district that is resource efficient, beautiful and human-friendly. In the winning design proposal it is suggested that neighbours share winter gardens. Another design proposal relating to social aspects is that community houses, where people can meet and interact, should be built. In the quality program these design ideas are realized in form of a community house and a green house in every block. We also find demands for the building companies regarding outdoor lightening, easy access to nature, and the use of health-friendly materials.

Many of the above-mentioned examples of social aspects also have a connection to *environmental aspects*. In the vision for physical and social planning in Sweden we see the call for efficient public transport infrastructure and decreased motor traffic in the urban district as examples of ways to encourage and support an overall resource-saving lifestyle. A strive for increased energy efficiency and a fossil-free electrical energy system are other highlighted goals. In the idea program this is translated to innovations in energy effective buildings, locally produced electricity, and sustainable construction material. Environmental aspects are thus discussed in rather general terms. However, in the competition program it is stated that the district should make it easy for the individual to act climate smart. In order to emphasize the environmental aspects bikes and public transportation should be prioritized instead of cars. The goal is to build a dynamic and robust environment that should be sustainable and easy to adjust to new demands. In the winning design proposal this is converted into a car pool and electric car charging stations together with good public transportation. Another idea is that the residents should grow vegetables locally and, thus, decrease the need for transportation. By building for densified, close living energy efficiency will increase and a CO_2 neutral district is aimed to be a reality in 2025. In the quality program we see how these ideas are formulated in a planning that supports walking, biking and public transportation. Car pools are suggested and parking by houses is not allowed. Smart meters are installed in all houses and electricity surplus should be possible to deliver to the power grid.

ICT aspects are treated in rather general terms in the vision for physical and social planning in Sweden. It is stated that communication infrastructure is a robust pre-condition for services and information flows, and that e-services are important tools to connect citizens and public sector agencies. Mobile devices are also mentioned as important in order to communicate both in cities and in rural areas. In the idea program this is described as smart and innovative ICT solutions which should be used in order to decrease consumption of natural resources. Another effect of using ICT should be increased availability, service and social presence. In the competition program this is concretized to mobile solutions that will enable people to work at home, in cafés and public places. It is also mentioned that smart grid technology should be implemented. The winning design proposal suggests that smart grid technology should be used in the district in order to enable both energy production and consumption. In the quality program ICT aspects are not explicitly mentioned at all. The concept "climate smart" is mentioned, but it is not stated what constitutes smartness in this case.

When comparing the main view of ICT in the analyzed documents a picture arises where the high level policy starts with discussing ICT in broad terms. We see traces of digitization in the intelligent home where smart energy use is in focus. When turning to the concrete policy level and the idea program, which is the most visionary document among the project documents, we find an explicit ambition to build a climate smart district. However, neither in the idea program nor in the competition program ICT solutions are explicitly mentioned. The winning design proposal states that smart electricity meters will be implemented in the buildings. Finally in the quality program (local plans) ICT is not mentioned at all. This is a clear example of the situation we described in the beginning of this paper; that ICT aspects are neglected, taken for granted or seen as so unproblematic that they do not need to be commented on. In Table 1 above, the found expressions of social, environmental, and ICT aspects in the studied documents are summarized.

5 Discussion

From this analysis of policy documents we find that rather few ICT solutions and innovations are expressed in high level policies and even fewer seem to survive during the transfer to concrete policy level. Instead, sustainability solutions are dominating when we come closer to the concrete urban development project. The ICT dimension of smartness does not reach out the entire way, and instead smart resource use, without ICT, ends up being in focus. The policy documents do not offer any new visions or ideas when it comes to ICT innovation. Of course we should not regard ICT as an end in itself, but it is definitely an important means to create and realize the visions of the smart city [1, 10, 12]. There might be many reasons for this situation to arise. In the studied policy documents there seem to exist several, partly competing, values such as social sustainability, inclusion, integration and ecological sustainability. ICT is not put forth by any policy-making actor or framework of rules, etc. Furthermore, it seems as the building industry has a rather conservative view of ICT (because of rules and regulations, but also organizational and professional culture), thus, the ICT aspects of smartness seem to be neglected or reduced to existing technologies (e.g. smart grid and smart meters) in the local plans.

From an institutional theory perspective [22] we identify that important pillars and elements are carried in different ways and by different expressions and actors in the studied policy documents. There are several *rules* regarding how to plan and build that are present in different stages of the policy process, and the plans that are expressed in the studied documents. Rules are *regulative* and constraints what is possible to do in a formal plan and building process (regarding e.g. compulsory and necessary steps to be taken as a part of an institutional process). *Normative* elements are also present affecting what is to be considered as legitimate and desirable. It is also expressed in terms of values of sustainability (e.g. environmental aspects in Table 1 above) in all types of documents analyzed above. Environmental aspects are part of the core of legitimizing the smart city and the means to reach certain objectives [cf. 22]. These elements travel all the way through the policy documents, as stated above, and are an evident part of the policy-making from national strategies to the local project. *Cultural-cognitive* elements in the form of symbols are evident here, since words carry different ideals, such as sustainability in ecological or social terms. These elements are also carried by several strong actors, who make them "survive" throughout the process together with activities in the same line. Social aspects, in Table 1 above, are also carried throughout the process and expressed as what is preferred and/or desirable. Normative elements are clear regarding e.g. the community ideal, interaction and integration. These ideals are also carried by symbols (words) and significant actors in the studied project.

When analyzing the policy documents also from an institutional point of view, we identity that values and norms regarding ICT artefacts are not that evident. ICT is not a significant part of the prefix smart at any level or setting in the studied documents. There are ideals and meaning of ICT being part of a communication infrastructure, a carrier of services, and a precondition for mobile solution on a general and national policy level, but these ideals and ideas are not that evident in documents throughout the process, and not carried further in a clear and convincing way. The visionary ideas, or to put it in other words, the ICT edge is lost. There are signs of ICT being a part of grids and mobile applications, but more as one means among others, to achieve e.g. sustainability. ICT is not an objective or significant artefact that constitutes the smart concept. The analysis reveals that the local policy documents are dominated by values and norms connected to the building process and strong actors in this field carrying those ideal, rather than ICT related relational system structures (e.g. strong governance structures or power systems supporting ICT as an important aspects in a smart city project). This goes in line with the underpinning from the institutional perspective and the perspective in this study, that all carriers are non-neutral and carry the values, preferences, and social constructions given to or implemented in them [21, 22].

Activities, as another carrier, do not support ICT as a key component of the smart city concept in the development process. In that sense ICT is overruled by other values and norms as a part of a policy process dominated by environmental and social aspects (Table 1), not ICT aspects. The ICT related values and norms are not effectively carried throughout the different documents representing the policy process from a strategic level to a local level. Maybe this is not surprising since building processes are highly regulated and institutionalized. The innovative dimension of the smart city concept, however, can be threatened when not using ICT as an active and symbolic element in policy-making processes.

6 Conclusions

In this paper we have analyzed how five policy documents on different abstraction levels express social, environmental, and ICT aspects connected to the urban development process. The purpose of this study has been to explore how policy documents function to carry and institutionalize smart city ideas from high policy level to concrete policy level in this kind of projects. By applying the theoretical concept of institutional carriers [21, 22] to our findings, we have discussed possible explanations to the fact that social and environmental aspects dominate in the policy documents while ICT aspects are almost non-existing. It is interesting to notice that even though ICT is perceived as an important smart city component in literature [1, 10, 12] it does not have the same prominence neither on high policy level nor on concrete policy level. In this paper we have shown that policy documents carry and institutionalize social and environmental ideas and ideals. However, as carriers of how ICT can contribute to increased sustainability in urban development, the policy documents do not seem to function very well. We have searched for expressions of how ICT is envisioned to support the smart city, but found very little evidence of this. One could expect a leak of ideas during the transfer between policy levels and documents, but if the ICT aspects are not there from the beginning they will not emerge during the process.

An important finding in this study is that the ICT aspects are not put forth by any policy-making actor, neither on national nor on local level. The notion of institutional carriers helped us to see that if no one is responsible for focusing on ICT it is easy to forget or lose sight of technology. Thus, ICT disappears from the view, is taken for granted or underestimated as uncomplicated [14]. A theoretical contribution is, thus, that researchers need to theorize about the role of ICT artefacts in order to achieve "smartness" in urban development. A practical implication of this is that in order for future urban development projects to reach the high expectations of smart cities solving grand challenges of urbanization, globalization, and climate changes, ICT must be focused. ICT can be used to combine social and environmental aspects in innovative ways and, thus, realize the ideas and ideals of the smart city, but ICT can also be the carrier of such ideas in the smart city context. ICT is not an end in itself, but an important means for realizing the smart city.

Applying institutional theory to empirical data from an urban development project has helped us to discuss policy documents as carriers of smart city ideas in a promising way. In future studies a more thorough analysis of findings from both policy and practice levels would be interesting to conduct in order to further understand the meaning of ICT in smart cities. These studies can also include other regional and national contexts in order to challenge and handle the limitations of studying only one context above.

Acknowledgements. This study has been financially supported by the Swedish Energy Agency.

References

1. Alawadhi, S., et al.: Building understanding of smart city initiatives. In: Scholl, H.J., Janssen, M., Wimmer, M.A., Moe, C.E., Flak, L.S. (eds.) EGOV 2012. LNCS, vol. 7443, pp. 40–53. Springer, Heidelberg (2012)
2. Angelidou, M.: Smart city policies: a spatial approach. Cities **41**(1), S3–S11 (2014)
3. Baskerville, R.: Editorial: reviving the IT in the IS. Eur. J. Inf. Syst. **21**(6), 587–591 (2012)
4. Berger, P.L., Luckmann, T.: The Social Construction of Reality – A Treatise in the Sociology of Knowledge. Anchor Books, Random House Inc., New York (1967)
5. Caragliu, A., Del Bo, C., Nijkamp, P.: Smart cities in Europe. J. Urban Technol. **18**(2), 65–82 (2011)
6. COM – Communication from the commission: Europe 2020: a European strategy for smart, sustainable and inclusive growth. European Commission (2010)
7. Gil-Garcia, J.R., Helbig, N., Ojo, A.: Being smart: emerging technologies and innovation in the public sector. Gov. Inf. Q. **31**(1), 11–18 (2014)

8. Gosain, S.: Enterprise information systems as objects and carriers of institutional forces: the new iron cage? J. Assoc. Inf. Syst. **5**(4), 151–182 (2004)
9. Granath, M., Axelsson, K.: Stakeholders' views on ICT and sustainable development in an urban development project. In: Proceedings of the European Conference on Information Systems (ECIS) 2014, Tel Aviv, Israel, 9–11 June 2014 (2014). ISBN 978-0-9915567-0-0
10. Hollands, R.G.: Will the real smart city please stand up? intelligent, progressive or entrepreneurial? City: Anal. Urban Trends Cult. Theory Policy Action **12**(3), 303–320 (2008)
11. Kievani, R.: Reflections on Rio: perspectives on the World Urban Forum 5. Int. J. Urban Sustain. Dev. **2**(1–2), 141–148 (2010)
12. Nam, T., Pardo, T.: Conceptualizing smart city with dimensions of technology, people, and institutions. In: Proceedings of the 12th Annual International Conference on Digital Government Research (Dgo 2011), pp. 282–291 (2011)
13. Nierotti, P., De Marco, A., Cagliano, A.C., Mangano, G., Scorrano, F.: Current trends in smart city initiatives: some stylised facts. Cities **38**, 25–36 (2014)
14. Orlikowski, W.J., Iacono, S.: Research commentary: desperately seeking the "IT" in IT research - a call to theorizing the IT artifact. Inf. Syst. Res. **12**(2), 121–134 (2001)
15. Parsons, D.W.: Public Policy: An Introduction to the Theory and Practice of Policy Analysis. Edward Elgar Publishing Ltd., Cheltenham (1995)
16. Potter, J., Wetherell, M.: Discourse and Social Psychology: Beyond Attitudes and Behaviour. Sage Publications, London (1987)
17. Powell, W.W., DiMaggio, P.J.: The New Institutionalism in Organizational Analysis. University of Chicago Press, Chicago (1991)
18. Rees, W.: Ecological footprints and appropriated carrying capacity: what urban economics leaves out. Environ. Urban. **4**(2), 121–130 (1992)
19. Robey, D., Boudreau, M.: Accounting for the contradictory organizational consequences of information technology: theoretical directions and methodological implications. Inf. Syst. Res. **10**(2), 167–185 (1999)
20. Scott, W.R.: Institutions and Organizations, 2nd edn. Sage, Thousand Oaks (2001)
21. Scott, W.R.: Institutional carriers: reviewing modes of transporting ideas over time and space and considering their consequences. Ind. Corp. Change **12**(4), 879–894 (2003)
22. Scott, W.R.: Institutions and Organizations, 4th edn. Sage Publications Inc., London (2014)
23. United Nations Population Fund. www.unfpa.org. Accessed 11 Mar 2016
24. Walsham, G.: Interpretive case studies in IS research: nature and method. Eur. J. Inf. Syst. **4**(2), 74–81 (1995)
25. Walsham, G.: Doing interpretive research. Eur. J. Inf. Syst. **15**(3), 320–330 (2006)
26. Walsham, G.: Are we making a better world with ICTs? Reflections on a future agenda for the IS field. J. Inf. Technol. **27**(2), 87–93 (2012)
27. Yanow, D.: Accessing local knowledge. In: Hajer, M.A., Wagenaar, H. (eds.) Deliberative Policy Analysis. Understanding Governance in the Network Society, pp. 228–246. Cambridge University Press, Cambridge (2003)

Towards a "Smart Society" Through a Connected and Smart Citizenry in South Africa: A Review of the National Broadband Strategy and Policy

More Ickson Manda[(⊠)] and Judy Backhouse

The University of Witwatersrand, Johannesburg, South Africa
moreikson@gmail.com

Abstract. Broadband has been recognised as an enabling technology in connecting government and citizens in transitioning towards a smart society. However, governments, especially in developing countries, continue to face challenges in their bid to connect citizens. This study provides an understanding of how institutional pressures have influenced policy implementation to advance the "smart agenda" in a developing country context, using South Africa as an exemplary case study. The study is an interpretive qualitative case study, using documentary evidence as data. Institutional theory is used as a lens for interrogating the issues confronting government in implementing "smart" initiatives. We conclude that policy alone is not sufficient if not supported by a strong implementation plan and other supporting institutional mechanisms such as leadership to coordinate, and direct resources and activities in the institution.

Keywords: Smart citizen · Smart society · E-government · Institutional theory

1 Introduction

Governments around the world have realised the great potential of using Information and Communication Technologies (ICTs) to create so called "smart societies" for social and economic development [37]. Broadband internet access has been recognised as an enabling technology for connecting people, businesses and governments in the smart society [23]. The adoption of inclusive and effective broadband policies has thus been identified as a critical step in enhancing digital connectivity [23].

In this study we explore the implementation of broadband and other relevant policies aimed at assisting South Africa to realise its vision of a smart and connected society by 2030. Lofgren [29] argues that "mainstream e-government literature rarely goes beyond basic descriptions of the policy ideas and the actors behind them. The bargaining and negotiations between policy actors (both inside and outside the government), which initiate the policy, set the agenda, as well as actually implement the policy, has been notably overlooked in the literature of e-government." This is the gap this study is hoping to close by contributing new knowledge through the use of institutional theory as a lens for understanding institutional forces that have impacted policy implementation in a developing country context.

© IFIP International Federation for Information Processing 2016
Published by Springer International Publishing Switzerland 2016. All Rights Reserved
H.J. Scholl et al. (Eds.): EGOV 2016, LNCS 9820, pp. 228–240, 2016.
DOI: 10.1007/978-3-319-44421-5_18

In the last decade, South Africa has made progress towards building a "smart society", realising the value of ICT in the social and economic development of the country. It is one of the few countries in Africa that has adopted the "smart" agenda through initiatives such as "smart cities" which include efforts to enhance connectivity through broadband, digital access and e- literacy of residents [3]. The National Development Plan (NDP) is South Africa's national strategic framework which sets a vision for the development of the country, including developing an ICT infrastructure for stimulating social and economic development. A concern that the NDP seeks to address is that *"South Africa's ICT sector has not brought affordable, universal access to the full range of communications services and has lost its status as continental leader in internet and broadband connectivity"* [45]. Only 49 % of South Africa's population is using the internet, ranking 40th among 144 developing countries. Access to fixed broadband per 100 capita still remains low at 3.3 with an overall ranking of 110 out of the 189 International Telecommunications Union member states [23].

Smart societies are being brought about as "society is moving towards a socio-technical ecosystem in which physical and virtual dimensions of life are inter-twined and where people interactions ever more take place with or are mediated by machines" [40]. The concept of smart society is based on the idea of how the techno-social trends can be leveraged towards addressing some of the challenges facing modern society [21]. A smart society is thus an advanced stage of the information and knowledge society characterised by communities with diverse values, needs and skills yet linked by a common identity [26, 40]. It is also defined as "one that successfully harnesses the potential of digital technology and connected devices and the use of digital networks to improve people's lives" [27]. From these definitions, it is clear that smart societies are driven by technology, digital connectivity, knowledge, skills, common goals and innovation to institute political, social and economic development.

Policy implementation remains one of the significant challenges in governing the "smart" environment [41]. The purpose of this study is therefore to provide an understanding of how institutional pressures in government have influenced policy implementation in the "smart" era. We conducted this study in a developing country context, where few such studies have been conducted and findings will strengthen policy implementation through a better understanding of forces impacting e-government.

The **main question** shaping this study is:

- What institutional barriers is the South African government facing in its bid to create a connected and smart citizenry that is responsive to the smart society?

The **main objectives** of the study are to:

- *Understand barriers confronting the South African government in its bid to create a smart citizenry that is responsive to the demands of a smart society.*
- *Examine how policy implementation impacts broadband penetration to increase citizen connectivity in realising the vision of a smart society in South Africa.*

This paper is divided into two sections; the first section reviews literature on increasing citizen participation in a smart society. The second section discusses challenges in smart society development in South Africa using institutional theory as a lens to explain and understand issues confronting government in policy implementation.

2 Methodology

The study is a qualitative interpretive case study as its purpose is to understand the complex social, cultural, economic and political issues surrounding policy implementation in South Africa. A review of literature and documentary evidence were used as the main methods of gathering data. Literature on smart societies and government to citizen e-government was reviewed so as to help understand some of the issues confronting governments in their bid to develop smart societies. We reviewed literature published between 2000 and 2015 because the "smart agenda" is still a fairly new concept in e-government research. Literature searches using key words such as "smart society", "smart citizen", "smart government", "broadband penetration" and "e-participation" were conducted across four databases namely Google scholar, Science direct, IEEE explore and Wiley online. For documentary evidence, we reviewed the national broadband policy and other strategic national policies addressing the "smart agenda" published in the last 10 years (2005–2015) so as to understand institutional pressures impacting smart initiatives in South Africa (see Table 1). Relevant government and media reports were also used as sources of data. International reports such as the United Nations e-government report, Alliance for Affordable Internet and International Telecommunications Union (ITU) broadband reports were also consulted. Documents often contain rich information about institutions and their actions which may be difficult to gather through other methods such as interviews.

Table 1. E-government and ICT policy framework South Africa

Policy/strategy	Key elements
Digital migration policy (2008)	The Policy seeks to enable South Africa to emerge as a global leader in harnessing ICTs for socio-economic development
National development Plan (2012)	A long term strategic plan for South Africa which provides a broad strategic framework to guide key choices and actions including the development of e-government
National infrastructure plan (2012)	The plan seeks to transform the economic landscape through provision of key national infrastructure such as ICT, transport etc. to strengthen service delivery
Integrated ICT policy (2013)	The policy integrates the telecommunications, broadcasting and ICT framework into one policy framework due to convergence of Technology
National broadband policy (2013)	Provision of broadband services to ensure social and economic inclusion

Thematic analysis was used for analysing qualitative data and it involved identifying general themes in the data. Closed (deductive) coding was used to identify and classify themes of interest coming through from literature and theory.

3 Theoretical Framework

The study is underpinned by institutional theory which helps in understanding the interlinked and complex relationships inherent in institutional mechanisms, technology, social, and economic context, and institutional factors in which they are embedded [30]. We examine how internal and external institutional pressures have influenced policy implementation in support of smart society development in South Africa. Institutional theory is used as a lens for understanding how institutional elements, including regulative, normative and cultural-cognitive elements, together with their associated resources and activities identified by Scott [42] have influenced progress towards the smart agenda in South Africa. We also explore the three mechanisms identified by DiMaggio and Powell [14], through which isomorphic change occurs to understand institutional pressures influencing the smart agenda. These include coercive isomorphism that stems from formal and informal political influence to institutionalise certain rules and practices, mimetic isomorphism which results from pressure to imitate other organisations as standard responses from uncertainty and the need to minimise risk, and normative isomorphism associated with professionalisation of organisational actors. Institutional theory was used for identifying themes in the data for analysis. The adoption of institutional theory is particularly appropriate given the multidisciplinary nature of this study. This study crosses disciplines such as information systems, public administration and information science in the investigation of societal, technological and political issues central in the study of e-government.

4 Increasing Citizen Participation in a Smart Society

The country's citizens have been recognised as the most important beneficiaries of a connected and smart society [45]. E-government services worldwide have tended to shift towards being citizen centric as the successful transition towards a smart society relies on the ability of citizens to participate fully in government's smart initiatives [9, 39]. There are few definitions of "smart citizen" appearing in academic and practitioner literature. Smart citizen has been defined as "the citizen with wisdom and virtue based on collective opinion" [33]. It has also been defined as "the one who is healthy, having morals and create smart plan for all activities in best manner" [28]. From these two definitions it is clear that the concept of "smart citizen" has not been approached from the socio-technical perspective. It is against this background that we propose the following definition in the e-government context: A smart citizen is *"a technologically savvy citizen who has access to information and knowledge which they use to make informed choices in participating in social, economic, political and other activities in a smart society"*. Citizen engagement and participation in government activities is one of the key features of smart societies. Electronic participation (e-participation) is defined as the use of ICTs to enhance citizen engagement and participation in government [18, 35]. The use of sophisticated ICTs in government has "little social value if citizens are not able to use services or interact in political processes in meaningful ways" [22]. Citizen participation has however been compromised by a complexity of factors such as mistrust of government, mistrust of technology, low e-literacy and low access to technology [4, 12]. In the next sub-section we discuss several factors that have been identified in literature as important in developing a smart and connected citizenry that is responsive to the demands of smart society.

4.1 Technology: Information and Communication Infrastructure

At the heart of the convergence of ICT, telecommunications and broadcasting is the need for modern high-tech telecommunication infrastructure [20], such as broadband [10]. Broadband technologies have the potential to enhance the quality of life of citizens and improve connectedness between governments, businesses and their societies [19]. Broadband technologies promote the transition to smart societies by "modernizing economies and societies by stimulating the use of the internet and enabling the use of feature-rich applications and services" [52]. It is therefore clear that for smart societies to work, smart citizens need to be connected and broadband is needed for the levels of connectivity envisaged.

Broadband penetration is affected by supply side factors such as legislation, regulation, infrastructure and competition. It is also affected by demand factors such as affordability, its perceived value to citizens and business and socio-cultural factors such as e-readiness and acceptance of new technologies in society [5, 17, 19, 38, 52].

Despite the recognition of broadband as a key enabler in creating a smart citizenry, the reality is that broadband penetration has been slow in developing countries as compared to developed economies. Lack of economic development, low Gross Domestic Product, low personal income levels and other socio-economic factors contribute to this [52]. Developing countries are still grappling with challenges such as poverty and poor health and hence connectivity is not an immediate priority [23]. More than two billion people in developing countries are being "priced out" of accessing the internet [1]. Population and demographic characteristics such as population density and urban versus rural populations were also found to have an impact [23, 52]. Expanding infrastructure to areas outside of urban areas, into remote and rural areas is one of the significant supply side challenge [23]. This is especially true in developing countries where a significant population still lives in rural areas. In South Africa for example an estimated 40 % of the population live in rural areas [46].

4.2 E-Skills for a Connected and Smart Citizenry

The e-skills of citizens is one of the important factors that influence citizens' ability to leverage the benefits of a smart society. Leading countries in broadband penetration such as Singapore, were found to have higher e-skills levels [8]. Citizen participation in smart societies is generally higher in countries with high levels of e-skills, compared to countries that are still struggling with low levels of e-skills [8]. Many governments have developed e-skilling initiatives for citizens to address this concern. Citing successes in developed countries, studies on the accessibility of e-services in South Africa found that the level of ICT skills and literacy among citizens has a major role in the successful participation in e-services, by influencing the ability of citizens to access and use information [31, 34]. This is clear evidence of mimetic pressure at play, which in some cases including in South Africa, has influenced policy decisions.

4.3 Role of Government in Broadband Diffusion: Broadband Policies, Strategies, Regulation and Infrastructure

Governments play a major role in establishing regulative mechanisms such as policy and legislation for promoting the development of broadband for socio-economic prosperity by improving the framework conditions, stimulating demand and indirectly supporting the supply side [17]. Developed countries such as Singapore, USA and Sweden have increased broadband penetration through supportive policies that promote infrastructure development, competition and regulate the sector [5, 7, 16]. Here we see the use of coercive mechanisms to promote the growth of socio-economic infrastructure. Developing countries have liberalised the telecommunications sector and established independent telecommunications regulators to promote a telecommunications regulatory environment that is in line with global best practices [6, 25]. This is evidence of the mimetic mechanism at work where developing countries have copied developed countries in their efforts to increase broadband penetration.

4.4 Security, Privacy and Trust Concerns in a Smart Society

Citizens' security and privacy concerns in the connected and smart environment are a major threat to the success of smart initiatives due to increased mistrust of smart initiatives by citizens [4]. Legal and social concepts of a citizen's "right to privacy" which are intertwined with the challenge of security and the benefits of smart initiatives, have posed a significant challenge for governments [15]. Governments have responded by developing policies, legislation and other mechanisms for addressing security, privacy and trust concerns [2]. Addressing citizens' concerns is critical in promoting citizen participation and trust in a smart society. The development of such regulative mechanisms can be viewed as governments' response to external pressures from citizens, who are one of governments' most important stakeholders.

5 Results

We discuss five key national projects implemented by the South African government aimed at increasing citizen connectivity to support the vision of a smart society.

5.1 Broadband Implementation in South Africa: "SA Connect" Project

To progress towards the goal of universal access, in 2013, South Africa launched a national broadband project "SA Connect", the country's broadband strategy and policy. The broadband strategy and policy's objective is to ensure affordable broadband access for all by addressing both supply-side issues such as e-readiness, skills and availability and demand side issues such as infrastructure, regulation and competition. The strategy aims to bridge the gap between the currently poor status of broadband in South Africa, and the country's vision of a seamless network that will make broadband universally accessible at an affordable cost to all. This is an example of the use of policy as a normative mechanism in achieving desired goals by proposing amendments to the institutional framework necessary for effective regulation of an environment of open and fair competition. The four-pronged strategy includes:

(i)   Digital readiness: This pillar addresses institutional, regulatory and environmental reforms necessary to create a fair and competitive environment.
(ii) Digital development: The focus is the smart procurement of quality infrastructure and services in order to address public sector broadband demand.
(iii) Digital future: The focus is on the introduction of an open access wireless broadband network and wholesale fibre through public-private partnerships.
(iv) Digital opportunity: The focus is on e-readiness programmes, development of local content and ICT entrepreneurship as strategies to stimulate demand.

South Africa is multi-cultural and multi-lingual with eleven official languages which government needs to cater for. The production of content in local languages is important in ensuring that citizens can fully participate in and benefit from smart initiatives. This is important in offering equivalent services to all citizens as well as reducing long-standing hostilities perpetrated by socio-historic injustices [31]. Cultural and linguistic inclusivity in this case is used as a basis for achieving institutional legitimacy. We observe government's attempt to influence desired social behaviour through e-participation as well as strategies to stimulate demand as attempts to establish social norms with the long-term goal of embedding new cultural-cognitive assumptions in South African society.

The inclusion of the informal sector and ICT entrepreneurship in the national broadband policy is of importance because the informal sector plays an important role in the South African economy. The South African economy is currently struggling to absorb college and university graduates with unemployment currently at 25 % with a low absorption rate of 43.5 % [50]. ICT entrepreneurship and innovation are key features of a smart and connected society [36]. We argue that normative pressure on government to meet their social obligations has influenced government to find innovative responses in addressing some of these socio-economic challenges.

5.2   Strategic Infrastructure Projects

The Strategic Infrastructure Projects (SIPs) support government's goals of using ICT to "underpin the development of a dynamic and connected information society that is more inclusive and prosperous" [46]. SIP 15: *Expanding access to communication technology* aims to enhance connectivity and access to information by providing for broadband coverage to all households by 2020 [44]. Despite the establishment of SIP 15, internet access is still low in South Africa with only 10.8 % of the population accessing internet at home due to high costs [49]. We argue that infrastructure development alone is not sufficient in increasing citizen connectedness if it remains unaffordable. The adoption of smart technologies does not guarantee success of smart initiatives [32]. A holistic approach is needed to yield a positive result.

5.3 Smart Cities Initiative

The "smart cities" initiatives are part of government's project of developing South Africa's major cities into world class cities. The government is embarking on several national initiatives such as "e-schools" and free wireless broadband in public areas so as to support the national goal of creating a smart society. As part of their "smart cities" agendas, several cities in South Africa such as Johannesburg, Cape Town and Pretoria have embarked on projects to roll out free wireless broadband in public areas to provide connectivity and access to all residents. The Gauteng provincial government's R2-billion "paperless classrooms" project, for example, aims to provide learners in public schools with digital connectivity [11]. Resources and associated activities are thus critical in realising the goal of a connected and smart citizenry.

5.4 Digital Migration Programme

To promote digital access to all South Africans, the government is migrating the broadcasting infrastructure from analogue to digital, a move which is key in enabling faster broadband services. To ensure inclusion of all citizens, the government will provide free set-top boxes to 5 million poor households [13, 43]. Social obligation thus plays a major role in influencing policy decisions aimed at addressing social and economic inequalities. The need for digital migration derives from the International Telecommunications Union (ITU) resolution where countries were given a June 17 2015 deadline to migrate [24]. Here we observe the role of coercive isomorphic pressure in influencing policy direction. Delays in implementation resulted in South Africa missing the deadline. Inefficiencies and a leadership crisis since the split of the former Communications Department into the Department of Telecommunications and Postal Service and Department of Communications have been cited by government leadership as some of the challenges [48]. It appears that coercive isomorphic pressure is unlikely to lead to desired behaviour if not accompanied by sufficient supportive normative and cultural cognitive mechanisms such as leadership, resources and trust.

5.5 E-Readiness Programme (E-Skills and E-Literacy)

E-readiness (e-skills and e-literacy) are among the key success factors in moving towards a smart and connected society. The success of e-government in Singapore for example has been attributed to the e-readiness of its citizens among other factors [8]. E-readiness enables citizens to fully leverage the benefits of a smart society as well as participate fully in smart initiatives. In recognition of the importance of e-readiness, South Africa established the Ikamva National e-Skills Institute (iNeSI) to co-ordinate the development of an e-skilled and e-empowered society and delivers on the goals of the NDP. This is a significant example of the positive role of mimetic pressure in influencing desired behaviour. Social obligation is the basis for attaining legitimacy in this instance. The implementation of e-readiness programmes for citizens, despite several strategies and initiatives put in place, have been hampered due to a fragmented approach, poor resourcing and inefficiencies in coordination. This reiterates the importance of supportive institutional mechanisms and their associated resources and activities in driving institutional priorities to achieve success and legitimacy [42].

6   Discussion

6.1   Poor Implementation: Integrated E-Strategy Challenge

South Africa still lacks an integrated e-strategy to guide and coordinate the development of ICT in government, business and society [13, 47]. This is a stumbling block in the implementation of policies geared towards developing a smart society, which require a much more coordinated approach. This has often resulted in inefficiencies due to poor coordination of institutional resources and activities and delays in implementing critical projects such as the Strategic Infrastructure and "SA Connect" projects. Poor capacity due to leadership and resource constraints in institutions tasked with the implementation of policies has compromised planning and associated activities in implementation. This is a threat to government's NDP vision of ensuring that by 2030, *"A seamless information infrastructure will be universally available and accessible and will meet the needs of citizens"* [45] and prevents the NDP from being fully implemented. South Africa is failing to meet some of its short and medium term targets set out in the NDP due to poor implementation. The presence of normative and regulative institutional mechanisms such as policies and legislation are therefore not a panacea if these are not supported by effective implementation mechanisms.

The slow implementation of legislation aimed at addressing privacy and security in the "smart" era is also concerning. The Protection of Personal Information Act aimed at protecting personal information privacy came into law in 2013 but is still yet to be fully implemented. The Cybercrimes and Cybersecurity Act aimed at protecting critical information infrastructure is still in draft and is yet to be finalised and implemented, leaving South Africa vulnerable to cyber-attacks that have been on the increase globally. This compromises citizens' trust of the "smart" environment because of the perception that it is intrusive to their privacy and increases security risks.

6.2   Institutional Leadership Challenges

Despite the existence of coercive isomorphic mechanisms such as policy and legislation, and normative mechanisms such as appeals to social justice, South Africa continues to face challenges in achieving its goal of universal access in transitioning to a smart society. The Broadband Council, composed of high level experts set up to stir broadband development, is dysfunctional and has been rocked by resignations of experts citing lack of guidance from government [51]. A leadership challenge in the department of Telecommunications and Postal services, the department responsible for coordinating the broadband project and ICT in government, has also been a major blow. To indicate the gravity of the matter, on the 3rd of August 2015, the Minister of Telecommunications and Postal services initiated an independent public service inquiry into the management affairs of the Department of Telecommunications and Postal Services [13] Institutional mechanisms fail in the face of incompetence and self-interest, creating significant setbacks to the success of government's vision of a smart and connected society. Such failures are likely going to lead to citizens' mistrust of government as an institution driving the smart agenda.

6.3 Socio-Economic Challenges

South Africa is still battling with socio-economic challenges such as poverty, inequality and high unemployment [50]. Broadband, telecommunications and connectivity tariffs remain unaffordable to most South African citizens, some of whom still lack decent housing, healthcare and clean water. Broadband connectivity is therefore the lowest priority for the majority of citizens. South Africa is described as a "dual economy" where an advanced capitalist economy co-exists with an informal traditional economy [31]. Despite the government making some progress in addressing poverty, social injustices and inequality, these remain significant challenges and are threatening South Africa's successful transition towards a smart society.

Economic challenges have resulted in broadband roll-out having a lower priority as evidenced by insufficient funding. In the Medium Term Expenditure Framework (MTEF) for 2015/2018, despite requesting R1.4 billion (US$95 million) for broadband rollout, the SA connect project was only allocated R739 million (US$47 million) by National Treasury. This figure falls short of requested funds and casts a shadow of doubt on South Africa's ability to reach its target of 100 % broadband connectivity by 2020. Resourcing thus remains important in supporting other institutional mechanisms and activities in implementation of policy, without which implementation is bound to be compromised.

6.4 Infrastructure Roll-Out Challenges

Infrastructure roll-out has largely been biased towards urban areas where citizens are already economically advantaged compared to their rural counterparts. Even within cities, the focus has been on wealthier suburbs. This is despite the fact that policy clearly prioritises rural areas in infrastructure roll out. Social obligation in this instance is seen as having a profound influence in policy decision making but there is less evidence of such in implementation. This has the potential to increase inequalities by widening the digital divide and is a threat to achieving the national vision of smart society as access and connectivity remain low in marginalised areas. Several metropolitan cities in South Africa (including Pretoria, Johannesburg and Cape Town) are already enjoying free WiFi rollout in public places and in some public schools. Rural areas are not developing at the same pace as South Africa's major cities. This is concerning considering an estimated 40 % of the population lives in rural areas [46].

7   Conclusions

South Africa has made some progress in transitioning towards a smart society through a connected and smart citizenry. Government has played a significant role by developing an enabling policy framework, implementing regulative and normative measures such as the broadband project and e-readiness programmes. Poor leadership, socio-economic barriers such as affordability and the slow and poor implementation of policy and programmes are some of the barriers discussed. Government efforts are at times uncoordinated and fragmented, hence threatening the success of smart initiatives. The slow pace of development in rural and poor areas will further increase the connectivity divide. This has compromised government's efforts in realising its vision of a smart society through the provision of a smart and seamless information infrastructure. What is clear is that policy alone is not sufficient if not supported by a strong implementation plan and other appropriate institutional mechanisms such as leadership to direct resources and activities in the institution. We also observed the influence of mimetic and coercive pressure in policy direction in South Africa, where the international community has directed best practice and policy decisions. The socio-cultural, socio-economic and socio-historic contexts in developing countries like South Africa however make it impractical to follow these so called "best practices". Governments often find themselves doing a balancing act between domestic priorities and international best practices in policy and governance. This may lead to poor conceptualisation and implementation of policy.

References

1. Alliance for Affordable Internet: Affordability Report (2015). http://a4ai.org
2. Al-Omari, H., Al-Omari, A.: Building an e-government e-trust infrastructure. Am. J. Appl. Sci. **3**(11), 2122–2130 (1996)
3. Backhouse, J.: Smart city agendas of African cities. In: Proceedings of 1st African Conference on Information Systems and Technology (ACIST), Accra, 7–8 July 2015
4. Belanger, F., Hiller, J.S.: A framework for e-government: privacy implications. Bus. Process Manag. J. **12**(1), 48–60 (2006)
5. Belloc, F., Nicita, A., Rossi, M.A.: Whither policy design for broadband penetration? Evidence from 30 OECD countries. Telecommun. Policy **36**(5), 382–398 (2012)
6. Berg, S., Pollitt, M., Tsuji, M.: Private Initiatives in Infrastructure: Priorities, Incentives and Performance, pp. 202–220. Edward Elgar Publishing Inc., Northampton (2002)
7. Cava-Ferreruela, I., Alabau-Munoz, A.: Broadband policy assessment: a cross-national empirical analysis. Telecommun. Policy **30**(8), 445–463 (2006)
8. Chan, C.M., Lau, Y., Pan, S.: E-government implementation: a macro analysis of Singapore's e-government initiatives. Gov. Inf. Q. **25**(2), 239–255 (2008)
9. Chen, Y.C.: Citizen-centric e-government services: understanding integrated citizen service information systems. Soc. Sci. Comput. Rev. **28**(4), 427–442 (2010)
10. Chochliouros, I.P., Spiliopoulou, A.S.: Broadband access in the European Union: an enabler for technical progress, business renewal and social development. Int. J. Infonom. **1**(1), 5–21 (2005)

11. City of Johannesburg: Gauteng Gets Paperless Classrooms (2015). www.joburg.org.za
12. Colesca, S.E.: Understanding trust in e-government. Eng. Econ. **63**(4), 1–9 (2009)
13. Department of Telecommunications and Postal Services: Integrated ICT Policy Discussion Paper (2015). http://www.dtps.gov.za
14. DiMaggio, P.J., Powell, W.: The iron cage revisited-Institutional Isomorphism and collective rationality. Am. Sociol. Assoc. **48**(1), 147–160 (1983)
15. Elmaghraby, A.S., Losavio, M.: Cyber security challenges in smart cities: safety. Secur. Priv. J. Adv. Res. **5**(4), 491–497 (2014)
16. Eskelinen, H., Frank, L., Hirvonen, T.: Does strategy matter? A comparison of broadband rollout policies in Finland and Sweden. Telecommun. Policy **32**(6), 412–421 (2008)
17. Falch, M.: Penetration of broadband services – the role of policies. Telemat. Inform. **24**(4), 246–258 (2007)
18. Fedotova, O., Teixeira, L., Alvelos, H.: E-participation in Portugal: evaluation of government electronic platforms. Procedia Technol. **5**(1), 152–161 (2012)
19. Firth, L., Mellor, D.: Broadband: benefits and problems. Telecommun. Policy **29**(2), 223–236 (2005)
20. Gunasekaran, V., Harmantzis, F.C.: Emerging wireless technologies for developing countries. Technol. Soc. **29**(1), 23–42 (2007)
21. Hartswood, M., Grimpe, B., Jirotka, M., Anderson, S.: Towards the ethical governance of smart society. In: Miorandi, D., Maltese, V., Rovatsos, M., Nijholt, A., Stewart, J. (eds.) Social Collective Intelligence, pp. 3–30. Springer International, Heidelberg (2014)
22. Helbig, N., Gil-García, J.R., Ferro, E.: Understanding the complexity of electronic government: implications from the digital divide literature. Gov. Inf. Q **26**(1), 89–97 (2009)
23. International Telecommunications Union: The State of Broadband (2015). http://www.broadbandcommission.org/documents/.../bb-annualreport2015.pdf
24. International Telecommunications Union: ITU Activities on Digital Migration. Digital Migration & Spectrum Policy Summit, Nairobi, Kenya, 29 November 2011
25. Jayakar, K., Martin, B.: Regulatory governance in African telecommunications: testing the resource curse hypothesis. Telecommun. Policy **36**(9), 691–703 (2012)
26. Lapo, M., Pennarola, F., Za, S.: From Information to Smart Society: Environment, Politics and Economics. Springer International Publishing, Heidelberg (2015)
27. Levy, C., Wong, D.: Towards a Smart Society. The Big Innovation Centre, London (2014)
28. Liyanage, C.P., Marasinghe, A.: Planning smart meal in a smart city for a smart living. In: Biometrics and Kansei Engineering International Conferernce, pp. 166–171. IEEE (2013)
29. Lofgren, K.: The governance of e-government: a governance perspective on the Swedish e-government strategy. Publ. Policy Adm. **22**(3), 335–352 (2007)
30. Luna-Reyes, L.F., Gil-García, J.R.: Using institutional theory and dynamic simulation to understand complex e-government phenomena. Gov. Inf. Q. **28**(3), 329–345 (2011)
31. Maumbe, B.M., Owei, V., Alexander, H.: Questioning the pace and pathway of e-government development in Africa: a case study of South Africa's Cape Gateway project. Gov. Inf. Q. **25**(4), 757–777 (2008)
32. Nam, T., Pardo, T.A.: Smart city as urban innovation: focusing on management, policy, and context. In: International Conference on Theory and Practice of E-Governance (2011)
33. Noh, K.S., Lee, S.H.: A study on innovative model for communication system of political parties in Korea by using big data. Int. J. Adv. Comput. Technol. **5**(13), 342–348 (2013)
34. Ngulube, P.: The nature and accessibility of e-government in Sub Saharan Africa. Int. Rev. Inf. Ethics **7**(9), 1–13 (2007)
35. Panopoulou, E., Tambouris, E., Tarabanis, K.: Success factors in designing eParticipation initiatives. Inf. Organ. **24**(4), 195–213 (2014)

36. Paskaleva, K.A.: The smart city: a nexus for open innovation? Intell. Build. Int. **3**(3), 153–171 (2011)
37. Phang, C.W., Kankanhalli, A.: A framework of ICT exploitation for e-participation initiatives. Commun. ACM **51**(12), 128–132 (2008)
38. Picot, A., Wernick, C.: The role of government in broadband access. Telecommun. Policy **31**(10), 660–674 (2007)
39. Purao, S., Seng, T.C., Wu, A.: Modeling citizen-centric services in smart cities. In: Ng, W., Storey, V.C., Trujillo, J.C. (eds.) ER 2013. LNCS, vol. 8217, pp. 438–445. Springer, Heidelberg (2013)
40. Scekic, O., Miorandi, D., Schiavinotto, T., Diochnos, D.I., Hume, A., Giunchiglia, F.: Smart society: a platform for collaborative people-machine computation. IEEE (2015)
41. Scholl, H.J., Scholl, M.C.: Smart governance: a roadmap for research and practice. In: iConference 2014 Proceedings, pp. 163–176 (2014)
42. Scott, W.R.: Institutions and Organizations. Sage, Thousand Oaks (2014)
43. South Africa: Digital migration policy. In: Government Gazette 31408, vol. 958, pp. 1–19 (2008)
44. South Africa: National Infrastructure Plan (2012). www.gov.za/issues/key-issues
45. South Africa: National broadband policy. Government Gazette 37119, vol. 953, pp. 1–62 (2013)
46. South Africa: National Development Plan (2013). www.gov.za/issues/key-issues
47. South Africa: Integrated ICT policy. Government Gazette 37621, vol. 34, pp. 1–102 (2013)
48. South Africa: Inquiry into the affairs of the DTPS (2015). http://www.dtps.gov.za
49. Statistics South Africa: General Household Survey. Statistics South Africa, Pretoria (2014)
50. Statistics South Africa: Quarterly Labour Force Survey. Statistics South Africa, Pretoria (2015)
51. Times Live: Experts Quit Broadband Council (2016). www.timeslive.co.za
52. Trkman, P., Blazic, B.J., Turk, T.: Factors of broadband development and the design of a strategic policy framework. Telecommun. Policy **32**(2), 101–115 (2008)

Social Smart City: Introducing Digital and Social Strategies for Participatory Governance in Smart Cities

Robin Effing[1,2]([⊠]) and Bert P. Groot[2]

[1] University of Twente, P.O. Box 217, 7500 AE Enschede, The Netherlands
[2] Saxion University of Applied Sciences, P.O. Box 70.000,
7500 KB Enschede, The Netherlands
r.effing@saxion.nl

Abstract. Cities increasingly face challenges regarding participatory governance in order to become a "smart city". The world's best cities to live in are not the ones with the most advanced technological layers but cities that create an atmosphere where citizens, companies and government together build a vital and sustainable city. This study compares various definitions of smart cities and integrates current insights from the field of e-participation. Five best-practice examples from over the world illustrate the various ways participation can be developed from various leadership perspectives. A new conceptual framework, the Social Smart City framework, is derived from both e-participation theory and these best-practice examples. The framework comprises of a set of digital strategies for participatory governance in smart cities.

Keywords: Smart city · Electronic participation · Governance · Participatory governance

1 Introduction

What is the city but the people? Today, nearly 4bn people live in cities and it is expected that this number will increase by 2.5bn in the year 2050 according to The Economist [1]. People increasingly prefer to live and work in urban environments. Cities face enormous challenges in terms of attractiveness, social cohesion, safety, city marketing and so on [2]. One of the related challenges is citizen participation [4,5]. Life in cities tends to become more and more individualistic and citizens often lack interest in taking part in city debate or local politics [6]. As a result, the social cohesion is affected and cities cannot make use of the full potential of the capabilities of their citizens. The rise of online tools could contribute to address these challenges [7–9]. Particularly, the rise of web 2.0 and social media provides cities with enhanced digital opportunities to reshape the relationship with their inhabitants [10].

© IFIP International Federation for Information Processing 2016
Published by Springer International Publishing Switzerland 2016. All Rights Reserved
H.J. Scholl et al. (Eds.): EGOV 2016, LNCS 9820, pp. 241–252, 2016.
DOI: 10.1007/978-3-319-44421-5_19

In the near future, co-creation in the city by governments, companies and cities will be of increased importance [20]. In many cases, the local government will become part of a network of stakeholders instead of the leading authority [2,3]. Partnerships and cooperation strategies among main stakeholders are required in order to reach full potential of research and innovation [10]. Therefore, more research regarding effective strategies for the participatory governance of cities, including smarter ways to use the potential of citizens and companies, is necessary. However, to our knowledge, there is currently a lack of knowledge regarding these effective smart city participation strategies.

Therefore the main question of this article is; By using what digital strategies can cities effectively involve citizens and companies in the policy and development process of the city in order to become a smarter city?

The main aim of this article is to develop a "Social Smart City Framework", to create a more comprehensive theoretical understanding of the participatory governance aspect with regard to smart cities. The starting point of the analysis in the assumption that the best cities of the world to live in are not the ones with the most advanced technological layers but cities that create an atmosphere were citizens, companies and government build a vital and sustainable city in close collaboration.

The remainder of this article is structured as follows. In Sect. 2, we will introduce a theoretical background including definitions of smart cities and a literature review. Second we will propose the theoretical framework that can be useful to derive various participation strategies in relation to digital participation ambitions. Section 3 contains a discussion of several best-practices. Finally, we will present both a conclusion and discussion section.

2   Theoretical Background

There is currently a large body of literature addressing the concept of smart city. Yet little consensus consists among researchers about the exact definition, scope and meaning of a smart city [7,8]. In this section we will pay attention to definitions and key concepts from literature. We will elaborate upon the key related concepts of participation ladders, digital divide and network participation.

2.1   Definitions

Early definitions of smart cities were largely technology-driven [8]. For example, Hall et al. defines smart city as: "a city that monitors and integrates conditions of all of its critical infrastructures" [11]. The big system integrator companies such as IBM, Siemens and Cisco were eager to jump quickly on the bandwagon of smart cities to present their ICT solutions. IBM played an important role in the first years of smart cities and contributed significantly to the thinking behind smart cities [12,13]. IBM defines smart city as an: "instrumented, interconnected and intelligent city" [14]. It goes without saying that ICT companies like IBM and Siemens focus largely on delivering the ICT infrastructures enabling cities to be smart. However, when we only address a smart city from the technological perspective there is a risk that the city is not becoming smart at all. Just introducing technology is not enough to become a smart city.

There are also authors that take a more integrated view on smart cities. For example, Caragliu, Del Bo and Nijkamp [4] provide us with a comprehensive definition of smart cities. "We believe a city to be smart when investments in human and social capital and traditional (transport) and modern (ICT) communication infrastructure fuel sustainable economic growth and a high quality of life, with a wise management of natural resources, through participatory governance." On top of ICT technology as an enabler for city development it is emphasized that smart cities should contribute to better quality of life and stronger economies. Additionally, various authors stress that participatory governance is also an essential part of smart cities [4,15].

As Neirotti et al. made clear, a smart city can only be really smart when the city is capable of addressing real-life challenges and when it is able to bear the fruit of the social capital of the people involved in that city [16]. In recent years we have seen a development in definitions of smart cities towards more integral ones including the social factor of people, quality of life and economic benefits [17]. ITU-T, a telecom think tank from the United Nations with experts from over the world, investigated a list of more than 100 definitions in 2014 and introduced the term of Smart Sustainable City. As a result of analysis, they provide us with the following definition: "a smart sustainable city (SSC) is an innovative city that uses information and communication technologies (ICTs) and other means to improve quality of life, efficiency of urban operation and services, and competitiveness, while ensuring that it meets the needs of present and future generations with respect to economic, social and environmental aspects" [18]. The involvement of citizens and other non-governmental actors is essential. Smart citizens play a crucial role in smart cities by their participation in smart governance [20].

2.2   Key Concepts Related to Smart Cities and Participatory Governance

As Caragliu et al. [4] made clear in their definition, participatory governance is one of the essential aspects of smart cities. The electronic support of participatory governance has received a considerate amount of attention in the field of electronic participation. In its body of literature there has been emphasis on frameworks and models to understand the various levels of citizen participation in relationship to governmental tasks. First, we will discuss existing theories about so called Participation Ladders as firstly introduced by Arnstein [19,20]. Various theories were developed from the foundations of Arnstein to measure and compare electronic forms of citizen participation. A selection of them will be discussed below. Additionally, we will pay attention to the concepts of digital divide and network-based participation.

e-Participation Ladders. In general, electronic participation ladders are theoretical models or frameworks to define and categorize various levels of citizen participation by electronic means. Many authors address the issue of defining and measuring e-participation. From our literature selection, 11 different e-participation ladders were identified but no consensus exists within them [21–31]. As the overview in Table 1 makes clear, the e-participation ladders include levels of participation from low to high.

Table 1. e-Participation ladder theories

Stages/Theory	IAP2/Tambouris [24, 30]	Macintosh [24, 29, 31]	OECD [24, 28, 29, 31]
	1. e-Informing	1. e-Enabling	1. Information
	2. e-Consulting	2. e-Engaging	2. Consultation
	3. e-Involving	3. e-Empowering	3. Active participation
	4. e-Collaborating		
	5. e-Empowerment		

Because of the inconsistent and various ways of defining and measuring participation (as Table 1 shows) in the literature, it is difficult to measure and compare levels of e-participation. A problem with existing e-Participation models is that central concepts are not clearly defined and measurement scales are, consequently, not clear and often confuse different measures [24]. In general the evaluation of e-participation is not well developed [32]. Macintosh [24] created a comprehensive participation ladder with three stages of online participation, which is useful to understand levels of participatory governance in smart cities. Macintoshs model seems most suitable for describing participation levels in a smart city environment. The borders between the steps on the ladder are relatively clear in comparison to other models and it is capable of distinguishing the levels for various stages of participation within electronic tools. Firstly, there is e-Enabling. This stage is mainly about providing access to existing data and information for citizens and companies. The second stage is e-Engaging. During this stage, people can interact with the organization and start a dialogue. People being consulted for certain projects, decisions or activities for instance with forums and polls. The third stage is e-Empowering. This stage is about working together with citizens and companies; Empowering them with responsibilities, tasks and options to allow them to collaborate with the local government.

While these e-participation ladders help to understand the extent to which citizens can take part in government decision making and its ownership, the current ladders predominantly focus on a two-way relationship between citizen and government. However, as we saw in the discussion of the definitions of smart cities, smart city challenges are not only a case of governments and citizens. Companies, nonprofit organizations and other city stakeholders such as schools and institutions in the city also are part of the network of influencers [3, 10]. Therefore, we argue that the current e-participation ladders have shortcomings for effectively describing various forms of participatory governance in smart cities. The European Union has introduced the concept of Gov 3.0 where the city government is one of the partners in the city and this breaks the paradigm of the government that should always lead and control the future of a city in solitude [33]. As a result, we should consider whether the current e-participation ladders have to be updated to meet these new reality in smart cities.

Digital Divide. Another concept in literature that is strongly related to participatory governance by using digital tools, is the concept of digital divide. Online participation is not representing all groups from society equally. Certain groups of people take more interest in working together with the government while others are more difficult to reach such as young people [34]. According to various authors, those active on the web and willing to participate in government tasks are well-educated males with relatively high incomes and high age [35–37]. Another aspect of the divide is the knowledge and accessibility necessary to participate. There is some evidence available to show that the digital divide is reducing, levering potential engagement of citizens with an increased participation of women and younger people [38] but the divide is still something to take into account when deploying digital tools for participation.

Network-Based Participation. Governments and citizens are not completely isolated from other organizations and institutions in local society. Castells' terminology of the network society is increasingly relevant in contemporary cities: as an historical trend, dominant functions and processes in the Information Age are increasingly organized around networks [39]. Feedback of multiple stakeholders is essential in a network approach [3]. This marks an important shift in contemporary societies including life in cities. Increasingly, people take part in various communities and networks. Just like what we discussed in the previous section, this makes that participatory governance should not be reduced to the government and citizen relationship [2]. A more complete way of addressing the participation of networks of partners in cities is the Quadruple Helix: The Triple Helix innovation model focuses on university-industry-government relations. The Quadruple Helix embeds the Triple Helix by adding as a fourth helix the media-based and culture-based public and civil society [40].

3 Preliminary Study of Best Practices

To illustrate various digital strategy examples we have conducted preliminary study. The main objective was to identify best-practice examples from the world, where different forms of participatory governance where applied with remarkable outcomes.

As part of a project in collaboration with a municipality, partner universities and selected business partners we started identifying leading examples of smart city projects from a participation perspective. This exploratory part of the project was conducted in the period November 2015 until January 2016. We retrieved 20 examples from literature after an extensive, multi-disciplinary literature review. We have also used the snowball method to find additional resources. The following selection criteria were used to select five best-practice examples:

- Description of the example in literature where it received the verdict of best practice, good example, leading example or similar recommendation.
- The city is well-known worldwide and one of the top 5 largest cities of the country.
- There was a significant impact of the project as demonstrated by recognizable effects on the city life.

We did not strive for completeness here but we focused on five examples that highlight various strategies behind participatory smart city projects. While we could have chosen for another selection, we believe that these five projects work best as illustration here. The five best practice examples of Beijing, Seoul, Berlin, Reyjavik, and Krakow will now be presented below.

3.1   Bejing: Participatory Airbox

The PiMi Airbox is a small sensor box developed by the Chinese Tsinghua University of Beijing [41]. The box is an instrument that measures the quality of the air in the surroundings in which it is placed. An advantage of individual measuring instruments like the PiMi Airbox is that they achieve a high level of accuracy.

The PiMi airbox was provided to citizens of Beijing on a voluntary basis. In the first day of availability already five hundred households volunteered. For the volunteers the PiMi-boxes provide information about the indoor air quality in the interior of their houses. The data as collected by the boxes generate an accurate map of air quality by the process of crowdsourcing. The map is a powerful and low-cost tool for the local government to access air quality data and adjust policies.

The project is developed by a university and enables new data that could enable people to take part in active policy making and social movements. It could therefore be placed in the category of e-Enabling.

3.2   Seoul: Sharing City

In 2012, the South Korean capital Seoul declared itself a "sharing city". The Seoul Metropolitan Government (SMG) developed the Seoul Metropolitan Government Act for Promoting Sharing and translated this in a comprehensive project called Share Hub. The Share Hub project aims to stimulate as much sharing activities as possible.

According to the 2014 annual report this initiative already resulted in the designation and support of 57 sharing organizations and aims to promote 300 businesses in the years to 2018 [42].

Due to the comprehensive character of the project, it reaches a wide variety of people and stakeholders who are stimulated to start new sharing initiatives. For example, sharing initiatives in sharing cars, knowledge, clothing, parking lots, public buildings, and business ideas were created in the past few years. The government intends to further stimulate sharing initiatives and also invests in education about sharing, to create an adaption of the concept of sharing from childhood on.

The Share Hub project itself is operated in a cooperation of the SMG and Creative Commons Korea. Due to the cooperation and the wide variety of initiatives generated by the project, the project can be characterized as a network-driven initiative. The project empowers citizens to create new initiatives and co-create and co-work in more efficient and sustainable environment. It therefore can be characterized as an e-empowering initiative.

3.3   Berlin: Open Data Portal

In 2013, the City of Berlin introduced a new web portal (Berlin Open Data) on which open data sets of the city of Berlin are gathere an freely shared. Most of these data sets were released under some form of the Creative Commons license. This warrants that interested parties including citizens and companies can freely access these open data sets and work on them. The data sets are gathered from nine governmental organizations in Berlin [43].

As of March 2016, 934 data sets, divided in 22 categories, are published on the dataportal. This resulted in 32 new applications, initiated by non-governmental parties (daten.berlin.de). The organizations that developed applications using the data form the dataportal vary from individual citizens, universities, businesses and startups and contains parties of all four helixes in the Quadruple Helix approach.

The initial initiative to create the data portal came from the local government of Berlin. The availability of the portal resulted in initiatives from a wider range of actors. Those initiatives sometimes generate other new initiatives or strengthen each other mutually as an open data ecosystem [43]. This initiative has all the characteristics of a networked form of development. The platform enables several new initiatives and parties to create new tools and could therefore be categorized as e-enabling.

3.4   Reykjavik: Better Reykjavik Agenda Setting

In 2010, the platform Betri Reykjavk (Better Reykjavik) was launched. Better Reykjavik is a website where the citizens of the Icelandic capital can propose policy ideas and proposals to the local government. Since the opening of the website, it generated the participation of over 70,000 people. This is a large share of the total inhabitants of the approximately 120,000 headed city.

Ideas that are posted to the website can be reviewed by inhabitants of the city and can be voted in favor or against. The municipality of Reykjavik uses this platform to feed the policy agenda and political agenda, therefore providing a citizen generated policy agenda.

Remarkably, since the founding of the website, 256 new ideas of citizens were officially accepted and executed by the city council (betrireykjavik.is).

The project was started by the local government itself, but it currently largely drives on initiatives from local citizens. The city council uses the content on the website to engage the inhabitants of the city to generate ideas to create a better Reykjavik. This initiative could therefore be categorized as e-Engaging.

3.5 Krakow: Participatory Budgeting

In 2013, the Polish city of Krakow introduced a pilot project to create an open and participatory way of budgeting. By doing this, the city gathered information about civic priorities, set by their inhabitants whilst at the same time giving citizens more power in allocating the city budgets.

This project gave the inhabitants of various districts in the city the possibility to decide how parts of the local budget should be spent. By choosing the district as the governmental scale of the project, the project created possibilities for local administrators to gain insight in the desires and needs of inhabitants. Furthermore, the local administration came in close touch with their citizens.

This participatory form of governance resulted in more efficient and effective public spending and a growing understanding of the needs and priorities of Krakows civic society [33].

The pilot project was an initiative of the municipality of Krakow and empowered citizens to set parts of the local budget. It could therefore best be characterized as a form of e-Empowering.

4   Introducing Digital and Social Strategies for Participatory Governance in Smart Cities

We noticed that a comprehensive conceptual framework to study and compare participatory governance strategies in smart cities was lacking. Therefore we propose a new framework here in Fig. 1. The Social Smart City framework is derived from both the theoretical findings and the example cities as described in this article. The framework can be used to have a more systematic way of studying current practices in cities. Furthermore the framework can be used to describe and compare the participatory governance progress of various cities towards becoming a smart city. We draw upon the e-participation ladder of Macintosh [24] to distinct various levels of participation. This is the horizontal axis in Fig. 1. On the vertical axis we display the aspect of leadership and control by government, citizens or networks. Each field in the matrix comprises of a different example of a digital participation strategy. The bottom right corner of the matrix is considered to be the highest ambition for cities who aim to be smart in terms of participatory governance. However, as the matrix makes clear also the top left corner still needs a considerable amount of attention for governments to open up their information resources (e.g. open data sets) for the public and meet transparency goals. The data can be opened in order to meet open government transparency policies [11, 10] Open government as a phenomenon is one of the approaches to inform the people and enable citizens and companies to participate [3]. Moreover, opening up government data potentially increases participation, interaction and social inclusion [45]. Figure 1 also shows various possible digital strategies for each combination of leadership and level of participation.

stage / leadership	e-enabling	e-engaging	e-empowering
government initiatives	web information sharing strategy	digital consultation strategy	crowdsourcing strategy
citizen initiatives	digital e-literacy and digital access strategy	e-petitioning strategy	change movement support strategy
network initiatives	open data strategy	open knowledge consultation strategy	open innovation strategy (co-create)

Fig. 1. Social Smart City framework

5   Conclusion

The Social Smart City framework provides us with a refined way to look at digital strategies for participatory governance in cities that aim to become smart cities. This framework provides us with an overview of various digital strategies for participatory governance in smart cities. However, the overview has to be further developed and refined in future studies. In addition to the known participation ladders, the framework gives a broader perspective on participatory governance than a two-way relationship between citizen and government. The framework shows various examples of digital strategies within smart cities. Although the framework provides us with an refined way to look at digital strategies for smart cities, it should be used with care as a tool to assess smart city progress. A city probably has to support several e-empowering initiatives to become smart in that respect. Also, the framework should be further applied and validated in studies to refine its contents. Additional strategies could be added that are not yet present within our overview. Potentially, the framework could be extended to become a benchmarking tool for participatory initiatives various smart cities. Validation in future empirical comparative studies could help to assess the completeness and validity of the framework.

6 Discussion

This study has several limitations that should be addressed in future studies. First, it is necessary to underpin the various possible strategies in our framework with empirical data. For example, the proposed framework could be employed in comparative case studies. Secondly, there could have been other best practices of participatory governance in smart cities that were not yet identified. Other examples could enhance the explanatory function of our framework. In the near future we will continue studying the various innovative ways of participatory governance in smart cities. We have designed the framework from the perspective of governmental users. As a result the network initiatives in the framework show examples of strategies that governments could employ. We have deliberately designed the framework in such a way.

In the end, even with solid digital strategies from local governments, the future of cities is largely an outcome of a set of decisions of multiple stakeholders in an open network. We follow the words of Castells since there will be open structures, able to expand without limits, integrating new nodes as long as they are able to communicate within the network, namely as long as they share the same communication codes [39]. The complexity of the ownership, leadership and decision making processes in our future cities will be tremendously high. People increasingly make short-term commitments in changing communities of interest and changing goals that meet their expectations (e.g. Latour, Reassambling the social [6]). The time has come to explore new effective participatory strategies using digital tools in order to really become a smart city that benefits from it's human capital.

Acknowledgements. This study was supported and partly funded by the Province of Overijssel in the Netherlands as part of a research project: "Tech For Future Brid.ge". http://www.smartcitystrategy.eu

References

1. Economist: Tomorrows Cities, Creating Optimal Environments for Citizens, London (2015). http://www.economistinsights.com/infrastructure-cities/analysis/tomorrows-cities
2. Gil-Garcia, J.R., Pardo, T.A., Nam, T.: What makes a city smart? Identifying core components and proposing an integrative and comprehensive conceptualization. Inf. Polity **20**, 61–87 (2015)
3. Dawes, S.S., Vidiasova, L., Parkhimovich, O.: Planning and designing open government data programs: an ecosystem approach. Gov. Inf. Q. **33**, 15–27 (2016)

4. Caragliu, A., Del Bo, C., Nijkamp, P.: Smart cities in Europe. J. Urban Technol. **18**, 65–82 (2011)
5. Mellouli, S., Luna-Reyes, L.F., Zhang, J.: Smart government, citizen participation and open data. Inf. Polity **19**, 1–4 (2014)
6. Latour, B.: Reassembling the Social. Oxford University Press, Oxford (2005)
7. Townsend, A.M.: Smart Cities: Big Data, Civic Hackers, and the Quest for a New Utopia. W. W. Norton and Company, New York (2013)
8. Jorna, F.B.A., Veenstra, M.J.A.: Setting up smart cities ecosystems, essential building blocks. In: Proceedings of the IADIS International Conference Connected Smart Cities (2015)
9. Sivarajah, U., Irani, Z., Weerakkody, V.: Evaluating the use and impact of Web 2.0 technologies in local government. Gov. Inf. Q. **32**, 473–487 (2015)
10. Schaffers, H., Komninos, N., Pallot, M., Trousse, B., Nilsson, M., Oliveira, A.: Smart cities and the future internet: towards cooperation frameworks for open innovation. Future Internet Assembly **6656**, 431–446 (2011)
11. Hall, R.E., Bowerman, B., Braverman, J., Taylor, J., Todosow, H., Von Wimmersperg, U.: The vision of a smart city. In: 2nd International Life Extension Technology Workshop, Paris (2000)
12. Nam, T., Pardo, T.A.: Conceptualizing smart city with dimensions of technology, people, and institutions. In: Proceedings of 12th Annual International Digital Government Research Conference Digital Government Innovation Challenging Times - dg.o 2011, p. 282 (2011)
13. Paroutis, S., Bennett, M., Heracleous, L.: A strategic view on smart city technology: the case of IBM smarter cities during a recession. Technol. Forecast. Soc. Change **89**, 262–272 (2014)
14. Harrison, C., Eckman, B., Hamilton, R., Hartswick, P., Kalagnanam, J., Paraszczak, J., Williams, P.: Foundations for smarter cities. IBM J. Res. Dev. **54**, 1–16 (2010)
15. Kennedy, R.: E-regulation and the rule of law: smart government, institutional information infrastructures, and fundamental values. Inf. Polity **21**, 77–98 (2016)
16. Neirotti, P., De Marco, A., Cagliano, A.C., Mangano, G., Scorrano, F.: Current trends in smart city initiatives: some stylised facts. Cities **38**, 25–36 (2014)
17. Saunders, T., Baeck, P.: Rethinking Smart Cities from the Ground Up. Nesta, London (2015)
18. Kondepudi, S.N.: Smart Sustainable Cities Analysis of Definitions, ITU-T (2014)
19. Arnstein, S.R.: A ladder of citizen participation. J. Am. Inst. Plann. **35**, 216–224 (1969)
20. Granier, B., Kudo, H.: How are citizens involved in smart cities? Analysing citizen participation in Japanese smart communities. Inf. Polity **21**(1), 1–16 (2016)
21. Anadiotis, G., Alexopoulos, P., Mpaslis, K., Zosakis, A., Kafentzis, K., Kotis, K.: Facilitating dialogue - using semantic web technology for eparticipation. In: Aroyo, L., Antoniou, G., Hyvönen, E., ten Teije, A., Stuckenschmidt, H., Cabral, L., Tudorache, T. (eds.) ESWC 2010, Part I. LNCS, vol. 6088, pp. 258–272. Springer, Heidelberg (2010)
22. Conroy, M.M., Evans-Cowley, J.: E-participation in planning: an analysis of cities adopting on-line citizen participation tools. Environ. Plann. **24**, 371–384 (2006)
23. French, S., Insua, D.R., Ruggeri, F.: e-Participation and decision analysis. Decis. Anal. **4**, 211–226 (2007)
24. Grönlund, Å.: ICT is not participation is not democracy – eParticipation development models revisited. In: Macintosh, A., Tambouris, E. (eds.) ePart 2009. LNCS, vol. 5694, pp. 12–23. Springer, Heidelberg (2009)

25. Hansen, H.S., Reinau, K.H.: The citizens in e-participation. In: Wimmer, M.A., Scholl, H.J., Grönlund, Å., Andersen, K.V. (eds.) EGOV 2006. LNCS, vol. 4084, pp. 70–82. Springer, Heidelberg (2006)
26. Koh, J., Kim, Y., Butler, B., Bock, G.: Encouraging participation. Commun. ACM **50**, 69–74 (2007)
27. Loureno, R.P., Costa, J.P.: Incorporating citizens views in local policy decision making processes. Decis. Support Syst. **43**, 1499–1511 (2007)
28. Loukis, E., Xenakis, A.: Evaluating parliamentary e-participation. ICDIM **2008**, 806–812 (2008)
29. Medaglia, R.: Measuring the diffusion of eParticipation: a survey on Italian local government. Inf. Polity **12**, 265–280 (2007)
30. Sæbø, Ø., Rose, J., Molka-danielsen, J.: eParticipation: designing and managing political discussion forums. Soc. Sci. Comput. Rev. **28**, 403–426 (2010)
31. Sommer, L., Cullen, R.: Participation 2.0: a case study of e-participation within the New Zealand government. In: 42nd Hawaii International Conference on System Sciences 2009 (2009)
32. Sanford, C., Rose, J.: Characterizing eParticipation. Int. J. Inf. Manag. **27**, 406–421 (2007)
33. Both, M., Kommers, P., Verhijde, M.: OpenGovEU Project: Handbook Best Practices (2015)
34. Bridges, F., Appel, L., Grossklags, J.: Young adults online participation behaviors: an exploratory study of web 2.0 use for political engagement. Inf. Polity **17**, 163–176 (2012)
35. Lilleker, D.G., Pack, M., Jackson, N.: Political parties and web 2.0: the liberal democrat perspective. Polit. Stud. **30**, 105–112 (2010)
36. Hibberd, M.: E-participation broadcasting and democracy in the UK. Converg.: Int. J. Res. New Media Technol. **9**, 47–65 (2003)
37. Moreira, A.M., Moller, M., Gerhardt, G., Ladner, A.: E-society and E-democracy. In: eGovernment-Symposium 2009 (2009)
38. Holt, K., Shehata, A., Stromback, J., Ljungberg, E.: Age and the effects of news media attention and social media use on political interest and participation: do social media function as leveller? Eur. J. Commun. **28**, 19–34 (2013)
39. Castells, M.: The Rise of the Network Society: The Information Age: Economy, Society, and Culture. Wiley-Blackwell, Chichester (2009)
40. Carayannis, E.G., Barth, T.D., Campbell, D.F.: The Quintuple Helix innovation model: global warming as a challenge and driver for innovation. J. Innov. Entrep. **1**, 2 (2012)
41. Nesta: PiMi Airbox: a low-cost air quality monitor which creates a crowd-sourced map of indoor air pollution in Beijing. https://www.nesta.org.uk/news/10-people-centred-smart-city-initiatives/pimi-airbox
42. Sharing City Seoul Annual Report 2014. http://sharehub.kr/2014/en/
43. Seibel, B.: Open Data in der Praxis. Technologie Stiftung Berlin, Berlin (2016)
44. Janssen, M., van den Hoven, J.: Big and open linked data (BOLD) in government: a challenge to transparency and privacy? Gov. Inf. Q. **32**, 363–368 (2015)
45. Zuiderwijk, A., Janssen, M.: Open data policies, their implementation and impact: a framework for comparison. Gov. Inf. Q. **31**, 17–29 (2014)
46. Scholl, H.J.: Five trends that matter: challenges to 21st century eGov. Inf. Polity **17**, 317–327 (2012)

Beyond Bitcoin Enabling Smart Government Using Blockchain Technology

Svein Ølnes

Western Norway Research Institute, Sogndal, Norway
sol@vestforsk.no

Abstract. The new technology Bitcoin has got a lot of attention since it was presented in late 2008 and implemented early 2009. However, the main attention has been to the currency and not so much the underlying blockchain technology. This paper argues that we need to look beyond the currency and investigate the potential use of the blockchain technology to enable smarter governments by utilizing the secure, distributed, open, and inexpensive database technology. The technology is discussed in the perspective of an information infrastructure to investigate its full potential. After a literature review of Bitcoin publications, with a special emphasis on eGovernment literature, the paper presents a relevant use case highlighting the innovation potential of the new technology. The literature review shows that Bitcoin is absent from the e-Government literature. The use case presented shows that Bitcoin could be a promising technology for validating many types of persistent documents in public sector.

Keywords: e-Government · Bitcoin · Blockchain · Information infrastructure

1 Introduction

Once in a while technological breakthroughs occur that open up a whole new world of possibilities. Internet itself was a breakthrough like this, and the invention of the web, with its HTTP protocol built on top of the Internet the protocols, likewise opened up a new world of possibilities. To many the breakthrough in trustless commerce and payment made possible with the Bitcoin protocol holds a bit of the same potential as the aforementioned examples [1]. For the first time in history a system has been made that enables secure transactions to be carried out in an unsecure, unreliable environment like the Internet without the need for a trusted third-party. The way this is done is explained in more detail in section two.

Public sector faces a number of challenges, not least in more cost efficient use of ICT and better interoperability between systems, as Codagnone and Wimmer (eds.) states [2]. Dawes et al. looks at information boundaries and the necessity of going from "need to know" to "need to share" and suggests public sector knowledge networks [3]. For higher education, which is the sector where the use case discussed in this paper comes from, the accelerating trend of globalization [4] puts even more pressure on finding solutions that are interoperable on a global scale. Proving the authentication of documents is a general issue for public sector and finding smarter solutions that scale globally and is cost efficient can help both cutting public sector costs and increase the quality of these services.

© IFIP International Federation for Information Processing 2016
Published by Springer International Publishing Switzerland 2016. All Rights Reserved
H.J. Scholl et al. (Eds.): EGOV 2016, LNCS 9820, pp. 253–264, 2016.
DOI: 10.1007/978-3-319-44421-5_20

The Bitcoin blockchain has global reach and can be viewed as an open, distributed, and trustless database on the Internet. Trustless means that it requires no third-party to secure transactions; the trust lies in the software only. Bitcoin can be seen as a system for proving ownership both to assets and currencies [5]. It was invented by Satoshi Nakamoto [6], presumably a pseudonym for a person or a group of persons. The peer-to-peer system was released as open source software in 2009 and it enables users to transact directly without an intermediary [7].

Currently the Bitcoin blockchain is limited to handle a theoretical maximum of seven transactions pr. second [8] and is therefore not, as yet, ideal for high volume transactions. However, for efficient storing of more persistent objects and assets it is ideal. The low cost of transactions (transaction fees are typically a few cents) combined with a high degree of security makes promises for a cost efficient and secure way of storing assets of various types and in addition achieve a better interoperability due to the open, distributed, and global architecture. This can also comprise public sector assets like certificates, diplomas, licenses and more.

The research objectives of this paper thus is

- to give an overview of the Bitcoin literature in general and in e-Government in particular
- to study the potential for using Bitcoin technology in public sector services

The objectives will be met by first carrying out a thorough literature review related to Bitcoin and then to study the Bitcoin technology in an information infrastructure perspective. Finally a relevant use case from higher education will be explored to shed light on the possible use of this technology in public sector.

Bitcoin is used throughout the paper as a proxy for crypto-based currency systems. Bitcoin is both a distributed infrastructure (the blockchain) and a currency and the paper tries to be consistent in denoting Bitcoin the infrastructure with a capital 'B' and bitcoin the currency with a small case 'b'.

The following section gives a brief explanation of the Bitcoin technology, to the extent necessary for the paper. This is a conceptual paper and the main method of a systematic literature review is described in section three together with a discussion of the use case method. In section four Bitcoin as an information infrastructure and platform for innovation is discussed to investigate Bitcoin's broader potential. A use case relevant for public sector is explored and discussed in section five before, finally, Sect. 6 concludes with open problems and suggestions for further research on the use of this promising technology.

2   What is Bitcoin?

Bitcoin is a virtual currency connected to a distributed ledger (the blockchain) first presented to the Cryptography mailing list by the posting of a white paper [9] from the author named Satoshi Nakamoto. The white paper was titled "Bitcoin – A Peer-to-Peer Electronic Cash System" [6]. The Bitcoin system enables users to transact directly on an open and unsecure network, like the Internet, without the use of an intermediary.

Like most innovations Bitcoin also builds upon earlier innovations. David Chaum introduced blind signatures when creating DigiCash, the first digital cash system [10]. Adam Back's *HashCash* method presented in 1997 [11] and introduced a hash-based proof-of-Work method also used in Bitcoin [7]. Wei Dai's *b-money* [12] took Back's ideas further and suggested a crypto anarchy system where full anonymity was the central feature. Finally Nick Szabo presented his idea of *Bit gold*, a system that comprised most of the previous mentioned systems in a digital gold system that was very close to the final Bitcoin system [13].

However, the fundamental problem with avoiding double-spending was still unsolved until the advent of Bitcoin. The problem of establishing trust among untrusted parties, like a transaction between two unknown parties on the Net, is generally known as the Byzantine Generals' Problem and was first formulated by Lamport et al. [14]. The problem was related to computer systems' handling of conflicting information from different parts or components. How can the computer, or in Bitcoin's situation the network, decide which message is the correct one when it gets conflicting messages? Bitcoin has solved this in a proof of concept way.

Bitcoin solved the problem in an elegant way by using the afore-mentioned proof-of-work method inspired by HashCash and combined with a consensus based system among the Bitcoin peers [6]. In Bitcoin the users effectively "vote" with their computing power to prevent double-spending attacks [15]. The security relies on the presumption that the cost of compromising the system must outweigh the profit of doing so.

The most interesting feature with Bitcoin seen from an eGovernment perspective thus is the blockchain technology. Although the blockchain marks the really interesting technology it is crucial to understand the deep interlinking between the currency bitcoin and the underlying blockchain technology [7]. One cannot exist without the other (ibid.). Even if the blockchain can hold assets other than the currency bitcoin, the currency is the central component in transferring ownership of assets and it is the incentive for the miners who guarantee the security of the system (ibid.).

Bitcoin relies on two fundamental technologies from cryptography: public key cryptography for making digital signatures [16] and hash functions for validation [5]. A Bitcoin transaction is a digital signature which signs a transaction containing the payers address, the recipients address, and the amount (of bitcoins) transferred [7]. The transaction is propagated to the Bitcoin network, e.g. the nodes comprising all users of the Bitcoin core program, and eventually bundled with other transactions to be included in a block [7]. The new block is attached to the blockchain through a mining process where computer power is used to solve a mathematical puzzle, the proof of work (PoW) part [7]. The blocks can also store other information and instructions and this is where the asset component comes in.

Although the virtual currency itself could have a place in public sector use, this paper looks at the potential use provided by the blockchain technology. Bitcoin provides an infrastructure on which new applications and services can be built. The Internet itself represents an important information infrastructure for permissionless innovation both in private and public sector, and the Bitcoin infrastructure holds many of the same promises in its field, as will be elaborated further on in section four.

3 Methodology

The paper is of explorative and conceptual nature and relies on a systematic literature review [17] of Bitcoin-related papers. In addition to the systematic approach a "snowball" method has also been used (ibid.). For the illustration of potential use of Bitcoin technology in public sector a selected use case with special relevance to public sector has been studied.

It is important to emphasize that the conceptual style of the paper is necessary since the use of Bitcoin is almost non-existent in public sector, something the literature study also shows. The only part of Bitcoin paid attention to by public sector is understandably regulatory questions concerning the currency.

For the Bitcoin status in eGovernment literature the newly updated e-Government Research Library[i] (EGRL) v. 11.5, was used as the primary resource. The EGRL library has an extensive overview of e-Government related research currently containing 7,899 of predominantly English-language, peer-reviewed work in the study domains of electronic government and electronic governance [18]. For the broader coverage of Bitcoin-related academic publishing the Thompson Reuters' Web of Science and Google Scholar were chosen. Finally the source "Bitcoin Academic Research" compiled by Brent Scott [19] was categorized into major research disciplines. Scott's compilation using well-known literature resources like JSTOR, Science Direct, Springer Link, SSRN, Taylor & Francis, Google Scholar, Wiley Online Library and many more shows a growing number of Bitcoin-related publications (Table 1).

Table 1. The growth of academic Bitcoin publications [19]

Year	No. of publications
2008	1[a]
2009	0
2010	1
2011	8
2012	21
2013	63
2014	208
2015	325
2008–2015	**627**

[a]Satoshi Nakamoto: «Bitcoin – A Peer-to-Peer Electronic Cash System» [6]

The table below shows a categorization of the papers found using different sources. For the three first sources; the EGRL, Google Scholar, and Web of Science, only search phrases related to Bitcoin/blockchain and e-Government is shown. For the Bitcoin Academic Research source the whole catalogue was categorized into the categories technology, economy, and legal and regulatory. The categories were a result of the screening of the papers. The categorization was done based on the title, the summary of the papers, and the journal. In case of ambiguity the complete paper was downloaded and examined (Table 2).

Table 2. Categorization of Bitcoin publications from different sources

Category	EGRL 11.5	Google Scholar	Web of Science	Bitcoin Academic Research
Search phrases	"bitcoin" "block-chain"	"bitcoin e Government" "blockchain e-Government"	[same as for Google Scholar]	-
Economy	0	0	0	244
Technology	0	0	0	241
Legal, regulatory	0	0	0	107
Other	0	0	0	35
Irrelevant	-	-	-	-
Total	**0**	**0**	**0**	**627**

Searches for "bitcoin" or "blockchain" in the e-Government literature database EGRL 11.5 did not give any results nor did the searches for "bitcoin e-Government" or "blockchain e-Government" in Google Scholar or Web of Science. In addition to "e-Government" the word "eGovernment" was also included.

The categorization of the Bitcoin Academic Research compilation [19] shows that most of the publications listed fall within the fields of technology and economy with an almost perfect balance between the two research fields. There are also quite a few publications dealing with legal questions like regulation and governance. The category "other" contains work in different research fields, e.g. environmental issues, social science etc.

From the literature search we can conclude that Bitcoin and crypto currency technology is absent from e-Government research.

We have also used a case study approach [20] and studied a relevant use case to shed light on the possibilities for using Bitcoin technology in public sector services. The use case was chosen because of its high relevance for public sector. The use case method is especially useful in situations where the researcher has little or no control over the object to be studied, and for its usefulness in answering "how" and "why" questions [20]). This is the case for Bitcoin in e-Government context where there to date are no obvious use cases to study.

4   Bitcoin as an Information Infrastructure

In order to be a potential valuable technology for use in public sector Bitcoin needs to be more than a payment solution. The technology needs to be a platform capable to foster innovative derivatives. Kazlan et al. [21] define a digital platform as "*a proprietary or open modular layered technological architecture that support efficient development of innovative derivatives*". Bitcoin is published as open source software and is thus an open technological architecture. A number of alternative digital currencies have been created

Table 3. Bitcoin as an information infrastructure

Property	Information infrastructure (in general)	Bitcoin as an II
Shared	Universally and across multiple IT capabilities	Yes Bitcoin is universally shared (one only need an Internet connection and download/install a wallet to use/take part)
Open	Yes, allowing unlimited connections to user communities and new capabilities	Yes Bitcoin is open for any users and offering an infrastructure for "permissionless innovation"
Heterogenous	Increasingly heterogeneous both technically and socially	To a certain extent. Bitcoin has already generated many new applications and platforms (thousands of altcoins, emerging sidechains, foundation for new platforms like Ethereum[b])
Evolving	Yes, unlimited by time or user community	Yes, although it is a bit early to say Although a new technology, Bitcoin bears the signs of an unlimited evolvement. The particular Bitcoin system can wither, but the technology will be brought forward by others
Organizing principles	Recursive composition of IT capabilities, platforms and infrastructures over time	Showing signs of recursive composition. Bitcoin itself is fairly new (seven years), but already a recursive composition of IT-capabilities (e.g. different wallets), platforms (e.g. different altcoins), and infrastructures (e.g. Ethereum and lightning network) have found place [23, 24]
Control	Distributed and dynamically negotiated	Distributed and dynamically negotiated. Bitcoin is a distributed system based on open source software and changes are dynamically negotiated among the user community (e.g. substantial changes need to have a majority of "votes" in order to be accepted)

[b]Ethereum is a derivative of Bitcoin that focuses on smart, programmable contracts. It uses a separate blockchain with its own currency; named ether [23]

on the basis of Bitcoin's source code, all with their special features separating them from Bitcoin itself. This shows that Bitcoin is able to support efficient development of innovative derivatives and that Bitcoin as such meets the requirements applied to an open, digital platform.

Information infrastructures (IIs) on the other hand represent another level of complexity by combining social and technical dimensions [22]. Hanseth and Lyytinen (ibid.) define an information infrastructure as "*a shared, open and unbounded, heterogeneous, and evolving socio-technical system consisting of a set of IT capabilities and their user, operations, and design communities*". This definition highlights what they call the emerging properties of IIs. In addition they also point to the structural properties, e.g. organizing principles and control. Examples of IIs are Internet itself, electronic market places, EDI, and wireless service infrastructures to mention a few (ibid.). Hanseth and Lyytinen [22] point to the considerable benefits successfully constructed and implemented IIs hold, as exemplified by Internet, but also at the potential risks involved in designing such systems, again exemplified by the nation-wide e-health system i UK, the ICT part of the National Health Service (NHS). If Bitcoin can be showed to share some of the core properties of an II we can assume that the potential for far-reaching application, including public sector, is high.

IIs distinguish themselves from traditional classes of IT solutions such as IT capabilities, applications, and platforms by being more complex [22]. IIs are thus seen as a more complex unit than platforms. A main difference between an II and a digital platform is the central control of platforms in contrast to the distributed and dynamically negotiated control of IIs [22] (Table 3).

Bitcoin can be seen as an information infrastructure in that it meets the definition. The characteristic properties of an information infrastructure and how these applies to Bitcoin is showed in the table below and discussed in more detail below the table. The table builds on Hanseth and Lyytinen [22, p. 3].

An II is *shared* across multiple communities in a multitude of ways [22] and should in principle exhibit unbounded *openness* by including new components in many, including also unexpected, ways. Bitcoin is universally shared by adhering to the protocols of the web (the HTTP protocol) and is released as open source software. Components added to the Bitcoin network range from several types of wallets (e.g. desktop wallets, mobile wallets, hardware wallets, paper wallets), a range of exchange services (e.g. physical ATMs, online exchange services), and mining components. Everybody can run a Bitcoin full client and such be a peer in the network, or on the other hand one can also use a light-weight version of Bitcoin; typically a mobile wallet. The mining operation of the Bitcoin system is also open although at present it requires specialized hardware in order to gain more than the cost of equipment.

Because of the openness an II should also be *heterogeneous* implying that social and technical diversity should increase during the lifetime [22]. Bitcoin is a fairly new technology, but already we see great social and technical diversity with applications and platforms like altcoins (more than 3,300 to date[1]), smart contracts [23], sidechains for reducing the load on the main Bitcoin blockchain [25], micro payments systems

---

[1] http://www.cryptocoincharts.info/coins/info.

built on top of Bitcoin [24], coloured coins to represent different types of assets [26], Bitcoin blockchain for secure domain name handling [27] and many more digital implementations as well as physical constructions like ATMs.

Also because of the openness IIs should *evolve* constantly (ibid.). Again Bitcoin, including the blockchain technology, is not mature. However, already in the first seven years the technology has shown a remarkable development from being used by a handful of persons the first year to today's millions of users (nodes) and links [28], high investment rate indicating lots of start-ups, and a continuous expansion also in terms of diversity of components and services added to the technology.

When looking at the structural properties the *organizing principle* of an II should be a recursive composition of IT capabilities, platforms and infrastructure over time [29]. The bootstrapping process by experimenting is also evident in the Bitcoin development first designed as a payment method and later having evolved into a range of possible uses. The bootstrapping process for Bitcoin and other crypto currencies is also special since it is both a technology and a financial structure. The system is especially vulnerable in the bootstrapping process due to the proof of work method. It will be relatively easy to compromise such a system in the beginning because of the low requirements for PoW resources. This will also increase the "first mover advantage" because over time the infrastructure will grow more and more robust while competing systems will have trouble bootstrapping.

Finally the structural property of *control* typical for an II is distributed and dynamically negotiated one [30]. Bitcoin is clearly a distributed technology with no central control. The main purpose of its design was to avoid central control in the form of a trusted third-party. It was presented as a peer-to-peer technology from the beginning [6]. The recent debate over the block size [31] also shows that no party is in control of changes to be made and that these changes must be negotiated dynamically: miners have their say, full node clients have their say, and core developers also have their say, but none of the groups can dictate the terms. This has been, and is, a very heated debate and the community has not reached a conclusion yet [32].

The use case presented in the next section will be discussed in light of digital platforms and information infrastructures.

5   Use Case: Academic Certificates Stored on the Blockchain

Andreas Antonopoulos is one of the most experienced Bitcoin technologists and the author of "Mastering Bitcoin" [7]. In addition to serving on the advisory board for many start-up companies in Bitcoin technology he is also a Teaching Fellow at the University of Nicosia where he teaches the online courses in digital currencies. After finishing the first teachings of the MOOC-based[2] course "Introduction to Digital Currencies" he decided to store the academic certificates for all the students who successfully completed the course on the Bitcoin blockchain [33]. After all, one of the great promises of the blockchain technology is that it can serve as a decentralised,

---

[2] MOOC = Massive Open Online Courses.

permanent, and utterly secure store for all types of assets, not just as a currency. That is what makes it interesting also for public sector use.

The following basic requirements were set up before the project of storing the academic certificates on the blockchain started: (a) the process should involve no other services or products other than the Bitcoin blockchain, (b) the process should allow someone to authenticate a University of Nicosia certificate without having to contact the University of Nicosia, and (c) The process should allow someone to complete the process even if the University of Nicosia, or more likely their website, no longer existed. The University of Nicosia is a private university, but this use case is just as relevant for a public university.

The process of storing the academic certificates on the blockchain followed these steps [33]:

Hash of the Individual Certificates. A hash of a certificate is at the core of the process. A hash function is a one-way function that takes any arbitrary data as input and produces a string with a fixed number of characters [16]. In Bitcoin the SHA-256 hash function is used [7].

Index Put on the Blockchain. Instead of storing each individual certificate on the blockchain an index document containing the hashes of all the certificates were created and the hash value of the index document stored on the blockchain. The hash of the index document was entered to the blockchain in an unspendable Bitcoin transaction to serve as the permanent record underpinning the whole approach.

Timing and Instructions. The certificates had to be self-verifying the timing of entering of the hashed index on the blockchaincritical.

Public Access. The index document containing the hashes of all the individual certificates is published on the University of Nicosia homepage. But if this was all, there would be no use for the blockchain. For the process to be truly decentralised people should be able to find a copy of the index document anywhere on the web and compare it to the index document on the blockchain.

The verification process is carried out in two steps; one for verifying the index document and the second for verifying the particular certificate:

Verifying the Index Document. Ensure that a valid index document from the University of Nicosia is used. The hash of the index document should be the same as the hash stored on the blockchain, in the specified timeframe.

Verify the Certificate. Once the index document has been verified, a SHA-256 hash of the certificate (in pdf) should be compared to the hash of the same certificate listed in the index document. If the hash values are similar, the certificate is authentic. Of course, the comparison of the hash values only guarantees the authenticity of the certificate, not that the person who sent the certificate is the same as the person on the certificate. That has to be validated in other ways.

The use case above has shown one possible use of the Bitcoin blockchain technology for public sector. All organizations issuing certificates, licenses etc. could benefit from the new technology, as this use case shows. The use case from the University of Nicosia has pointed to a couple of challenges that should be investigated more in depth in order to arrive at a best practice for storing certificates and licenses on the blockchain.

The Bitcoin technology fits the definition of a digital platform and the characteristics of an information infrastructure can also be found in the technology, as shown in Table 3. Its dispersed and distributed "ownership" is in line with the central attribute of an II. *Installed base* is another key element in an information infrastructure and denotes technical and non-technical elements illustrating the network effects determining the development of the infrastructure [22]. The installed base in this case is the organisational, economic, and legal factors governing today's public service II. The legal factors are of special importance, as is also discussed in many of the publications listed in section three. However, the legal and regulatory factors discussed in these papers are mostly about regulating the currency and the payment system. The use case described above, and similar uses of Bitcoin, escapes these worries since the payment part is just a necessary side effect and not the goal itself. That is the case with all use cases belonging to so-called "smart contracts" use of Bitcoin. The currency is used only as a token in these cases.

An information infrastructure without direct Government control might seem scary for public sector. When considering Bitcoin as an interesting technology in e-Government we need to review history and be reminded of the "battle" between global network standards in the end of the 1980s, beginning of 1990s. Governments had the choice between the controlled OSI protocol and the Internet protocol, and most of them chose the OSI protocol. USA's Government OSI Profile – GOSIP – became the standard for many other nations' OSI profiles, e.g. NOSIP – Norwegian OSI Profile [34]. Internet's rise in popularity made it a de facto standard that soon overrun the OSI protocol, not least because the OSI standards struggled to deliver working and interoperable services [34]. Internet became the national and international standard for global communication not because of national priorities, but despite them. This is something to bear in mind when considering a technology that uses the same distributed model that Internet itself.

6 Conclusions and Further Research

This paper has shown that the topic Bitcoin technology is absent from e-Government literature. The major part of academic publishing on Bitcoin has been in the fields of technology, economy, and regulation. Of course, one explanation why Bitcoin and blockchain is absent from the e-Government literature could be that the technology does not have any potential benefit for public sector, but that is hardly likely. At least researchers should provide arguments for why this could be the case.

Bitcoin meets most of the core requirements for an information infrastructure and is thus well positioned to have a broad impact on future digital innovation. The use case detailed and analyzed in the chapter above shows that Bitcoin also has a great potential for use in public sector. Storing certificates on the block-chain is a cost-effective way of storing and securing vital information. The use case shows that this is possible for certificates, but also that this could be a promising technology for all types of permanent, or relatively permanent, public documents. Other examples could include contracts of different types (e.g. procurement contracts), licenses (e.g. driving licenses), and many more given its information infrastructure capabilities.

Having a great potential is not the same as having a great success. There are quite a few examples of technologies with great potential nevertheless failing to be embraced and included in the technologies used for everyday service provision.

However, given the promising benefits the Bitcoin technology holds it is important that also researchers in the e-Government field starts to investigate it. There are a lot of questions that need to be answered by doing more research. Among the many research questions are how can the Bitcoin blockchain technology help innovate the development of digital services from public sector? How should the currency and the blockchain part of the Bitcoin protocol be handled by public agencies? Should public sector use a separate sidechain and if so, what would be the major threats to such a strategy? What are the important factors determining the adoption of Bitcoin technology in public sector? And with regard to Bitcoin as an information infrastructure: what is the crucial installed base determining whether Bitcoin will succeed or not in public sector?

These questions are not that different from the questions of public sector's use of Internet and the web in the beginning of the 1990s. Perhaps going back 25 years and looking at how these questions were answered can give us an idea of how public sector should approach the Bitcoin technology.

Acknowledgement. Thanks to Satoshi Nakamoto for giving us this radical technology to build on.

References

1. Andreessen, M.: Why Bitcoin matters. New York Times, 21 January 2014
2. Codagnone, C., Wimmer, M.A.: Roadmapping e-Government Research: Visions and Measures Towards Innovative Governments in 2020. Guerinoni Marco & Co., Clusone (2007)
3. Dawes, S.S., Cresswell, A.M., Pardo, T.A.: From 'need to know' to 'need to share': tangled problems, information boundaries, and the building of public sector knowledge networks. Pub. Adm. Rev. **69**(3), 392–402 (2009)
4. Altbach, P.G., Reisberg, L., Rumbley, L.E.: Trends in Global Higher Education: Tracking an Academic Revolution. UNESCO Pub. Sense, Paris (2009)
5. Böhme, R., Christin, N., Edelman, B., Moore, T.: Bitcoin: economics, technology, and governance. J. Econ. Perspect. **29**(2), 213–238 (2015)
6. Nakamoto, S.: Bitcoin: a peer-to-peer electronic cash system. Consulted **1**(2012), 28 (2008)
7. Antonopoulos, A.M.: Mastering Bitcoin - Unlocking Digital Cryptocurrencies. O'Reilly Media, San Francisco (2014)
8. Zohar, A.: Bitcoin: under the hood. Commun. ACM **58**(9), 104–113 (2015)
9. Karlstrøm, H.: Do libertarians dream of electric coins? The material embeddedness of Bitcoin. Distinktion: Scand. J. Soc. Theory **15**(1), 23–36 (2014)
10. Chaum, D.: Blind signatures for untraceable payments. In: Chaum, D., Rivest, R.L., Sherman, A.T. (eds.) Advances in Cryptology, pp. 199–203. Springer, New York (1983)
11. Back, A.: Hash cash: a partial hash collision based postage scheme (2001). http://www.hashcash.org

12. Dai, W.: B-money. Consulted, vol. 1 (1998)
13. Szabo, N.: Bit gold. Website/Blog (2008)
14. Lamport, L., Shostak, R., Pease, M.: The Byzantine generals problem. ACM Trans. Program. Lang. Syst. (TOPLAS) 4(3), 382–401 (1982)
15. Gervais, A., Capkun, V., Capkun, S., Karame, G.O.: Is Bitcoin a decentralized currency? (2014)
16. Schneier, B.: Applied Cryptography-Protocols, Algorithms, and…. Wiley, New York (1994)
17. Briner, R.B., Denyer, D.: Systematic review and evidence synthesis as a practice and scholarship tool. In: Handbook of Evidence-based Management: Companies, Classrooms and Research, pp. 112–129 (2012)
18. Scholl, H.J.: e-Government Reference Library (EGRL) version 10.5. University of Washington (2015)
19. Scott, B.: Bitcoin Academic Research. The Heretic's Guide to Global Finance: Hacking the Future of Money, 30 December 2014
20. Yin, R.K.: Case Study Research: Design and Methods. SAGE Publications, Thousand Oaks (2013)
21. Kazan, E., Tan, C.-W., Lim, E.T.: Towards a Framework of Digital Platform Disruption: A Comparative Study of Centralized & Decentralized Digital Payment Providers (2014)
22. Hanseth, O., Lyytinen, K.: Design theory for dynamic complexity in information infrastructures: the case of building internet. J. Inf. Technol. 25(1), 1–19 (2010)
23. Wood, D.G.: Ethereum: A Secure Decentralised Generalised Transaction Ledger. Ethereum (2014)
24. Poon, J., Dryja, T.: The Bitcoin lightning network: scalable off-chain instant payments. Technical report (draft) (2015). https://lightning.network
25. Back, A., Corallo, M., Dashjr, L., Friedenbach, M., Maxwell, G., Miller, A., Poelstra, A., Timón, J., Wuille, P.: Enabling blockchain innovations with pegged sidechains (2014). http://www.opensciencereview.com/papers/123/enablingblockchain-innovations-with-pegged-sidechains
26. Rosenfeld, M.: Overview of colored coins. White paper, bitcoil.co.il (2012)
27. Ali, M., Nelson, J., Shea, R., Freedman, M.J.: Blockstack: design and implementation of a global naming system with blockchains
28. Kondor, D., Pósfai, M., Csabai, I., Vattay, G.: Do the rich get richer? An empirical analysis of the Bitcoin transaction network. PLoS ONE 9(2), e86197 (2014)
29. Edwards, P.N., Jackson, S.J., Bowker, G.C., Knobel, C.P.: Report of a workshop on "history & theory of infrastructure: lessons for new scientific cyberinfrastructures". In: Understanding Infrastructure: Dynamics, Tensions, and Designs (2007)
30. Weil, P., Broadbent, M.: Leveraging the New Infrastructure. Harvard Business School Press, Boston (1998)
31. Croman, K., Decker, C., Eyal, I., Gencer, A.E., Juels, A., Kosba, A., Miller, A., Saxena, P., Shi, E., Gün, E.: On scaling decentralized blockchains. In: Proceedings of 3rd Workshop on Bitcoin and Blockchain Research (2016)
32. Pilkington, M.: Blockchain technology: principles and applications. In: Olleros, F.X., Zhegu, M. (eds.) Research Handbook on Digital Transformations. Edward Elgar, Northampton (2016)
33. University of Nicosia: Academic Certificates on the Blockchain, M.Sc. in Digital Currency - University of Nicosia (2014). http://digitalcurrency.unic.ac.cy/certificates. Accessed 01 July 2015
34. Ness, B.: Tilkoplet - En fortelling om Internett og Forskningsnettet i Norge. Fagbokforlaget (2013)

Making Computers Understand Coalition and Opposition in Parliamentary Democracy

Matthias Steinbauer[✉], Markus Hiesmair[✉], and Gabriele Anderst-Kotsis[✉]

Institute of Telecooperation, Johannes Kepler University of Linz,
Altenbergerstrasse 69, 4040 Linz, Austria
{matthias.steinbauer,gabriele.kotsis}@jku.at,
markus.hiesmair@tk.jku.at
http://www.tk.jku.at/

Abstract. In recent years a tremendous raise in the establishment of Open Data initiatives can be observed, aiming at more transparency in government and public institutions. One facet of this trend are data from legislative bodies, including records and archived transcripts of plenary sessions as a measure of transparency and accountability. In this paper the system design and a prototypical implementation of an information system that makes use of these data is presented. From session transcripts naive metrics such as when and how often representatives participate in political discourse but also network metrics as in with whom representatives engage in consenting and opposing discourse can be derived. The objective of the system is to make those relationships visible and accessible to the user in an intuitive way. The system neither can nor attempts to interpret the data, this is left to the user. This paper discusses how data analytics, data visualisation, and network analytics can be facilitated to make the transcripts of legislative bodies more accessible for this purpose. The findings are underpinned by first observations over a proof-of-concept prototype which exploits data available from the Austrian parliament.

Keywords: Data visualisation · Open data · Network analytics

1 Introduction

Technological, political, and sociological developments in recent years are leading to a situation where public bodies, governments, but also many other organisation with extensive influence on the general public aim for higher transparency in their management. In democracy a certain degree of transparency is achieved by making the legislative process public and in other bodies key data is made available to the public through Open Data platforms.

A tool for larger transparency in parliamentary democracy are the transcripts of debates in the different legislative bodies. These transcripts are created during debates by stenotypists, are then typeset and published as continuous volumes. Depending on the country these volumes are distributed to policy makers

H.J. Scholl et al. (Eds.): EGOV 2016, LNCS 9820, pp. 265–276, 2016.
DOI: 10.1007/978-3-319-44421-5_21

and subscribers via mail, and are available for reading in libraries. Today many legislative bodies provide such debate transcripts as part of their Open Data initiatives.

Although this already allows very detailed and good insight into the democratic decision making process the transcripts bear some detriments. First of all the sheer volume of text and data found in these transcripts makes it time consuming to analyse the political discourse such that the general public needs to rely on more condensed information formats as provided by daily political news papers and news shows. Direct analysis of the transcripts remains in the domain of professionals such as political analysts, researchers, and journalists.

Further, also professionals might find it hard to analyse simple metrics in the given data. The extraction of information interesting to the general public, such as how often their elected representatives engage in discussions and which political positions they take, will often require manual analysis of large volumes of transcripts.

Finally, from the mere text interesting structures in the political landscape are hard to observe. Revealing the structure of the political discussion and finding links between individual policymakers would usually require analysts with informed background.

In the given work the authors claim that by lending methodologies from automated information extraction, data modelling, and graph analytics one is able to generate structured data about the political discourse in parliamentary democracy. The structured data allows to objectively compute metrics over the observed system and by creating agreeable visualisation allows clear insight into the political system for the general public.

It is believed that by employing a process which (1) continuously retrieves transcripts from a legislative body, (2) extracts the relationships between actors in the discourse, and (3) visualizes the results, an important contribution to political transparency can be made. Politically interested are able to make more informed decisions. These will still be base based on information as received through media, however, arguments can be questioned and verified in the available data.

A public software system that follows the process described above can provide simple metrics on the members of political parties and the participants of political discourse. The system can provide data on how often individual members attended sittings of a council, and if attended how actively they took part in discussions.

Through taking part in discussions policymakers induce relationships. These relationships can be tracked in a network (sociogram) which can be modelled as a temporal graph. By visualizing this graph relationships between politicians and political parties become visible, groups of politicians (supposeably with similar attitudes) can be found, and formal groups (parties, coalition, and opposition) can be analysed for their homogeneity.

Future legislative periods in democratic systems might become rateable; the electorate might assess the performance of the delegates through political performance indicators just as companies now use key performance indicators in their informed decisions. With mathematical models and machine learning approaches it might even be possible to make predictions.

The remainder of this paper is structured as follows. In Sect. 2 inspiring work from automated analytics of political systems and relevant foundational material from the relevant fields such as Information retrieval and temporal graph analytics is discussed. Section 3 discusses the system design of a software system as proposed in this work, and Sect. 4 presents a real-world prototypical implementation in greater detail. In Sect. 5 the use of the system on the example of the Austrian parliament and first observations are presented. Finally Sect. 6 provides pointers towards future work and concludes the paper.

2   Related Work

The analysis of political debate and reflection upon the performance of public bodies are key tasks of political science and social sciences. Traditionally these sciences afford high expert involvement. Manual review of literature, transcripts, and datasets are often used as methods.

Recent progress in computer science, the boom of the social web, and transparency efforts towards Open Data lead to a spiked interest in political analysis from other fields of research such as computer science. Ultimately nurturing efforts towards automated analytics of political structures starting with pure lexical analysis of political debate [13] and stopping at structural analytics of Big Data resources [14].

2.1   Open Data

Open Data in the context of public bodies is defined as data which is non-privacy-restricted and non-confidential that was generated with public money. It becomes Open Data when made available without any restrictions on its usage or distribution. It is assumed that Open Data closes gaps between public organisations and citizens thus nurturing discourses and the exchange between public bodies and citizens is seen as constructive. Open Data can coarsely be categorized into political and social data, economic data, and operational and technical data [8]. The data used in this paper falls into the first category.

Although governments worldwide are at different levels of installing Open Data initiatives some early adopters can already look back at a history and lessons learned from Open Data. For instance Shadbolt et al. [9] are able to reflect on the benefits gained from the linked open government data platform http://data.gov.uk installed in the United Kingdom. As an important finding it becomes clear that the state transforms to a service provider. The vision of an Internet of linked open data and thus also linked open government data makes us believe that systems such as the one described in this paper will become easy to implement in the future.

2.2   The Social Web

However, not only official state bodies provide political analytics with data. Also a vast amount of services which invite their users to social interaction form another pool of information. In general social networks, their structure and especially information diffusion are topics which are very well studied [10]. In the context of this paper political discourse in online social networks are of particular interest.

Exemplary studies that address political discourse on the popular sites Twitter and Facebook are given in [11,12]. In Hsu et al. the micro-blogging service Twitter was used to scrape information on a distinct political topic in South Korea. The study shows that a limited number of opinion leaders are the main drivers in the political discussion around this topic. This is clear through the fact that thousands of users interact with the artefacts on the site which were created by the opinion leaders. From the 20 identified key users several results were derived. (1) The users were categorized and some of the most popular key users refer to large Korean media outlets which are already opinion leaders in other media (print, TV, radio broadcast, etc.). (2) Central keywords were derived from the discourse and clusters were derived from them such that the political position of the key users becomes visible. (3) Finally, the keyword clusters and key users were visualized as network diagrams such that the links between them become visible [11].

In contrast Kushin et al. discuss the computer mediated communication possible in online social networks. These systems have been criticised for isolating disagreeing persons from engaging in discussions and for fostering atmosphere of uncivil behavior due to a perceived feeling of anonymity and distance between the actors. Although political discussions on the web have been taking place since the very beginning of the public Internet and thus also the analysis of it is a long standing topic of interest, systems such as Facebook allow for deeper insight. Whereas in the past discussions where scattered over many different platforms such as web forums and Usenet groups some of which accessible only to a technically proficient audience, now systems like Facebook and Twitter are used by a wide demographic. In online social networks different aspects of political engagement are possible and according to Kushin et al. will lead to different reactions. Users can be-friend politicians, can express their interest in political content posted on sites, and can directly comment on political content posted by other users.

2.3   Structural Analytics

In fall 2013 Renzo Luicioni created several graph visualisations that highlight voting relationships between US senators from the 101st congress throughout the 113th congress [1]. The data was scraped from GovTrack.us [4] converted to graph structures which were then automatically layouted by an implementation of the ForceAtlas algorithm [7] as found in the Gephi graph visualisation workbench. The results impressively document how the political landscape in

the US morphed from a collaborating scene towards a polarized political landscape. In the recent visualisations one can get the impression that the two major
forces (Democrats, and Republicans) are almost dictating the voting schemes.
The work of Luicioni was picked up by Yahoo News [2] and since it spiked large
interest was later featured in a short piece in The Economist [?]

Although the work of Luicioni gained much public attention there has been
earlier work in the field of structural analysis of political networks. Naturally
the field of graph analytics has interest in this area. Well known metrics such as
centrality measures, graph partitioning, and graph clustering can also be applied
on political networks. In 2005 Porter et al. [5] were able to successfully demonstrate the application of graph clustering algorithms on data originating from
the U.S. house of representatives. The outcome of their studies are dendrograms
representing the hierarchical structure of the different communities within the
political bodies. Their results also underpin the visual results of Luicioni as the
clusters in their data show a high degree of separation.

Based on the findings of Porter et al., Amelio and Pizzuti [6] studied the
voting behavior in the Italian parliament. In the first part of their study similar
results are presented. Also the Italian parliament shows community structure
which can be broken down into a dendrogram. However, further metrics such
as the cohesion of political parties and the similarity in voting behavior were
analysed. An interesting finding was that the cohesion within the governing parties decreased in relevant time-spans of the observed dataset. On the other hand
cohesion within opposition increased. Ultimately the political landscape changed
and government was not reelected. This leaves room for the interpretation that
future automatic analytics systems might predict probabilities of government
reelection.

Where the previously mentioned related work base their analysis on structured data of political systems, the work of [14] works in a larger context. The
described software pipeline is able to detect election-related articles in large
corpora of news articles and political information systems, parses them. After
parsing key actors, objects, and actions are identified and used to form a network
structure of political key players and topics.

3   System Design

In the following the overall system design of the analysis platform is discussed.
The system lends its general processing structure from the well known ETL
(extract, transform, load) steps as found in business intelligence applications.
The ETL process is then continued by a processing and visualisation step. The
process is outlined in Fig. 1.

The phase *Extract* is responsible to retrieve relevant data from a data source
such as an Open Data repository. Depending on the actual implementation of
the repository a variety of different methods can be used. For instance many
large public bodies are starting to adopt data platforms such as CKAN[1] which

---

[1] The Comprehensive Knowledge Archive Network (CKAN): http://ckan.org.

Fig. 1. General structure of the processing pipeline

amongst others provides REST based APIs. Other data might have access paths based on the RDF Site Summary (RSS) framework or might be presented in other open or even proprietary formats. Hence the *Extract* component is tightly interlinked with the data resource it is bound to. This is indicated in the pipeline with grey filling of the box.

Also the *Transform* phase has a tight binding on the actual data source. Data about political debate is available in many different formats. For instance the transcripts of the Austrian parliament are available as HTML and PDF documents[2], the Italian parliament provides structured voting records on their site[3], and for the US the site govtrack.us[4] provides structured data and full text from many governmental bodies.

Observing the landscape of data sources it becomes clear that the two data-bound phases (*Extract* and *Transform* marked in grey) need to be adapted to specific data providers. However, for all of the resources it is possible to transform them into a set of structured data which contains representatives, and their voting and discourse patterns. This structured data is the input for the *Load* phase which uses the structured data and loads them to a query-able data repository such as a relational database management system. The *Load* phase reads input data in a generic data-format or through standardised APIs such that a general implementation of this phase can be used regardless the data-source.

On top of the loaded data model typical data analysis tasks can be run. Such as computing relevant metrics in the *Process*, and creating human-readable interpretations of the data in the *Visualize* phase. Metrics computed over the available data can be roughly discriminated into two groups. The first group are metrics that provide simple indicators over records found in the datasets. Exemplary indicators in this group for individual politicians are: the total number of years the representative is in service, degree of attendance in sessions, number of speeches and interactions in the plenary. We call these indicators naive indicators or metrics.

Further more complex indicators can be derived from the interaction network that is formed by representatives engaging in discussions with each other. Network metrics such as the node centrality, and betweenness centrality can be used to determine which actors are at the core of groups or who acts as a hub between individual groups. Further, methods from community detection can be

---

[2] Austrian Parliament Session Transcripts: https://www.parlament.gv.at/PAKT/STPROT/.

[3] Italian Parliament Open Data: http://parlamento17.openpolis.it.

[4] govtrack.us: https://www.govtrack.us.

applied to reveal the groups that form within the network. These are of particular interest if compared to formal groups that are expected to be found in the network such as coalition, opposition, and political parties.

Depending whether naive or network metrics are of interest different tactics can be applied to visualize the data for the user. Naive metrics can mostly be reflected through the use of standard charts such as bar-charts or scatter-plots. The network data can be visualized through automatically layouted graph representations. Additional information in this case must be color coded.

As the process described above is designed to be fully automated it can be repeated on a regular basis. This leads to a system that is constantly fed with current information and allows the creation of a user-facing dashboard that can be used to analyse the current but also past situations.

The current landscape of Open Data in combination with the ETL and processing steps described above and the use of methods from graph analytics allows the creation of a prototype system that gives a first impression as of how in future the insight into public bodies can be significantly improved.

4 Proof-of-Concept Prototype

To demonstrate the mere technical feasibility of our approach and to allow first usability tests with focus groups, a proof of concept prototype for the presented system design was created. In this first prototype openly available data from the Austrian parliament, was used. The prototype uses politician profiles and transcripts of the sessions of the national council which are both publicly available as HTML files. With these data sources, general data of politicians (birth date, ...), their membership in political parties and their activities and absences during sessions of the national council can be derived. Furthermore, relations among politicians and parties can be calculated through meta data of the speeches held in the parliament.

An important aspect while building the prototype was extendibility, especially the *Extract* and *Transform* phase of the processing pipeline must be adaptable. The prototype was built for the national council of the Austrian parliament, but in general the system has been held modular and therefore legislative systems of other countries can be targeted as well, if the data is available in sufficient quality and of an overall similar structure.

The prototype was implemented with state of the art Java and Spring standard frameworks and consists of the following modules:

Extractor: Loads the raw HTML-Files from the Data Source (in our case the Austrian Parliament Web Site). The data-source provides an RSS feed which can be used to get up-to-date information.

Transformer: Downloaded HTML files are parsed in the transformer module. Depending on the input file different output is generated. From politician profiles the parser is able to derive a structured profile, from session transcripts the parser finds votes and debates and assigns politician profiles to the actors.

Loader: Loads the data-source independent records provided from the transformer into a relational database system.

Analyzer: Calculates basic measures and generates the relation graphs for politicians and parties. The relationship graph is built by analysing how politicians expressed sentiment towards topics discussed in the plenary. For the dataset used vast amounts of speeches and contributions from the auditorium are marked pro and contra arguments. The normalized edge weight of relationships between actors is used to express the overall pro and contra disposition between any two actors.

Community Detector: Automatically detects communities in the relation graph using a label propagation algorithm [15]. The algorithm can be configured to consider only edges in a certain weight-range such that more global or local communities can be found.

Web Visualization: Contains mainly the user interface which presents the computed metrics and provides graph visualisation.

As intended by the system design other legislative systems can be connected through replacing the extractor- and transformer-module with implementations for the respective data source. All other modules will work for other systems without the need for a change.

The real world implementation of the prototype is available as open source software. The code can be found online at Github[5]. Screenshot in Fig. 2a gives a first impression for the graphical representation of a legislative period. It gives rough overviews on session meta-data and highlights some of the naive metrics. Interested users can drill down for instance to politician profiles as presented in Fig. 2b. The profile puts the selected politician in context with other politicians in the legislative body. Graph visualisation is discussed in the next section.

(a) Overview over a period   (b) Politician profile

Fig. 2. Prototype screenshots

5   Observations

During the course of creating the prototypical implementation for the political information system presented in this paper it became clear semi-automated and

---

[5] Austrian Parliament Analyzer https://github.com/hias234/AustrianParliament Analyzer.

automated analysis of legislative bodies is already technically feasible. Open Data platforms provide the required data which can easily be processed and analysed with state of the art methods from data analytics, data visualisation and in this case also network analytics.

As for our showcase scenario we can also report that the data extraction process from text / HTML based transcripts works surprisingly well. Once in the showcase in-depth profiles from politicians are available actors in the transcripts can be looked up in an index which leads to a completely correct mapping of actor names to politician profiles in the observed dataset. Obviously over the years the formatting of the transcripts continuously improved such that parsing mechanisms need to adapt as well. In the observed dataset there is one major technology change. Old versions of the transcripts are actually scanned text documents instead of HTML. If these were to be analysed optical character recognition techniques would be required. For transcripts from other legislative bodies also some annotations such as the pro/contra indicators found for the Austrian parliament might be missing. In this case advanced methods from text processing such as automated sentiment analysis will be required.

Already the naive metrics presented in period overviews and politician profiles provide interesting insight. However, politician interaction network graphs as presented in Fig. 4 provide even deeper insight. The graphs have been automatically layouted by a force driven layout algorithm [7]. The algorithm in general tries to place nodes as far apart as possible, however the weighted edges create a opposing pull force. This leads to a layout process where politician profiles with similar attitudes get pulled close together and opposing attitudes drawn apart. In the output it is clearly shown that the network is clustered.

In Fig. 4 the periods 22 and 25 were chosen on purpose because these two graphs both show two clearly distinct clusters. In both visualisations the left cluster is formed by profiles in the coalition government and the right cluster contains profiles from the oppositions parties. In the 25th period we can see that in the opposition the green nodes (profiles from the Austrian Greens) are a little closer to the government than the blue nodes (Freedom Party of Austria). In general the nodes in the opposition cluster are less densely layouted than in the coalition government. This is conform with the opposing political agenda of the opposition parties. In the 22nd period however a different coalition government was formed (black, blue, and orange nodes). Again one can observe two clearly distinct clusters, however both clusters are far more dense.

The very same clusters are detected by the community detection algorithm chosen in our experiments [15]. The community detection algorithm was run exemplary on periods 20 through 25 of the dataset and the community labels assigned to the individual political profiles were compared with the official politician profiles. The algorithm in [15] describes an iterative process, in our experiments ten iterations led to stable communities. Further a threshold for edge selection was used such that only edges with an absolute edge-weight above 3 were considered during community detection. This number was determined throughout multiple experiment runs and is a parameter which most likely needs to be adjusted for other datasets. Most of the Austrian representatives are organised in clubs such that it is save to assume that a politician who is a member of a governing party is part of the government. However, there are rare cases where politicians change clubs and thus move from government to opposition during a period. The chart in Fig. 3 shows that in worst case the community detection algorithm assigned more than 91 % of the profiles to the correct group but on average (98 %) it is doing far better.

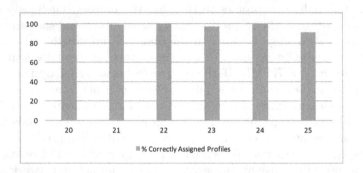

Fig. 3. % of correctly assigned profiles

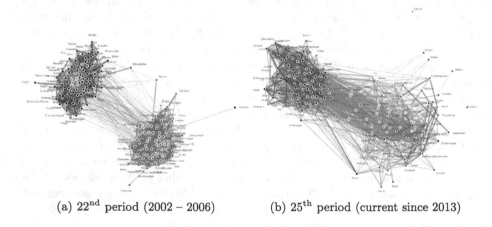

(a) 22nd period (2002 – 2006)   (b) 25th period (current since 2013)

Fig. 4. Politician relation graphs (Color figure online)

6   Conclusions

In this paper the rationale behind and the necessary steps for building an online system that allows network analysis on top of parliamentary political discourse were presented. It is highlighted how such systems may contribute to more transparent policy making in the future by allowing laymen to visualise and analyse interlinks between political figures and topics. The architecture of a computer system was presented that allows for automatic information retrieval from relevant Open Data repositories, the parsing and conversion of the data into network data, and allows the application of methods from graph theory and graph visualisation in final analysis steps. The more technical feasibility of the architecture was demonstrated by implementing an Open Source prototype of this architecture and its practical feasibility was demonstrated by putting the system in use with data scraped from the transcripts available at the Open Data repository of the Austrian parliament.

The presented approach, the architecture, and the resulting software system are work in progress. In future work the presented system can be extended in multiple ways. (1) With the continuous trend towards Open Data hopefully future transcripts of parliamentary discourse are already pre-annotated such that a higher data quality can be reached and errors in the loading process can be reduced to a minimum. (2) The presented software prototype and its analysis mechanisms are just the tip of the iceberg of which would be possible in the future. Users could enter the system through different analytics paths such as looking up all contributions to discourse of politicians, browsing through topics and finding relevant key players, and cross-referencing the official political discourse with material found in mass-media. Further, more metrics such as the automatic estimation cohesion and clout seem logical next steps, however, would require input and verification from other disciplines.

Although studies of various political institutions exist from the U.S. and Europe this is the first approach to build a generic framework that allows to import data from different countries. In future iterations it is believed that an application framework like the presented can be used to compare political bodies of different countries. This is also the first study that applies network analysis over data provided by the Austrian parliament.

Due to online social networks that allow direct political discourse among citizens, the trend towards Open Data, and systems like the presented that make use of the available data, future citizens have powerful tools at hand that shed clear light into the decision making process of governmental bodies.

References

1. Lucioni, R.: Senate Voting Relationships. Private Blog, December 2013. http://www.renzolucioni.com/senate-voting-relationships/. Accessed 8 Mar 2016
2. Krumboltz, M.: The Splitting of the Senate (Now in Convenient GIF Form). Yahoo News, November 2013. http://news.yahoo.com/the-splitting-of-the-senate-now-in-convenient-gif-form-213908185.html. Accessed 8 Mar 2016
3. United States of Amoeba: The Economist. Print 7th edn. December 2013
4. GovTrack: Civic Impulse LCC. https://www.govtrack.us/data/congress/. Accessed 8 Mar 2016
5. Newman, M., Warmbrand, C.: A network analysis of committees in the U.S. House of Representatives. Proc. Natl. Acad. Sci. **102**(20), 7057–7062 (2005)

6. Amelio, A., Pizzuti, C.: Analyzing voting behavior in Italian parliament: group cohesion and evolution. In: Proceedings of the IEEE/ACM International Conference on Advances in Social Networks Analysis and Mining, pp. 140–146 (2012)

7. Jacomy, M., Heymann, S., Tommaso, V., Mathieu, B.: ForceAtlas2, a graph layout algorithm for handy network visualization, TR, gephi consortium (2011). http://webatlas.fr/tempshare/ForceAtlas2_Paper.pdf

8. Janssen, M., Charalabidis, Y., Zuiderwijk, A.: Benefits, adoption barriers and myths of open data and open government. Inf. Syst. Manag. (ISM) 29(4), 258–268 (2012)

9. Shadbolt, N., O'Hara, K., Berners-Lee, T., Gibbins, N., Glaser, H., Hall, W., schraefel, M.C.: Linked open government data: lessons from Data.gov.uk. IEEE Intell. Syst. 27(3), 16–24 (2012)

10. Guille, A., Hacid, H., Favre, C., Zighed, D.A.: Information diffusion in online social networks: a survey. ACM SIGMOD Record 42(2), 17–28 (2013)

11. Hsu, C.-L., Park, S.J., Park, H.W.: Political discourse among key Twitter users: the case of Sejong City in South Korea. J. Contemp. East. Asia 12(1), 65–79 (2013)

12. Kushin, M.J., Kitchener, K.: Getting political on social network sites: exploring online political discourse on Facebook. First Monday 14(11) (2009). http://firstmonday.org/article/view/2645/2350

13. Bara, J., Weale, A., Bicquelet, A.: Analysing parliamentary debate with computer assistance. Swiss Polit. Sci. Rev. 13(4), 577–605 (2007)

14. Sudhara, S., Veltri, G.A., Cristianini, N.: Automated analysis of the US presidental elections using big data and network analysis. Big Data Soc. 2, 1–28 (2015)

15. Raghavan, U.N., Albert, R.: Near linear time algorithm to detect community structures in large-scale networks. Phys. Rev. E 76(3), 036106 (2007)

Digital Networks in Public Administration:
The Case of #Localgov

Panos Panagiotopoulos[1] and Dennis De Widt[2]

[1] School of Business and Management, Queen Mary University of London, London, UK
P.Panagiotopoulos@qmul.ac.uk
[2] University of Exeter Business School, Exeter, UK
D.DeWidt@exeter.ac.uk

Abstract. Digital networking has been shaping interactions between governments and their respective publics over the last years. At the same time, networking spaces have become hosts to informal communities of public sector professionals engaging in discussions that remain largely unexplored. This papers looks at the dynamics of interaction between public sector professionals in digital networking spaces using a dataset of tweets that contain the hashtag #localgov. This hashtag is used by a variety of accounts mainly within the UK local government. An analysis of 235,681 tweets posted during 2013–2015 shows how #localgov facilitates interactions and the sharing of expertise within the context of intense financial cuts imposed by the UK government. We discuss how networking spaces like #localgov support open discourses as part a network of practice outside organisational barriers.

Keywords: Social media · Digital networks · Networks of practice · Budget cuts · Local government finance

1 Introduction

The study of networks and networking relationships has been popular in public administration research e.g. [1– 3]. Public sector networks generally include policy, collaborative and governance networks which vary in their aims but all entail interactions within or across government agencies and other actors like interest groups, businesses, professional associations and non-profits. More recently, there is increased interest in networks that emerge in more informal settings and enable individuals to share expertise according to their interests [4–6].

Many of these networks are emerging in social networking spaces where public sector professionals share insight about their work, connect to colleagues and even collectively discuss policy issues. Such communities include permanent (e.g. blogs, LinkedIn groups) or more ad hoc spaces (e.g. Twitter) that facilitate personal networking outside organisational boundaries [7]. It is often the case that informal networks on social media reflect trends and processes of institutional change in government agencies [8]. So far, research on social media in the public sector has focused on adoption practices

H.J. Scholl et al. (Eds.): EGOV 2016, LNCS 9820, pp. 277–286, 2016.
DOI: 10.1007/978-3-319-44421-5_22

within government agencies or explored the impact on citizen-government relationships e.g. [8–11]. Beyond communications with the public, there still more to learn about social media within the public sector. As part of this, it is important to explore the new dynamics of interaction between public sector professionals in digital networking spaces.

This paper presents an analysis of the #localgov Twitter hashtag that is mainly used within the UK local government. A dataset captured within a period of almost two years (June 2013 to May 2015) includes 235,681 tweets posted by 37,592 users. This retrospective mapping of online interactions takes place within a period of extended change caused by the UK government's financial decisions that led to significant reductions in local government budgets. Specifically, the dataset tracks reactions to budget reductions from the Spending Review announcement in June 2013 by the Chancellor of the Exchequer (Finance Minister) to the Queen's speech that identified key priorities for the newly elected government in May 2015.

The analysis shows a wide variety of exchanges amongst local government actors about the impact of the cuts and appropriate responses by local government (e.g. joining-up services). Conversations were found to be mainly driven by the need to localise the centrally imposed agenda of budget reductions. This suggests that informal networks like #localgov can facilitate the sharing of expertise even if there is no evidence that they directly drive institutional change. We briefly discuss the implications of these findings including the methodological ones.

2   Digital Networks of Practice in Public Administration

Networks in public administration mostly involve formal organisational structures classified as policy, collaboration or governance networks [1, 4, 12]. Studies of digitally-enabled networks have also remained within the context of interorganisational collaborations. Janowski et al. [13] introduce Government Information Networks where actors use ICTs to connect to others and build, manage or sustain relationships. Dawes et al. [14] describe Public Sector Knowledge Networks as sociotechnical systems that facilitate interorganisational knowledge learning in tackling complex public management problems. Both these concepts refer to organisational networks where interpersonal relationships are embedded within clearly defined professional tasks (e.g. emergency management or service delivery).

In this paper, we turn our attention to digital networks that enable individual connections on the basis of their professional identity. An established concept to describe informal interpersonal networks can be found in "networks of practice", which are spaces of collective learning that involve interactions between participants within professional practice [15]. Networks of practice are driven by individuals based on a loose professional identity to facilitate knowledge exchange across organisations without relying on existing relationships. Within public administration, such structures have emerged in contexts like forensic scientists in government crime laboratories [5] and advice networks between school teachers [6]. Both Binz-Scharf et al. [5] and Siciliano [6] conclude that informal networks deserve attention because they can have largely positive effects in public organisations – not only they facilitate knowledge sharing amongst highly-skilled professionals but also allow crossing organisational barriers in ways that have otherwise not been possible.

When considering digital networking relationships, a highly relevant stream of work can be found in digital or electronic networks of practice [16 19]. Digital networks of practice are generally open, self-organised and without formal controls [16, 17]. They allow individuals interact with others to exchange advice and ideas with others based on common interests related to their practice. Public or semi-public spaces like forums, knowledge portals, intranets and social networking groups are common spaces where such networks emerge. Participants tend to contribute when they think that it enhances their professional reputation, when they have something important to share and when they feel a structural part of the network – expectations of reciprocity from other participants may not even be necessary [18]. As a result, digital networks of practice have been found to facilitate connections between regional networks in traditionally fragmented areas of professional practice like agriculture [20].

These features suggest that digital networks of practice can facilitate the formation of relationships between individuals within but also across the strict boundaries of professional practice within the public sector (e.g. forensic scientists, school teachers). As such, these spaces can arguably facilitate the transfer of knowledge through network relationships across institutions [21, 22]. For example, Mergel and Bretschneider [8] discuss how the adoption of social media applications is often the result of informal exchanges across agencies where challenges are discussed collectively (e.g. good practice, challenges, resource implications). In this respect, digital networks can drive forthcoming trends in the public sector due to knowledge sharing across institutional barriers. As a result, it is important to look further into the dynamics of interaction between public sector professionals in these spaces.

3   Study Methodology

User-generated content from social media applications can be an important source of data e.g. [23]. Twitter hashtags usually form on a dynamic basis around events like national elections, emergencies or popular television shows [24]. Hashtags were initially self-assigned by Twitter users but soon became a key element of Twitter's unique proposition as an immediate information sharing platform. In professional networking, hashtags can facilitate rapid information sharing and links to resources than the exchange of in-depth opinions within long conversations. This feature makes Twitter hashtags different than social networking groups were membership is stable and clearly defined.

The Twitter hashtag #localgov provides an interesting context to study the role of informal networks particularly during the period 2013-2015. #Localgov is the most popular Twitter space used by professionals involved in different aspects of local government in the UK (e.g. policy actors, officers, elected representatives, service providers, consultants and journalists). The use of #localgov is not exclusive to the UK local government but an estimated 70–80 % of the tweets that use the hashtag are related to this context. This was also confirmed by our data analysis.

Twitter posts tagged with #localgov were collected from June 2013 to May 2015 using Chorus Analytics, which is a set of applications designed to facilitate social science research [25]. Chorus captures data from Twitter's application programming interface that is publicly available to developers. Keyword-based searches can retrieve tweets posted up to a week before each search. To update the database of tweets from #localgov, searches took place automatically and on a daily basis during the period of study within 2013–2015.

Following a data cleaning and validation step, the final dataset contained a total of 235,681 tweets posted by 37,592 unique accounts. This dataset includes all original tweets and retweets that were posted in this period and contained '#localgov' within their text. The analysis was carried out in several steps. For the analysis reported in the paper we focus on the following:

- *Overview of #localgov activity:* mapping the volume of tweets over time in relation to their structure (e.g. mentions, retweets, hashtags) and content (main topics of discussion). The latter involved keyword frequency queries using the qualitative analysis software NVivo 11. To facilitate the analysis, the dataset was divided into four roughly equal parts based on a 6-month interval within the near two years of data collection.
- *Social networking analysis:* to extract and visualise networking relationships between user accounts within the dataset in the form of mentions or retweets. The open source tool Gephi was used to visualise networking relationships.

4   Findings

About 2.2 million people are employed by local government authorities in the UK [26]. The institutional structure of local government is diverse with different administrative authorities having responsibilities related to transportation, planning, social care, housing and waste management – the main entities are known as councils. Councils are strongly reliant upon central government funding at the levels of 70 % on average [27]. As a result, budget decisions at the UK central government level have a strong impact on the financial position of local authorities. Because of this reliance, it is not surprisingly that relationships between central and local government actors have been traditionally tense.

The 2008 financial crisis and its consequences on the wider economy have put significant pressure on UK public finances. In the period 2010–2015, local government expenditure experienced unprecedented budget cuts under the Conservative-Liberal Democrat coalition government. Real local government expenditure was reduced by an estimated 40 % in real terms over this period [28]. Related to the timeframe of the tweets collected, the central level budget events during the parliamentary year 2013–14 resulted in significant reactions from local government, particularly in June 2013 when further cuts were proposed in an official Spending Review announcement by the Chancellor of the Exchequer (Finance Minister). This was the starting point of our data collection. The end point is May 2015 after the national elections with the Queen's speech that set areas of priority for the newly elected government. This is the context within which our Twitter data can reveal how #localgov acts as an information sharing and discussion space.

4.1 Overview of #Localgov

Table 1 shows the overview of of tweets tagged with #localgov. The 235,681 tweets correspond to approximately 331 tweets per day – a daily posting frequency that kept increasing during the period of capturing. The volume of tweets tagged with #localgov peaks during weekdays at the levels of 400–500 tweets while weekends generate fewer tweets at the levels of 100. Daily peaks of activity were related to a combination of events like the joint local government and European elections on 22/5/2014 (986 tweets), other elections, political events, adverse weather conditions and financial announcements. For example, the Spending Review announcement on 26/6/2013 with 1,178 tweets sparked a plethora of predictions, previews of key points commentaries, official responses and other reactions.

Table 1. Overview of #localgov activity

Period	Total tweets	Tweets per day	Retweets	Direct Mentions	Tweets with links	Accounts
20/06/2013 to 31/12/2013	56,762	291	23,154 (40.8 %)	4,067 (7.2 %)	37,567 (66.1 %)	11,142
01/01/2014 to 30/06/2014	58,085	321	24,722 (42.6 %)	4,459 (7.7 %)	42,062 (72.4 %)	11,826
01/07/2014 to 31/12/2014	63,335	344	29,949 (47.3 %)	4,235 (6.7 %)	45,150 (71.3 %)	13,731
01/01/2015 to 31/05/2015	57,499	381	28,558 (49.6 %)	3,650 (6.3 %)	42,617 (74.1 %)	14,408
Total	235,681	331	106,383 (45.1 %)	16,411 (7 %)	167,396 (71 %)	37,592 (unique)

As shown in Table 1, an increasing proportion of tweets over time, around 65–75 %, contain links to resources in the form of commentaries, news websites, blogs or other sources. The accompanying tweets can be simply informational, ironical, critical or political. There is also a steady increase in the proportion of retweets during the time of study from about 41 % to almost 50 %, which to some extent accounts for the increased number of users contributing to the hashtag. The proportion of direct mentions to other users fluctuated around 7 % and slightly decreased mainly in the last period – this is not unexpected in the months before the UK elections of May 2015.

We can also observe a steady increase in the number of accounts contributing in each period up to a total of 37,592 unique contributors. This might reflect three different trends: (1) increasing interest in the hashtag itself (network effects), (2) the growing base of Twitter users in the UK and (3) increasing use of Twitter for professional networking amongst different groups related to local government.

In terms of content, taking into account only original tweets (no retweets), contributions to #localgov focused heavily on topical and temporal keywords. Keywords like "council", "local", "new", "government", "public", "services", "social", "city" and "today" were mentioned at least 2,000 or more times. This was followed by similar themes containing "people", "committee", "meeting", "report", "digital" and "future" that received over 1,000 mentions. These more general themes were followed by terms more specific to local government finances including "cuts", "care", "communities", "funding", "sector", "elections", "finance", "tax", "leaders", "budgets", "labour" and "housing" all of which were mentioned at least 500 times.

Taking retweets into account, as expected, themes that are more nationally relevant receive more attention via reposting. For example, "cut" and "cuts" receive over 10,000 mentions combined. The overall conclusion from the keyword analysis is that, except general keywords that every council or local government officer could use, the dominant theme of discussion was centred around financial cuts and their impact. Although this conclusion can be expected, it is interesting to see how discussions took place as a conversational network of mentions between users.

4.2 Networks Within #Localgov

Networking relationships of accounts that contribute to #localgov can be visualised as a map of interactions in the form of mentions or retweets. Extracting this information from the 235,681 tweets led to a network that has 15,014 nodes (different accounts) and 38,509 edges (mentions or retweets). This network is very diverse in its composition

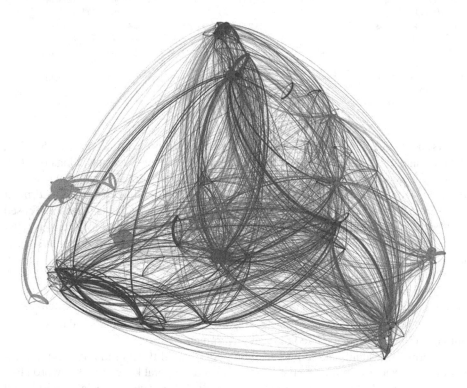

Fig. 1. Network of accounts that received at least 10 mentions or retweets during the whole period.

and contains hundreds of different communities or clusters. Such diversity is expected in a hashtag as broad as #localgov over two years. It is interesting to observe how inter-actions between accounts that contribute to #localgov represent certain groups within this open network and how they reflect specific conversations during the period of study. Given the complexity of such a task, we show here one example of networking analysis.

Figure 1 represents a network of accounts that received and made at least 10 mentions or retweets. This most interactive core of the network contains 176 nodes (1.17 % of the total) and 2,886 edges (7.49 % of the total). The different colours are indicative of the main clusters that exist within this network. The yellow, slightly disconnected cluster represents accounts outside the UK like @icma, the @theCPBB and @careersingov. The blue cluster represents main media accounts that receive high number of references in informational tweets like popular UK media accounts (e.g. @Guardian_Local and @GdnLocalLeaders). The green and red clusters represent frequent interactions between a large group of influencers in the local government community including think tanks, the Local Government Association, magazine editors and other leaders that receive a lot attention.

Furthermore, it is important to note that central government and other political actors have an "implied" but not active presence in these networks; for example, the account of Eric Pickles (former secretary for the Department of Communities and Local Government) received over 200 mentions but made fewer than 5.

5   Concluding Remarks

The dynamics of interaction in #localgov reveal the existence of an open community that reflects many of the characteristics of professional networking (e.g. decreased activity over weekends). Conversations within #localgov are driven by both endogenous (what happens in local authorities) and exogenous sources (central government financial measures). Many of the posts are purely informational (e.g. retweeting news items), but we also find a large amount of direct interactions and exchange of opinions. Existing local government networks and organisations, civil society actors, news and media accounts act as main hubs in different topics but discussions are not highly centralised around a few key contributors. This is not unexpected given that local government is a large tier of administration that brings together sub-communities around common professional interests (e.g. care services, local development, financial planning).

This open, dynamic and highly flexible nature makes #localgov much different from networks that exist within formal organisational and institutional structures [13, 14]. At the same time, the extent to which contributors experience #localgov as a network of practice certainly fluctuates. Twitter hashtags remain unexplored in this context but literature within networks of practice indicates that members have can varying levels of participation, unclear membership and strong motivations to increase their reputation [16–19]. In #localgov, levels of participation change depending on the topic, for example, in themes like budget reductions activity peaked when there was high interest to discuss the impact of the cuts. Reliance on existing relationships is minimal although it is likely that conversations tagged with #localgov are also determined by "following" relationships or result in new connections between users. While conversations and relationship formation takes place in a very open way, #localgov still exhibits some boundaries. Central policy actors are mentioned in the network but do not engage in discussions, which reflects the traditional setting of intergovernmental relationships especially in England.

The contribution of this study lies in improving our understanding of how networking relationships in the public sector are moving on digital spaces where new types of interactions are being enabled. In particular, open networks like Twitter allow both collective discourses to take place and the ad hoc formation of ties between participants. For public managers, it is important to be aware of how digital networking relationships affect knowledge sharing across public organisations and tiers of government. At the next level, they might need to consider facilitating those relationships with or without claiming institutional ownership. For example, the way the central-local government duality was reflected in our networking analysis is an interesting starting point.

Methodologically, the study applies emerging digital research methods to new phenomena that have gradually gained importance. Understanding the evolution of digital discussions is challenging due to the novelty of the phenomena and the exploratory nature of the analysis. As a result, the study has limitations inherent to most digital research methods where inferences are attempted between online and offline activity. Information flows in a popular hashtag like #localgov are driven by a large number of events that might be difficult to understand using summary measures like keyword analysis and network visualisation. The choice of #localgov, motivated by intense discourses over local government finances during the study, increases the complexity of analysis compared to more contained hashtags.

Finally, as a self-assigned hashtag, #localgov might not even include all relevant tweets and is certainly an intentional tagging method for users that want to increase the reach of their tweets. We cannot know what motivated each individual user to assign #localgov to their tweets and the extent to which they monitor other discussions within the hashtag. These issues have to be taken into account in more in-depth interpretations of findings while further work is needed to map and understand digital interactions in social networking spaces.

Acknowledgments. The dataset used in this study was collected and analysed with the help of Chorus software, which is an analytics suite designed to facilitate social science research using Twitter data. The authors gratefully acknowledge the Chorus team: Timothy Cribbin, Julie Barnett, Philip Brooker and Hiran Basnayake.

References

1. O'Toole, L.J.: Networks and networking: the public administrative agendas. Public Adm. Rev. **75**, 361–371 (2015)
2. Agranoff, R., McGuire, M.: Big questions in public network management research. J. Public Adm. Res. Theor. **11**, 295–326 (2001)

3. Provan, K.G., Lemaire, R.H.: Core concepts and key ideas for understanding public sector organizational networks: using research to inform scholarship and practice. Public Adm. Rev. **72**, 638–648 (2012)
4. Isett, K.R., Mergel, I.A., LeRoux, K., Mischen, P.A., Rethemeyer, R.K.: Networks in public administration scholarship: understanding where we are and where we need to go. J. Public Adm. Res. Theor. 21, 157–173 (2010)
5. Binz-Scharf, M.C., Lazer, D., Mergel, I.: Searching for answers: networks of practice among public administrators. Am. Rev. Public Adm. **42**, 202–225 (2011)
6. Siciliano, M.D.: Advice networks in public organizations: the role of structure, internal competition, and individual attributes. Public Adm. Rev. **75**(4), 548–559 (2015)
7. Mergel, I.: The use of social media to dissolve knowledge silos in government. In: O'Leary, S.K., Van Slyke, D.M. (eds.) The Future of Public Administration, Public Management and Public Service Around the World, pp. 177–187. Georgetown University Press, USA (2010)
8. Mergel, I., Bretschneider, S.I.: A three-stage adoption process for social media use in government. Public Adm. Rev. **73**, 390–400 (2013)
9. Mergel, I.: Social media adoption and resulting tactics in the U.S. federal government. Gov. Inf. Q. **30**, 123–130 (2013)
10. Panagiotopoulos, P., Bigdeli, A.Z., Sams, S.: Citizen–government collaboration on social media: the case of Twitter in the 2011 riots in England. Gov. Inf. Q **31**(3), 349–357 (2014)
11. Criado, J.I., Sandoval-Almazan, R., Gil-Garcia, J.R.: Government innovation through social media. Gov. Inf. Q. **30**, 319–326 (2013)
12. Kapucu, N., Hu, Q., Khosa, S.: The state of network research in public administration. Adm. Soc. (advanced online publication)
13. Janowski, T., Pardo, T.A., Davies, J.: Government information networks - mapping electronic governance cases through public administration concepts. Gov. Inf. Q. **29**, S1–S10 (2012)
14. Dawes, S.S., Cresswell, A.M., Pardo, T.A.: From "need to know" to "need to share": tangled problems, information boundaries, and the building of public sector knowledge networks. Public Adm. Rev. **69**, 392–402 (2009)
15. Brown, J.S., Duguid, P.: Knowledge and organization: a social-practice perspective. Organ. Sci. **12**, 198–213 (2001)
16. Wasko, M., Faraj, S., Teigland, R.: Collective action and knowledge contribution in electronic networks of practice. J. Assoc. Inf. Syst. **5**(11) (2004)
17. Wasko, M., Teigland, R., Faraj, S.: The provision of online public goods: examining social structure in an electronic network of practice. Decis. Support Syst. **47**, 254–265 (2009)
18. Wasko, M., Faraj, S.: Why should I share? Examining social capital and knowledge contribution in electronic networks of practice. MIS Q. **29**, 35–57 (2005)
19. Vaast, E., Walsham, G.: Trans-situated learning: supporting a network of practice with an information infrastructure. Inf. Syst. Res. **20**(4), 547–564 (2009)
20. Oreszczyn, S., Lane, A., Carr, S.: The role of networks of practice and webs of influencers on farmers' engagement with and learning about agricultural innovations. J. Rural Stud. **26**, 404–417 (2010)
21. Lowndes, V.: Something old, something new, something borrowed… Policy Stud. **26**, 291–309 (2005)
22. Crouch, C., Farrell, H.: Breaking the path of institutional development? Alternatives to the new determinism. Ration. Soc. **16**, 5–43 (2004)
23. Halfpenny, P., Procter, R.N.: Innovations in Digital Research Methods. Sage, London (2014)
24. Bruns, A.: How long is a tweet? Mapping dynamic converstation networks on Twitter using Gawk and Gephi. Inf. Commun. Soc. **15**, 1323–1351 (2012)
25. Chorus: Chorus analytics data harvesting and visual analytics suite. http://chorusanalytics.co.uk/

26. Office for National Statistics: Quarterly Public Sector Employment Survey, London (2013)
27. Pratchett, L., Leach, S.: Local government: selectivity and diversity. Parliam. Aff. **56**, 255–269 (2003)
28. Hastings, A., Bailey, N., Gannon, M., Besemer, K., Bramley, G.: Coping with the cuts? The management of the worst financial settlement in living memory. Local Gov. Stud. **41**(4), 601–621 (2015)

Construction of Enterprise Architecture in Discourses Within the Public Sector

Juha Lemmetti[✉]

Department of Information Management and Logistics,
Tampere University of Technology, Tampere, Finland
juha.lemmetti@iki.fi

Abstract. Enterprise Architecture (EA) has been employed in the public sector to improve efficiency and interoperability of information systems. Despite their daily use in the public sector, the concepts of Enterprise Architecture and efficiency are ambiguous and lack commonly accepted definitions. The benefits and outcomes of using EA in the public sector have been studied with mixed results. This study examined the use of EA in the Finnish basic education system using critical discourse analysis (CDA). The research revealed how the role and rationale of EA is constructed in the speech of public sector officials. Three orders of discourse, each having its own views on EA, were found. While there were commonly accepted functions for EA, there were also areas where the concepts were not mutually understood or accepted.

Keywords: Enterprise architecture · Public sector · Efficiency · Discourse analysis · CDA

1 Introduction

Improving public sector efficiency has attracted an enormous amount of management attention in western economies [24], especially since the introduction of New Public Management (NPM) [6]. NPM demands the public sector to operate in a more 'business-like' manner, stressing performance, reduction of costs, efficiency and audits [3]. While the term efficiency is widely used, it is often unclear what it means in the context of the public sector [24].

Regardless of whether a public sector official advocates NPM [3], the digitalization of services and the use of interoperable information systems reduces the need for workforce by automating tasks and creating new, easier means of service delivery [32]. However, public sector information systems have experienced problems with issues such as interoperability, information silos and systems that are not user friendly.

Enterprise Architecture (EA) has been seen as a promising tool for improving information systems interoperability, standardization and business-IT alignment in the rapidly changing world of public administration [5, 23]. However, experiences in using EA in the public sector are mixed [10, 13, 18].

© IFIP International Federation for Information Processing 2016
Published by Springer International Publishing Switzerland 2016. All Rights Reserved
H.J. Scholl et al. (Eds.): EGOV 2016, LNCS 9820, pp. 287–298, 2016.
DOI: 10.1007/978-3-319-44421-5_23

EA was employed to improve interoperability of information systems and to help coordinate and develop new information systems and services for the Finnish public sector. The use of EA and the Finnish National Enterprise Architecture framework have been mandatory in the Finnish public sector since 2011. The performance audit done in 2015 revealed that EA work has 'not been integrated into existing management and planning processes and structures'.[1]

As EA generally has not fulfilled its expectations nationwide, a study was conducted to determine the reasons and rationale for using or not using EA in daily public sector activities. A critical research approach [28] using Fairclough's critical discourse analysis (CDA) [7] was chosen to gain insight into the use of EA in the public sector. As EA is meant to be used nationwide [15, 23], a series of interviews was conducted vertically in the Finnish public administration, from the ministry level to the municipal level. The case organization selected for the research was the Finnish basic education system. While Fairclough's view on CDA does not require a research question—the starting point should be a social problem—the following question was posed to research data: '*How are the terms Enterprise Architecture and efficiency constructed and linked in the speech of public sector officials?*'

2   Background

2.1   Efficiency in the Public Sector

The terms efficiency, productivity and effectiveness are often used interchangeably in political discourse. Pollitt and Bouckaert define efficiency as the ratio of *output* to *input*, and effectiveness as the ratio of *outcomes* to output: 'Efficiency increase (or productivity gain) is usually defined as an improvement in the ratio of outputs to inputs.' [24].

Improving efficiency has attracted an enormous amount of management attention in western countries. However, different ways of measuring performance and efficiency are met with 'conceptual mess' [4, 24, 31]. Sometimes the output and input are mixed, and sometimes the concepts are too vague to be used consistently across the public sector (see [31]).

With the education sector, the situation is, if possible, even worse. While it would be possible to measure the ratio of outputs to inputs—i.e., the ratio of pupils educated per a given amount of money—such measurement quickly proves itself inadequate. More important than the number of pupils is what they learn and how their education will help them later in life. Thus, the emphasis is on the outcomes of the education, not the outputs. With education, there also exist attribution problems [24]—how the effect of the school can be extracted, as research has shown that outcomes depend on the neighborhood [1] and parental involvement [9], just to name a few.

Regardless of the difficulties on measuring—or even defining—efficiency, the improvement of productivity and efficiency in the public sector is a popular topic in political speeches and documents. The improvement of efficiency can be seen in Finnish

---

[1] National Audit Office of Finland, Audit report 7/2015.

Government Programmes since the 1990s. In the Government Programme of the current Finnish government (Sipilä I), *digitalization* is named as a way to improve the efficiency of the public sector.

2.2 Enterprise Architecture

Research on EA still lacks a common definition and common terminology [15, 28]. It can be viewed as an 'integrated representation of the business and information technology in past, current and future states' [28] or a 'coherent whole of principles, methods, and models that are used in design and realization of enterprise's organizational structure, business processes, information systems, and infrastructure' [16]. Several definitions present EA as linking business and IT, defining the key principles of organization while, on the other hand, acting as a normative restriction of design freedom [17].

Use of EA in the public sector has been researched widely [30], and it has been seen to improve the interoperability of Information Systems (IS) and the efficiency of operations [5, 12, 15], or even reduce failure in development projects [14]. EA is being used in many roles and for many purposes [21].

There have been attempts to clarify the concept of EA in the context of public administration. Janssen et al. conceptualized Government Architecture (GA), saying that 'GA consists of frameworks, principles, guidelines and standards to guide design projects and deal with complexity. These elements are used to direct and guide initiatives occurring at all levels of government.' [15]. Gregor et al. saw Enterprise Architecture as a tool for 'business' and IS/IT alignment within organizational units [5]. Larsson researched a case involving multiple organizations within the Swedish healthcare sector [18]. The case studies have shown that there are benefits to be gained through use of EA, but also that many ambiguities, problems and open questions exist [5, 12, 13, 18, 19, 31].

2.3 Critical Discourse Analysis

A critical approach is not common in information systems research [20, 25], although it is regarded as a third alternative to positivistic and interpretive research [22]. What differentiates a critical approach from an interpretive approach is its focus on *'critiquing existing social systems and revealing any contradictions and conflicts that may inhere within their structures'* [ibid.]. Critical discourse analysis (CDA) studies texts—written or spoken—as social events that are governed by underlying social structures. These social structures are in constant dialogue with social events—on one hand, the structures govern the ways the events may take place, and on the other hand, the events are constantly reiterating and recreating social structures. [7].

CDA has been used in IS research, e.g., [2, 11]. CDA methodology of Norman Fairclough was chosen because it stresses both the careful study of texts and linking them to their social context. The starting point of the research is 'social problem which has semiotic aspect' [7]. The difference between CDA methodology and interpretive linguistic research approaches and methodologies is that the actions and actual practices of the informants are not under study. Instead, the structures and truths governing the speech are the focal points of the research.

This research addresses two concepts—Enterprise Architecture and efficiency—that both lack a clear definition and are used ambiguously. In this research, these concepts are viewed as *socially constructed*, and the way in which they are rationalized and situated in the speech of public sector officials is examined. In terms of CDA, assumed background knowledge that governs the use of the concepts was sought. As an alternative to using only the interview texts as data, external sources were used to position the texts in their context.

3   Research Setting

3.1   Finnish Basic Education System

The structure of the Finnish public sector relevant to the basic education consists of two bodies—the state's central administration and local administration.[2] The highest central body in the hierarchy is the Ministry of Education and Culture. The Finnish National Board for Education operates under the Ministry's supervision. The local administration consists of 313 municipalities that are self-governing entities. Local self-government is based on the constitution of Finland. Thus, the central bodies have no direct authority over the municipalities. Their authority relies on the power to adopt acts that are decided by the Finnish Parliament, or give decrees and other binding instructions.

The Finnish basic education system consists of nine-year compulsory schooling that starts in the year when a child turns seven. Basic education is funded by municipalities, and 97 % of the schools are public.

Basic education is regulated by the central administration. The most important guideline is the national core curriculum determined by the Finnish National Board of Education.[3] On the municipal level, Finnish basic education is one of the largest responsibilities of the municipalities, typically the biggest after social welfare and healthcare expenses. Therefore, the schools in Finland are part of the organization of the municipality in which they operate. Each municipality has some kind of organization for governing its schools. As the population of a municipality in Finland ranges from under 1,000 to over 600,000, municipalities have devised various ways to organize their basic education.

The Finnish basic education system has been widely regarded as an exemplary way of organizing public education [26, 27]. Finland has been at the top of OECD Programme for International Student Assessment (PISA) rankings.

3.2   Enterprise Architecture in Finland

Enterprise Architecture was introduced to the Finnish public sector through the Act on Information Management Governance in Public Administration in 2011. Since then, all

---

[2] http://vm.fi/en/administrative-structures.
[3] http://www.oph.fi/english/curricula_and_qualifications/basic_education.

public organizations have been instructed to describe their operations according to the national EA framework, although it is not yet strictly mandatory [19].

Finland has created its own EA framework, called JHS-179. It is a simplified version of TOGAF. As suggested by [23], Finland has chosen a top-down approach for EA. While few national-level architectures exist to date, the design principles have been given and the responsible ministries have been named. A 2015 report of the National Audit Office of Finland states that 'The terminology used in the materials (of Finnish National Enterprise Architecture) is open to interpretation. The language used in the materials and the manner in which the information is presented are very difficult to understand and seem only to be intended for technical experts.'

The term National Enterprise Architecture (NEA) was chosen in this paper to refer to Enterprise Architecture in the Finnish Public sector, as mandated by the Act.

3.3 Research Data

The data used in this research comprised interviews conducted with public sector officials in touch with basic education. The officials had backgrounds in educative sciences, information and computer sciences, and in fields such as administrative sciences. A total of 12 interviews were conducted with officials in the Ministry of Education and Culture, the Finnish National Board of Education and two municipalities. The officials interviewed in the central administration were selected because of their knowledge of NEA in the basic education sector—typically, they were responsible for NEA in their sector or were participating in work on NEA. The officials at the municipal level were chosen so that their knowledge of both basic education and IT architecture were represented in the interviews.

The topic of the interview presented to the informants was "EA in the Finnish Public Sector." The letter inviting them to participate in the interview stated that the interview was not meant to be a measure of EA knowledge, a measure of EA maturity level, or a comparison to any given EA framework. No other background information about the research were given to the informants. The same letter was sent to all informants.

It was promised that the names and titles of the informants would be kept confidential. This was important in order to get the informants to speak freely about their impressions. The subjective estimate of the interviewer was that the interviews were open, and the informants gave their honest opinions about the state of EA work. In order to maintain the confidentiality of the interviews, the quotes used in this paper are anonymous.

3.4 Analytical Framework

In Fairclough's CDA methodology, discourse is defined as ways of representing [7]. From the interviews, words and concepts that were used to describe the work related to EA were identified as well as results of such work and rationale given for such work. In addition to the transcribed and recorded interviews, the ways in which the text was connected to discourses in the media and in research literature were investigated.

Discourses are constantly evolving and are constantly in dialogue with other discourses. Recontextualization is the process of internalizing ideas and concepts from other discourses. Recontextualization is not merely a borrowing—the actors actively appropriate the new concepts, and this process may lead to unpredictable transformations and outcomes [8]. In the research, concepts and parts of text that were 'borrowed' from other sources were analyzed.

The ways in which the informants differentiated themselves from other parties in their speech were also analyzed in the texts. As each discourse offers a representation of the world, it also conveys direct or subtle ways to differentiate between the speaker and others, or 'us' and 'them.' Often in these cases, the speaker uses generalization—i.e., a single individual or single act is generalized to represent a group of people. While generalization is used to describe the properties of 'others,' it also highlights the speaker's views on the 'normal' and 'desired' properties or ways of working.

Thus, a three-dimensional framework was used in the analysis. For the parts of the interviews discussing Enterprise Architecture, the ways used to *represent* EA, concepts and items that were *recontextualized,* and words with which the informants *differentiated* their positions from others were studied.

4 Findings

4.1 Discourses Found in the Interviews

In Fairclough's CDA, discourse is a way of representing aspects of the world [7]. The interviews described the use of Enterprise Architecture from multiple angles. The informants used different words, and all had various experiences with EA. When all three dimensions of the analysis framework were used, there were three groups of discourses that stood out from the data (see *orders of discourse* in [7]). The groups found were not homogenous—within one group, there were multiple conflicting opinions and ways of describing EA. Still, within the group, the extracts from the interview revealed common beliefs, values and ways of legitimation. The orders are summarized in Table 1 and explained below.

Table 1. The main three orders of discourse found in the interviews.

	ICT	Educational	Administrative
Representation	EA is a tool for rational decision-making	EA is a tool for communication and mutual understanding	EA is a tool for 'architectural steering' and governance
Recontextualization	Efficiency comes from well-designed information systems	Emphasis is on *digitalization*	Efficiency means that administration must use less money
Differentiation	Emphasis on knowledge, especially ICT-related skills	ICT is 'one requirement among hundreds'	Parties 'cling on to old habits and ways of working'

The first such group of discourses was named the *Information and Communications Technology (ICT) discourse.* In this discourse, the use of EA is legitimated by the fact that there exists room for improvement in current ICT systems. EA is seen as a way to combine the needs of 'function' and 'operation' in ICT systems. The discourses carry the rational view used in engineering sciences—that EA is a way to achieve 'better' systems. The resulting architecture is a *contract* or a *blueprint* [29].

One informant stated this as follows: '*We are missing the connection from architecture work to project management, which would bring the concreteness to this. Without it, it is just paper.*'[4] The informant went on to describe how new projects should always be checked against EA descriptions.

The second group was named the *educational discourse.* In this discourse, legitimacy comes from providing education to children. In the educational discourse, the role of EA was as a collaborative tool for education and IT professionals. The benefit of EA is that it increases mutual understanding: "*We have been happy to have this holistic (shared) view, with people with backgrounds from systems, machines, function, leadership, and even customers.*" The term *shared view* was used in many interviews in one form or another. Whereas in the ICT discourse the EA descriptions were seen as 'complete' descriptions, the educational discourse saw this in another light: '*If we have new development (projects), we have to somehow decide which are regarded as pilot projects and which go to the EA process.*' Thus, EA will not contain all ICT-related development within the basic education sector, but only those projects that require cooperation from IT departments.

In the educational discourse, EA was linked to the concept of digitalization. The concept of digitalization has a broader meaning than, for example, in the Government Programme. Digitalization in educational discourse is seen as the general increase of digital appliances, digital systems, Internet and connectivity. It is not something that can be controlled—it is an emergent and contingent phenomenon that teachers have to cope with. When considered from this perspective, EA is a tool for gaining insight into and knowledge of the issues concerning the information systems used in education. EA is a way to communicate—to share needs and plans with the IT department.

The third discourse was named the *administrative discourse.* This discourse is linked to public administration and to the way public administration is constructed. EA is shown as a means of *governance* and *steering.* The resulting documents of EA work are documents to which lower levels of administration must adhere. EA work is similar to all other administrative work.

All three groups of discourses could exist in a single interview. Thus, the informant could change his or her position in the interview. It was interesting to see that the discourses prominent in the interviews were not dependent on the informants' education. The informants typically came from the education sector or had background in ICT. However, the informants used mostly the discourse prominent in their job role, not their background.

---

[4] The quotes from the interviews are translated by the author.

4.2 Recontextualization in the Discourses

Recontextualization and intertextuality were present in all discourses—different discourses used the concepts from other discourses to legitimize their work and give rationale for the use of EA in their operation.

In the ICT discourse, the concept of *efficiency* was often discussed. Efficiency is recontextualized from the administrative discourse to the ICT discourse to mean more efficient information systems—not to mean layoffs and cuts to employee benefits. Inefficiency is seen in overlapping information systems, in systems that do not have proper interfaces, and in tasks that could or should be done digitally. Thus, efficiency is achieved by spending more money for the development of information systems—which will, in turn, save money in the long run. Information systems are seen as an investment, and increased efficiency is seen as a rationale for funding.

The link between information systems and efficiency was seen also in the administrative discourse. However, in this discourse, efficiency meant that the administration must operate literally with less money. Information systems are not seen as an investment, as in the ICT discourse. EA should be key to this by removing the need of simultaneous information system development in different municipalities. The information systems and interfaces should be developed once, and they should be usable nationwide.

The word efficiency was used hardly ever in the educational discourse. It was replaced by such concepts as *development, cooperation, mutual understanding* and *keeping up with digitalization*. This may be because the word efficiency is extensively used in neo-liberal discourses in the education sector, which are in conflict with the traditional view on independent teachers and quality of education. The educational discourse borrowed many terms and concepts from the ICT discourse, but generally the view was that of the school and the pupils. For example, it was suggested that digital technologies will put pupils in different situations based on their socio-economic background.

4.3 Ways of Differentiation

The ICT discourse emphasizes ICT skills and knowledge. For example, it can be seen that the ability to make informed decisions comes from knowledge about the subject, as evidenced in a quote from an informant: *"They are experts in their own domain (education) that have drifted to (ICT sector). If you have to explain the very basics of information systems design to them, how could they make informed decisions?"* While the expertise in the other domains is respected *per se*, it does not provide the authority to make decisions in IT systems.

In the educational discourse, the providing of education is seen as the essential value. EA is seen as 'one of the many' requirements posed to teachers and organizers of education. Thus, the value of EA is instrumental, whereas the value of education is intrinsic. The authority to make decisions that affect the education sector should rest solely in the educative sector. While instructions from IT departments are mandating, they can be regarded with comments such as *'Yes, from time to time there are new instructions from IT. I have such e-mails coming daily from more than a hundred different sources.'* So, while the speaker acknowledges the importance of the instructions, (s)he appeals to the fact that strictly abiding by all rules is not possible. In different levels of government, the same thing is said in different words, but the message is the same: The IT department does not have the authority to tell us how to conduct our work.

In the administrative discourse, education providers and IT staff of municipalities are seen as parties that *'cling on to their customary ways of working.'* The operations could be streamlined by standardizing different ways of working. The ICT discourse shares this view, but it is again recontextualized in the ICT discourse. Whereas the administrative discourse recognizes the autonomous nature of the municipalities, the ICT discourse carries the notion of mandated compliance to common norms. It was also noted that conditional clauses regarding EA were often used in the administrative discourse: *'The EA would be a great tool to achieve interoperability.'* Sometimes the 'but' was left out, and sometimes it was directly stated that it is not possible to achieve with current administrative structures.

5   Discussion

5.1   EA as Government Architecture

The role of EA as a resulting architecture, a blueprint that governs future operations, is highly contested. The ICT discourse relies on the fact that the IT department 'has a say' about new projects and pilots in the education sector. The educational discourse opposes the role of the architecture as a guiding tool. The education professionals have their own development methodologies, and EA is not seen as a replacement for them. However, also in the educational discourse, the need to link EA to an organization's strategy was seen as important. The administrative discourse acknowledges the difficulty related to putting EA into practice, as the independent organizations currently have no need to comply with national standards.

While the educational discourse effectively rejects the concept of efficiency, digitalization provides a rationale for EA usage. The informants see the effects of digitalization in the problems caused by the unprecedented and uncontrolled increase in the number of smartphones and other personal appliances. They demand training on how to use the new digital learning environments, and EA is seen as a way to put things 'under control.' However, EA is kept strictly out of the development of other educational activities.

The administrative discourse sees EA as a promising tool, but asserts that it should bring about tangible benefits—i.e., reduction of costs in the public administration. While the efficiency of the teaching itself is not at stake, there are several systems, like payroll and student registration, that are handled differently in each municipality. This causes overlap of IT development and is a waste of resources. However, the educational discourse sees this as 'operational agility'—when the processes are not fixed nationwide, there is room for pilot development and new innovations. ICT discourse sees these pilots mainly as nuisances, as they often come as a surprise and are not discussed with IT beforehand.

5.2 EA as Common Language

The educational discourse sees the role of the National Enterprise Architecture as a common language between educational staff and IT staff. It is a tool that can be used to describe and visualize IT systems and the desired future state. The ICT discourse recognizes this from its own standpoint. The EA can help to agree on the current state and the target state. The administrative discourse shares this view, but the context is in the organization between autonomous parties, while the educational and ICT discourses look at the situation within one organization.

This role of EA is uncontested in the interviews—the need for mutual understanding and common language is recognized in all discourses, but only in educational discourse does this arise as the most important function of EA. From the viewpoint of educational discourse, IT is just one of the requirements imposed on the school system. Other requirements and instructions come from all directions, and the schools have to balance them. Increasing common understanding so that IT departments can help them is an understandable wish.

On the other hand, the ICT discourse and administrative discourse simplify complex operations in the basic education sector as 'function' or 'special knowledge.' While the ICT discourse expresses the desire that EA acts more as a coordinating element, the accountability of the actions remains on the educational side.

6 Conclusion

The object of the research was to determine different ways of constructing Enterprise Architecture and efficiency in the speech of public sector officials. Three orders of discourse were found: ICT discourse, educational discourse and administrative discourse. While the ICT and administrative discourses had differing views of the concept of efficiency, the educational discourse did not see EA an as agent for improving efficiency.

The ambiguity of EA's role in practical work has also been noted in other research, such as [18]. The same ambiguity can be seen in this study, but due to the CDA methodology used, the ambiguity was seen to arise from different background knowledge and assumptions embedded in social structures. Hjort-Madsen studied the implementation of EA in the US government using an institutional lens, and found three strategies to cope with the mandated use of EA: accepters, improvers and transformers [13]. Here we see that the Finnish basic education sector has long traditions and is capable of 'defending itself' against requests from other sources—in fact, it is battling them constantly. However, digitalization in schools provides such an external shock to the system that it is seen as necessary to find new ways to cooperate with IT departments.

CDA was determined a suitable methodology for conducting research on a subject with so many 'free-floating' concepts, such as efficiency and newly introduced Finnish national enterprise architecture. By investigating the text and the social structures and practices regulating the speech simultaneously, the contradictions between different orders of discourse can be revealed.

This research focused on the construction of concepts. The discourses are in constant flux, and a single informant may use different—even conflicting—discourses in the course of an interview. Further research is needed on the power structures behind these discourses [11]—it is clear that the ICT discourse and the educational discourse must align themselves with the administrative discourse when they are applying for funding, but it is not yet clear what effects this has on discourses and daily operations.

References

1. Aaronson, D.: Using sibling data to estimate the impact of neighborhoods on children's educational outcomes. J. Hum. Resour. **33**(4), 915–946 (1998)
2. Albert, C.S., Salam, A.F.: Critical discourse analysis: toward theories in social media. In: The 19th Americas Conference on Information Systems (2013)
3. Diefenbach, T.: New public management in public sector organizations: the dark sides of managerialistic 'enlightenment'. Public Adm. **87**(4), 892–909 (2009)
4. Dunleavy, P., Margetss, H., Bastow, S., Tinkler, J.: New public management is dead—long live digital-era governance. J. Public Adm. Res. Theor. **16**(3), 467–494 (2005)
5. Gregor, S., Hart, D., Martin, N.: Enterprise architectures: enablers of business strategy and IS/IT alignment in government. Inf. Technol. People **20**(2), 96–120 (2007)
6. Hood, C.: The "new public management" in the 1980s: variations on a theme. Acc. Organ. Soc. **20**(3), 93–109 (1995)
7. Fairclough, N.: Analysing Discourse: Textual Analysis for Social Research. Routledge, London (2003)
8. Fairclough, N.: Critical Discourse Analysis: The Critical Study of Language. Routledge, London (2010)
9. Flouri, E., Buchanan, A.: Early father's and mother's involvement and child's later educational outcomes. Br. J. Educ. Psychol. **74**(2), 141–153 (2004)
10. Gaver, S.B.: Why Doesn't the Federal Enterprise Architecture Work? (2010). http://www.ech-bpm.ch/sites/default/files/articles/why_doesnt_the_federal_enterprise_architecture_work.pdf
11. Hekkala, R., Stein, M-K., Rossi, M.: "Omega-team is moving to another premise over my dead body…" power as discursive-material practice in an IS project. In: The 35th International Conference on Information Systems (2014)
12. Hjort-Madsen, K.: Enterprise architecture implementation and management: a case study on interoperability. In: HICSS 2006 (2006)
13. Hjort-Madsen, K.: Institutional patters of enterprise architecture adoption in government. Transforming Gov.: People Process Policy **1**, 333–349 (2007)
14. Janssen, M., Klievink, B.: Can enterprise architectures reduce failure in development projects? Transforming Gov.: People Process Policy **6**(1), 27–40 (2012)
15. Janssen, M., Flak, L.S., Sæbø, Ø.: Government architecture: concepts, use and impact. In: Proceedings of 2nd IFIP WG 8.5 International Conference, EGOV 2013, pp. 135–147 (2013)
16. Land, M.O., Proper, E., Waage, M., Cloo, J., Steghuis, C.: Enterprise Architecture—Creating Value By Informed Governance. Springer, Heidelberg (2009)
17. Lankhorst, M.M.: Enterprise Architecture at Work. Springer, Berlin Heidelberg (2005)
18. Larsson, H.: Ambiguities in the early stages of public sector enterprise architecture implementation: outlining complexities of interoperability. In: Proceedings of 10th IFIP WG 8.5 International Conference, EGOV 2011, pp. 367–377 (2011)

19. Lemmetti, J., Pekkola, S.: Understanding enterprise architecture: perceptions by the Finnish public sector. In: Scholl, H.J., Janssen, M., Wimmer, M.A., Moe, C.E., Flak, L.S. (eds.) EGOV 2012. LNCS, vol. 9248, pp. 162–173. Springer, Heidelberg (2012)
20. Myers, M.D.: A set of principles for conducting critical research in information systems. MIS Q. **35**(1), 17–36 (2011)
21. Niemi, E., Pekkola, S.: Using enterprise architecture artefacts in an organisation. Enterp. Inf. Syst. 1–26 (2015)
22. Orlikowski, W.J., Baroudi, J.J.: Studying information technology in organizations: research approaches and assumptions. Inf. Syst. Res. **2**(1), 1–28 (1991)
23. Peristera, V., Tarabanis, K.: Towards an enterprise architecture for public administration using a top-down approach. Eur. J. Inf. Syst. **9**, 252–260 (2000)
24. Pollitt, C., Bouckaert, G.: A Comparative Analysis—New Public Management, Governance, and the Neo-Weberian State. Oxford University Press, New York (2011)
25. Richardson, H., Robinson, B.: The mysterious case of the missing paradigm: a review of critical information systems research 1991–2001. Inf. Syst. J. **17**, 241–270 (2007)
26. Sahlberg, P.: Education policies for raising student learning: the finnish approach. J. Educ. Policy **22**(2), 147–171 (2007)
27. Simola, H.: The finnish miracle of PISA: historical and sociological remarks on teaching and teacher education. Comp. Educ. **41**(4), 455–470 (2005)
28. Simon, D., Fischbach, K., Schoder, D.: An exploration of enterprise architecture research. Commun. Assoc. Inf. Syst. **32**, 1–72 (2013)
29. Smolander, K., Rossi, M., Purao, S.: Software architectures: blueprint, literature, language or decision? EJIS **17**, 575–588 (2008)
30. Tamm, T., Seddon, P., Shanks, G., Reynolds, P.: How does enterprise architecture add value to organisations? Commun. Assoc. Inf. Syst. **21**, 141–168 (2011). Article 10
31. Van de Walle, S.: The state of the world's bureaucracies. J. Comparable Policy Anal. **8**(4), 437–448 (2007)
32. West, D.M.: E-government and the transformation of service delivery and citizen attitudes. Public Adm. Rev. **64**(1), 15–27 (2004)

Towards Trusted Trade-Lanes

Joris Hulstijn[1(✉)], Wout Hofman[2], Gerwin Zomer[2], and Yao-Hua Tan[1]

[1] Delft University of Technology, Delft, Netherlands
j.hulstijn@tudelft.nl
[2] TNO, The Hague, Netherlands

Abstract. Customs administrations are exploring system-based approaches to regulatory supervision, taking the entire set of controls in a process into account. In addition to Trusted Traders, which are recognized by a certification process, customs are considering to identify so called Trusted Trade Lanes: companies that collaborate in a trade lane in a reliable manner. In this paper we explore the concept of a trusted trade lane. We identify essential characteristics of a trusted trade-lane, and develop various scenarios in which trade lanes may develop and find ways to demonstrate to the authorities and commercial partners that they conform to these requirements. The characteristics have been evaluated in a workshop with experts. The scenarios are tested against three pilot projects, that aim to improve supply chain visibility.

Keywords: Regulatory supervision · Customs · Supply chain visibility

1 Introduction

Customs administrations face two opposing challenges. One the one hand they must improve regulatory compliance, specifically related to safety and security, while on the other hand reducing administrative burden and facilitating trade. To meet these challenges, customs administrations are adjusting their regulatory supervision models. They increasingly rely on the compliance efforts of the companies themselves [1]. This often involves a so called system-based approach to regulatory supervision, which – by contrast to the currently dominant transaction-based approach – takes the entire system of internal controls into account [2]. This includes the way in which companies choose to collaborate in a value chain, their business processes and logistics operations, as well as their information systems and security devices.

In practice, those companies that can demonstrate to be 'in control' of the risks, are recognized as so called trusted traders and receive benefits in terms of reduced inspections [3]. Certification schemes exist to recognize trusted traders, like AEO in the European Union. However, supply chain risks and challenges, such as sustainability or resilience, affect the entire trade lane and can't be solved by individual companies alone. For this reason, recent vision documents suggest a customs supervision approach that is based on the concept of a *trusted trade lane* [4]: a collaboration of supply chain partners who maintain a system of control measures in order to cover the risks of the entire trade-lane, which makes the trade lane trustworthy, both

H.J. Scholl et al. (Eds.): EGOV 2016, LNCS 9820, pp. 299–311, 2016.
DOI: 10.1007/978-3-319-44421-5_24

to the authorities and to commercial partners. It is an open question how to characterize a trusted trade-lane. Regulators are actively debating this issue.

In this paper we discuss what it would mean to form a trusted trade lane and how trustworthiness can be demonstrated. What makes a group of trading companies trustworthy to themselves, their commercial parties and to the authorities? Based on a discussion of the literature on supply chains, regulatory supervision and internal controls, and extrapolating from observations about current trusted trader initiatives like AEO, we propose a set of essential characteristics of a trusted trade-lane.

It is uncertain how the companies in a trade-lane will organize themselves and how they will demonstrate to the regulator that they are trustworthy. In particular, we see several scenarios ranging from a dominant party scenario, in which a company forces its suppliers to join and adopt the necessary controls, through a cooperative scenario, offering services to its members, towards a data-driven scenario in which patterns of behavior can be identified to show trustworthiness empirically.

To validate the proposed characteristics, we have held an evaluation workshop with supply chain experts. In addition, we compare the scenarios with observations from three real-life demonstrator projects that aim to develop supply chain visibility infrastructures, see e.g. [5]. These can be seen as real-life cases.

The remainder of the paper is structured as follows. Section 2 identifies essential characteristics of trusted trade-lanes. Section 3 develops several scenarios for setting up and demonstrating trustworthiness. Section 4 discusses the evaluation workshop. Section 5 contains some early observations made in the context of three demonstrator projects that will serve as initial validation of the characteristics.

2   What Are Trusted-Trade-Lanes?

In general, why do people obey the law? Economic approaches to regulation assume that parties calculate what is in their best interest. A violation may lead to a sanction, so the decision to violate a norm is made on the basis of the expected likelihood of being caught and the severity of the sanction. However, experimental research shows that subjects are more than economic agents [6]. Citizens, or companies for that matter, have all kinds of additional motivations to obey the law: economic, social, ethical but also practical. An important practical aspect concerns the costs of compliance. New regulatory approaches try to reduce costs of compliance, based on the idea that for a subject to be compliant, he or she must (i) know the regulations, (ii) must be willing and (iii) must be able to comply, see OECD [7]. For this reason, much effort has been put into making it easier to be compliant, for instance by reducing complexity of regulations, or introducing a single-window [8]. In the remainder of this section we briefly review literature on regulatory supervision, that is relevant to the regulatory approach adopted by customs administrations.

Self-regulation. The regulator has delegated some regulatory tasks to the party being regulated: setting the norm, implementing the norm, and monitoring [9]. Only a kind of meta-supervision, to test whether the company is indeed 'in control' remains. Self-regulation makes sense when the interests of the company are aligned with those of society, for example in work safety regulations, where companies also benefit from a reduced number of accidents. This also holds for security in international trade.

Responsive Regulation. The regulator has a choice how to respond to subject behavior. The response (e.g. education, feedback, warning, penalty) is based on the specific compliance behavior of the party being regulated [10], p. 35. For instance, incidental violations may lead to a warning, but do not immediately lead to a penalty. Repeated violations, however, do lead to sanctions. They show a breach of trust.

Risk-Based Regulation. The regulatory response takes the risk for society into account [11]. A higher risk leads to a more severe response. For example, in the customs domain, risk assessments determine whether a container will be selected at the border for scanning or for physical inspection. The assessments are based on data from the Entry Summary Declaration (ENS), which must be filed by the carrier 24 h before loading the goods at the port of departure.

System-Based Regulation. This type of regulatory supervision takes the entire system of controls into account that influence the processes and systems that generate the behavior [2]. This approach is opposed to transaction-based supervision, commonly used for fiscal matters and therefore also for many customs supervision tasks. A particular example of system-based supervision in the supply chain domain is the self-assessment and review procedure to obtain the AEO certificate (see below), but it is also common for supervising specific customs licenses, like a bonded warehouse. Such licenses are only granted after a full IT audit of the relevant systems, processes and organizational measures.

2.1 Customs Supervision: Mixed Methods

These regulatory approaches from the literature are rather abstract. How can these be combined into a practical approach? The key is to distinguish different categories of subjects, or in this case, different streams of goods, and treat each of these differently.

The Netherlands Customs Administration has laid down its vision on regulatory supervision for the future [4], also visible on Youtube. Figure 1 shows a screenshot. The customs administration already makes use of mixed regulatory methods. For all streams, a combination of administrative checks, physical inspections, and X-ray scanning is used, but the relative proportion of methods depends on the type of trader. This is illustrated in Fig. 1. White dots show information. On the basis of pre-arrival data, the stream of goods is separated into three kinds.

- Blue: unknown trader (traditional). Only origin and goods description are known. Mostly physical inspections and additional X-ray scans. Administrative verification for fiscal matters. Note that physical checks are more resource intensive and typically lead to logistics disruptions and delays.
- Green: trusted trader (AEO since 2007; customs licenses). Mostly administrative verifications, with occasional audits or physical inspections to verify reliability.

- Yellow: trusted trade lane (future). Mostly administrative verification of data from supply chain visibility platforms (data pipeline). Occasional audits or inspections to verify reliability.

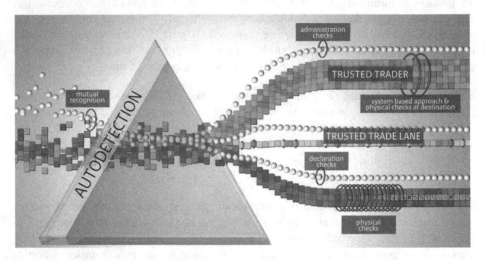

Fig. 1. Customs administration of the Netherlands' vision on regulatory supervision.

2.2   On Trust and Control

Supply chain parties collaborate in a network. Parties depend on each other. Parties must therefore trust each other. Trust is originally seen as a personal attitude or characteristic of a person (trustor) towards another person (trustee), but it can also be attributed to an organization [12]. Here we will follow the economic literature, which defines trust as "the willingness of a party to be vulnerable to the actions of another party based on the expectation that the other party will perform a particular action important to the trustor, irrespective of the ability to monitor or control that other party" [12], p. 712. Trustworthiness, on the other hand, depends on properties of the trustee. Traditionally these properties are ability, integrity, and benevolence [13].

How can parties improve their trustworthiness? They have to signal that they possess these properties. But what is the value of a signal from the trustee itself? This explains the need for an independent auditor to assess reliability of reports. To do so an auditor requires certain precautions built into the organization, processes and information systems: internal controls [14]. Consider for example segregation of duties, an audit trail, access control, baseline security, supervision and monitoring, etc. In practice an auditor – or customs officer – must verify whether the system of internal controls of a company is adequate to meet the risks in that line of business, whether it has been properly implemented and has been operationally effective for the duration of the period under investigation. Only under such conditions, the regulator may rely on the records of the company. This suggest a form of self-regulation, where the internal controls are specified, implemented and monitored by the company. Only a form of meta-supervision remains for the regulator [1]. The reason is that controls are highly context dependent. A regulator cannot specify beforehand precisely which controls are necessary in, say, the petrochemical industry.

2.3 Trusted Trader

A trusted trader is a trading company that is officially recognized by the authorities to be trustworthy. The concept was made popular by the SAFE framework of standards, that is influential in customs supervision [3]. In principle, distinguishing trusted from non-trusted traders allows the regulator to redirect its efforts to those subjects, which pose a higher risk to society. In return, the trusted trader may expect benefits in terms of reduced administrative burden (less inspections; less uncertainty).

A well-known example is the AEO framework that operates in the European Union since 2007 [15]. To become Authorized Economic Operator (AEO), a company must demonstrate the following properties: customs compliance, appropriate record-keeping, financial solvency and, where relevant, appropriate security and safety standards. Similar initiatives exist elsewhere, such as Australia, or the US CTPAT.

Countries have developed different ways of granting AEO status. For example, the CTPAT scheme in the US is based on inspections with detailed checklists. Initially, The Netherlands and Sweden were among the few countries that opted for a self-assessment of the risks and controls, followed by an audit. However, the UCC, the upcoming new customs legislation, has now also adopted the self-assessment model. Moreover, AEO status will now be a necessary requirement to obtain other customs simplifications. One could say that the AEO initiative is relatively successful. For example, in 2014 AEO operators were involved in 54 % of imports, 68 % of exports and in 54 % of transits[1]. Is that enough to meet the regulatory challenges of today?

There have also been complaints about AEO. For example, the European Shippers Council (ESC) filed a manifesto (July 2014), to express dissatisfaction with the way the AEO framework is being operated. The perception is that there are not enough benefits in terms of trade facilitation and reduced administrative burden to counter the investments in internal controls. There is no legal certainty attached to the certificate.

2.4 Challenges for Supply Chains

The trusted trader concept is directed to individual companies. However, companies cannot solve the risks and challenges that face international supply chains by themselves. Some form of public-private collaboration is necessary [16].

– **Supply chain visibility** concerns awareness of and control over end-to-end goods movements in supply chains – including insight in sources of data and whereabouts of goods – enabling agile, resilient, sustainable as well as compliant and trusted supply chains [17]. Stakeholders may have limited control over end-to-end movements. They may have outsourced tasks or only contribute to part of the chain. Supply

---

[1] Fact sheet European Union: http://ec.europa.eu/taxation_customs/.

chain visibility can be achieved by sharing sensor data (e.g. using Internet of things [18]), and by sharing data extracted from trade documents. It requires uniform semantics. A particular approach to achieve data visibility is the vision of a data pipeline [5].

- **Sustainability.** Collaboration in a supply chain was always motivated by the economic need not to waste resources [19]. Later environmental and social concerns were added as objectives in their own right. Collaboration is necessary to achieve these objectives. Consider the carbon footprint of a product. Efforts to reduce transport emissions are useless if production produces ten times as much. In order to detect and address inefficiencies, information needs to be shared.
- **Supply chain resilience.** Resilience is the ability of a supply chain to respond to disturbances by resisting damage and recovering quickly [20]. By collecting data with respect to the environment and subscribe to particular events signaled by external providers, an organization will be able to take proper mitigation measures. In general, resilience also requires a way to handle dependencies and reduce complexity. For instance, try to do things locally if possible [21].

Note that information sharing and supply chain visibility also contribute to solutions of the other challenges. Parties need to communicate to overcome these challenges.

2.5 Characterizing Trusted Trade-Lanes

What makes a trusted trade lane? What are the essential characteristics?

First, the notion of a trusted trade lane is an extension of the trusted trader concept. If we extrapolate on the current practice of assessing and granting AEOs, we can expect a focus on risk and controls, self-assessment and audits. In particular, there are two kinds of controls that matter in the customs domain. (a) Physical controls are needed to secure the goods. Essentially, customs supervision is about integrity of the flow of goods [3]. Measures must be taken to prevent adding goods to the flow (smuggle) or taking goods out (theft). Consider for example container security devices (CSD), RFID devices to establish a causal chain between the goods and their records, or a secure consolidation point as part of the logistics operations. (b) Administrative controls are needed to make sure customs can rely on the records. Compare the objective of 'appropriate record keeping' for AEO. Consider for example a data visibility infrastructure, which provides access to data from packing list, pro-forma invoice, purchase order, certificates, etc. [5].

Second, the notion involves an entire trade lane, so a group of companies which collaborate together. For this reason, the stability of the collaboration itself affects trust [12], see also [16]. Parties who invest in a trade lane, depend on each other. We expect that members will also have to be individually trustworthy.

Third, the task of implementing controls to mitigate global supply chain risks creates a fundamental challenge, as traditionally controls are internal and are the responsibility of central management, and do not cover inter-organizational aspects [22]. In practice, under this view, a trade lane requires some governance structure, to identify risks and assign controls to mitigate those risks to specific partners. There is not much literature on distributing risks and controls in networks, except for [23].

Moreover, because being part of a trusted trade lane will have legal consequences (e.g. benefits in reduced inspections) it is likely that some party will have to act as legal representative of the trade lane, for instance to request to be recognized as such. Some party will also need to do secretarial duties, record which partners have entered and have left, and help to collect revenues, distribute costs, and generally organize and assign tasks, such as internal and external communication.

Thus we identify three essential characteristics of a trusted trade-lane. These properties must be demonstrated, for a trade lane to be considered trustworthy.

(1) Members are known and individually trustworthy.
(2) There is long-term and stable collaboration among members, motivated by a viable business proposition, and coordinated by a governance structure that provides a party who can act as legal representative.
(3) There is an adequately designed, well implemented and operationally effective system of control measures to ensure
    (a) physical integrity of the goods, and
    (b) reliable trade data, to be made available to the authorities.

3   Scenarios

It is unknown in which way trade lanes will choose to demonstrate to the regulator that they are trustworthy. An analogy can be dawn with the early days of the AEO initiative, in 2007, when no guidelines were given on how to adopt the requirements. We envision various scenarios. Some scenarios are based on formal controls, whereas other scenarios could be based on data analytics to analyze behavior and establish trustworthiness empirically. In practice, there will probably be mixtures of both.

Dominant Party Scenario. In many industries, a commercially dominant party drives innovation by forcing its suppliers to adopt specific technologies. Such a player can take the role of supply chain orchestrator and can act as representative for a trade lane. Steinfield et al. [24] call this a private coordination hub.

Suppose a manufacturer extends its efforts of supplier selection to also include customs compliance, in additional to usual selection criteria like cost and product quality. The data that needs to be shared to make this happen is also used for risk analysis by customs and other regulators (piggy backing) [25]. In this case, the business case is based on that of the dominant party. As suppliers are dependent, they have to follow. The information technology is expected to be proprietary.

Data-Driven Scenario. Partners innovate their supply chain and logistics operations by implementing technology that allows them to collaborate and share data reliably, facilitated by a platform that acts as a kind of information broker. Consider a kind of Uber or AirBnB for logistics services. There is a commercial reason to join the platform, for example to reduce uncertainty and delays. In this way a network of small specialist companies can jointly offer sophisticated services. Steinfield et al. [24] call this a shared coordination hub. Data from the platform can be re-used for regulatory purposes (piggy backing) [25]. The host of the platform acts as a legal representative, or helps to elect a representative.

The controls to make the network trustworthy are embedded in the business model of each stakeholder and in that of the platform host; they are not added for the sake of regulatory compliance. Collaboration can be relatively dynamic, with parties entering and leaving the network as they see fit. Because of this dynamics, the software applications for information exchange can only be built on open standards.

Cooperative Scenario. Supply chain partners collaborate with each other and with public agencies to improve compliance and reduce administrative burden. Trust is based on acquaintance. Formal agreements are drawn up at a later stage. Business cases are developed, but are based on estimates only. Subsidies may be necessary to overcome an initial hurdle. Technology for information exchange only follows after the agreements have been made, and is therefore likely proprietary.

For example, imagine a cooperative (such as the Flora Holland flower auction house) acting as representative. Member firms are legally independent of the cooperation, but Flora Holland can offer 'assurance' services to its members, and may make membership conditional on certain requirements. Flora Holland would have substantial influence over its members; enough to warrant increased trustworthiness.

These scenarios are characterized by different organizational structures of power or influence (Fig. 2). For example, we foresee a hierarchical, peer-to-peer, or a hybrid membership topology. In each case, different kinds of partners will act as a representative. For example, the dominant partner scenario will have a hierarchical topology, with a clear representative, who is also in a position to distribute risks and controls. By contrast, the data-driven scenario has a peer-to-peer topology. There is no dominant partner, and whoever acts as representative is elected. The cooperative scenario has a structure of membership that implies influence, but no formal power.

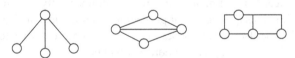

Fig. 2. Network topologies: (a) hierarchical, (b) peer to peer, (c) membership

4   Evaluation Workshop

In order to discuss what constitutes a trusted trade-lane we organized a workshop, held in the context of a meeting of the European project CORE [25]. It was held in Leiden on 9 December 2015. The audience consisted of about 20 participants, including representatives from businesses, branch organizations, research institutes and several customs authorities; all were experts on safety and security for international supply chains. An introductory text was distributed among participants with two questions to be discussed in small groups.

(1) How do you define a trusted trade lane? Mention five essential characteristics that make a trade lane trustworthy, to commercial partners and the authorities.
(2) You are working on a specific case. Please consider how your approach helps to demonstrate that a trade lane is to be trusted.

Although there was limited time, groups were actively discussing. In response to question 1, the groups suggested characteristics. All of the mentioned characteristics can be seen as rephrases of the characteristics (1)–(3) above. For example, several groups listed supply chain visibility, which corresponds to 3(b). In response to question 2 several practical suggestions were made, which also helped to further detail the scenarios explained above. In particular, suggestions were made about dealing with risk and control in networks. Groups were actively discussing the notion of a trusted trade-lane and the expected advantages and disadvantages. The following issues were raised in the discussion.

Issue 1. What trade facilitation will be given to a trusted-trade lane? There is already some dissatisfaction among shippers about the current AEO framework, witness the ESC Manifesto (July 2014). The customs response to this concern, was that a trusted trade-lane should first of all be trustworthy for commercial reasons, because there is a business proposition in being more reliable. Once established, a trusted trade-lane can be recognized by the customs authorities as such, and once demonstrated, reliability can be translated into reduced inspections.

Issue 2. Talking about supply chain visibility requires a common understanding of the way a supply chain is functioning. We have to consider the fundamentals of supply chains, so that standards can be agreed on to share information. Syntactic interoperability is not enough; it also concerns the meaning and practical usage of the data. In addition, we need to standardize how to define and assess risks.

Issue 3. Extrapolating from experiences with the AEO initiative, we expect that the recognition process of a trusted trade lane will be a kind of dialogue between businesses and customs. In this process businesses need guidance on what is expected, otherwise there will be no level playing field. The response by customs was that it is too early for guidance. First companies must take the initiative and develop best practices. We must find out what the characteristics of a trusted trade-lane are.

Issue 4. Do we really need a legal representative and what does it mean to be a representative? Participants agreed that the representative would not have to be legally liable for what members of the trusted trade-lane are doing, but must be responsible in some sense. For example, Flora Holland are not officially importing the goods; the growers do. However, as a cooperative they can take some responsibility for their members. Note in this respect that they import under DDP or CIF incoterms.

Issue 5. To be trustworthy as a trade lane, it is crucial to reduce variability. Delays can be handled, as long as they can be predicted. Variability leads to unpredictability and uncertainty. Reducing variability has large additional benefits, which may be the dominant business driver for a trusted trade lane.

5   Observations from Demonstrator Projects

In this section we describe three initiatives to develop supply chain visibility infrastructures, which are studied as demonstrators or living labs in the CORE project [25]. The demonstrators can be seen as cases of potential trusted trade lanes. In general, the case study method makes sense when research is exploratory and the phenomenon investigated is intertwined with the context [26]. That is the case here.

The cases were selected by convenience: from a total of nine demonstrator work packages we selected active demonstrators where we have access to informants. Note that demonstrators in a large EU project are a kind of subsidized experiments. Properties of collaboration in a project may differ from purely commercial initiatives. Nevertheless, the technical and governance issues that need to be tacked are the same.

Data was collected by participating observation, as the authors are also part of the CORE consortium, and by lengthy unstructured interviews with key participants. In particular, we spoke with representatives of the Netherlands Customs Administration.

Earlier we noted that supply chain visibility is a prerequisite for solving other supply chain challenges, besides customs compliance. That is why these supply chain visibility initiatives are indeed potential cases of emerging trusted trade lanes. We look in particular at three of the essential characteristics of a trusted trade lane: (1) governance structure, (2) business model and reason to collaborate, (3) IT infrastructure. At this stage in the project, it is too early to say much about the controls for physical integrity and data reliability and how these are to be achieved.

Case 1. SIP. This case is about the Shipping Information Pipeline (SIP), that is developed by MAERSK. The goal is to position SIP as a 'common good' type of connectivity infrastructure: costs will be shared by MAERSK with the other stakeholders, namely the global ocean carriers, global terminal operators and even freight forwarders. For such large players, standardization and a common infrastructure to share data is potentially very beneficial. (1) Based on the current market position, MAERSK can be seen as a dominant party. We observe a hierarchical structure. However, in the long run, the service could develop into a kind of information broker. (2) Initially, parties will join because MAERSK induces them to do so, but if the platform is successful and becomes a de facto standard, there will be additional business reasons to join. (3) The information technology is based on open standards. However, the data set that will be shared is relatively limited. It will mostly concern data about events, such as data about departure and arrival times, or data about opening and closing the container. So the scope of the project is limited.

Case 2. Flora Holland. This case is about the *Flora Holland* auction house, which is responsible for several large trade lanes of cut flowers being transported from Kenya to the Netherlands, either by air, or recently also by refrigerated sea container. The pilot project aims to build a customs dashboard for sharing data from official trade documents to facilitate administrative checks and border controls: export declaration, phytosanitary certificate, pro-forma invoice (which contains much of the data required by customs) and various types of event data. (1) Flora Holland is a cooperative, who want to offer new services to their members, the growers. Hence we find a membership structure. There are also contractual relations to commercial partners. (2) Members have joined the pilot project because they are curious about the results and because they want good relations with the Netherlands Customs Administration, who actively support the project. In the long run, it is expected that commercial benefits of data visibility may be demonstrated, in particular reduced delays, reduced uncertainty and less administrative burden. (3) The information technology is based on open standards, but needs to be connected to proprietary systems. This is not trivial, as we have to coordinate several regulators (customs and plant protection organizations), each with their own standards and practices.

Case 3. Felixstowe. This case is about a data pipeline initiative that is supporting four different trade-lanes that run through the port of Felixstowe. Members have implemented data-pipeline software and connected their proprietary systems. The initiative started in the CASSANDRA project that preceded CORE, but has now been taken on by commercial players. In particular, the Destin8 port community system has taken the role of information broker. HMRC, the British Customs, have not connected to the data pipelines directly, but do want to link their OneGov at the Border initiative. (1) Currently, we find an ad-hoc power structure, based on the governance of the pilot project, and the emerging information broker role of Destin8. (2) Parties have mainly joined for commercial reasons. In some specific cases commercial benefits of improved data visibility have already been demonstrated. Improved control over the supply chain was said in one case to have resulted in a 30 % reduction of supply chain costs. (3) The pipelines are run by separate commercial parties, but they all use the same data model and interoperability standards, based on UN/CEFACT and WCO data model. So here too, standardization is crucial [16].

6 Conclusions

In this paper we discuss the concept of a trusted trade lane. Trusted trade lanes will be identified by customs authorities using a system-based approach to regulatory supervision: the entire system of controls in processes, systems and logistics operations is taken into account, including in particular commercially motivated controls. We identified three essential characteristics of a trusted trade-lane: members must be individually trustworthy, there must be a stable collaboration and governance structure, and a system of control measures must ensure physical integrity of the goods and reliable trade data, to be made available to the regulator.

We have held an initial evaluation workshop, which confirmed these characteristics, but also raised issues for discussion. In particular, guidance is needed on how to become a trusted trade-lane. Reduction of variability is likely to be a business driver. To arrive at a trusted trade-lane, we envision different scenarios. We consider a dominant party forcing its suppliers to be more reliable, a cooperative providing services for its members, or a data-driven scenario facilitated by a platform.

Elements of these scenarios were also identified in three demonstrator cases, as they are studied in the CORE project. In particular, we find evidence of a hierarchical scenario, and a cooperative scenario. A data-driven scenario may develop from current commercial initiatives for information brokers.

Acknowledgments. Thanks to participants of the EU project CORE for their input.

References

1. Burgemeestre, B., Hulstijn, J., Tan, Y.-H.: Value-based argumentation for justifying compliance. Artif. Intell. Law **19**(2–3), 149–186 (2011)
2. May, P.J.: Regulatory regimes and accountability. Regul. Gov. **1**(1), 8–26 (2007)
3. WCO: SAFE Framework of Standards to Secure and Facilitate Global Trade (version 2015). World Customs Organization, Brussels (2015)
4. Customs Administration of the Netherlands: Pushing Boundaries: The Customs Administration of The Netherlands' Point on the Horizon for the Enforcement on Continuously Increasing Flows of Goods. The Hague (2014)
5. Klievink, B., et al.: Enhancing visibility in international supply chains: the data pipeline concept. Int. J. Electron. Gov. Res. **8**(4), 14–33 (2012)
6. Gneezy, U., Rustichini, A.: A fine is a price. J. Legal Stud. **29**(1), 1–17 (2000)
7. OECD: Regulatory Enforcement and Inspections: OECD Best Practice Principles for Regulatory Policy. Organisation for Economic Co-operation and Development (2014)
8. Wimmer, M.A.: Integrated service modelling for online one-stop government. Electron. Mark. **12**(3), 149–156 (2002)
9. Rees, J.: Self regulation: an effective alternative to direct regulation by OSHA? Policy Stud. J. **16**(3), 602–614 (1988)
10. Ayres, I., Braithwaite, J.: Responsive Regulation: Transcending the Deregulation Debate. Oxford University Press, Oxford (1992)
11. Black, J., Baldwin, R.: Really responsive risk-based regulation. Law Policy **32**(2), 181–213 (2010)
12. Mayer, R.C., Davis, J.H., Schoorman, F.D.: An integrative model of organizational trust. Acad. Manag. Rev. **20**(3), 709–734 (1995)
13. Gefen, D.: Reflections on the dimensions of trust and trustworthiness among online consumers. ACM SIGMIS Database **33**(3), 38–53 (2002)
14. COSO: Internal Control - Integrated Framework. Committee of Sponsoring Organizations of the Treadway Commission (1992)
15. EC: AEO Guidelines. European Commision, DG Taxation and Customs Union, Brussels (2007)
16. Klievink, B., Bharosa, N., Tan, Y.-H.: The collaborative realization of public values and business goals. Gov. Inf. Q. **33**, 67–79 (2016)
17. Wieland, A., Wallenburg, C.M.: The influence of relational competencies on supply chain resilience: a relational view. Int. J. Phys. Distrib. Logist. Manag. **43**(4), 300–320 (2013)
18. Brous, P., Janssen, M.: Advancing e-Government using the internet of things: a systematic review of benefits. In: Tambouris, E., et al. (eds.) EGOV 2015. LNCS, vol. 9248, pp. 156–169. Springer, Heidelberg (2015)

19. Beske, P., Seuring, S.: Putting sustainability into supply chain management. Supply Chain Manag.: Int. J. **19**(3), 322–331 (2014)
20. Ouabouch, L.: Supply chain resilience. Mat. Manag. Rev. 16–18, July 2015
21. Helbing, D.: Globally networked risks and how to respond. Nature **497**, 51–59 (2013)
22. Kartseva, V., Gordijn, J., Tan, Y.-H.: Towards a modelling tool for designing control mechanisms in network organisations. Int. J. Electron. Commer. **10**(2), 57–84 (2005)
23. van Wijk, Y.W., et al.: Assurance in collaborative ICT-enabled service chains. In: 16th International Conference on Enterprise Information Systems, pp. 368–375. Lisbon (2014)
24. Steinfield, C., Markus, M.L., Wigand, R.T.: Through a glass clearly: standards, architecture, and process transparency in global supply chains. J. Manag. Inf. Syst. **28**(2), 75–107 (2011)
25. Klievink, B., Zomer, G.: IT-enabled resilient, seamless and secure global supply chains: introduction, overview and research topics. In: Janssen, M., et al. (eds.) I3E 2015. LNCS, vol. 9373, pp. 443–453. Springer, Heidelberg (2015). doi:10.1007/978-3-319-25013-7_36
26. Yin, R.K.: Case Study Research: Design and Methods. Sage Publications Inc., Los Angeles (2003)

Author Index

Printed in the United States
by Baker & Taylor Publisher Services